ADOLF KRISCHANITZ

ADOLF KRISCHANITZ

Mit Beiträgen von / With essays by

Ákos Moravánszky

Gottfried Pirhofer

Elisabeth von Samsonow

und Gesprächen zwischen / and conversations between

Adolf Krischanitz und / and Otto Kapfinger

HATJE
CANTZ

Buchkonzept / Conception: Otto Kapfinger, Adolf Krischanitz
Redaktion / Editors: Anna Dabernig, Otto Kapfinger, Katharina Ráček
Lektorat / Copyediting: Dawn Michelle d'Atri, Uta Hasekamp
Übersetzungen / Translations: Amy Klement, Erik Smith
Grafische Gestaltung / Graphic design: Loys Egg
Schrift / Typeface: Bembo, GillSans
Herstellung / Production: Heidrun Zimmermann, Hatje Cantz
Reproduktionen / Reproductions: studio_02 Wien, Markus Rothbauer
Papier / Paper: Claro silk, 170 g/m^2
Gesamtherstellung / Printing and binding: Grasl Druck & Medien GmbH, Bad Vöslau

Erschienen im / Published by
Hatje Cantz Verlag
Zeppelinstrasse 32
73760 Ostfildern
Deutschland / Germany
Tel. +49 711 4405-200
Fax +49 711 4405-220
www.hatjecantz.com
A Ganske Publishing Group company

Hatje Cantz books are available internationally at selected bookstores.
For more information about our distribution partners, please visit our website at
www.hatjecantz.com.

ISBN 978-3-7757-3482-0

Printed in Austria

Umschlagabbildung / Cover illustration: Dachausbau / Roof Conversion for the
Oesterreichische Kontrollbank, Wien / Vienna (Foto / photo: Lukas Roth)
S. / p. 6: Museum Rietberg, Zürich / Zurich (Foto / photo: Heinrich Helfenstein)
S. / p. 250: Liska Pelzmodengeschäft 2, Flughafen Wien / Vienna Airport
(Foto / photo: Wolfgang Thaler)

Gefördert durch das Land Niederösterreich und das Land Salzburg /
Supported by the Province of Lower Austria and the Province of Salzburg

INHALT / CONTENTS

Ákos Moravánszky

Kippungen
Stoffwechsel im Werk von Adolf Krischanitz

1. Einführung
»Baldachine von Smaragd« ist das von den Architekten Adolf Krischanitz und Alfred Grazioli gewählte Motto für den Eingangspavillon des Museum Rietberg in Zürich, der die neuen unterirdischen Ausstellungsräume mit der Villa Wesendonck verbindet. Es stammt aus »Im Treibhaus«, einem von Richard Wagner vertonten Gedicht aus der Feder der ersten Bewohnerin der Villa, Mathilde Wesendonck. Der neue Pavillon befindet sich im Rieterpark an der Stelle des ehemaligen Palmenhauses, einem Ort, der für Mathilde Wesendonck mit dem Gefühl des Fremdseins verbunden war: »Ich weiss es, arme Pflanze: Ein Geschicke teilen wir, ob umstrahlt von Licht und Glanze, unsre Heimat ist nicht hier!«[1]
Die mit einem smaragdgrünen Kristallgitter durchzogene Glasfassade des neuen Pavillons erscheint im Rieterpark wie eine Studie des Unheimlichen, das auch sein (scheinbares) Gegenteil, das Heimliche, mit einschließt. Nicht nur das Spiel der Interferenzen der sich hinter dem Pavillon befindenden und sich in der Fassade spiegelnden Bäume, der transluzente Schleier und die Durchblicke tragen zum Effekt einer Fata Morgana bei. Wichtiger ist das Aufscheinen einer wienerisch-orientalischen Opulenz und Drapierungsfreude in Zürich, wo solche Effekte – dem protestantischen Geist der Stadt entsprechend – eigentlich fremd sind. Die Fassade des Pavillons mit dem großen Π-Schriftzeichen des Eingangs löscht die Bedeutung der Grenze als Limit aus und suspendiert sie in den esoterischen Raum der Wiener Secessionisten, das Ver Sacrum. Auch das Betonrelief von Helmut Federle im Foyer, das die Besucher mit Goldfolien schmücken können, oder die Decke aus durchscheinenden Onyxplatten gehören eher in das Wien Gustav Klimts und der Secession, zu der Welt der unergründlichen Referenzen, der strömenden Farben und Formen, die in magischen Augenblicken zum Stillstand kommt.
»Für mich liegt das potenzielle Fleisch der Architektur im Aufspannen von Bedeutungsfeldern beidseits entlang einer Grenze«,[2] schreibt Adolf Krischanitz. Im Rieterpark besteht die Fassade des Eingangspavillons aus tragenden Glasplatten – das Verhältnis zu einem »aufgespannten« Baldachin ist rein mimetisch. Wo einst das Palmenhaus stand, blitzt heute ein feiner Schleier auf – übertragen in eine feste Konstruktion, welche auch die Abweichung, die Differenz zu diesen Vorbildern klar vor Augen führt.

Tipping Points
Metabolism in the Work of Adolf Krischanitz

1. Introduction
"Canopy of emerald" is the motto selected by the architects Adolf Krischanitz and Alfred Grazioli for the entrance pavilion of the Museum Rietberg in Zurich, which connects the underground exhibition spaces with the Villa Wesendonck. The motto comes from "Im Treibhaus" (In the Hothouse), a poem penned by the first resident of the Villa, Mathilde Wesendonck, which was set to music by Richard Wagner. The new pavilion is located in the Rieterpark on the site of the former palm house, a place that, for Wesendonck, was associated with a feeling of displacement: "Well I know it, poor plant! We share the same fate. Although the light shines brightly round us, our home is not here!"[1]
In Rieterpark, the glass façade of the new pavilion, which is coated with an emerald-green crystal lattice, seems to be a study of the uncanny, but one that also incorporates its (apparent) opposite, the earthly. It is not only the play of the interferences of the trees located behind the pavilion and reflected in the façade, the translucent veil, and the vistas that contribute to the effect of a fata morgana. What is more important is the appearance of a Viennese-Oriental opulence and a penchant for drapery in Zurich, where such effects—in line with the Protestant spirit of the city—are actually quite alien. The façade of the pavilion with the large Π sign at its entrance eliminates the significance of the boundary as limit and suspends it in the esoteric space of the Vienna Secessionists, the Ver Sacrum. The concrete relief by Helmut Federle in the foyer, which visitors may decorate with gold foil, or the ceiling made of translucent plates of onyx belong much more to the Vienna of Gustav Klimt and the Secession, to the world of inscrutable references, of flowing colors and forms, which come to a standstill in magical moments.
"In my opinion, the potential materialization of architecture lies in the fields of meaning on either side along a boundary,"[2] writes Adolf Krischanitz. In Rieterpark, the façade of the entrance pavilion consists of load-bearing plates of glass; the relationship to a "spanned" canopy is purely mimetic. Where the palm house once stood, today a fine veil sparkles—inscribed in a solid construction that also clearly shows the deviation, the difference from these role models.
Like his friend Gottfried Semper, Richard Wagner was also part of the circle of those "foreigners" in

1 Mathilde Wesendonck, »Im Treibhaus«, in: dies., *Fünf Gedichte für eine Frauenstimme (Wesendonck-Lieder)*, Leipzig 1962.
1 Mathilde Wesendonck, "Im Treibhaus," in *Fünf Gedichte für eine Frauenstimme (Wesendonck Lieder)* (Leipzig, 1962). English translation by Thomas A. Quinn (Phonogram International B.V., Baarn, The Netherlands).

2 Adolf Krischanitz, *Architektur ist der Unterschied zwischen Architektur*, Ostfildern 2010, S. 40.
2 Adolf Krischanitz, *Architecture Is the Difference between Architecture* (Ostfildern, 2010), p. 41.

3 Gottfried Semper, »Vorläufige Bemerkungen über bemalte Architektur und Plastik bei den Alten«, in: ders., *Kleine Schriften*, Berlin und Stuttgart 1884, S. 223–225; Richard Wagner, *Das Kunstwerk der Zukunft*, Leipzig 1850.
3 Gottfried Semper, "Preliminary Remarks on Polychrome Architecture and Sculpture in Antiquity," in *The Four Elements of Architecture and Other Writings*, trans. Harry Francis Mallgrave (Cambridge, 1989), pp. 45–73; Richard Wagner, *Das Kunstwerk der Zukunft* (Leipzig, 1850).

4 Krischanitz 2010 (wie Anm. 2), S. 76.
4 Krischanitz 2010 (see note 2), p. 77.

5 Ebd., S. 140.
5 Ibid., p. 141.

6 Wesendonck 1962 (wie Anm. 1).
6 Wesendonck 1962 (see note 1).

7 Krischanitz 2010 (wie Anm. 2), S. 164.
7 Krischanitz 2010 (see note 2), p. 165.

Wie sein Freund Gottfried Semper gehörte auch Richard Wagner zum Kreis jener »Fremden« in Zürich, die Deutschland 1848 wegen ihrer Beteiligung an der Märzrevolution verlassen mussten. Die Wesendoncks unterstützten sie, bis Wagners Ehefrau vom Verhältnis ihres Mannes mit Mathilde Wesendonck erfuhr – sie war Wagners Isolde, auch die Vertonung des Gedichts »Im Treibhaus« war als musikalische Vorstudie zur Oper *Tristan und Isolde* gedacht.

Semper und Wagner, zwei herausragende Denker und Schöpfer des Historismus, haben die räumliche Kontinuität der Kunst, die Idee des Gesamtkunstwerks ins Zentrum ihres Schaffens gestellt.[3] Im Gesamtkunstwerk werden nicht nur die Grenzen zwischen den Kunstgattungen aufgelöst, sondern auch die konkreten Inhalte und Sinnzusammenhänge der Bestandteile vernichtet – geblieben sind die überzeitlich gültigen, typenhaften Ausprägungen der Ideen wie »das Tempelhafte« oder – wie im gegebenen Fall – »das Pavillonhafte« als »Eindruck des bergenden Raumes in der zerstörerischen Zeit«, wie Adolf Krischanitz das von ihm und Otto Kapfinger restaurierte Ausstellungsgebäude der Wiener Secession charakterisiert.[4] Deshalb bleibt der Typus des Pavillons ein ständiges Thema seiner Arbeit; »Nähe und Ferne bedienend«, sind Pavillons vertraut und fremd zugleich: »Der Pavillon als Wahrnehmungsapparat stilisiert sich zur transitorischen Erscheinung am ›falschen‹ Ort und erzeugt damit möglicherweise ein richtiges Bewusstsein.«[5] Die unheimliche Wirkung des Rietberg-Pavillons entsteht auch durch die Ornamentalität der Fassade, der Umwandlung eines flüchtigen Vor-Bildes, bekannt aus der islamischen Kultur, in eine anorganische Schrift, in welche auch das von Mathilde Wesendock heraufbeschworene »organische« Bild der Palmenkronen, die »Zeichen in die Luft« malen, eingeflochten ist.[6] Diesen Transformationsprozess beschreibt Krischanitz mit Hinweis auf die Theorie Gottfried Sempers als Stoffwechsel: »Nach den Semperschen Prinzipien der Bekleidung und des Stoffwechsels übernehmen Ornamente in der Architektur weit über den eigentlichen Verwendungszweck hinausgehende, architektonische Aufgaben. Es vollzieht sich nicht nur eine Verwandlung des Gebäudes, sondern auch die von der Applikation der Dekoration zur Emanation. Das Ornament als Schmuck transzendiert das funktionale Sosein eines Gebäudes genau wie ein ornamentierter Rahmen ein monochromes Bild verändert.«[7]

2. Stoffwechsel

Gottfried Semper hat mit seiner Stoffwechseltheorie Schienen gelegt, auf denen immer noch Züge ver-

Zurich who had to leave Germany in 1848 as a result of their involvement in the March Revolution. The Wesendoncks supported them until Wagner's wife learned of her husband's relationship with Mathilde Wesendonck—she was Wagner's Isolde, and the setting to music of the poem "Im Treibhaus" was also intended as a preliminary musical study for the opera *Tristan und Isolde*.

Semper and Wagner, two outstanding thinkers and creators of historicism, made the spatial continuity of art, the idea of the *Gesamtkunstwerk* (total work of art) central to their work.[3] In the total work of art, not only are the boundaries between art forms dissolved, the concrete contents and contexts of the components are also eliminated—what remain are supratemporally valid, typical forms of ideas related to types such as the "temple" or, like in the case given, "the pavilion" as an "impression of space as a harbor in the ravage of time," as Adolf Krischanitz characterized the exhibition building of the Vienna Secession that he and Otto Kapfinger restored.[4] It is for this reason that the type of the pavilion remains a constant theme in his works; "serving both distance and proximity," pavilions are intimate and strange at the same time: "The pavilion as a perceptual apparatus is stylized to a transitory appearance in the 'wrong' location and thereby possibly generates a correct consciousness."[5]

The uncanny effect of the Rietberg pavilion also arises from the ornamentality of the façade, the transformation of a fleeting earlier model familiar from Islamic culture into an inorganic script into which the "organic" image of palm crowns "tracing signs in the air" evoked by Mathilde Wesendock is woven.[6] With reference to Gottfried Semper's thesis, Krischanitz describes this process of transformation as metabolism: "According to the Semperian principles of covering and metabolism, ornaments assume architectonic tasks in architecture far beyond the actual (intended) purpose. Not only does a transformation of the building occur, but also that of application of decoration to emanation. The ornament as decoration transcends the functional essence of a building just like an ornamented frame changes a monochromatic picture."[7]

2. Metabolism

With his thesis of *Stoffwechsel* (metabolism, literally "material change"), Gottfried Semper laid tracks on which trains continue to travel—as Friedrich Achleitner once claimed.[8] Today, Adolf Krischanitz is the most powerful locomotive on these tracks. Metabolism is one of those terms that cause interferences between different areas of knowledge—it is thus no surprise that the word, which is borrowed

kehren – behauptete einmal Friedrich Achleitner.[8] Adolf Krischanitz ist heute die stärkste Lokomotive auf diesen Schienen. Stoffwechsel ist einer jener Begriffe, die Interferenzen zwischen verschiedenen Gebieten des Wissens auslösen – kein Wunder also, dass das aus der Biologie übernommene Wort, wo es den Austausch der Materialien in der Natur bezeichnet, in den Texten von Krischanitz oft vorkommt.

Semper suchte die Erklärung für ein Phänomen, das in der Architekturgeschichte seit ihren Anfängen bemerkt und interpretiert wurde: die Übertragung der charakteristischen Formen eines Materials auf einen anderen Stoff. Vitruv behauptete in *Zehn Bücher über Architektur*, dass die Formen der Säulen und Gebälke des griechischen Tempels aus dem Holzbau hervorgegangen sind. Imitation, Nachahmung – die alte These von Mimesis als Aufgabe der Kunst wird zu oft auf die Darstellung der Wirklichkeit in der Malerei oder Skulptur reduziert, obwohl sie auch in der Architektur allgegenwärtig ist. Mit dem Gedanken, dass Architektur als Kunst das unmittelbare Bedürfnis »abstreifen« muss, nahm Friedrich Schelling eine zentrale These Sempers vorweg. Stoffwechsel ist ein Mittel, um Architektur aus den Klammern des im Bedürfnis verankerten, materialgerechten Bauens zu befreien, damit sie zur Baukunst, zur »erstarrten Musik«,[9] werden kann.

Für Semper war Stoffwechsel keine Täuschung oder Unfähigkeit zum Ausbruch aus den Formkonventionen, sondern ein Prinzip, das den Objekten Erinnerungsfähigkeit und eine kulturelle Bedeutung gibt, die den Wert ihrer alltäglichen Brauchbarkeit bei Weitem übertreffen. Die Bedeutung von »Stoff« als Sujet (Thema), also Rohmaterial für das Drama, war ihm wichtig, um die Notwendigkeit der künstlerischen Bearbeitung zu betonen. Er wies darauf hin, dass »der zu behandelnde Stoff« selbst als Schicksal eines Individuums umgestaltet, erhöht, monumentalisiert werden sollte, um uns als Ausdruck des allgemein-menschlichen Schönen und Großen zu berühren.

»Der Sempersche Begriff ›Stoffwechsel‹ bezeichnet die Emanzipation der Form vom Stofflichen und vom reinen Zweck. Das Funktional-Technische wird damit zur Kunstform, die Architektur zur Kunst. Das ehemals funktional-konstruktive, wie das materialrelevante Gestaltungsprinzip, ist ebenso aufgehoben wie auch bewahrt in den Kategorien der Bekleidung und des Stoffwechsels, und ergibt somit das messbare Wahrnehmen einer Differenz. Bis zu einem gewissen Grad ist die Aufhebung von Realität erforderlich, wo sich Form als bedeutendes Symbol, als ›eigenständige‹ humane Schöpfung zeigen soll. Reale Formzusammenhänge müssen in ideell

from biology, where it refers to the exchange of materials in nature, is often found in Krischanitz's texts. Semper was looking for an explanation for a phenomenon that has been noted and interpreted since the beginnings of architectural history: the transfer of the characteristic forms of one material to another substance. In *The Ten Books on Architecture*, Vitruvius claimed that the forms of the columns and entablature of Greek temples developed from wooden structures. Imitation, simulation—the old theory of mimesis as a task for art is too often reduced to the representation of reality in painting or sculpture, although it is also omnipresent in architecture. With the thought that architecture as an art has to discard direct necessities, Friedrich Schelling anticipated one of Semper's central theories. Metabolism is a means for liberating architecture from the hold of material-appropriate construction anchored in necessity so that it is able to become the art of building, to become "frozen music."[9]

For Semper, metabolism was not an illusion or an inability to break with design conventions, but rather a principle that gives objects an ability to remember and a cultural significance that go far beyond the value of their everyday utility. The significance of "material" as a topic, thus as a raw material for drama, was important to him in emphasizing the need for artistic handling. He referred to the fact that "the material to be treated" should itself be transfigured, monumentalized as the fate of an individual, in order to touch us as an expression of general human beauty and capacities.

"'Metabolism' is the Semperian term, which designates the emancipation of form from material and purely utilitarian considerations. The functional-technical form thereby becomes a form of art and architecture itself art. The formerly functional-constructive, like the material relevant design principle, is as much suspended as it is maintained in the categories of cladding and of metabolism, with a difference that can be measured. Up to a certain extent, a suspension of reality is required, where form as a meaningful symbol should appear as an 'independent' human creation. Real conjunctions of form have to be transformed into ideally inspired shapes," writes Adolf Krischanitz in his text on Semper's thesis of metabolism.[10] In other essays, he emphasizes the "sublimation energy"[11] that can be built up through the destruction of "physical existence."[12]

It is thus understandable that plasterwork plays a paradigmatic role in Krischanitz's thinking. Fritz Schuhmacher, an advocate of material truth, accused plasterwork of a moral inferiority: "Plasterwork, which easily and effortlessly makes it possible to

8 Friedrich Achleitner, »Franks Weiterwirken in der neueren Wiener Achitektur«, in: *UmBau 10*, August 1986, S. 125.
8 Friedrich Achleitner, "Franks Weiterwirken in der neueren Wiener Achitektur," *UmBau 10* (August 1986), p. 125.

9 Friedrich Wilhelm Joseph von Schelling, »Philosophie der Kunst« (1802/03), in: ders., *Ausgewählte Schriften*, Band 2, Frankfurt am Main 1985, S. 421.
9 Friedrich Wilhelm Joseph von Schelling, "Philosophie der Kunst" (1802–03), in: *Ausgewählte Schriften*, vol. 2 (Frankfurt am Main, 1985), p. 421.

10 Krischanitz 2010 (wie Anm. 2), S. 68.
10 Krischanitz 2010 (see note 2), p. 69.

11 Ebd., S. 70.
11 Ibid., p. 71.

12 Ebd., S. 114.
12 Ibid., p. 115.

13 Fritz Schumacher, *Das Wesen des neuzeitlichen Backsteinbaues*, München 1920, S. 46.
13 Fritz Schumacher, *Das Wesen des neuzeitlichen Backsteinbaues* (Munich, 1920), p. 46.

14 Krischanitz 2010 (wie Anm. 2), S. 44.
14 Krischanitz 2010 (see note 2), p. 45.

15 Ebd.
15 Ibid.

16 Ebd., S. 116.
16 Ibid., p. 117.

17 Ebd., S. 70.
17 Ibid., p. 71.

18 Ludwig Wittgenstein, *Philosophische Untersuchungen*, Frankfurt am Main 1971, S. 24.
18 Ludwig Wittgenstein, *Philosophical Investigations*, trans. G. E. M. Anscombe (Oxford, 1958), p. 8.

19 »Gute Architektur kann beschrieben, sie müsste nicht gezeichnet werden. Das Pantheon kann man beschreiben.« In: Heinrich Kulka (Hrsg.), *Adolf Loos. Das Werk des Architekten*, Wien 1931, S. 18.
19 "Good architecture can be described, it need not be drawn. One can describe the Pantheon." Cited from *Adolf Loos: Das Werk des Architekten*, ed. Heinrich Kulka (Vienna, 1931), p. 18.

inspirierte Gebilde verwandelt werden«, schreibt Adolf Krischanitz in seinem Text zu Sempers Stoffwechseltheorie.[10] Er betont in anderen Essays die »Sublimierungsenergie«,[11] die man durch die »Zerstörung der Physis«[12] gewinnen kann.

So ist es verständlich, dass der Putz im Denken von Krischanitz eine geradezu paradigmatische Rolle einnimmt. Fritz Schuhmacher, ein Verfechter der Materialwahrheit, warf dem Putz eine moralische Minderwertigkeit vor: »Der Putzbau, der leicht und mühelos erlaubt, jeder unreifen Laune Gestalt zu geben, ist […] ein geradezu verführerisches Material. Allen geilen Instinkten der Unfähigkeit und Anmaßung kommt er willig entgegen«, schrieb er.[13] Für Krischanitz dagegen ist der Putz der Inbegriff eines immensen gestalterischen Potenzials. Der neutrale Charakter des Putzes erlaubt ihm etwa bei der Wohnanlage Monte Laa in Wien eine große Übertragungsfähigkeit, eine »kulturelle Überarbeitung beziehungsweise Überformung«[14]: »Gerade die Moderne hat gezeigt, dass die Verwendung einer homogenen Oberflächenstruktur (Verputz) auf die nächste Ebene verweist, auf die geschlossene, fugenlose, körperhafte, skulpturale Form. Oft wird die ins Material Verputz eingeschriebene Neutralität mit Charakterlosigkeit gleichgesetzt und dabei das enorme Gestaltungs- und Übertragungspotenzial unterschätzt. Jedes Material ist an sich dumm, es sei denn man setzt es intelligent ein. Gerade die Universalität des Materials Verputz führte in neuerer Zeit meistens zu einer flachen, missbräuchlichen, den Möglichkeiten des Materials nicht angemessenen Verwendung.«[15]

Krischanitz extrapoliert den Semper'schen Stoffwechselbegriff, um eine Durchlässigkeit zwischen den Kategorien Stadt, Typus, Struktur und Ornament oder »Schrift« festzustellen. Er spricht etwa über die Verwendung von Begriffen, die – selbst wenn sie politisch leicht missbraucht werden können – »dynamische ›Stoffwechselvorgänge‹« ermöglichen,[16] oder über »stadtstrukturelle Stoffwechselapparate«, die unterschiedliche Nutzungsszenarien unterstützen können[17].

3. Verschriftlichungen

Die Sprachlichkeit der Architektur, oder besser: die Architektonik der Sprache, war ein ständiges Thema des Philosophen Ludwig Wittgenstein. Er verglich die Sprache mit einer alten Stadt, ein »Gewinkel von Gässchen und Plätzen, alten und neuen Häusern, und Häusern mit Zubauten aus verschiedenen Zeiten«.[18] Auch Adolf Loos' Bonmot über die »Beschreibbarkeit« von guter Architektur ist wohlbekannt.[19] Die »Stoffwechselvorgänge« zwischen Sprache, Schrift und Stadt beschäftigen auch Adolf

give form to every immature fancy, is . . . an almost seductive material. It willingly accommodates all lustful instincts of inability and arrogance," he wrote.[13] For Krischanitz, in contrast, plasterwork is the epitome of immense design potential. The neutral character of plasterwork allows him, for example, in the case of the residential complex Monte Laa in Vienna, a great capacity for negotiation, a "cultural revamping and metamorphosis."[14] "Modernism has shown that the employment of a homogenous surface structure (plasterwork) refers to the next level, to the closed, seamless, body-like and sculptural form. The neutrality imprinted in plasterwork is often equated with a lack of character so that the enormous design and transfer potential is underestimated. Each material is in itself mute until one utilizes it intelligently. It is precisely the universality of plasterwork that has recently led to a mostly flat material misuse that fails to reflect its possibilities."[15]

Krischanitz extrapolates from Semper's concept of metabolism to specify a kind of permeability between the categories of city, type, structure, and ornament or "writing." He speaks, for example, about the use of terms that—even when they might easily be misused politically—make possible "dynamic 'metabolic processes'"[16] or are capable of supporting diverse usage scenarios by way of an "urban structural metabolic apparatus."[17]

3. Scriptualizations

The language of architecture—or better: the architectonics of language—was a constant topic for the philosopher Ludwig Wittgenstein. He compared language with an old city, a "maze of little streets and squares, of old and new houses, and of houses with additions from various periods."[18] Adolf Loos's bon mot about the "descriptiveness" of good architecture is also well known.[19] "Metabolic processes" between language, text, and city also interest Adolf Krischanitz. Based on the example of James Joyce's descriptions of Dublin, he determined that "language certainly is capable of sketching a thoroughly complex and multilayered image of a city street. . . . Because this abstraction of language achieves something akin to making that liveliness fluid, and that then crystallizes as writing, as language, as a book, and will be able to evaporate and be interpreted again sometime . . . writing as possibility apparently really fascinated us."[20]

Here, one indeed must first reflect on the artistic and literary practices of the *flâneur*, on the chance encounters ranging from nineteenth-century Paris to Surrealist strategies and the *détournements* of the Situationists, on a type urbanity without a master

Krischanitz. Am Beispiel von James Joyces Schilderungen von Dublin stellt er fest, dass »die Sprache sehr wohl in der Lage ist, ein vollkommen komplexes und vielschichtiges Bild einer Stadtstrasse zu zeichnen. [...] Weil diese Abstraktion der Sprache ist so etwas wie eine Verflüssigung von Lebendigkeit leistet, die sich dann wieder als Schrift, als Sprache, als Buch kristallisiert und irgendwann wieder verflüssigbar und interpretierbar sein wird [...] die Schrift als Möglichkeit, das hat uns offensichtlich sehr fasziniert.«[20]

Man muss hier wohl zuerst an die künstlerischen und literarischen Praktiken des Flaneurs denken, an die zufälligen Begegnungen, die des Paris des 19. Jahrhunderts über surrealistischen Strategien zu den »détournements« der Situationisten, an eine Urbanität ohne Masterplan. Krischanitz spricht allerdings von »Verschriftlichung« und macht damit den Unterschied zwischen einem semiotischen und einem eher typografischen Verständnis der Architektur sichtbar. Es gibt keinen Widerspruch zwischen diesen Verwendungen des Begriffs Beschreibung, als sprachliche Schilderung und als Überzug der Oberfläche mit einer ornamentalen »Schrift«, wie es bereits Joseph Maria Olbrich, der Architekt der Wiener Secession, tat, um trotz der intendierten »Zerstörung der Schachtel« dem visuellen Auseinanderbrechen des Volumens »mit einem genialischen grafischen ›Scribble‹« entgegenzuwirken.[21]

Die Schrift ist die visuell wahrnehmbare Form, die Oberflächenstruktur der Sprache, deren Bedeutung nur für jene verständlich ist, die sie lesen können. Die »Schrift« der Stadt bleibt jedoch hermetischverschlossen, was wir wahrnehmen können, ist die Intention zur Mitteilung. In den Entwürfen für die Wiener Donau City oder neues bauen am horn in Weimar wird das Verhältnis Architektur / Stadt durch eine kryptisch wirkende »Typografie« geregelt. Der Begriff trifft zu: Es geht um ein Schreiben *(graféin)* mit prägenden und geprägten Grundformen *(typos)*. Der typografische »Satz« mit seinem Versprechen von Bedeutung schafft Verbindung zwischen individuellen Zeichen und der Prägung der Stadt als Ganzem. »Die inhaltliche Ebene des Textes ist [...] sekundär.«[22] Die Schrift ist nur in dem Sinne Bedeutungsträger, als sie die Präsenz eines Sinns suggeriert.

Krischanitz' Programm der »Verschriftlichung des Stoffes« geschieht im Sinne der Semper'schen Theorie, wo die wichtigste, die kulturelle, bedeutungstragende Funktion der Architektur in letzter Konsequenz von der immateriellen oder fast immateriellen, ornamental beschrifteten oder polychromen »Hülle« übernommen wird. Er ist überzeugt, dass dieser epochale »Stoffwechsel« im Zeitalter der

plan. Krischanitz, however, speaks of *Verschriftlichung* (scriptualization) and hence makes visible the difference between a semiotic and a more typographic understanding of architecture. There is no contradiction between these uses of the term description, as a linguistic depiction and as an overlaying of the surface with ornamental "writing"—like Joseph Maria Olbrich, the architect of the Vienna Secession, already did in order to counteract the visual breaking apart of volume "with an inspired, graphic 'scribble'" despite the intended "destruction of the box."[21]

Text is the visually perceptible form, the surface structure of language, whose meaning can only be comprehended by those who are able to read it. The "text" of the city, however, remains hermetically closed, and what we are able to perceive is the intention to communicate. In the designs for the Donau City in Vienna or the neues bauen am horn in Weimar, the relationship of architecture / city is structured by a cryptic-seeming "typography." It is an apt term, for what is concerned is a text *(graféin)* with characterizing and characterized basic forms *(typos)*. With its promise of meaning, the typographic "sentence" creates a connection between individual symbols and the imprinting of the city as a whole. "The content level of text is secondary."[22] Text is only a bearer of meaning in the sense that it suggests the presence of a meaning.

Krischanitz's program of scriptualizing matter is understood in the sense of Semper's thesis, in which the most important function of architecture—the cultural, meaningful one—is ultimately assumed by the immaterial (or virtually immaterial), ornamentally inscribed, or polychromatic "shell." He is convinced that this epochal "metabolism" will first be completed in all of its radicalness in the age of digitization: "The analogue digital transformation is dispensing with material reality, an inscription of substance. In this sense, the new universal language, like Latin in the Middle Ages, is the exclusive metalanguage. It means dissolution of substance. The discovery is based on the irrelevance of the semantic and the discovery of a common deep structure: everything is structure, code. Strictly speaking, the 'inscription' of work means that this, like the books in a public library, work is generally accessible, is collective property."[23] The consequences of metabolism will thus fundamentally alter the concrete and symbolic economy of the world. In fact, theoreticians of digital production such as Bernard Cache make reference to Semper's thesis of metabolism as well.[24]

Among the key texts that document modern philosophy's turn to language, and that have set the

20 Interview mit Angela Hareiter, Otto Kapfinger und Adolf Krischanitz, Wien, 23. März 2002, in: *The Austrian Phenomenon. Architektur Avantgarde Österreich 1956–1973*, Basel 2009, S. 934.
20 Interview with Angela Hareiter, Otto Kapfinger, and Adolf Krischanitz, Vienna, March 23, 2002, published in *The Austrian Phenomenon: Architecture Avantgarde Austria 1956–1973* (Basel, 2009), p. 197.

21 Otto Kapfinger und Adolf Krischanitz, *Die Wiener Secession. Das Haus. Entstehung, Geschichte, Erneuerung*, Wien u. a. 1986, S. 68.
21 Otto Kapfinger and Adolf Krischanitz, *Die Wiener Secession: Das Haus: Entstehung, Geschichte, Erneuerung* (Vienna et al., 1986), p. 68.

22 Krischanitz 2010 (wie Anm. 2), S. 10.
22 Krischanitz 2010 (see note 2), p. 9.

23 Ebd., S. 138.
23 Ibid., p. 139.

24 Bernard Cache, »Digital Semper«, in: Cynthia Davidson (Hrsg.), *Anymore*, Cambridge, Massachusetts, 2000, S. 190–197.
24 Bernard Cache, "Digital Semper," in *Anymore*, ed. Cynthia Davidson (Cambridge, MA, 2000), pp. 190–97.

25 Wittgenstein 1971 (wie Anm. 18), S. 78.
25 Wittgenstein 1958 (see note 18), p. 46e.

26 Krischanitz 2010 (wie Anm. 2), S. 108.
26 Krischanitz 2010 (see note 2), p. 109.

Digitalisierung erst in seiner ganzen Radikalität vollzogen wird:

»Die Analog-digital-Wandlung ist ein Dispens der stofflichen Realität, eine Verschriftlichung des Stoffes. In diesem Sinn ist die neue Universalsprache wie das Latein des Mittelalters die höherwertige Metasprache, sie bedeutet die Ablösung vom Stoff. Die Entdeckung beruht auf der Irrelevanz des Semantischen und der Entdeckung einer gemeinsamen Tiefenstruktur: Alles ist Struktur, Code. Streng genommen läuft die ›Schriftwerdung‹ von Arbeit darauf hinaus, dass diese, ähnlich wie in den öffentlichen Bibliotheken, allgemein zugänglich wird, kollektiver Besitz.«[23] Die Konsequenzen dieses Stoffwechsels werden also die konkrete und symbolische Ökonomie der Welt grundlegend verändern. In der Tat beziehen sich heute Theoretiker der digitalen Herstellung wie Bernard Cache auf Sempers Stoffwechseltheorie.[24]

Zu den Schlüsseltexten, die die Hinwendung der modernen Philosophie zur Sprache dokumentieren und für Weichenstellungen im Denken über Metaphysik und Epistemologie sorgten, gehören Ludwig Wittgensteins *Tractatus logico-philosophicus* (1918) und *Philosophische Untersuchungen* (1953). Den *Tractatus*, der als zentrales Dokument des logischen Positivismus gilt, hat der junge Wittgenstein zwischen seinem Studium in Cambridge und seinem Soldatendienst an der italienischen Front geschrieben. Die postum veröffentlichten *Untersuchungen* sind allgemein als eine Korrektur der zu engen Definition der Sprache im *Tractatus* betrachtet worden. Im *Tractatus* geht es um die Grenzen der Sprache; er trennt sorgfältig Fragen, mit denen sich die Philosophie sinnvoll auseinandersetzen kann, von jenen, die sinnlos oder tautologisch sind. In den *Philosophischen Untersuchungen* sind diese Grenzen nicht mehr so klar gezogen. Es geht nicht mehr um Sinn oder Unsinn, sondern um die alltägliche Praxis des Sprechens, um die Frage des Gebrauchs. In einem schönen Satz vergleicht er diese Perspektivwechsel mit einer räumlichen Drehung: »Das *Vorurteil* der Kristallreinheit kann nur so beseitigt werden, daß wir unsere ganze Betrachtung drehen. (Man könnte sagen: Die Betrachtung muß gedreht werden, aber um unser eigentliches Bedürfnis als Angelpunkt.)«[25] Adolf Krischanitz bezeichnet diese Wende hin zum Bedürfnis in Wittgensteins Philosophie nicht als Drehung, sondern als »Kippung«, ein typisches »Phänomen für Wiener Denk- und Konzeptstrategien«.[26] Das eigene Werk zeigt eine entscheidende Kippung nach der ersten, gesellschaftskritischen Phase. Architekten, die ihre Praxis in den 1970er-Jahren als »experimentelles Entwerfen« bezeichneten, gerieten, als sie ein Jahrzehnt später die ersten

course for reflection on metaphysics and epistemology, are Ludwig Wittgenstein's *Tractatus Logico-Philosophicus* (1918) and *Philosophical Investigations* (1953). The young Wittgenstein wrote the *Tractatus*, which is considered to be a central document of logical positivism, between studying in Cambridge and serving as a soldier on the Italian front. The posthumously published *Investigations* have generally come to be seen as a correction of the too narrow definition of language in the *Tractatus*. In the *Tractatus*, it is the boundaries of language that are addressed; Wittgenstein carefully differentiates questions that philosophy is reasonably able to examine from those that are senseless or tautological. In the *Philosophical Investigations*, these boundaries are no longer drawn as clearly. What is at issue is no longer sense or nonsense, but rather the everyday practice of speaking, the question of use. In a beautiful sentence, he compares this change of perspective with a rotation in space: "The *preconceived idea* of crystalline purity can only be removed by turning our whole examination round. (One might say: the axis of reference of our examination must be rotated, but about the fixed point of our real need.)"[25]

Adolf Krischanitz does not describe this inclination to necessity in Wittgenstein's philosophy as a turn but instead as *Kippung*, or "tipping over," a typical "phenomenon of Viennese thinking and concept strategies."[26] Krischanitz's own work shows a decisive overturning after the initial socially critical phase. Architects who described their practice in the nineteen-seventies as "experimental design" found themselves in a position that seemed to call their credibility into question when they received their first construction contracts a decade later. The architecture scene in Vienna was particularly interesting in this respect since the representatives of the radical avant-garde were able to erect, of all things, business portals and shop interiors on the shopping streets of the city center as "architectural anarchist cells."[27] Otto Kapfinger, a partner of Adolf Krischanitz in the Missing Link architectural group along with Angela Hareiter, has described the earlier position as a "rebellious mistrust of conventional function programs and inspired architectural demands."[28] The "incredibly aggressive potential" that Adolf Krischanitz always had to expect in connection with interventions by Missing Link[29] drained away at the latest after the Kuoni travel agencies of Krischanitz and Kapfinger (1980)—an intervention that, in comparison to Hans Hollein's celebrated Retti candle shop, seems almost fragile. The glazed façade layer introduced does not conceal the old façade system, and the large metal letters that

Bauaufträge erhielten, in eine Lage, die ihre Glaubwürdigkeit infrage zu stellen schien. Die Wiener Architekturszene war in dieser Hinsicht besonders interessant, da die Vertreter der radikalen Avantgarde als »architektur-anarchistische Zellen«[27] ausgerechnet Geschäftsportale und Ladeneinrichtungen in den Einkaufsstraßen der Innenstadt errichten konnten. Otto Kapfinger, neben Angela Hareiter Partner von Adolf Krischanitz in der Architektengruppe Missing Link, beschrieb die frühere Position als ein »rebellische[s] Misstrauen gegen konventionelle Funktionsprogramme und geniehafte Baukunstansprüche«.[28] Das »ungeheuere Aggressionspotenzial«, mit dem Adolf Krischanitz bei den Performances von Missing Link immer rechnen musste,[29] wich spätestens nach dem Kuoni-Reisebüro von Krischanitz und Kapfinger (1980) – einem Eingriff, der im Vergleich zu Hans Holleins zelebriertem Retti-Kerzenladen geradezu fragil erscheint. Die vorgestellte, gläserne Fassadenschicht verdeckt das alte Fassadensystem nicht, die großen Metallbuchstaben, die am Rand der neuen Fassadenmembran stehen, lehnen sich an die alte Fassade an, indem sie diese nur leicht berühren. Ähnlich vorsichtig gehen die Architekten mit den bestehenden Räumen um, mit Achsenverschiebungen spielend. Es scheint, dass die Architekten von Missing Link – die Materialaktionen realisierten, die ihrer Meinung nach »eine extrem aggressive Haltung«, ja sogar eine »relativ brachiale Gewalt« zeigten[30] – sich jetzt vorsichtig und einfühlsam jener Kultur des Konsums näherten, die sie früher unter dem Einfluss der Frankfurter Schule und Theodor Adornos ablehnten. Das Verhältnis zu dieser zugelassenen Realität wurde zum Grundproblem ihrer Architektur. Der Hohn, der für »geniehafte Baukunstansprüche« und für die Arbeit an der architektonischen Form galt, musste »sublimiert« werden. Die Radikalität dieser Umstellung war nur durch theoretische Arbeit zu meistern, indem die Form verflüssigt oder »verschriftlicht« wurde oder als Container betrachtet, der beliebige Inhalte aufnehmen kann. Jedenfalls finden wir in den zur Ausführung bestimmten Arbeiten diese Relativierung der Form zugunsten des »Alltags«, der Multiplizität der Nutzungen, der Performanz des Objekts.

Die Gefahr, auf diese Situation entweder zynisch oder pathetisch-verklärend zu reagieren, wurde gebannt – möglicherweise durch die für Wien typische Ununterscheidbarkeit von Lob und Ablehnung begünstigt.

Wenn Adolf Krischanitz heute für große Konzerne wie Swiss Re oder Novartis baut, bewegt er sich nicht in James Joyces Dublin, sondern in Als-ob-Städten, deren »Öffentlichkeit« aus Managern, Angestellten und Gästen besteht. Die Fassade seines

stand on the edge of the new façade membrane do not lean on the old façade since they only touch it lightly. The architects dealt with the existing spaces in a similarly cautious manner by playing with shifts of axes. It seems that the Missing Link architects—who realized material actions that, in their opinion, indicated "an extremely aggressive attitude," indeed even a "fairly brutal violence"[30]—now cautiously and perceptively approached that culture of consumption that they had previously, under the influence of the Frankfurt School and Theodor Adorno, rejected. The relationship to this tolerated reality became the fundamental problem in their architecture. The derision expressed with regard to "inspired architectural demands" and to work on the architectural form had to be "sublimated." It was only possible to cope with the radicalness of this shift by means of theoretical work, since the form became liquefied or "inscribed," or was seen as a container that is capable of assimilating any desired content. In any case, in the realization of particular works, we find that this relativization of form benefits "everyday life," the multiplicity of uses, the performance of the object. The risk of reacting to this situation in either a cynical or emotionally transfiguring manner was averted—possibly supported by the indistinguishableness of praise and rejection that is typical of Vienna.

When Adolf Krischanitz today builds for large companies such as Swiss Re or Novartis, he is not active in James Joyce's Dublin but rather in "as-if" cities whose "public" consists of managers, employees, and guests. As a folding screen, the façade of his laboratory building on the Novartis campus turns the primarily negative meaning of the provisional upside down in the "ideal city" of Novartis with its arcades, gardens, artworks, and their perfect details and high-quality execution. The curtain walls of classical corporate architecture, which, at least in name, also make reference to the textile origins of architecture claimed by Semper, in reality stand for liberation from the tectonic function. At the same time, the constructively liberated "garment" is placed in the service of the search for a corporate image, for iconicity. In this situation, Krischanitz again deliberately utilizes the image of the folding screen, of the provisional, as a metaphor. The "ideal" structure of the company city is split into many reflected, transparent, or translucent facets that mirror the sky, trees, and buildings nearby and allow for a glimpse into the offices.

"The sentence 'architecture is the difference between architecture' is programmatic and presented in the sense of a rolling stone, whose sides are always visible due to the rotation of the stone but which

27 *The Austrian Phenomenon* 2009 (wie Anm. 20), S. 929.
27 *The Austrian Phenomenon* 2009 (see note 20), p. 193.

28 Krischanitz 2010 (wie Anm. 2), S. 106.
28 Krischanitz 2010 (see note 2), p. 107.

29 *The Austrian Phenomenon* 2009 (wie Anm. 20), S. 932.
29 *The Austrian Phenomenon* 2009 (see note 20), p. 195.

30 Ebd.
30 Ibid.

Laborgebäudes am Novartis Campus kehrt als ein »Folding Screen« die primär negative Bedeutung des Provisorischen in der »Idealstadt« Novartis mit ihren Arkaden, Gärten, Kunstwerken und ihren perfekten Details und hochwertigen Ausführungen um. Die Curtain Walls der klassischen Corporate Architecture, die zumindest im Namen ebenfalls auf die von Semper behaupteten textilen Ursprünge der Architektur hinweisen, stehen in Wirklichkeit für eine Befreiung von der tektonischen Funktion. Gleichzeitig wird das konstruktiv befreite »Gewand« in den Dienst der Suche nach einem Corporate Image, nach einer Ikonizität gestellt. Bewusst mobilisiert Krischanitz in dieser Situation wieder das Bild des Folding Screens, des Paravents, des Provisorischen als Metapher. Die »ideale« Ordnung der Firmenstadt wird in viele gespiegelte, transparente oder durchscheinende Facetten aufgesplittet, die den Himmel, die Bäume und Bauten der Nachbarschaft widerspiegeln und Blicke in die Büros erlauben.

»Der Satz ›Architektur ist der Unterschied zwischen Architektur‹ ist ein Programm, das sich im Sinn eines rollenden Steins darstellt, dessen charakteristische Seiten durch die Eigendrehung zwar immer wieder sichtbar werden, sich jedoch bereits insgesamt an einem anderen Ort befinden.«[31] Der rollende Stein, der immer andere Seiten zeigt, dessen Identität sich im ständigen Wechsel, in ständig neuen Konfigurationen mit dem Grund entfaltet. In der ständig wechselnden Positionierung zu dem, was es bereits gibt, enthüllt sich der Sinn der Architektur von Adolf Krischanitz.

already are located as a whole at another location."[31] This is the rolling stone that always shows other sides, whose identity develops through constant change, through ever new configurations with the ground. In the perpetually changing positioning in relation to that which already exists, Adolf Krischanitz's sense of architecture is revealed.

31 Krischanitz 2010 (wie Anm. 2), S. 6.
31 Krischanitz 2010 (see note 2), p. 7.

0301
Laborgebäude / Laboratory Building, Novartis Campus
Basel
Lampion-Kunststoffelemente: Plattenteilung mit Rautenmuster für den Siebdruck / Plastic lampion elements: sheet division with diamond pattern for screen printing

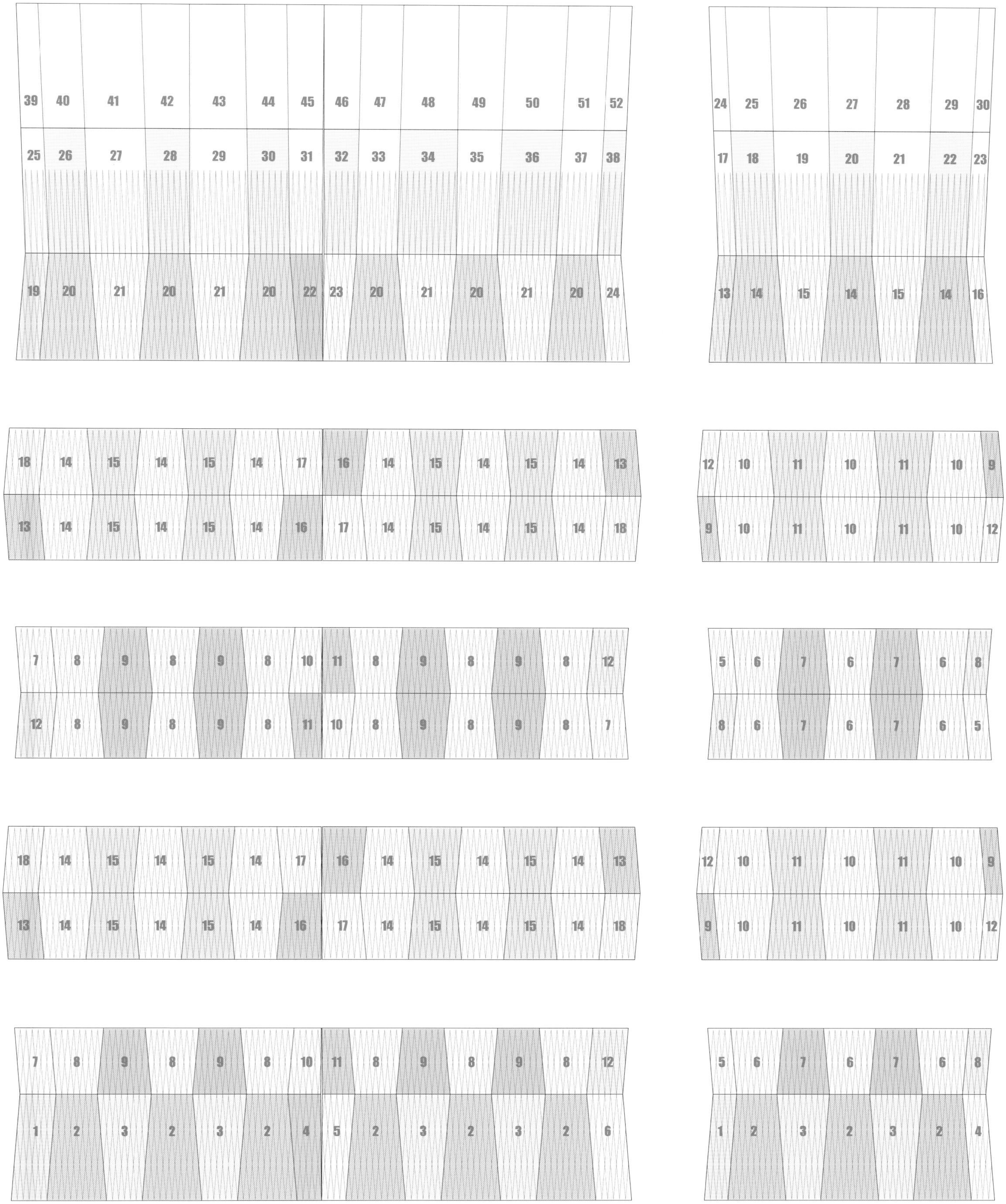
39 40 41 42 43 44 45 46 47 48 49 50 51 52
25 26 27 28 29 30 31 32 33 34 35 36 37 38
19 20 21 20 21 20 22 23 20 21 20 21 20 24
24 25 26 27 28 29 30
17 18 19 20 21 22 23
13 14 15 14 15 14 16
18 14 15 14 15 14 17 16 14 15 14 15 14 13
13 14 15 14 15 14 16 17 14 15 14 15 14 18
12 10 11 10 11 10 9
9 10 11 10 11 10 12
7 8 9 8 9 8 10 11 8 9 8 9 8 12
12 8 9 8 9 8 11 10 8 9 8 9 8 7
5 6 7 6 7 6 8
8 6 7 6 7 6 5
18 14 15 14 15 14 17 16 14 15 14 15 14 13
13 14 15 14 15 14 16 17 14 15 14 15 14 18
12 10 11 10 11 10 9
9 10 11 10 11 10 12
7 8 9 8 9 8 10 11 8 9 8 9 8 12
1 2 3 2 3 2 4 5 2 3 2 3 2 6
5 6 7 6 7 6 8
1 2 3 2 3 2 4

Der architektonische Raum ist ein komplementäres Behältnis.
Es schützt vor der Okkupation durch die Natur in der Zeit.
Die Zeit ist in jedem Fall ein Potenzial für Veränderung und
letztendlich Zerstörung. Der Raum ist von der Architektur gegen
den Eindringling Natur aufgeboten. Die Besetzung durch Architektur
bildet die Rahmenhandlung für das exkludierte und auch inkludierte
Potenzial von Natur. Die Kulturhaltung wird zur Raum(er)haltung
in der Zeit. Die Architektur als Zustand der Grenze reflektiert
die Welt in der Welt.

The architectonic space is a complementary receptacle. It protects
against the occupation by nature over time. Time is in any case a
potential for change and thereby, in the end, destruction. Space is
deployed by architecture against the invader nature. The occupation
by architecture provides the framework plot for the excluded and also
incorporated potential of nature. The cultural disposition creates
the spatial condition in time. Architecture as a state of boundary
reflects the world within a world.

Adolf Krischanitz

IM GESPRÄCH
Adolf Krischanitz – Otto Kapfinger

Otto Kapfinger: Am Beginn der Arbeit zu diesem Buch stand der Wunsch: Das soll nicht die übliche Werkschau werden; du möchtest etwas anderes als ein grafisches Schema von Text-, Foto- und Planzuordnungen.

Adolf Krischanitz: Ich sehe es eher als Lesebuch, angelegt in der Art eines Bild- und Textgartens: offen, informell und assoziativ, zum Flanieren einladend.

Wir hatten zwischendurch die optimistische Vorstellung, das Buch wie ein Stadtviertel zu konzipieren, mit Fotogruppen, welche die Plätze, die Räume, Halte- und Aussichtspunkte dieser »Stadt« bilden.

Ja, und als Verbindung dieser unterschiedlichen Räume, als Straßen und Gassen: die Texte, die Textflächen eines Gesprächs, das wir sozusagen im Flanieren, im Assoziieren zu diesen Bereichen mit mehreren Interviews entwickelten und dann im schriftlichen Austausch konkretisierten …

PAVILLONS

Das Thema steht nicht zufällig am Beginn unseres Gesprächs. Es zieht sich wie ein roter Faden durch Dein Œuvre. Das begann 1988 mit dem Traisenpavillon. In mehreren Publikationen hast du sehr prominent das Bild von dessen Baustelle im Auwald von St. Pölten verwendet. Das war wohl eine Anspielung auf Bilder der sogenannten Urhütte in den Traktaten der klassischen Architekturtheorie. Wie kam es zu diesem Auftrag, was war das Spezifikum?

Der Pavillon von St. Pölten war im wahrsten Sinne des Wortes eine Urhütte, durchaus verwandt den bekannten Zeichnungen in den Traktaten von Laugier oder Viollet-le-Duc. Er entstand im Auftrag des Donaufestivals als eine Art Versuchsstation nach der zwei Jahre zuvor erfolgten Ernennung von St. Pölten zur Landeshauptstadt Niederösterreichs. Bauherr war die damals gegründete Landeshauptstadt-Planungsgesellschaft. Diese Hauptstadtwerdung war mit schlagartiger Bedeutungsakkumulation verbunden – mit einer ganz neuen Qualität, einem utopischen Anspruch. Darauf musste und wollte man das Land, die Stadt erst einstimmen. Und dazu diente die Errichtung

IN CONVERSATION
Adolf Krischanitz—Otto Kapfinger

Otto Kapfinger: When work on this book began, you felt it should stand apart from the conventional presentation of works. You wanted something different than a graphic schema containing collations of texts, photos, and plans.

Adolf Krischanitz: I see it more as a book for people to read, laid out in the form of a garden of images and texts—open, informal, and associative—which invites people to take a stroll through it.

At one point, we had the optimistic notion of designing the book like a district of a city, with groups of photos constituting the squares, spaces, stopping and vantage points of this "city."

Yes, and as an interface between these different spaces, as roads and backstreets: the texts, the blocks of texts of a conversation that we developed, so to say, while strolling, while establishing associations to these areas through multiple interviews, which we then put into concrete terms as a written exchange . . .

PAVILIONS

This theme is not at the beginning of our conversation by chance, since it runs through your oeuvre like a unifying thread. It all began in 1988, with the Traisen Pavilion. You have used a picture of its construction site in the alluvial forest of St. Pölten prominently in several publications. This was perhaps an allusion to images of the so-called primitive hut in treatises on classic architectural theory. How did this commission come about, and what were the specific aspects?

The pavilion of St. Pölten was a primitive hut in the truest sense of the word, closely akin to the well-known drawings found in the treatises of [Marc-Antoine] Laugier or [Eugène] Viollet-le-Duc. It was commissioned by the Donaufestival as a type of experimental station after St. Pölten had been named capital of the Province of Lower Austria two years earlier. The client was the then established Landeshauptstadt-Planungsgesellschaft (State Capital Planning Association). Becoming the capital was connected with a sudden increase in significance—with a completely new

Der erste Bau / The First Building,
aus / from:
Eugène Emmanuel Viollet-le-Duc,
Histoire de l'habitation humaine,
Paris 1875

Rudolf Wondracek
Strukturplan / Structural Plan
St. Pölten, 1936

St. Pölten
52.000 Einwohner, 108 km², Hauptstadt von Niederösterreich (1,5 Mio. Einwohner, 19.000 km²), größtes der neun Bundesländer von Österreich (7,6 Mio. Einwohner, 84.000 km²)

St. Pölten
52,000 inhabitants, 108 km², capital of Lower Austria (1.5 million inhabitants, 19,000 km²), largest of the nine federal states in Austria (7.6 million inhabitants, 84,000 km²)

eines nicht näher definierten Gebäudes für Ausstellungen und Veranstaltungen, oder besser gesagt: Der provisorische Bau sollte das verträumte, etwas verwilderte Parkgelände am Flussufer östlich vom Stadtkern in dieser Richtung stimulieren.

Zu diesem Zeitpunkt war nicht einmal klar, wo das neue Regierungs- und Kulturviertel gebaut werden sollte! Die Situation war wirklich utopisch, der städtebauliche Wettbewerb kam ja erst danach. So war der Traisenpavillon ein fast mythischer Akt, ein Probe- und Versuchsraum zur geistigen Orientierung.

Die Umwertung der kleinen Bezirksstadt, die als Bischofssitz, Industrieort und Schulzentrum des Bezirks eine interessante, aber gewiss nicht spektakuläre Geschichte aufwies, wurde damals von Teilen der Bevölkerung als willkürlich empfunden. Es ging unter anderem um die Übersiedlung von mehr als 3000 Beamten, die bisher im Zentrum von Wien ihre Schreibtische hatten – samt den dazugehörigen Einrichtungen administrativer, repräsentativer und infrastruktureller Art. Der Pavillon war somit ein Symbol der Antizipation, er war eine Umsteigstation in eine unbekannte, jedoch unausweichlich kommende Entwicklung.

Du hast dort zwei elementare Bautypen aneinandergesetzt: ein prismatisches Langhaus – ein mehrstöckiges »Regal« – und einen kreisrunden Zentralbau – eine Halle mit zylindrischem Lichtauge mitten im Dach.

Einerseits war das utopische Moment der Nichtverortung ein wesentlicher Faktor des Entwurfsgedankens. Andererseits war die funktionale Unbestimmtheit mangels Vorgaben durchaus Programm. Diese inhaltliche Offenheit war freilich gepaart mit Kostenlimits – der Preis des Pavillons durfte nur dem eines kleinen Einfamilienhauses entsprechen! Die Emanzipation vom Ort und von fixierten Nutzungen bot die Chance einer gewissen Idealisierung. Es war ein Moment von Autonomie ohne Pathos, eine »fröhliche Unschuld im Mangel«. Gleichzeitig mit der Konkretisierung der Planung entwickelten EichingeroderKnechtl, Georg Schöllhammer und Dietmar Steiner Ideen zur Bespielung. Das besteigbare Regal und der Versammlungsraum inszenierten gleichsam den arkadischen Auftakt der Hauptstadtwerdung. Im grünen Erholungsraum der Stadt, am Hochwasser-Schutzdamm der Traisen gab es dann, so exotisch wie ein Zirkusbesuch, eine anspruchsvolle Ausstellung als »tour d'horizon« zum Thema und eine Reihe von Veranstaltungen, Symposien.

quality, a utopian ambition. But first it was important to attune the province and the city to this idea. And that was the purpose of erecting a building not defined in any further detail for exhibitions and events, or put more precisely: the provisional building was thus meant to stimulate the languorous, somewhat overgrown park area along the bank of the river to the east of the city center.

At that point, it wasn't even clear where the new governmental and cultural quarter was supposed to be built! The situation was truly utopian; the urban-planning competition was held later of course. So the Traisen Pavilion was a virtually mythical act, and a space for trial and experimentation with respect to ideational orientation.

Some segments of the population saw the revaluation of this small county seat as being somewhat high-handed, considering that, with a bishop's see, industrial center, and school center for the county, it had an interesting but certainly not spectacular history. What was concerned, among other things, was the relocation of over three thousand civil servants, who up to that point had their desks in the center of Vienna—along with the corresponding administrative, representative, and infrastructural facilities. The Traisen Pavilion was therefore a symbol of anticipation, a transfer station into an unknown but inevitably imminent development.

You positioned two elemental building types next to each other there: a prismatic longhouse, which is a several story "shelving unit"; and a circular central building, or a hall with a cylindrical eye in the center of the roof for light.

On the one hand, the utopian moment of non-location was a significant factor in coming up with ideas for the design. On the other, the functional indeterminateness due to the absence of guidelines specified the agenda. This openness in terms of content was, of course, paired with cost limits—the price of the pavilion was not supposed to be higher than the price for a small single-family house! The emancipation from the location and from fixed utilization offered the opportunity for a degree of idealization. It was a moment of autonomy without pathos, a "blithe innocence in privation." At the same time, as the planning became more concrete, Eichinger oder Knechtl, Georg Schöllhammer, and Dietmar Steiner developed ideas for use. The multistory shelving unit

Du hast für den Pavillon ein minimalistisches Stahl-gerüst aus Standardprofilen und -knoten entworfen. Das Dach über der Halle nutzte das Prinzip des Speichenrades mit leerer Mitte, hier in die Horizontale gekippt und ohne Schubkräfte zu erzeugen auf die 24 Stützen der Hallenwand gelegt. Dieses Rahmenwerk war in strahlenden Farben gestrichen und mit gewellten Kunststoffplatten sowie gefärbten Eternit-Platten umhüllt.

Die gemeinsam mit Professor Ziesel entwickelte Konstruktion und der Kostendruck erbrachten eine Assemblage von Alltäglichem: Stahl, Scobalit, Eternit; Holzbohlen für die »Regalböden«. Das Ganze erhielt dann eine signalhafte Verfremdung durch das Farbkleid nach dem Konzept von Oskar Putz. Zusätzlich erzeugten die gewellten Kunststoffplatten eine irisierende optische Wirkung, die einer Membran zwischen Innen und Außen.

Oskars Farben – weder die »reinen« Töne der klassischen Moderne noch die der heute gängigen Standardpalette – steigerten die rohe Einfachheit des Baus in abstrakt-frische, festliche Künstlichkeit, emanzipierten sich aber auch von der Idylle des Auwaldes. Dem fügten die halbtransparenten Lichtwellplatten etwas Eigenartiges hinzu …

Ich empfand den Blick durch das Scobalit, hinaus auf die nahen Bäume oder hinein in die Etagen der Ausstellung wie die stark eingeschränkte Tiefenschärfe von Polaroid-Fotos. Er hatte partielle Schärfe, eingebettet in generelle, lichterfüllte, luminöse Unschärfe. Und das passte sowohl zum damaligen Status der Hauptstadtdiskussion als auch zum traumhaften Charakter eines Pavillons – zum Fata-Morgana-Effekt einer solchen »folie«, wie das Gauklerhafte, das Transrationale von Gartenpavillons im französischen Begriff für diese angesprochen wird.

Der spontane Anlass

Du hast oft formuliert, Pavillons seien »Gebäude am falschen Ort zur Entwicklung eines richtigen Bewusstseins«. Der Traisenpavillon hatte viele Fans (die ihn Jahre später noch als permanenten Raum erhalten und winterfest ausrüsten wollten), provozierte aber auch viel Kritik, sogar Aggression. Der kleine Kunstbau von John Whiteman neben dem Ausstellungs-Regal wurde eines Nachts komplett niedergebrannt.

Pavillons sind Objekte, die unabhängig vom Ort diesen »unerwartet« prägen. Sie stehen nur mittel-

8804
Ausstellungspavillon an der Traisen /
Exhibition Pavilion on Traisen River
St. Pölten, 1988

and the assembly room staged, as it were, the Arcadian prelude to becoming the capital city. In the city's green leisure space, at the site of the protective dam against flooding on the Traisen River, there was then—as exotic as a visit to the circus—an ambitious exhibition as a *tour d'horizon* on the theme, along with a series of events and symposia.

S. / p. 30

For the pavilion, you designed a minimalist steel framework using standard profiles and nodes. The roof over the hall used the principle of a spoke wheel with an empty center, here tilted onto the horizontal plane and positioned along the twenty-four supports of the walls of the hall without producing thrusts. This framework was painted in bright colors and encased in Scobalit corrugated plastic and tinted Eternit panels.

The structure developed in cooperation with Professor Ziesel along with the cost pressure resulted in an assemblage of everyday materials: steel, Scobalit, Eternit, and wooden planks for the "shelves." The color scheme based on Oskar Putz's concept then evoked a signal-like alienation. Moreover, the corrugated plastic panels produced an iridescent visual effect, like a membrane between the inside and outside.

Oskar's colors—neither the "pure" shades of classical modernism nor those of the palette standard today—not only augmented the raw simplicity of the building with an abstract, fresh, festive artificiality, but they were also emancipated from the idyll of the alluvial forest. The semi-transparent corrugated panels added something quirky to it …

I found that the view through the Scobalit onto the nearby trees or into the floors of the exhibition building resembled the very limited depth of field of Polaroid photos. It had a partial sharpness, embedded in general, light-filled, and luminous blurriness. And that was consistent both with the

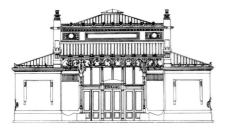
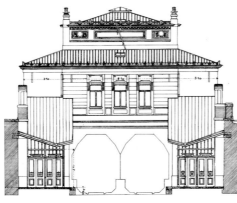

Otto Wagner
Stadtbahn Wien,
Haltestelle Normaltype, 1898
Straßenansicht, Bahn in Tieflage /
Street view, city railcar at sublevel

»Die Pavillons der Wiener Stadtbahn
von Otto Wagner«,
eine Studie von Missing Link,
Kapfinger & Krischanitz,
im Auftrag des Museums des
XX. Jahrhunderts, publiziert in:
Toni Michlmayr,
Fotoserie einer Zerstörung.
Abbruch Station Karlsplatz,
Ausst.-Kat. Museum des
XX. Jahrhunderts, Wien 1978

bar mit dem Standort in Verbindung, gleichgültig, ob sie nun im Kontext aufgehen oder ob es kontrastierende, autonome Gebilde sind.

Bemerkenswert ist, dass es innerhalb der durchstrukturierten Gesellschaft oft Anlässe gibt, ephemere Gründungsgebäude oder Festzeichen zu setzen. Wenn man die Wiener Stadtentwicklung betrachtet, gab es immer wieder solche Anlässe, etwa die Stationen des Makart-Festzuges 1879 und der diversen Kaiserjubiläen, oder die Pavillons für Messen und Weltausstellungen, die nur einer kurzzeitigen, aber signifikanten Verwendung dienten. Ihre Standorte waren im Augenblick »falsch« und meist mit Bauverbot belegt, erhielten nur befristete Genehmigungen, waren langfristig für andere Nutzungen vorgesehen – jedoch immer einem Brennpunkt nahe, um ein Ereignis zu begleiten, ein vorübergehendes Bedürfnis zu bedienen. Der spontane Anlass, die Kurzfristigkeit des Ereignisses, die subversive Unterbrechung des Alltags, die Maximierung der Wirkung mit geringem Aufwand sind Bedingung und Parameter. Pavillons sind frei vom Anspruch der Dauer, sind sozusagen unernst. Sie durchbrechen die Normalität, erzeugen spontane Heterotopien, lassen unerwartete Perspektiven aufblitzen. Pavillons sind wie Kalligrafien, zum Bild verdichtete Texte, mit einer schnelleren und eindringlicheren Sprachfähigkeit als andere Bauten.

Zufall oder nicht – Pavillons zählten zu den ersten typologischen Untersuchungen, die wir in den 1970er-Jahren gemeinsam unternommen haben: die Pavillons der Wiener Stadtbahn von Wagner, die Hochbahn-Station Gumpendorferstraße, die Tiefbahn-Pavillons am Karlsplatz, allesamt transitorische Räume, Umsteigstationen im flüchtigen Muster des urbanen Alltags ...

Der Kunstwissenschaftler Otto A. Graf hat in seiner Dissertation über Otto Wagner die Stadtbahnpavillons »Gebäude zum Verlassen« genannt.

status of the capital city discussion at the time and with a dreamlike pavilion—with the fata morgana effect of such a *folie*, similar to the way the traveling entertainer quality, the transrational character of garden pavilions, is addressed in the French term.

The Spontaneous Occasion

You have often said that pavilions are "buildings in the wrong place for cultivating proper awareness." The Traisen Pavilion had many supporters (who continued to maintain it for years as a permanent space and wanted to equip it for use throughout the year). But it also provoked a lot of criticism, even aggression. The small art building by John Whiteman next to the shelving unit for exhibitions was completely burned down one night.

Pavilions are objects that "unexpectedly" shape the place where they are located independently of it. They are only indirectly connected with the location, regardless of whether they then merge with the context or remain contrasting, autonomous entities.

It's worth noting that, within a tightly structured society, occasions frequently arise for constructing ephemeral original buildings or those erected in conjunction with special occasions. If we consider the urban development of Vienna, there have been such occasions time and again, for instance the Makart-Festzug in 1879 (the pageant to mark the silver anniversary of the imperial couple) and the various imperial jubilees, or the pavilions for fairs and world expositions, which only served a significant purpose for a short period of time. Their locations were "wrong" at the moment, and there was generally a ban on construction imposed on them. They received only temporary permits because they were planned for other uses in the long term—but they were always located near a focal point in order to accompany an occasion, to serve a temporary need. The spontaneous occasion, its short-term nature, the subversive disruption of everyday life, and the maximization of effect with little expense are both condition and parameter. Pavilions are free from the requirement of permanence, which implies that they are unserious, as it were. They disrupt normality, produce spontaneous heterotopias, and allow unexpected perspectives to arise. Pavilions are like calligraphy, text concentrated to become an image, with a faster and more emphatic faculty of speech than other structures.

An den Karlsplatz-Pavillons faszinierte uns die Fusion des elementaren Typus mit dem schmetterlingshaften Gewand, diese grelle Vergegenwärtigung von archaischen Zuständen, die Erinnerung an uralte Rituale und zeitlose Symbole angesichts modernster Technik und Infrastruktur.

Die elastische Lösung

Dazu fällt mir auf: Es gibt eine weitere Bedeutungsachse. Der Pavillon als temporärer Halte- und Schutzpunkt im mythologischen Paradies, im »hortus conclusus«, ist auch ein Archetyp der humanen Kulturwerdung innerhalb und gegenüber der inhumanen Natur. Könnte man die Serie deiner Pavillons nun auch so lesen: als heiter-gelassene Umsteigstationen in der Inhuman-Landschaft heutiger Stadträume zur Kultivierung »richtigen« Bewusstseins?

Die Anlässe dieser Projekte waren in der Regel nicht heiter-gelassen, sondern geprägt vom Eindruck, dass nichts mehr geht! Am Anfang stand meist ein spürbarer Mangel, der sich einer konventionellen Lösung kurzfristig entzog. So ging es schlicht darum, eine elastische Lösung zu finden, gewitzt mit Bedingungen, mit absurden Reglementierungen und minimalen Budgets umzugehen.

Kürzlich las ich in einer Pavillons gewidmeten Ausgabe von *werk, bauen + wohnen*, dass im Japanischen das Wort Schrein ein Synonym für die Farbe Weiß und all ihre Konnotationen ist. Passt da nicht zum Beispiel der weiße Innenraum deiner temporären Kunsthalle in Berlin perfekt dazu?

Mies van der Rohe baute einen gläsernen Schrein für Edith Farnsworth: die Stilisierung von Stahl und Glas zu einer hochtechnischen hieratischen Urhütte – ein Raum, der zwischen sich und die umgebende Natur nur mehr eine Glasscheibe setzen musste und sich so, in totalem Blickkontakt mit ihr, endgültig aus der Natur in die Künstlichkeit, in eine »zweite«, menschgeschaffene Natur entfernte.

Allerdings: Ist nicht schon die »erste Natur« ein kosmetisches (oder mentales) Konstrukt, das da kalkuliert in den gläsernen Pavillon einbezogen wird? So wird Natur selbst zur omnipräsenten Wand, zur »domestizierten« Umhüllung des Habitats, dessen physische Präsenz wiederum fast verschwindet.

Das Gegenteil des gläsernen ist der fensterlose Pavillon, der sich quasi durch Kunst verstellt, sich in

Coincidence or not—pavilions were one of the subjects of the first typological examinations we undertook together in the nineteen-seventies: Otto Wagner's pavilions for Vienna's city railway, the Gumpendorferstrasse elevated railway station, the underground railway pavilion at Karlsplatz, all of them transitory spaces, transfer stations in the fleeting pattern of everyday urban life . . .

In his dissertation on Otto Wagner, the art historian Otto A. Graf called the city railway pavilions "buildings for leaving." At the Karlsplatz pavilion, we were fascinated by the fusion of the elemental type with the butterfly-like raiment, this flamboyant realization of archaic conditions, the memory of ancient rituals and timeless symbols while confronted with the most modern technology and infrastructure.

The Elastic Solution

What also strikes me is that there is another axis of meaning. The pavilion as a temporary stopping point and site of protection in the mythological paradise, in the *hortus conclusus*, is also an archetype for becoming a human culture within and in relation to inhuman nature. Might one then also read your series of pavilions in such a way: as sanguine, serene transfer stations for cultivating "proper" awareness in the inhuman landscape of contemporary urban spaces?

The occasions for these projects were usually not sanguine and serene, but instead shaped by the impression that nothing else worked! In the beginning, there was generally a noticeable lack, which made a conventional solution impossible in the short term. It was then simply a matter of finding an elastic solution for dealing shrewdly with marginal conditions, absurd regulations, and minimal budgets.

In an issue of *werk, bauen + wohnen* dedicated to pavilions, I recently read that, in Japanese, the word shrine is a synonym for the color white and all its connotations. Doesn't that apply perfectly to the example of the white interior of your Temporäre Kunsthalle (Temporary Art Hall) in Berlin?

Mies van der Rohe designed a glazed shrine for Edith Farnsworth: a stylization of steel and glass as a highly technical, hieratic primitive hut—a space that only had to place a sheet of glass between itself and surrounding nature in order to distance itself once and for all from nature, thus moving

Personifikation der Architektur mit der Urhütte / The Personification of Architecture and the Primitive Hut,
aus / from: Marc-Antoine Laugier, *Essai sur l'architecture*, Paris 1753

barocker Weise von der profanen Außenwelt abschottet, um innen einen ganz anderen Kosmos zu schaffen. Bei meinen provisorischen Kunsthallen in Wien und Berlin hatte ich sowohl die Innen- als auch die Außenseiten als Kunstträger konzipiert. Diese Pavillons waren tatsächlich Paravents: innen und außen synchron, »vorne« und »hinten« synonym. Betrachtet man einen solchen Paravent-Bau als Vexierschachtel zur Herstellung von Imaginationen, so erschließt sich in den Doppelrollen der Wand – Innen / Außen beziehungsweise Stütze / Schutz / Bild – die ganze Bandbreite architektonischen Vermögens: vom Gebrauchswert bis zum Ausstellungswert.

Die engste Synchronizität von Architektur und Kunst entstand in Berlin mit der Installation *Compass* von Allora & Calzadilla (2009). Da wurde in einer Höhe von 2,40 Metern eine Decke eingezogen, auf der sich während der Ausstellungsdauer Tänzer und Tänzerinnen nach einer eigenen Choreografie bewegten und im Ausstellungsraum darunter ausschließlich die Bewegungsgeräusche hörbar waren.

Die Kunsthalle als Vexierschachtel

Gehen wir nochmals zurück nach Wien, zur Entstehung der Kunsthalle am Karlsplatz, die dort ja einige Zeit gewaltig Staub aufgewirbelt hat.

Die Urfassung war eine Indoor-Halle im Wiener Messepalast zum Anlass der internationalen Ausstellung der Wiener Festwochen 1990 *Von der Natur in der Kunst*, kuratiert von Peter Weiermair. Das Areal der barocken Hofstallungen, später als Messegelände genutzt und ausgebaut, war schon als künftiges Museumsquartier vorgesehen. Die Stadt nutzte die alten Hallen zwischenzeitlich für Ausstellungen. 1989 hatte Hermann Czech in der historistischen Reithalle die Schau *Wunderblock. Eine Geschichte der modernen Seele* gestaltet. Dieselbe Halle brauchte im Jahr darauf für großformatige Kunstwerke neutrale Wände, kontrolliertes Licht und Klima. So wurde es eine »Halle in der Halle« – ein Container aus zerlegbarer Stahlkonstruktion mit Plattenverkleidung und Oberlichtdecke, innen stützenfrei, mit einer Stahl-Glas-Röhre, die den Zugang vom Hof durch die alten Foyers inszenierte und als »halbblinder« Tunnel den Kunstraum durchquerte. Schon damals kam die Idee auf, während der langen Zeit der Museumsquartier-Baustelle eine temporäre Kunsthalle in zentraler Lage zu bespielen. Ich hatte die Adaptierung, das Weiterleben der Indoor-

9008
Indoor-Halle, Wien, 1990
Messepalast, ehemalige Winter-
reitschule / former Winter Riding
School, Modell / model

S. / pp. 40 / 41

into artificiality, into a "second" nature created by humans, while still maintaining total visual contact.

However, isn't the "first nature" already a cosmetic (or mental) construct that is incorporated into the glazed pavilion in a calculated way? Nature itself therefore becomes the omnipresent wall, the "domesticated" encasement of habitat, whose physical presence then virtually disappears.

The opposite of the glazed pavilion is the windowless pavilion, which is quasi dissembled through art, sealing itself off from the profane outside world in a baroque manner in order to create a completely different cosmos. In the case of my provisional art halls in Vienna and Berlin, I designed both the inside and outside as supports for art. These pavilions were in fact screens: with inside and outside synchronous, "in front" and "behind" synonymous. If you see such screen structures as puzzle boxes for stimulating imagination, in the dual roles of the wall—inside/outside or support/protection/image—the entire spectrum of architectural patrimony therefore develops: from the utility value to the exhibition value. The closest synchronicity of architecture and art was produced in Berlin with Allora & Calzadilla's installation *Compass* (2009). There, a ceiling was installed at a height of 2.4 meters, on which male and female dancers moved according to choreographies of their own throughout the duration of the exhibition, and only the sounds of their movements could be heard in the exhibition space underneath.

The Art Hall as a Puzzle Box

Let's go back to Vienna again, to the creation of the Kunsthalle at Karlsplatz, which indeed caused quite a stir there for some time.

The original version was an indoor hall in Vienna's Messepalast (Trade Fair Palace) in conjunction with the international exhibition during the Wiener Festwochen (Vienna Festival) in 1990, *Von der Natur in der Kunst* (From Nature to Art), curated by Peter Weiermair. The grounds of the Baroque royal stables, which were later used and developed as an exhibition site, had already been designated for use as a future museum district. In the interim, the city was using the old halls for exhibitions. In 1989, Hermann Czech designed the show *Wunderblock: Eine Geschichte der modernen Seele* (Mystic Writing Pad: A History of the

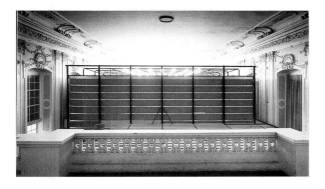

9008
Indoor-Halle
*Von der Natur in der Kunst / From
Nature to Art*, Messepalast, ehe-
malige Winterreitschule / former
Winter Riding School

9116
Kunsthalle Karlsplatz
Wien, 1992

Halle im Außenraum schon mitgedacht. Der Platz dafür war noch unklar. Bürgermeister Helmut Zilk und Kulturstadträtin Ursula Pasterk entschieden sich dann für den Karlsplatz.

In der Reithalle noch unscheinbar »verpuppt«, schlüpfte am Platz des alten Bauernmarktes bei der Secession dann ein knallgelber Schmetterling! Der Karlsplatz – von Otto Wagner als »Gegend« vor Fischer von Erlachs grandioser Kuppelkirche taxiert, trotz hunderter Projektideen seit Wagners Zeiten ein letztlich unbebaubarer zentraler Raum von Wien, über dem größten, außen unsichtbaren U-Bahn-Knoten, einem Brennpunkt der Drogenszene und Treffpunkt der Heimatlosen, rings umstellt von Ikonen der Hochkultur: Karlskirche, Technikum, Musikverein, Secession, Künstlerhaus, Wien Museum, und dazwischen die Asphaltbänder einer innerstädtischen Hauptschneise des Autoverkehrs ...

Die Kunsthalle Karlsplatz hatte die denkbar schlechtesten Prognosen bezüglich eines erfolgreichen Betriebes. Die bei den U-Bahn-Passagen ansässige Drogenszene und das fehlende Vorstellungsvermögen vieler Wiener für einen Neubau im Sichtkreis der Karlskirche hätten den Start fast verhindert. Es gab wilde Polemiken in den Medien gegen den »Schandfleck«, der angeblich die Kirche verdeckte. Man ätzte über den Bau, kritisierte aber in Wahrheit, dass damit die offensive, zeitgenössische, sozialdemokratische Kulturpolitik unter der Ägide von Ursula Pasterk nun im Dunstkreis von Musikverein und Oper derart sichtbar wurde.
Doch sehr bald erreichte der gelb-blaue Container mit dem vorgelagerten Café Kultstatus. Aufgrund der langen Bauzeit des Museumsquartiers wurde die nur temporär gedachte und entsprechend »billig« ausgeführte Struktur schließlich zehn Jahre lang genutzt. Im neuen Museumsquartier entstand inzwischen die große permanente Kunsthalle der Stadt – als eher verkrampftes Implantat in die erwähnte, baugeschichtlich wertlose Reithalle, die

Modern Soul) in the historical riding hall. The following year, the same hall was in need of neutral walls and controlled lighting and climate for large-format artworks. It thus became a "hall within a hall"—a container made of a demountable steel structure with panel cladding and a skylight ceiling, without supports inside, and with a steel and glass tube staging the access from the courtyard through the old foyer and traversing the artspace as a "half-blind" tunnel. The idea of making use of a temporary art hall in a central location during the long period when the museum district was a construction site already arose at that time. I had already considered adapting and continuing the life of the indoor hall for outdoors. But the location for it was still unclear. The mayor, Helmut Zilk, and the city councilor for culture, Ursula Pasterk, decided on Karlsplatz.

Still inconspicuously "pupating" in the riding hall, a bright yellow butterfly then hatched on the square of the old farmers' market near the Secession! The Karlsplatz—appraised by Otto Wagner as an "area" in front of Johann Bernhard Fischer von Erlach's grand domed church, a place ultimately unfit for building despite hundreds of project ideas since Wagner's time, a central space in Vienna, situated above the largest subway hub which is invisible from the outside, a focal point for the drug scene and a meeting place for the homeless, surrounded by icons of high culture from all sides: the Karlskirche (Church of St. Charles), the Technikum (University of Applied Sciences), the Musikverein (Viennese Music Association), the Secession, the Künstlerhaus, the Wien Museum, and between them the asphalt bands of a main inner-city traffic route . . .

S. / pp. 31–33

The Kunsthalle at Karlsplatz had the worst prognoses imaginable for ever operating successfully. The drug scene flourishing in the subway passages and the lack of imagination of many Vienna residents regarding a new building within view of the Karlskirche nearly prevented the start.

23

9116
Kunsthalle Karlsplatz
Rohrbrücke über die Fahrbahnen,
im Hintergrund das Ausstellungshaus der Wiener Secession
von Joseph M. Olbrich (1898) /
Tubular bridge over the street,
with the Secession Building by
Joseph M. Olbrich (1898) in the
background

»Die Unmöglichkeit des Lebens ist
die Wirklichkeit der Kunst. Kunst
und Leben sind verbunden durch
eine sich gegenseitig ausschlie-
ßende Getrenntheit wie Leben
und Tod. Der Lorbeerbaum, Kuppel
der Wiener Secession, als Zerstörer,
als allgegenwärtige Natur, die sich
ins Menschenwerk einwächst, um
es schließlich zu überwinden, ist
nicht nur das Symbol des Verge-
hens der menschlichen Existenz,
sondern auch die Aufforderung
zur immer wiederkehrenden
Erneuerung.«

Adolf Krischanitz,
in: *Architektur ist der Unterschied
zwischen Architektur*,
Ostfildern 2010

man besser hätte abreißen sollen. Nach der Eröffnung des Museumsquartiers wurde der Pavillon
am Karlsplatz abgebaut und durch eine viel
kleinere, niedrigere Stahl-Glas-Variante ersetzt,
ebenfalls von meinem Büro geplant.

**Versuchen wir einmal eine Beschreibung der Dialek-
tik deiner Kunsthalle mit einem anderen, älteren
Kunstpavillon, der direkt gegenüber steht – dem
Ausstellungshaus der Secession. Beide Häuser waren
bei ihrer Errichtung extreme Zankäpfel der öffentlichen Meinung.**

Einige Jahre vor der Kunsthalle konnte ich die
Renovierung und Adaptierung der Secession
planerisch betreuen und den Olbrich-Bau in allen
Facetten und geschichtlichen Wandlungen studieren. Dabei kam heraus, dass auch dieses Monument der Wiener Moderne als temporärer Pavillon
auf fremdem Grund gedacht war. Die Künstler-
vereinigung hatte ihn 1897 für eine Nutzungs-
dauer von zehn Jahren konzipiert und das auch im
Vertrag mit dem Grundeigentümer, mit der Stadtgemeinde, so festgelegt!

**Die Secession bietet nach vorne, zum Platz, in Rich-
tung Karlskirche und Künstlerhaus, eine Schaufront
symbolhafter Elemente, zeigt sich nach hinten, zur
Akademie, dagegen ganz »industriell« alltäglich.**

Der Bau ist erstaunlich klein, entwickelt aber
durch Joseph Olbrichs spezielle Motivik, durch
seine Hermetik und die den Maßstab verschlei-
ernde Monumentalität eine raumbeherrschende
Ausstrahlung. Er ist eine Variante des Tor-Typus
von Otto Wagners Stadtbahn-Pavillons. Dort
war es ein Interface unterschiedlicher Geschwindig-
keiten, hier ist es eine kulturelle »Umsteigstation«.

**Deine Kunsthalle dagegen: völlig »kunstlos« aus dem
Stahlbau-Container-Katalog, auf wenigen Punktfun-**

There were wild polemics in the media against
the "eyesore" supposedly obscuring the church.
People commented bitingly on the building, but
were actually criticizing the fact that, with it, the
offensive, contemporary, social-democratic cultural
policies under the aegis of Ursula Pasterk were
now becoming strongly visible in the surroundings
of the Musikverein and Oper (Opera House).
The yellow and blue container with the café in
front nonetheless very soon achieved cult status.
Due to the long period of construction work on
the museum district, the structure, which was
originally only considered temporary and correspondingly realized "cheaply," was ultimately used
for ten years. In the meantime, the city's large
permanent Kunsthalle was under construction in
the new museum district—more as a cramped
implant in the, as already mentioned, architecturally worthless riding hall, which preferably should
have been demolished. After the opening of the
museum district, the pavilion at Karlsplatz was
dismantled and replaced by a much smaller and
shorter steel-and-glass variant, which was also
planned by my office.

**Let's try to describe the dialectic of your Kunsthalle
by considering another older art pavilion that stands
directly opposite it—the exhibition building of the
Secession. When they were erected, both buildings
were extreme bones of contention in terms of
public opinion.**

Some years prior to the Kunsthalle, I had the
chance to do the planning for the renovation and
adaptation of the Secession and to study the
Olbrich building in all its facets and historical
transformations. As it turned out, this monument
to Viennese modernism was also conceived as a
temporary pavilion on alien ground. In 1897, the
artists' association planned for an operating life
of ten years, and this was also stipulated in the
contract with the owner of the property and with
the municipality!

**To the front, toward the square, in the direction of
the Karlskirche and the Künstlerhaus, the Secession
offers a front with symbolic elements, while to the
back, toward the Akademie, it is, in contrast, rather
"industrially" quotidian.**

Though the building is surprisingly small, as a
result of Joseph Olbrich's special motifs, of its
hermetic quality and the monumentality obscuring
the dimensions, it develops a spatially dominating
aura. It is a variant on the portal type of Otto

damenten in der Wiese neben dem Verkehrsband abgestellt, allerdings gekleidet in die flüchtigste und abstrakteste und somit auch provokanteste Formenergie – die Farbe, mit der gelb-blauen Komposition aus der Palette von Oskar Putz »in der Nähe« des unmöglichen Möbelhauses und jener massentauglichen Wohnlichkeiten, die IKEA eben anbietet ...

Im Gegensatz zur auratischen, bei aller Umsturzrhetorik sehr »heiligen« Secession war meine Kunsthalle als industrieller Container, als bunte Schachtel auch leicht lesbar als Synonym für den banalen Warencharakter heutiger Kultur und Gesellschaft – und das empfanden die konservativen Gesellschaftskreise als zusätzliche Provokation im Zentrum der »Kulturhauptstadt« Wien. Der vordergründige Waren- und Paketcharakter des Pavillons bot aber eine überhaupt nicht so einfach kaufbare oder konsumierbare »Ware«: das künstlerisch stimulierte, emanzipatorische Erlebnis, das nicht verdinglichte, nicht verdinglichbare Bewusstsein.

Und im Durchstoßen des Pavillons mit der Gitterröhre wurde das nochmals überdreht. Die industrielle Röhre schlug eine Schneise des »spektakulären« Zugangs aus dem Massenverkehrsraum in den elitären Kunstraum hinein. Im Durchqueren der Halle wurde die Röhre blind, undurchsichtig, gewährte gerade keinen schnellen Einblick in die Kunst, in »das Andere« von Gesellschaft.

Eine Transparenz der Röhre auch im Inneren der Halle wäre ein populistischer Kurzschluss gewesen, ein Verrat dieser Dialektik an eine bloß oberflächlich argumentierbare »Popularisierung« künstlerischer Kritik- und Gegenwelten (so utopisch oder idealistisch diese Kunsthaltung heute auch sein mag).

Zwischen Labor und Depot

Der Pavillon der Kunsthalle war äußerlich auch ein »Gestell des Verschwindens« hinter verschiedenen, ebenfalls nur temporären, großformatig im Stadtraum präsenten Bemalungen durch Künstler.

Es gab eine Reihe großer und großartiger Ausstellungen. Die Halle war international berühmt, in Wien hat man sie immer unterschätzt und als zu wenig wertvoll erachtet. Doch das hat ihren Reiz ausgemacht, diese En-Passant-Qualität, die Neutralität irgendwo zwischen Produktionsstätte und Depot. Die Kunst musste sich hier nicht von der Architektur emanzipieren.

Wagner's city railway pavilion. There, it was an interface of different speeds, while here it is a cultural "transfer station."

Your Kunsthalle in contrast: assembled utterly "artlessly" from the steel-construction catalogue of containers, sited on a few point foundations in the grassy area next to the street, yet clad in the most fleeting and abstract, and therefore also most provocative, design energy—the color, with a yellow-blue composition from the palette of Oskar Putz, located near the outrageous furniture store and those mass-market home comforts offered by IKEA ...

Unlike the auratic Secession, which despite all the subversive rhetoric was held very "sacred," my Kunsthalle—as an industrial container, as a colorful box—was easy to read as a synonym for the banal commodity character of today's culture and society. Indeed, conservative circles in society perceived this as an additional provocation in the center of Vienna, the "capital of culture." But the superficial commodity and package character of the pavilion offered a "commodity" in no way as simple to purchase or consume: the artistically stimulated, emancipatory experience, a consciousness not reified and unable to be reified.

And in penetrating the pavilion with the latticework tube this was revved up once again. The industrial tube cleared a "spectacular" access path from the traffic space of the masses into the elite artspace. In traversing the hall, the tube became blind, opaque, provided, in particular, no quick insight into the art, into "the other" of society.

Also making the tube transparent inside the hall would have been a populist bypass, a betrayal of this dialectic in favor of a merely superficially justifiable "popularization" of artistic critique and parallel worlds (as utopian or idealistic as this artistic stance might seem today).

Between Laboratory and Depot

Outwardly, the Kunsthalle pavilion was also a "frame of disappearance" behind various large-format paintings, also only temporary, presented by artists in urban space.

There was a series of big and brilliant exhibitions. The hall was famous around the world, although it was always underestimated and viewed as being

9116
Kunsthalle Karlsplatz, Wien, 1992

»Die rationale Konstruktion ist wie aus dem Lehrbuch. Die Abspannungen verweisen unmissverständlich auf den provisorischen Charakter; für eine längere Lebensdauer würde man das nicht machen. Außen liegen das Skelett und die Sehnen; die neutrale Oberfläche für die Nutzung ist auf der Innenseite zu suchen. Derartige konstruktive Standardlösungen können auch von jenen verstanden werden, die nicht Fachleute sind. Nur ist ihre Anwendung für diese Bauaufgabe ungewohnt. [...]
Mag sein, dass dies die Leute ängstigt, diese rohe Kraft des Metallbaus, die Kraft, die in den Dingen zu stecken scheint. Diese Details sagen uns: ›So wird heute dort gebaut, wo ihr nie hinschaut.‹«

Walter Zschokke,
in: *Die Presse, Spectrum*,
14. August 1992

»Den Glanzpunkt des Eröffnungs-
tages der Frankfurter Buchmesse
setzte kein Schriftsteller, sondern
ein Architekt. Adolf Krischanitz hat
für den Österreich-Pavillon eine
raffinierte Balance zwischen Unauf-
dringlichkeit und selbstbewußter
Präsenz gefunden.«

Der Standard, 12. Oktober 1995

»Der ›Intimität und Offenheit‹
des Dialogs war der von Adolf
Krischanitz entworfene kreisrunde
Pavillon aus Stahl und Glas ver-
pflichtet, der eine Woche lang das
Auge des Messe-Zyklons bildete.«

Neue Zürcher Zeitung,
16. Oktober 1995

Auch in Berlin war es ein ähnlich aufgeladener Nicht-Ort und Diskussionsort – das stark debattierte Stadtschloss, die Museenballung ringsum –, und wir könnten da eine analoge Dialektik der Deutungen diskutieren.

Auch dort war die Strategie: Wir haben keine Chance, deshalb nutzen wir sie! Das Budget war fast lächerlich, die Sponsoren, ohne die es nicht gegangen wäre, haben wir selbst aufgestellt. Eines Tages kamen zwei junge Damen, Coco Kühn und Constanze Kleiner, auf mich zu und wollten, nachdem sie von der Wiener Kunsthalle gehört hatten, eine Anleitung zum Bau einer kostengünstigen Ausstellungshalle. Vorher hatte es eine Ausschreibung der Zeitschrift *Monopol* für eine Kunsthalle am Berliner Schlossplatz gegeben. Die interessanten Beiträge namhafter deutscher Architekten waren aber nicht finanzierbar. So wurde mein Vorschlag gemeinsam mit einem Projekt der Gruppe Graft in die engere Wahl einbezogen. Entscheidend war dann die Initia-tive des Industriellen Dieter Rosenkranz, der in großartiger Weise unser Projekt mit einer Million Euro und vielen sonstigen Zuwendungen unterstützte. Mir gelang es zusätzlich, Sach-spenden im Wert von 500.000 Euro von den beteiligten Firmen aufzutreiben. Durch das Engagement zweier junger Damen und eines Kunstmäzens hatte Berlin so zumindest für zwei Jahre eine Kunsthalle. Sie war aus Holz-Fertig-teilen geformt, jenseits aller so verführerischen formalen Allüren: eine Box für Ereignisse innen und als Leinwand für künstlerische Signale außen – das geometrische Wolkenbild von Gerwald Rockenschaub; die Blicke auf sich ziehend, nicht als Architektur, sondern als Ereignis; nicht als Skulptur, sondern als Produktionsort wechselnder Imaginationen.

of too little value in Vienna. Nonetheless, that was what gave it its appeal, this en passant quality, the neutrality somewhere between production site and depot. Here, the art did not have to emancipate itself from the architecture.

There was also a similarly charged non-location and place for discourse—the widely debated Stadtschloss or city palace, the concentration of museums all around—and we could also discuss an analogue dialectic of interpretation in this case.

The strategy there was also: We have no chance, so let's do it! The budget was almost ridiculous, and it wouldn't have worked without the sponsors, as we ourselves discovered. One day, two young ladies, Coco Kühn and Constanze Kleiner, came up to me and, after hearing about the Kunsthalle in Vienna, asked for instructions for erecting a cost-effective exhibition hall. A competition for designing an art hall at Schlossplatz in Berlin had just been announced in *Monopol* magazine. It was not possible, however, to finance the interesting contributions by distinguished German architects. My proposal was therefore shortlisted along with a project by the Graft group. What was then deci-sive was the initiative of the industrialist Dieter Rosenkranz, who generously supported our project with one million euros. I also managed to scrape up donations at a value of 500,000 euros from the companies involved. Through the com-mitment of two young women and a patron of the arts, Berlin therefore at least had an art hall for two years. It was made from prefabricated wooden components, quite removed from seductive formal affectations: a box for events on the inside and a canvas for artistic signals on the outside—Gerwald Rockenschaub's geometric cloud image; drawing attention to itself, not as architecture but as an

Bei allen Pavillons fällt auf: Nicht die Architektur erzeugt selbstbezüglich den Effekt der erwähnten »folie«, sondern dasjenige, dem die Architektur Raum gibt.

Ich kann rückblickend sagen, dass vor allem die Arbeit an und mit diesen ephemeren Hallen meinen latenten Hang zum Weder-Noch weiterentwickelt hat, meine grundsätzliche Auffassung von Architektur, die mehr und mehr die möglichst allgemeine, die nicht-subjektive Form sucht – und in dieser dann doch wieder die irritierenden Momente des Uneindeutigen.

Schauen wir uns im Vergleich den Wiener Karlsplatz, die Situation in Berlin und den Österreich-Pavillon auf der Frankfurter Buchmesse an: am Karlsplatz die temporäre Kiste in rohem Stahlbau, die Geste des Überschreitens der Verkehrswüste; bei der Kunsthalle Berlin »nur« die Raumhöhe, die Farbe, das Bodenmuster – und es genügt! Und in Frankfurt: der riesige Platz der Messehallen mit dem Obelisk – ein Phallus. Und deine Antwort – ein Ring aus Stahl und Glaswänden um den Obelisken herum, was zusammen ein Lingam ergab, das indische Symbol von Schöpfungskraft aus Vertikal und Horizontal.

Das Café samt Nebenräumen nutzte ein Hälfte des Ringes. In der anderen zeigten Cathrin Pichler und Johannes Schlebrügge eine feinsinnige Schau von Autografen und Utensilien österreichischer Autoren und Autorinnen. Und die Glaswände waren in großen Lettern mit einem Zitat von Robert Musil bedruckt; ein Nichts an Form und Intervention am Platz, und doch eine lässig funktionierende, mit Botschaften gesättigte Möblierung des Ortes für den Auftritt der Literatur aus Österreich bei der Buchmesse 1995.

Ein Pavillon kann heute nicht mehr Panoramen über die Stadtlandschaft bieten, er kann glaubhaft nur mehr Räume ins Imaginäre, ins Strukturelle öffnen …

… was Konzeptuelle Kunst, Arte Povera, Gender-Konzepte usw. längst tun. Und da liegt die Parallelität: in der Wende von der Spektakel-Architektur zur konzeptuellen Architektur, die materiell beziehungsweise gestalthaft das »Verschwinden« des Verdinglichten anbietet zugunsten des »Auftauchens« und des Erscheinens perzeptiver Grundstrukturen – eine Wende von virtuoser Waren-Ästhetik zum Strukturellen der Wahrnehmung, zu den Konstruktionsmustern von Wirklichkeit.

event; not as a sculpture, but rather as a production site for alternating ideas.

What's striking about all of the pavilions: it's not the architecture that self-referentially generates the effect of the aforementioned *folie*, but instead what the architecture provides space for.

Looking back, I can say that above all the work on and with these ephemeral halls further developed my latent penchant for neither/nor, my basic approach to architecture, which increasingly searches for the as-general-as-possible, for the non-subjective form—and, at the same time, contained therein are the irritating moments of the ambiguous.

Let's take a look at Karlsplatz in Vienna, the situation in Berlin, and the Austrian pavilion at the Frankfurt Book Fair: at Karlsplatz, the temporary box in a raw steel structure, the gesture of cutting across the traffic wasteland; in the case of the Kunsthalle in Berlin, "only" the height of the space, the color, the pattern of the floor—and that sufficed! And in Frankfurt: the huge plaza between the exhibition halls with the obelisk—a phallus. And your answer: a ring of steel-and-glass walls around the obelisk, which together created a lingam, the Indian symbol for creative energy, from the vertical and the horizontal.

The café took up one half of the ring. In the other, Cathrin Pichler and Johannes Schlebrügge presented a subtle show of autographs and utensils of Austrian authors. And the glass walls were printed with a quote by Robert Musil in large letters; a nothing with regard to form and intervention on the plaza, and nevertheless one that functioned nonchalantly, furnishings for the location saturated with messages for the appearance of literature from Austria at the Frankfurt Book Fair of 1995.

A pavilion today can no longer provide panoramas over the urban landscape; it can plausibly only open up more spaces in the imaginary, in the structural …

… which Conceptual Art, Arte Povera, gender concepts, and so forth have long since been doing. And that's where the parallelism lies: in the turn from spectacle architecture to conceptual architecture, which offers, materially and/or morphologically, the "disappearance" of the reified in favor of the "emergence" and appearance of more perceptual basic structures—a turn from a virtuoso commodity aesthetic to the structural facet of perception, to the patterns of constructing reality.

0703
Temporäre Kunsthalle Berlin

Letzte Ausstellung der Temporären Kunsthalle Berlin / Last Exhibition at the Temporäre Kunsthalle Berlin

»Jetzt hat John Bock ein fulminantes Finale gezündet. Die von ihm mit mehr als 60 Künstlern ausgerichtete Abschluss-Schau ›FrischGräten-MelkStand‹ ist das Beste, was in den letzten vier Jahren in Berlin an Gruppenausstellungen zu sehen war […]. Wie durch einen Termitenbau, der auf Mietshausformat vergrößert wurde, läuft man über vier Etagen auf elf Metern vertikaler Höhe, jedes Geschoss eine wuchernde Abfolge von Kabinetten, Emporen, Brücken und Schlupflöchern.«

Silke Hohmann,
in: *Die Welt*, 3. Juli 2010

8804
Ausstellungspavillon an der Traisen /
Exhibition Pavilion on Traisen River
St. Pölten, Aufbau / under construction

8804
Ausstellungspavillon an der Traisen /
Exhibition Pavilion on Traisen River

9116
Kunsthalle Karlsplatz
Wien / Vienna

9116
Kunsthalle Karlsplatz

9116
Kunsthalle Karlsplatz

mit Fassadengestaltungen von /
with façade designs by
Ed Ruscha
Gerhard Richter
Douglas Gordon
museum in progress

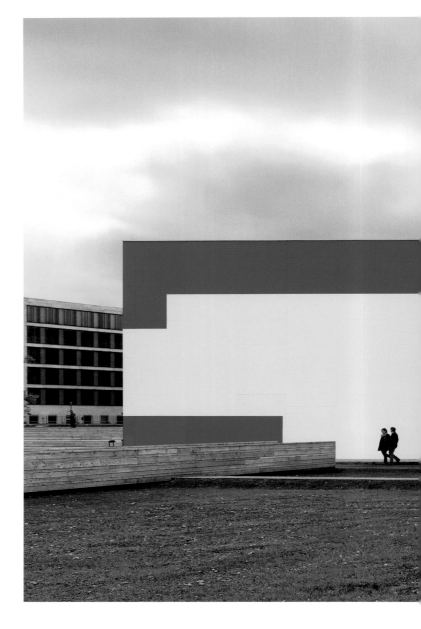

9406
Österreich-Pavillon Frankfurter Buchmesse /
Austrian Pavilion, Frankfurt Book Fair
Frankfurt am Main

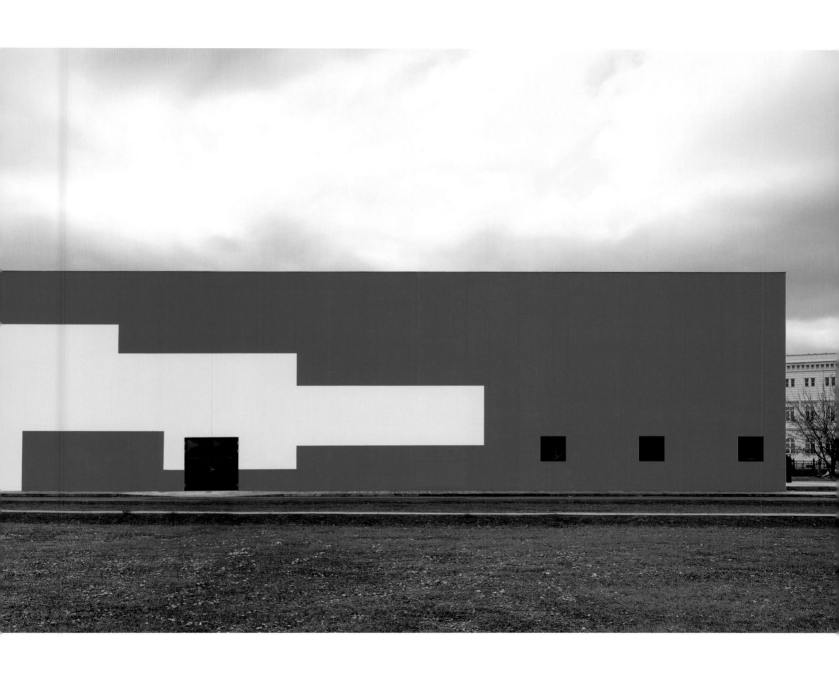

0703
Temporäre Kunsthalle Berlin
Fassade / Façade: Gerwald Rockenschaub

0703
Temporäre Kunsthalle Berlin
John Bock, Ausstellung / Exhibition *FrischGrätenMelkStand*, 2010

0703
Temporäre Kunsthalle Berlin >

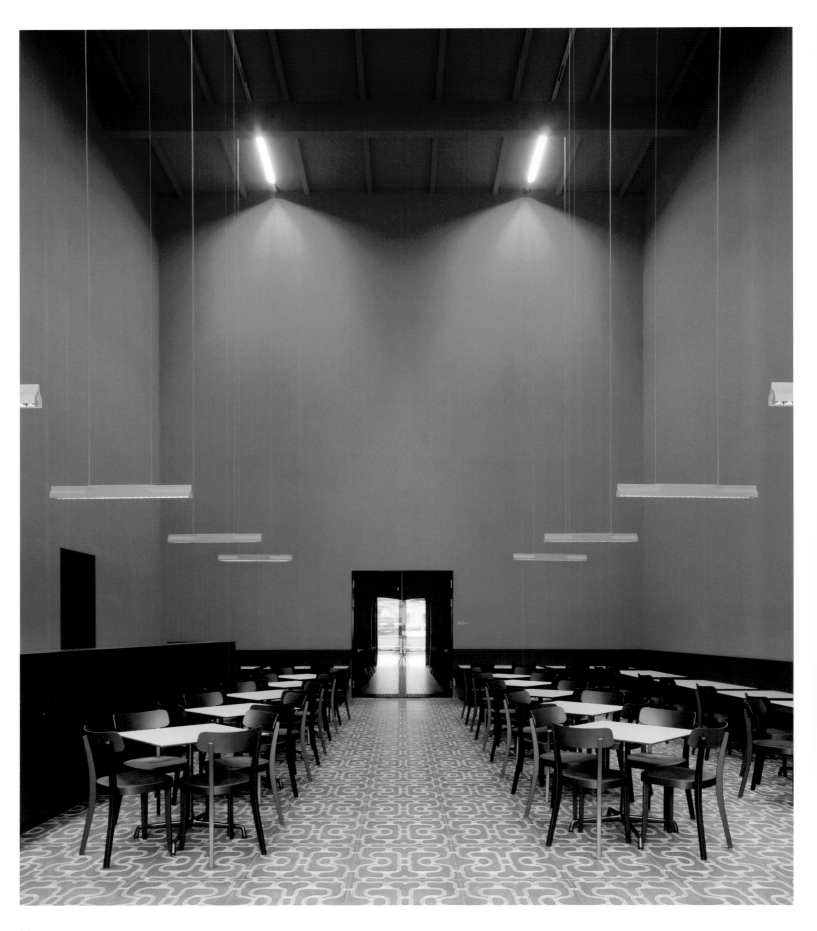

0703
Temporäre Kunsthalle Berlin, Installation *Compass,* Allora & Calzadilla, 2009

40

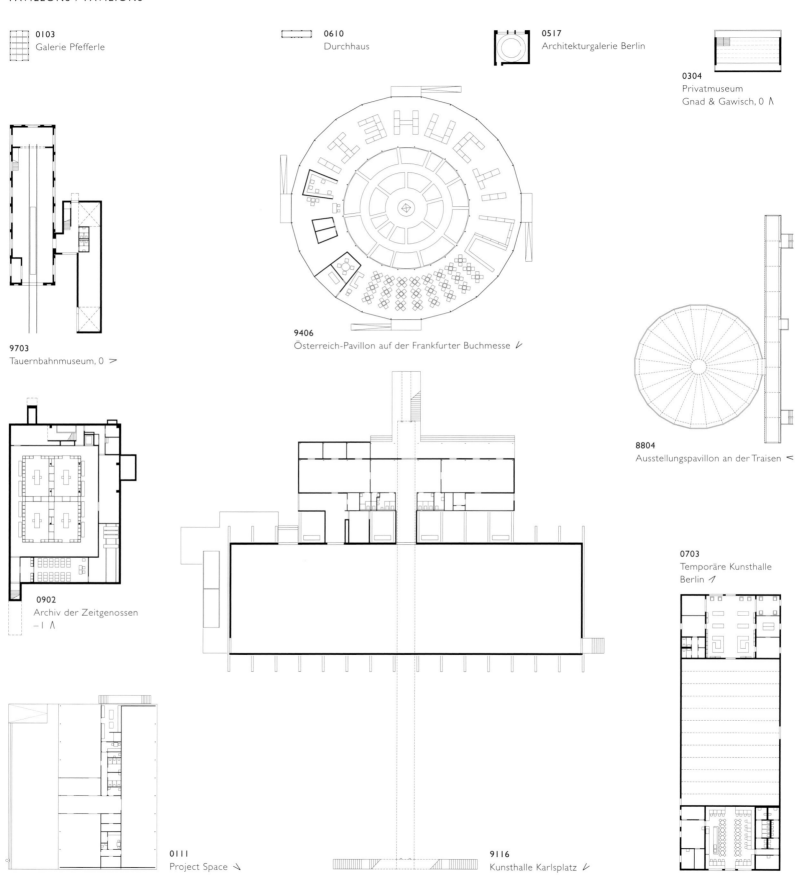

0103
Galerie Pfefferle

0610
Durchhaus

0517
Architekturgalerie Berlin

0304
Privatmuseum
Gnad & Gawisch, 0 ∧

9703
Tauernbahnmuseum, 0 ⟩

9406
Österreich-Pavillon auf der Frankfurter Buchmesse ⌄

8804
Ausstellungspavillon an der Traisen ⟨

0902
Archiv der Zeitgenossen
–I ∧

0703
Temporäre Kunsthalle
Berlin ⌐

0111
Project Space ⌄

9116
Kunsthalle Karlsplatz ⌄

Elisabeth von Samsonow

Sachliche Richtigstellung
Zur Beziehung zwischen Architektur und Kunst bei Adolf Krischanitz

Correction of Facts
On the Relationship between Architecture and Art in the Work of Adolf Krischanitz

I.

Es hatte damit begonnen, dass die Ergebnisse, die die Kunst aus der Minimal Art, der Abstraktion, der Installation – vornehmlich der Lichtinstallationen oder der Arte Povera, weniger der Trash-Scapes – verbucht hat, als Architektur wiederkamen. Während nämlich die Architektur in ihre postmoderne Phase eingetreten war, die Raum- und Konzeptkrise in einen neuen Eklektizismus beziehungsweise in die Entertainment- und Signalarchitektur umarbeitend, machten sich die Künste daran, sich hingebungsvoll dem Raum zu widmen und ihn mit allen möglichen Mitteln auszuloten. Es war sogar so, dass die Künste in ihrem Versuch, sich vom tonangebenden Medium des Bildes zu befreien, den Raum reklamierten, sich selbst imperativ als Überschreitung des Bildes oder des Bildformates ausgaben. Während also die ehrwürdige Architektur in das Stadium einer nie dagewesenen Polymorphose eintrat, ihren angestammten Ort als Verwalterin, Aufteilerin, Ordnerin, Deuterin des Raumes verlassend, tobten sich in diesem selben gewissermaßen die Kollegen von der bildenden Kunst aus. Während also die Architektur in eine Krise geraten war, nahmen sich die Künste wie selbstverständlich des Raumes an, allen voran die bildende Kunst, die ihrerseits ein Problem mit ihrem angestammten flachen Medium, der Malerei, hatte. Die Künste besetzten nun den Raum in allen möglichen denkbaren Formen: die Überwindung des Bildformats zielte in einem ersten Schritt zunächst auf eine Verräumlichung des Bildes, was sich in einer Ausdehnung in öffentliche und virtuelle Räume fortsetzte. Die Kunst wusste darüber hinaus jene Beziehung in die Waagschale zu werfen, die der Architektur abhanden gekommen zu sein schien, nämlich die innere Bezogenheit von Raum und Leib. In der Kunst schlug sich dies in einem bemerkenswerten Schub in Richtung performativer und installativer Praxis nieder. Die Architektur stand, um es einmal holzschnittartig auf den Punkt zu bringen, zugleich irritiert und hypnotisiert vor der Macht der Schrift, die ihr in etwa so den Rang abzulaufen drohte, wie Victor Hugo das in seiner drastischen Diagnose vorhergesagt hatte. Davon nun sahen sich die Künste keinesfalls bedroht oder eingeschränkt, die den Schriftkomplex entweder auf für sie profitable Weise der Kunstkritik überließen oder in die Multimedia oder Postmedia

I.

It began when Minimal Art, abstraction, installation—especially the light installations or Arte Povera, but less the trashscapes—returned as architecture. Because, namely, architecture had entered into its postmodern phase, in which the spatial and conceptual crisis was reworked into a new eclecticism and/or into entertainment and iconic architecture, and the arts set about devoting themselves with abandon to space and to exploring it with all means possible. The arts, in their attempt to liberate themselves from the tone-setting medium of the image, reclaimed space and imperatively presented themselves as transcending the image or the image format. Thus, while dignified architecture entered a stage of polymorphism that had never existed—leaving behind its traditional position as a steward, partitioner, bringer of order, interpreter of space—colleagues from the fine arts frolicked in this same position to a certain extent. So while architecture had entered a state of crisis, the arts quite naturally engaged with space, above all the fine arts, which for its part had a problem with the traditional flat surface, the painting. The arts now possessed space in all possible forms imaginable: in a first step, the transcending of the image format aimed at a spatialization of the image, which progressed to become an expansion into public and virtual spaces. Art, moreover, knew how to bring about the relationship that architecture seemed to have lost, namely, the interdependence of space and body. In art, this was reflected by a striking push in the direction of performative and installative practice. Architecture stood, putting it in a nutshell in a simplistic manner, simultaneously confused and hypnotized before the power of text, which, for example, as Victor Hugo had predicted in his drastic diagnosis, thus threatened to overtake it. Now, the arts, which either ceded the text complex to art critique in a way that was profitable for them or incorporated it in multimedia or postmedia, did not feel threatened or limited by this in any way. This situation can be summarized in a simple thesis: the arts desired space, and architecture desired surface (which can be grasped as a fetish dimension of text and of the virtual). It looks as if the arts and architecture had cleared space for each other, had performed an act of castling, after which they both found themselves changed. As a

hineinnahmen. Diese Situation lässt sich in einer einfachen These zusammenfassen: Die Künste begehrten den Raum, die Architektur die Fläche (welche als Fetischdimension der Schrift und des Virtuellen zu verstehen ist). Es sieht so aus, als hätten die Künste und die Architektur einander den Platz geräumt, eine Rochade durchgeführt, nach der sie sich beide verändert vorfanden. Sie wurden einander durch diese Transformationen aber nicht äußerlich, sondern um Beträchtliches bereichert. Die Interferenzen zwischen Kunst und Architektur hatten sich zusehends verstärkt, indem sie in neuen Zonen ineinandergeflossen waren. Der amerikanische Kunsthistoriker Hal Foster beleuchtet diese Vorgänge in seinem Buch *The Art-Architecture Complex* jedoch kritisch.[1] Er nimmt in der zeitgenössischen Architektur nach wie vor eine körperferne, zeichenhafte und sublimierende Tendenz wahr, unterstreicht aber die enge Verbindung zwischen Kunst und Architektur, deren Konstellation er um die »Global Styles« der »Pop Civics«, der »Crystal Places« und die »Light Modernity« rotieren sieht. Die Fusionen von Architektur und Kunst, die beispielsweise von Renzo Piano, Zaha Hadid, Frank Gehry oder Herzog & de Meuron angestrebt werden, betrachtet Foster eher skeptisch, als Versprechen, die nicht eingelöst würden. Die Bauaufgabe Museum hat sich prominent in den Vordergrund des ikonischen und skulpturalen Internationalen Stils geschoben, was der Beziehung zwischen Kunst und Architektur eine zusätzliche zeitgenössische Brisanz verleiht. Foster diagnostiziert im Museumsbau, sofern er nicht wie Frank Gehrys Guggenheim Museum in Bilbao oder Zaha Hadids MAXXI in Rom durch extreme Formgebung als neoavantgardistische Geste auftritt, eine Huldigung einer Bauauffassung, die er direkt aus der Minimal Art hergeleitet sieht. Diese Präferenz unterstreiche in besonderer Weise, so Foster, wie groß der Einfluss der visuellen künstlerischen Forschung auf die zeitgenössische Architektur ist.

II.
Adolf Krischanitz legt eine bemerkenswerte Fähigkeit an den Tag, diese Beziehung zwischen Architektur und Kunst jeweils von Projekt zu Projekt neu zu verhandeln und zu definieren. Schon auf den ersten Blick wird klar, dass es ihm nicht darum geht, Architektur wie ein Ausrufezeichen ins Spiel zu bringen, über welches sich dann der »Arty Touch« in Gestalt eines Dekorum oder eines formalen Extremismus legt. Die Performativität simulierenden Pseudoliquidifizierungen von Architektur liegen ihm nicht. Er bringt die Wiener Voraussetzungen mit, nämlich die Solidität der Wiener Moderne in Bezug auf die Art und Weise, wie Architektur mit Kunst zu

[1] Hal Foster, *The Art-Architecture Complex*, London 2011.
[1] Hal Foster, *The Art-Architecture Complex* (London, 2011).

result of these transformations, they were mutually enriched, but in terms of substantiality rather than in an outwardly way. The interferences between art and architecture became noticeably reinforced by flowing into each other in new zones.

The American art historian Hal Foster sheds critical light on these processes in his 2011 book *The Art-Architecture Complex*.[1] Although still discerning a remote-from-the-body, symbolic, and sublimating tendency in contemporary architecture, he nonetheless underlines the close connection between art and architecture. He comprehends this constellation as revolving around the "global styles" of "pop civics," "crystal palaces," and "light modernity." The fusions of architecture and art that, for example, Renzo Piano, Zaha Hadid, Frank Gehry, or Herzog & de Meuron strive for are something that Foster views rather skeptically as a promise that could not be fulfilled. The building project of the "museum" has prominently thrust itself into the foreground of the iconic and sculptural international style, which lends the relationship between art and architecture enhanced topicality in contemporary times. In the museum building, as long as it does not emerge as a neo-avant-garde gesture by extreme design, like Frank Gehry's Guggenheim Museum in Bilbao or Zaha Hadid's MAXXI in Rome, Foster diagnoses a homage to a concept of architecture that he sees as being derived directly from Minimal Art. According to Foster, this preference underscores how great the influence of visual, artistic research is on contemporary architecture.

II.
Adolf Krischanitz displays a remarkable ability to negotiate and define this relationship between architecture and art anew from project to project. It already becomes clear at first glance that he is not concerned with bringing architecture into play like an exclamation mark, over which the "arty touch" is then laid in the guise of décor or a formal extremism. Pseudo liquefaction that simulates performativity, as found in architecture, does not interest him. He brings the Viennese prerequisites with him, namely, the solidity of Viennese modernism with regard to the way in which he considers architecture to coalesce with art. And there, above all, Adolf Loos plays a role: for example, the Loos Bar and the Loos Residence, which are sculpture, ornamentation, and also *Bau* (building or structure) in equal measure, although the interior spaces are relatively small. Despite its small size, the Loos Residence has everything that an upscale home requires in terms of function and prestige, in order to suffice for both few and multiple residents, as well as for visitors

verschmelzen sei. Und da spielt vor allem Adolf Loos eine Rolle: Beispielsweise die Loos-Bar und die Loos-Wohnung, die ebenso Skulptur, Ornament wie »Bau« sind, obgleich es sich um relativ kleine Innenräume handelt. Die Loos-Wohnung besitzt trotz ihrer Kleinheit alles, was eine Wohnung an Funktion und Prestige braucht, um wenigen, aber auch vielen Bewohnern und Besuchern aus allen Schichten auszureichen. Und natürlich das Looshaus am Michaelerplatz mit dieser minutiös komponierten Fassade. Das Palais Stoclet von Josef Hoffmann – einer der wichtigsten Versuche, Architektur und Kunst zu vereinen – neigt sich schon gar nicht in die Richtung der bildenden Kunst, in der Weise, dass es aussähe wie ein Werk der Minimal Art, sondern in die Richtung Möbel, eher noch tendiert es in Richtung Kleinmöbel vom Typ Kästchen oder Schatulle. Die Möbel spielen in dieser Wiener Tradition eine besondere Rolle. Für Krischanitz ist die Relation zwischen den Raumhüllen, den inneren und den äußeren, von außerordentlicher Bedeutung, und man sieht seinen Entwürfen an, wie sehr ihn die Abstimmung dieser Dimensionen oder Raumfolgen beschäftigt. Diese Dimensionen dürfen nach Krischanitz durchaus als diskontinuierliche Schalen ineinanderstecken; es muss nicht der ganze Bau in allen seinen Dimensionen bis in die kleinste Maßstäblichkeit aus einem einzigen Guss sein, nicht bis in die kleinsten Partikel als Form durchgreifen. Die Möblierung kann einen Sprung in Bezug auf das Ganze machen, als wäre die innere Zone nicht erreichbar, nicht einfache Verlängerung der Öffentlichkeit oder des Außen. Ein eindrückliches Beispiel liefert die Innenraumgestaltung des Swiss-Re-Komplexes in Rüschlikon, die Krischanitz gemeinsam mit Hermann Czech in Angriff genommen hat. Erst aus der Spannung, der Inkongruenz, dem »Zittern« (wie Krischanitz diese Beziehung einmal selbst genannt hat), die sich aus dem Verhältnis zwischen Innenraum und Hülle ergibt, entsteht Bewohnbarkeit, die Entkoppelbarkeit von Raum als »Innen«.

III.

Insofern bringt Krischanitz im Unterschied zu den von Hal Foster aufgelisteten Beispielen eine Auffassung der Architektur-Kunst-Beziehung ins Spiel, die zwar oberflächlich den Typ Minimal Art favorisiert, aber auch andere Beziehungen zur Verfügung hat. Falls nun die Minimal Art einen Vektor bildet, so tut sie dies nicht, indem der Architektur selbst die Qualität einer Konstellation von Flächen zugeschrieben wird. Vielmehr ist diese Architektur aus einer Art Urkubus oder Schachtel gemacht, wobei die Minimal Art in der seriellen Gliederung und in

from all social strata. And, naturally, there is the Loos Building on Michaelerplatz with its meticulously composed façade. In the way that it looks like a work of Minimal Art, the Stoclet Palace by Josef Hoffmann—one of the most significant attempts to unite architecture and art—does not lean at all in the direction of visual art either, but rather in the direction of furniture, and it tends even more toward small pieces of furniture of the box or coffer type. In this Viennese tradition, furniture plays a special role. For Krischanitz, the relationship between spatial shells, the inner and the outer, is of utmost importance, and in his designs one sees how much the interaction of these dimensions or sequences of spaces interests him. According to Krischanitz, it is wholly permissible for these dimensions to be inserted into one another as discontinuous shells; the whole building in all its dimensions down to the smallest scale does not have to be cast from one single mold, does not have to penetrate as form down to the smallest particle. The furnishings can make a leap with respect to the whole, as if the inner zone were not reachable, were not a simple extension of the public or the outer form. The interior design of the Swiss Re complex in Rüschlikon, which Krischanitz realized in cooperation with Hermann Czech, provides an impressive example. It is first as a result of the tension, the incongruence, the *Zittern* (trembling or shaking)—as Krischanitz himself once called this relationship—arising from the relation between the interior space and the shell that habitability, the ability to decouple space as "interior," is created.

III.

In this respect, in contrast to the examples listed by Hal Foster, Krischanitz brings into play a concept of the architecture-art relationship that superficially favors the Minimalist Art type, but that, nonetheless, also has other relationships at its disposal. In the case that Minimalist Art now constitutes a vector, it does not do so through architecture itself being ascribed the quality of a constellation of surfaces. This architecture is instead made from a type of archetypal cube or box in which Minimal Art plays a role in the serial arrangement and in the relationships of the walls, as it is possible to see, for example, in the extension of the 21er Haus (21st House) in Vienna. Besides the relationship to the area of "furniture," which Krischanitz as an architect takes extremely seriously, he also plays off the valences of contemporary art in a field between Abstraction/Constructivism/Minimalism in such a way that the art-architecture relationship, which he then respectively establishes, is intensified to become a reciprocal

den Verhältnissen der Wände eine Rolle spielt, wie sich etwa in der Erweiterung des 21er Haus in Wien sehen lässt. Neben der Beziehung zum Bereich »Möbel«, der von Krischanitz als Architekt außerordentlich ernst genommen wird, spielt er die Valenzen der zeitgenössischen Kunst in einem Feld zwischen Abstraktion / Konstruktivismus / Minimalismus so aus, dass sich die von ihm jeweils dann gestiftete Kunst-Architektur-Beziehung in eine gegenseitige Interpretation, Erhöhung, Akzentuierung, Explikation der beiden Partner steigert. Das gilt insbesondere für jene Beziehung, der sich Krischanitz selbst nicht nur entwerfend annimmt, sondern in Kooperation mit bildenden Künstlern auseinandersetzt. Beispielsweise platziert er eine minimalistische blau-weiße Arbeit von Gerwald Rockenschaub auf der riesigen, monotonen Breitseite der Temporären Kunsthalle in Berlin (2008–2010) so, dass ihr Flächigkeitscode überhaupt erst richtig zur Geltung kommt. Diese verblüffend logische und zugleich leichte Kunsthalle besaß darüber hinaus gegenüber den (schwergewichtigen) Kunstmuseen von großen Kollegen den Vorteil, dass sie auf ihrer Wand oder als Wand ein Kunstwerk selbst zeigte oder besser: war. Das in Sachen Museumsbau auch des Öfteren als Konkurrenz zwischen Architektur und Kunst gewertete Verhältnis zwischen Form und Inhalt wird von Krischanitz mit dieser souveränen Geste sachlich richtiggestellt. Helmut Federles Betonrelief im Eingangsbereich des Ergänzungsbaus des Museum Rietberg in Zürich produziert wiederum gerade so viel Gedrängtheit im Raum, wie für eine Einstimmung in den zweistöckigen Abstieg in das unterirdische Museum vonnöten ist. Das formal schlanke, aber an das Vokabular der Megalithbauten anschließende Relief, das sich von den zahlreichen übrigen Gestaltungselementen der Eingangshalle nachdrücklich abhebt, ist zugleich Abbreviatur von Architektur, wie Rockenschaubs Arbeit Flächenkunst ist. Um diese Emphase oder Hebung geht es.

Über diese elaborierten, zum Teil selbst in die Fassadengestaltungen eingehenden Echo- oder Emphasebeziehungen zwischen Kunst und Architektur hinaus – an der Neue Welt Schule in Wien oder an der Fassade des Forschungslabors Novartis Campus in Basel – leistet Adolf Krischanitz eine höchst eigenständige Aneignung einer Grammatik eines avanciert naturwissenschaftlichen Ursprungs. Bemerkenswert in dieser Hinsicht die dekorative Versuche anderer Zeitgenossen weit hinter sich lassende Gestaltung des gläsernen Vorbaus des Museum Rietberg mit einem All-over aus dem Kristallgitter des Smaragds oder die Molekularstruktur in der Lobby des Novartis-Baus. Oder auch – wobei diese

interpretation, an accentuation, an explication of both partners. This applies in particular to the relationship that Krischanitz himself not only accepts in designing but also explores in cooperation with visual art. For example, he placed a Minimalist blue-and-white work by Gerwald Rockenschaub on the huge, wide, monotonous side of the Kunsthalle (Art Hall) in Berlin (2008–10) in such a way that its code of flatness first truly comes into its own at all. In comparison to the (heavy-weighted) art museums by great colleagues, this intriguingly logical and simultaneously light art hall, moreover, had the advantage that it showed an artwork itself on its walls or as a wall, or better, was an artwork. With respect to the museum building, Krischanitz matter-of-factly corrects the relationship of form and content, which is also often assessed as a competition between architecture and art. Helmut Federle's concrete relief in the foyer of the extension building at Museum Rietberg, on the other hand, even produces the degree of terseness in the space that is necessary in order to become prepared for the two-story descent into the underground museum. The formally slender relief, which is, however, connected to the vocabulary of megalithic structures and emphatically stands out from the numerous other design elements in the foyer, is also an abbreviation of architecture just as Rockenschaub's work is surface art. It is this emphasis that is significant.

Beyond these elaborated relationships of echo or emphasis between art and architecture, which are themselves incorporated into the design of the façade—at the Neue Welt Schule in Vienna or on the façade of the research laboratory of the Novartis Campus in Basel—Adolf Krischanitz realizes a highly individual appropriation of a grammar of an advanced, scientific origin. Worth noting in this respect is the design of the glazed front building of the Museum Rietberg with an allover from the crystal lattice of the emerald or the molecular structure in the lobby of the Novartis building, which both leave the decorative attempts of other contemporaries far behind. Or possibly—although this work belongs to another type, namely, the biomorphic one—the islands of green and water resembling huge, living lichens in the inner courtyard of the Lindengasse residential and business building. Perhaps one should also comprehend the latter example as a reference to the interior space, since the relationship between the long interior walls positioned unconventionally in the middle toward the front, toward the (carpet) islands, makes this room into an enormous, roofless space.

Adolf Krischanitz's architecture plays with the possibilities presented by modern and contemporary

Arbeit einem anderen, nämlich dem biomorphen Typus angehört – die riesigen, lebenden Flechten ähnelnden Inseln aus Grün und Wasser im Innenhof des Wohn- und Geschäftshauses Lindengasse. Wahrscheinlich sollte man letzteres Beispiel darüber hinaus auch noch als Referenz zum Innenraum auffassen, da das Verhältnis zwischen den eigenwillig in der Mitte sich nach vorne stellenden Längsinnenwänden zu den (Teppich-) Inseln diesen Raum zu einem gewaltigen dachlosen Zimmer macht.

Adolf Krischanitz' Architektur spielt mit den verfügbaren Möglichkeiten der nun bereits hundert Jahre bienenfleißig betriebenen Raumforschung der modernen und zeitgenössischen bildenden Kunst in der Weise, dass deren Ergebnisse die bauliche Solidität ästhetisch, logisch und praktisch erhöhen. Dies ist die doch außerordentlich begrüßenswerte Differenz zur gegenwärtigen Spektakelarchitektur des International Style, deren Signatur ihr kurzfristiges Ablaufdatum ist.

visual art's now already one-hundred-year-long, industriously practiced study of space in such a way that its results strengthen the structural soundness aesthetically, logically, and practically. This indeed is the extraordinarily welcome difference to the current spectacle architecture of the International Style, whose signature is its near-term expiration date.

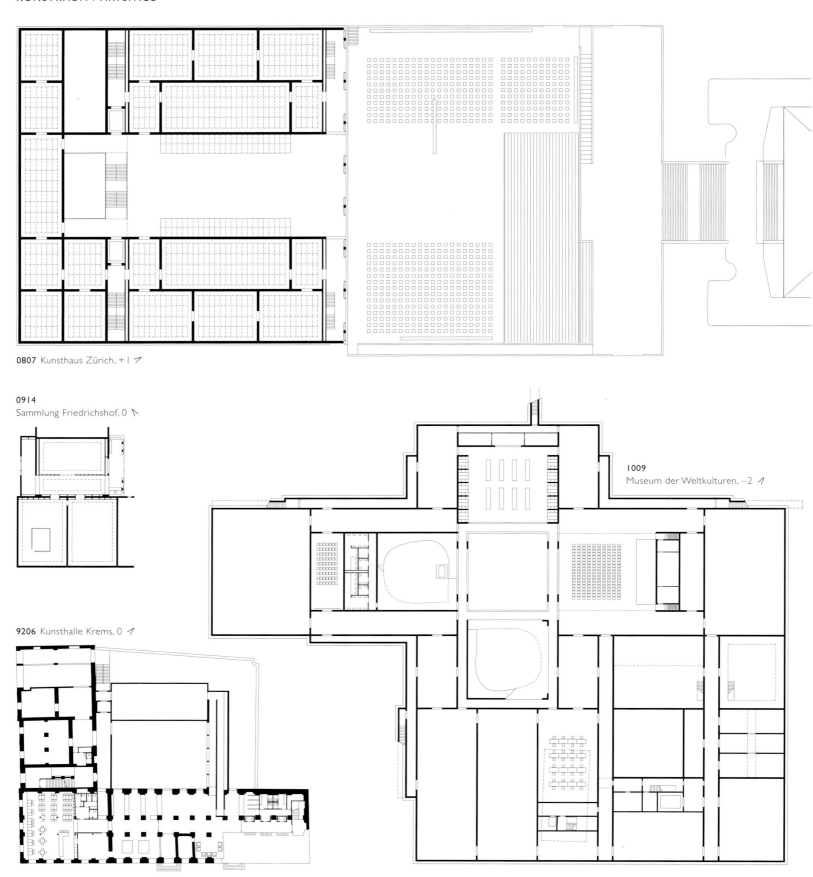

0807 Kunsthaus Zürich, +1 ↗

0914
Sammlung Friedrichshof, 0 ↖

1009
Museum der Weltkulturen, −2 ↗

9206 Kunsthalle Krems, 0 ↗

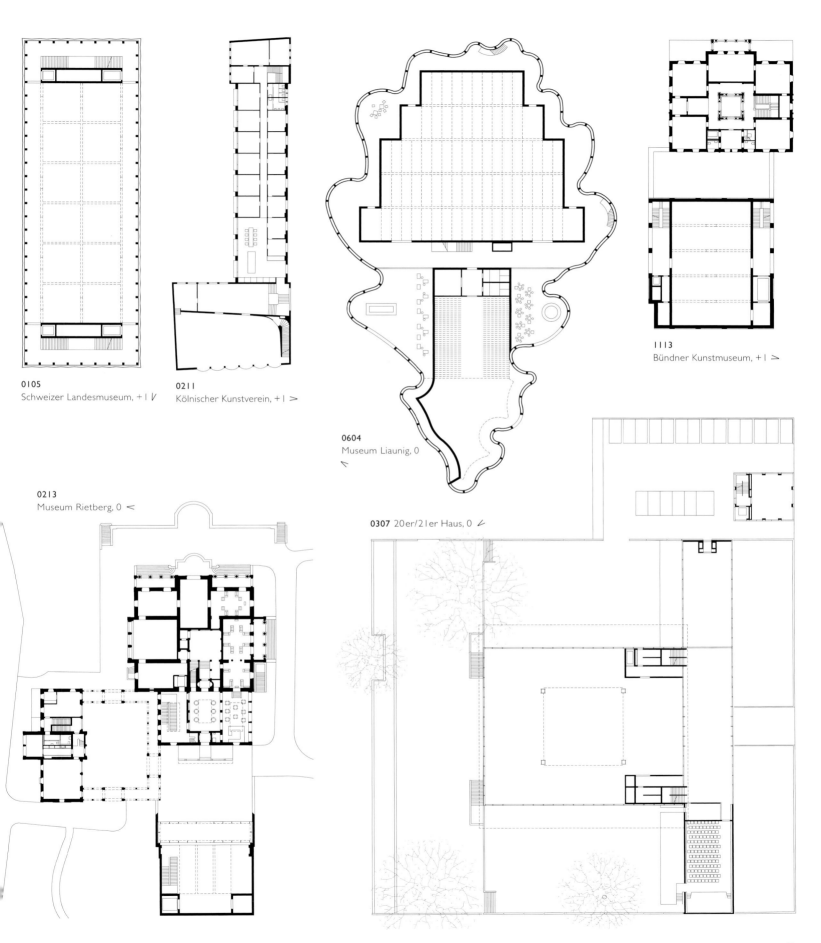

0105
Schweizer Landesmuseum, +1 ∨

0211
Kölnischer Kunstverein, +1 >

0604
Museum Liaunig, 0
∧

1113
Bündner Kunstmuseum, +1 >

0213
Museum Rietberg, 0 <

0307 20er/21er Haus, 0 ∠

49

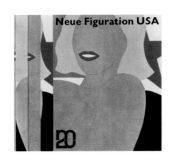

Neue Figuration USA,
Ausst.-Kat. / exh. cat.
Museum des 20. Jahrhunderts,
Wien 1969

Museums des 20. Jahrhunderts
Ausstellungen / Exhibitions,
Events, 1970:

Haus-Rucker-Co Live
Osteuropäische Volkskunst
Comic Strips
Die Epoche des überfließenden
Sehvermögens – Der Mensch
im Weltraum
Kinder malen, zeichnen, formen
Bruno Gironcoli
Bohuslav Kokoschka
Peter Pongratz
Konzerte der Arena 70
Ravi Shankar
Masters of Unorthodox Jazz
Jeunesse Musicale

Otto Kapfinger: Beginnend mit der Renovierung der Wiener Secession hast du mehrere Umbauten, Zubauten, Neubauten für Museen, für die Präsentation bildender Kunst ausgeführt. Die Anfänge dieser engen Beziehung zur Kunst waren von Widersprüchen geprägt. Wir hatten unsere gemeinsame Studienzeit rund um das »heiße« Jahr 1968, wo es ja auch extreme Kritik an Kunstinstitutionen und etablierten Kulturformen gab.

Adolf Krischanitz: 1968, die Jahre knapp davor und danach waren sehr interessant, sehr widersprüchlich. Sie waren einerseits getragen von der Entwicklung des studentischen Aufruhrs in Österreich und Deutschland, der unserer Studienzeit den Stempel aufdrückte. Andererseits haben wir uns neben der Gesellschaftskritik – und das war in Österreich nicht unbedingt ein Widerspruch – mit den Möglichkeiten der Kunst beschäftigt, die für politische Hardliner damals doch, sagen wir, verdächtig war. Anfangs übten wir Kritik an der politisch-gesellschaftlichen Realität, dann folgten Versuche der Verarbeitung der Differenz unterschiedlicher gesellschaftlicher Ansprüche mittels mehr oder weniger tauglicher künstlerischer Verfahren.

Ich war damals mit Bernhard Frankfurter und anderen an der Gründung der Aktion Wien beteiligt, einer studentischen Partei. Wegen dieser politischen Aktivitäten, darunter einige Scharmützel mit der observierenden Staatspolizei, habe ich das reguläre Studium ein Jahr lang unterbrochen, es später aber mit viel Engagement wieder aufgenommen. Unsere gemeinsame Arbeit mit Angela Hareiter als polymediale Gruppe Missing Link war sicher von diesen Erfahrungen und Zeitströmungen grundiert.

Es ist vielleicht typisch für Wien, vielleicht auch nur Zufall: In diesen Jahren war ein Ort der Hochkultur zugleich der einzige Raum, wo die gesellschaftliche Unruhe sofort in widerständigen künstlerischen Signalen, in seismografischen Ereignissen Platz fand. Ich meine vor allem das Wiener Museum des 20. Jahrhunderts – nicht nur ein Museum der Malerei und Skulptur, sondern der Mode, Wissenschaft, Musik, Architektur, Film, Technik des Jahrhunderts –, das 20er Haus unter der Leitung von Alfred Schmeller.

Diese Wiener Schizophrenie war, wenn man es heute betrachtet, ein Nährboden merkwürdiger Entwicklungen, die (wenn überhaupt) nur mehr unter dem Überbegriff Kunst abgehandelt werden

Otto Kapfinger: Starting with the renovation of the Vienna Secession, you have realized a number of building alterations, additions, and new museum structures for the presentation of visual art. The beginnings of this close relationship to art were characterized by contradictions. We were students together around the "hot" year of 1968, when there was indeed also extreme criticism of art institutions and established forms of culture.

Adolf Krischanitz: 1968—the years just before and after were very interesting, and very contradictory. On the one hand, they were carried along by the development of the student protests in Austria and Germany, which put its stamp on our time as students. On the other, besides the criticism of society—and, in Austria, this wasn't necessarily a contradiction—we were also preoccupied with the possibilities of art, which for political hardliners at the time was, let's say, quite suspect. In the beginning, we criticized the sociopolitical reality. This was followed by attempts to process the difference between various social demands using more or less suitable artistic methods.

At the time, along with Bernhard Frankfurter and others, I was involved in the founding of Aktion Wien, a student party. Due to these political activities, including some confrontations with the state police, which had us under surveillance, I interrupted my regular studies for one year but then resumed them again later with great commitment. These experiences and contemporary trends surely served as a primer for our work with Angela Hareiter as the polymedial group Missing Link.

Maybe it's typical for Vienna, but maybe it's only a coincidence: during these years, a location for high culture was really the only space where social unrest was immediately manifest in resistant artistic signals, in seismographic moments. I mean, above all, the Wiener Museum des 20. Jahrhunderts (Vienna Museum of the 20th Century)—not only a museum for painting and sculpture, but also for the fashion, science, music, architecture, film, and technology of the century—that is, the 20er Haus (20th House) under the direction of Alfred Schmeller.

If you think about it today, this Viennese schizophrenia was a breeding ground for peculiar developments, which (if at all) could only be dealt with under the umbrella term "art." As a student

konnten. Ich habe damals als Student die ersten öffentlichen Auftritte des Wiener Aktionismus miterlebt, das *Zock-Fest* und das *direct art festival* im Porrhaus, beide 1967. Das Erstere wurde durch einen makabren Polizeieinsatz abrupt beendet. Eine den aktuellen Strömungen freundlich gesonnene Institution dagegen war damals das Museum des 20. Jahrhunderts als Heimstätte für Außerordentliches.

Kunsterfahrung – Lebenspraxis

Wir waren allerdings nicht mehr Zeuge der legendären Ereignisse zu Beginn der 60er-Jahre in der Galerie nächst St. Stephan. Doch das 20er Haus war ab 1964 unter Werner Hofmann führend, zeigte im Herbst '68 schon Fotos, Plakate, Dokumente über den Mai '68 in Paris; es gab die Avantgarde-Konzerte der Wiener Festwochen; '69 die Personale von Roland Goeschl, schon unter der Direktion von Schmeller; '70 die legendäre Installation *Haus-Rucker-Co Live,* die Performances des Arena-Festivals draußen im Skulpturengarten usw. War nicht das 20er Haus ein Wohnzimmer oder eine WG unserer kulturellen Adoleszenz? Wir waren doch jede Woche dort, bei allen Ausstellungen und Vorträgen.

Es ist tatsächlich so, dass ich – damals mehr intuitiv – diese besonderen, emblematischen Räume völlig mit den Ereignissen identifizierte, weshalb sie zum Synonym meiner individuellen Emanzipation werden konnten. Die horizontale, tableauartige Offenheit des 20er Hauses prädestinierte es, zu einer Spielfläche für eine Kunst mit flacher Hierarchie, mit anti-auratischen Ansprüchen zu werden. Die fehlenden Wände, die bei zu hängender »Kunstware« erforderlich waren, mussten jeweils eigens errichtet werden. Dagegen gaben die Installationen, die diesen Ein-Raum ganz autonom bespielten, wie zum Beispiel die von Haus-Rucker-Co, Roland Goeschl, Walter Pichler und anderen, perfekte Antworten auf den Raumcharakter. Die permanente Sammlung von Malerei und Skulptur im ersten Stock musste durch die Installation von Hängeflächen zwischen den Geschossdecken erst etabliert werden. Das Fehlen von Wänden, die großen Glasfronten an allen Seiten trugen dem Haus ja den vorschnellen Ruf ein, als Ort für Malerei nicht wirklich geeignet zu sein.

Ein gutes Beispiel war 1971 die Ausstellung von Walter Pichler. Er schuf in der hellen Halle durch mit Mollino bespannte Lattengerüste kokonartige,

Art Experience—Life Practice

We didn't witness the legendary events in the Galerie nächst St. Stephan at the beginning of the sixties. But the 20er Haus led the way starting in 1964 and under Werner Hofmann already showed photos, posters, and documents from May 1968 in Paris during the fall of the same year, and then there were the avant-garde concerts during the Vienna Festival; in 1969 Roland Goeschl's one-man show, already under the direction of Schmeller; in 1970 the legendary *Haus-Rucker-Co Live* installation, the performances during the Arena Festival outside in the sculpture garden, and so on. Wasn't the 20er Haus sort of a living room or a commune for our cultural adolescence? We did go there every weekend, attending all the exhibitions and lectures.

As a matter of fact, I totally associated—at the time more intuitively—those special, emblematic spaces with the events, which is why they were able to become the synonym for my individual emancipation. The horizontal, tableau-like openness of the 20er Haus predestined it to become a playing area for art with a flat hierarchy, with anti-auratic pretensions. The walls necessary for "art products" that have to be hung were lacking and had to be erected specifically in each case. Then again, there were the installations that worked with this one room quite autonomously, such as the ones by Haus-Rucker-Co, Roland Goeschl, Walter Pichler, and others—perfect responses to the character of the space. The permanent collection of painting and sculpture on the first floor first had to be set up by installing hanging surfaces between the floor and the ceiling. The lack of walls, the large glass fronts on all sides, indeed prematurely gave the building the reputation of being a place that was not really suitable for painting.

A good example was the Walter Pichler exhibition in 1971. In the bright hall, he created cocoon-like, semitransparent "spaces within space" for his objects using lath frames covered with Mollino fabric. There was an extreme tension between the

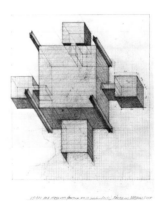

Walter Pichler
**Entwurf für die eigene Ausstellung /
Design for his own exhibition,**
Museum des 20. Jahrhunderts, 1971

51

semitransparente »Räume im Raum« für seine Objekte. Es gab eine extreme Spannung zwischen der offenen, technoiden Halle und der fragilen, zeitenthobenen, mit einfachsten Mitteln erzeugten Aura von Pichlers Intervention. Das tatsächliche oder vermeintliche Manko des Umraums war durch minimalistische, fast immaterielle Eingriffe in die unvergessliche Stimmung dieser Ausstellung verwandelt worden.

Das 20er Haus hatte diese schwellenlose, werkstatthafte Atmosphäre einer eleganten Industrie- oder Messehalle. Die Sammlung der klassischen Moderne, spannungsreich gruppiert im Obergeschoss, im milchweißen Licht der Okalux-Verglasung, wirkte gleichsam als sonntägliche Rückversicherung, als Vergewisserung gegenüber den schroffen, vitalen Manifesten und Konzentraten der Gegenwart im Parterre.

Das große, zum Park auf drei Seiten durchsichtige Erdgeschoss war Experimentierbühne für Alltag und Gegenwelten, war ein Hoffnungsraum, stufenlos von der Straße erreichbar und – ganz wichtig – nicht im Bannkreis der Ringstraße, sondern weit ab vom Schuss des Establishments, an der Rückseite des rauen Süd- und Ostbahnhofs, exterritorial im grünen Brachland, das man – was wir erst später verstanden – dem stadtfeindlichen Bauverbot um die nach der Revolution von 1848 errichteten k. u. k. Kasernen der Monarchie zu verdanken hatte.

Trausdorf, Untere Hauptstraße 18.
Muhr, Köb, Missing Link, 1972

Waren nicht unsere Begegnungen, zum Teil unsere Freundschaft mit den gerade ein paar Jahre älteren Künstlern viel profunder, viel wichtiger als das, was wir damals von unseren Architekturprofessoren geboten bekamen?

Vielleicht, aber ob das nicht unseren Architekturlehrern gegenüber ungerecht ist? Da waren immerhin Erich Boltenstern und vor allem Karl Schwanzer und Günther Feuerstein. Doch es stimmt schon. Das gemeinsame Arbeiten und Experimentieren mit Edelbert Köb am Institut für Zeichnen und Malen der Technischen Hochschule, mit ihm und Gotthard Muhr bei zusätzlichen Siebdruck- und Grafikseminaren und später mit Oskar Putz hat uns Einsichten in künstlerische Techniken und konzeptuelle Aspekte der Kunst gewinnen lassen, die über die Standardbeschäftigung von Architekturstudenten mit solchen Inhalten weit hinausreichten.

Wir lernten den Unterschied zwischen bloß gemalten Bildern einerseits und der Malerei als autonomem

open, technoid hall and the fragile, timeless aura of Pichler's intervention that had been created using the simplest of means. In the unforgettable atmosphere of this exhibition, the actual or alleged shortcoming of the surrounding space was transformed by means of minimalist, nearly immaterial interventions.

The 20er Haus had the wide-open, workshop-like atmosphere of an elegant industrial or exhibition hall. The collection of classic modernism, grouped to create exciting contrasts on the upper story in the milky-white light of the Okalux glazing, seemed to be dominical reassurance, as it were, to be confirmation, in contrast to the brusque, vital manifestos and concentrates of the present on the ground floor.

The ground floor, which is transparent on three sides toward the park, was the experimental stage for everyday life and parallel worlds, a space of hope, reachable without steps from the street and—very importantly—not in the Ringstrasse's sphere of influence. It was instead far away from the domain of the establishment, on the rough back side of the south and east train station, exterritorial in the green wasteland. This was—as we first understood later— thanks to the ban on building so inimical to the city around the monarchy's Imperial and Royal Arsenal, which was built after the Revolution of 1848.

Weren't our encounters, including our friendships with artists just a couple of years older than us, much more profound, much more important than the material offered to us by our architecture professors at the time?

Perhaps, but isn't that a bit unfair to our architecture teachers? There was, after all, Erich Boltenstern, and in particular Karl Schwanzer and Günther Feuerstein. But you really are right. Working and experimenting with Edelbert Köb at the Institute for Drawing and Painting at the Vienna University of Technology, with him and Gotthard Muhr in other seminars on silkscreening and graphic design, and later with Oskar Putz. All this allowed us to gain insight into artistic techniques and conceptual aspects of art extending far beyond the standard occupations of architecture students.

We learned the difference between pictures that were merely painted, on the one hand, and painting as an autonomous medium, on the other, as a highly complex language with its own rules. These were our first discoveries of the difference between gestural

Medium andererseits, als eigengesetzliche, hochkomplexe Sprache. Es waren erste Entdeckungen der Differenz zwischen der gestischen Dynamik, die eine Form zum Ausdruck bringt oder anschlägt, und der in tieferen Schichten grundlegenden Dynamik, die sich unabhängig von Formen zwischen Farben abspielt – sich zwischen Hell und Dunkel ereignet, zwischen Oberfläche und Tiefe von Bildschichten, zwischen Dichte und Leere in einem Bildraum.

Die frühe Auseinandersetzung mit unterschiedlichen Künstlern wurde für mich zu einer Erfahrung, die ins Existenzielle hineinreichte, in Kunst als Lebenspraxis. Mit Köb und Muhr habe ich viel Zeit an unterschiedlichen Orten im Burgenland und in den Wiener Ateliers verbracht. Vor allem im Burgenland, wo wir jeweils den Sommer über arbeiteten und leer stehende, abgewohnte alte Häuser und Höfe nutzten, war meine Rolle die des Quartiermachers. Ich hatte zum Beispiel des Öfteren einen Abort zu installieren oder bei simplen Instandsetzungsarbeiten zu helfen. Die Künstler arbeiteten unterschiedlich, von gegenständlich bis abstrakt, doch jeweils auf hohem Niveau. Sie haben gegenseitig und auch im Gespräch mit mir, mit uns, mit anwesenden Gästen ihre Arbeit sehr kritisch kommentiert, ständig reflektiert. Es war für mich eine künstlerische Grundlehre, durchsetzt von Phasen exzessiven Lebens. Und jeder war wechselweise Lehrer und Schüler in unterschiedlichen Situationen, Rollen.

Ich war da viel sporadischer involviert. Doch in Trausdorf haben wir immerhin dann einige Zeit auch mit Angela Hareiter gearbeitet und auf dem Atelierhof und in der Umgebung einige unserer Foto-Performances mit Alltagsrequisiten durchgeführt. Wir bewegten uns 1970/72 im Bereich von Concept Art, Performance, Object Art, Video – die jedoch werkten in Stein, Gips und Papier. Die ästhetischen und inhaltlichen Kriterien waren aber dieselben.

Die Kunst bot uns damals ein offenes, nicht näher definiertes und provozierendes Terrain, einen Freiraum im konservativen Umfeld, mit vielen leichten und zwanglosen internationalen Kontakten, eine Sphäre, in der man damals ohne wesentliche Einschränkungen experimentieren und sogar, wenn auch auf unterster Ebene, ökonomisch überleben konnte.

Wir waren anfangs mit Köb, Muhr und Putz und du allein später in der Secession mit Helmut Federle, Bart Prince, Kurt Kocherscheidt, Brigitte Kowanz, Ernst Caramelle und vielen anderen am Hängen von

dynamics, which express or forge one form, and fundamental dynamics in deeper layers, which take place in a pictorial space between colors independent of forms—evolving between light and dark, between the surface and depth of pictorial layers, between density and vacuity in pictorial space.

For me, encountering various artists early on became an experience that extended into the existential, into art as life practice. I spent a lot of time with Köb and Muhr at different locations in the Burgenland and in studios in Vienna. Above all in the Burgenland, where we worked over the summer and used vacant, dilapidated old houses and farms, my role was that of quartermaster. Quite often, for example, I had to install a toilet or help with simple repair jobs. The artists worked in different ways, from the figurative to the abstract, but each on a high level. They commented very critically on each other's work and were constantly reflecting, also in conversation with me, with us, and with guests who were there. For me, it was a basic lesson in art, interfused with phases of excessive life. And everyone was alternately teacher and student in different situations and roles.

I was involved much more sporadically. Although we did at least then also work for some time with Angela Hareiter in Trausdorf and did some of our own photo performances using everyday props at the studio farm and in the surrounding area. From 1970 to 1972, we moved in the areas of Conceptual Art, performance, Object Art, and video—and they worked in stone, plaster, and on paper. But the aesthetic and content-related criteria were the same.

At the time, art offered us an open, relatively undefined, and provocative terrain, a free space in the conservative surroundings, with lots of easy and informal international contacts, a sphere in which you could experiment at the time without major restrictions and even survive economically, if only on the lowest level.

At the beginning, we helped mount exhibitions with Köb, Muhr, and Putz, and you (on your own) later participated in the spatial organization of art events at the Secession with Helmut Federle, Bart Prince, Kurt Kocherscheidt, Brigitte Kowanz, Ernst Caramelle, and many others. What kind of experience did that bring?

When I was director of the Vienna Secession from 1991 to 1995, the board of directors and I carried out various tasks (and not only administrative

Missing Link, Ausst.-Kat. / exh. cat. Museum des 20. Jahrhunderts, Wien 1973

Missing Link, *Die andere Seite*, Aktion / Performance, Wiener Neustadt, 1973 Cover des Ausstellungskatalogs / Exhibition catalogue cover, Künstlerhaus Stuttgart, 2002

Ausstellungen, an der räumlichen Organisation von Kunstereignissen beteiligt. Was hat das an Erfahrung gebracht?

Als Leiter der Wiener Secession von 1991 bis 1995 fielen für mich und den Vorstand verschiedene nicht nur administrative Aufgaben an, von der Akquisition von Künstlern beziehungsweise Ausstellern über die Hängung der Arbeiten bis zur Katalog- und Texterstellung. Eines der größten Abenteuer in der Recherche und Konzeption von Ausstellungen war die Begegnung mit Dieter Roth. Nachdem Maria Lassnig mich in meinem Wunschtraum bestärkt hatte, ihn in die Secession einzuladen, waren, was die Erfolgsaussichten dieses Unterfangens betraf, die Prognosen seiner ehemaligen Wiener Freunde und Wegbegleiter absolut pessimistisch. Nach mehreren Anläufen, persönlichen Besuchen und skurrilen Momenten gelang die Ausstellung schließlich nach zweieinhalb Jahren. Der Kontakt und die Freundschaft zu ihm waren für mich eine Lehrzeit der ganz besonderen Art.

Paradigmenwechsel im Museumsbau

In unserer Adoleszenz im Kunstraum ging es doch immer um die Kehrseite des Positivismus, um die Dialektik von Form und Inhalt: ein Objekt, eine Performance, ein Stück Film hat nicht nur inhaltliche Aspekte – die »Erzählung« –, sondern vor allem die autonome, die interne Botschaft des Metiers: dessen Geschichte, dessen Brüche, dessen Regeln und Anti-Regeln, dessen immanente Kriterien – die Selbstreflexion von Kunst in der Moderne eben, herausgelöst aus der kultischen, metaphysischen, mimetischen Bedeutungsachse ...

Das war bis Mitte der 70er-Jahre auch die allgemeine, institutions- und selbstkritische Tendenz im Kunstbereich. Ende der 70er-, Anfang der 80er-Jahre gab es einen Paradigmenwechsel, rückte mit der aufkommenden Postmoderne der Museumsbau schlagartig ins Zentrum der Diskussion. Museen wurden wieder »die Orte« der Kunst. Eine der Ikonen dieser Phase war Hans Holleins Neubau des Museums Abteiberg in Mönchengladbach. Wir fuhren damals sofort gemeinsam hin und haben das Haus in einem umfangreichen Text für *UmBau 8* einer kritischen Analyse unterzogen, sowohl diese Art der Museumsarchitektur als auch die dort wieder ins Kommerzielle gebundene, auratische Kunstpräsentation. Es war ein absoluter Kontrast zu der erlebten Alltäglichkeit und

UmBau 8, 1984

S. / p. 85

ones): from acquiring artists and/or exhibitors, to hanging the works, to creating catalogues and texts. One of the biggest adventures in researching and designing exhibitions was the encounter with Dieter Roth. After Maria Lassnig encouraged me in my pipe dream of inviting him to the Secession, the prognoses of his former friends and associates in Vienna were extremely pessimistic as far as the prospects for this venture succeeding were concerned. After numerous attempts, personal visits, and bizarre moments, the exhibition finally became possible after two and a half years. For me, the contact and friendship with him were a very special kind of apprenticeship.

Paradigm Shift in Museum Architecture

In our adolescence in the realm of art, what was concerned was always the flip side of positivism, the dialectic of form and content. An object, a performance, a piece of film never had only content-related aspects—the "narrative"—but, above all, the autonomous, the internal message of the medium: its story, its discontinuities, its rules and anti-rules, its immanent criteria—simply art's self-reflection in the modern era, divorced from cultish, metaphysical, and mimetic axes of meaning ...

Until the mid-seventies, that was also the general, institution- and self-critical tendency in the realm of art. At the end of the seventies and in the early eighties, there was a paradigm shift, with museum architecture suddenly moving to the center of discussion in the face of advancing postmodernism. Museums once again became "the places" for art. One icon of this phase was Hans Hollein's new building for the Museum Abteiberg in Mönchengladbach. We immediately drove there together and, in an extensive text for the architecture journal *UmBau 8*, subjected the building to a critical analysis, both this type of museum architecture and the auratic presentation of art once again linked with the commercial there. It was a total contrast to the prosaicness and informal, hybrid porosity that we experienced during the events at the 20er Haus as mentioned earlier.

In this text we wrote together, at the beginning of one section you put some sentences recalling the archetype of cult locations, the transcendent experience in caves, underground caverns, in rock crevices, and in the grottos of antiquity—descending into an "underworld" of cult and art, just as it was also staged in Mönchengladbach.

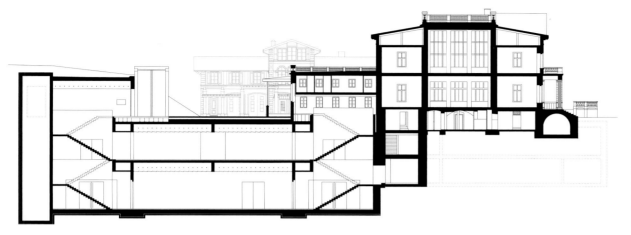

0307
Umbau und Erweiterung /
Renovation and Extension
Museum Rietberg, Zürich
Schnittplan / Cross section, 2007
mit der Villa Wesendonck (rechts)
und der Erweiterung (links) /
with Villa Wesendonck (right)
and the extension (left)

locker gemischten Durchlässigkeit der erwähnten
Events des 20er Hauses.

In diesem gemeinsam verfassten Text hast du an den
Beginn eines Kapitels Sätze gestellt, die an den Urtyp
der Kultorte, an die transzendente Erfahrung in Höh-
len, unterirdischen Kavernen, in Felsspalten, in den
Grotten der Antike erinnerten – an das Hinabsteigen
in eine »Unterwelt« von Kult und Kunst, so wie es
auch in Mönchengladbach inszeniert worden war.

Ich sagte in etwa das: »Im alten Griechenland
zeigte man Orte, an denen es in die Unterwelt
hinabging. Stätten mit hervorragenden topologi-
schen Eigenschaften wurden zur Manifestation der
Verehrung einer bestimmten Gottheit erklärt. An
solchen Punkten der Verschmelzung von Topos
und Mythologie wurden Altäre errichtet […]. Die
in den Naturzusammenhang eingefügten Anlagen
mit ihren vielfältig überlagerten Ordnungsprinzipien verkörperten die Aussöhnung des antiken
Menschen mit der Natur.«

20 Jahre später hat der mit Alfred Grazioli verfasste
Entwurf für das Museum Rietberg in Zürich genau
dieses Thema aufgegriffen und in ganz anders be-
gründeter, neuer Form realisiert.

Mönchengladbach war schon eine Voraussetzung
dafür, dass Alfred Grazioli und ich die unterirdische
Positionierung überhaupt ins Auge fassen konnten. Allerdings wollten wir Maßnahmen schaffen,
die das Unten und das Oben gewissermaßen
egalisieren. In das Wegenetz des Rieterparks
eingebunden präsentiert sich der neue Museums-
bezirk als Gruppierung von Baukörpern, die
Raumsequenzen aufspannen – von der Natur in
die Gebäude hinein und wieder zurück.
Der Glasportikus antwortet dort auf den Eingangstrakt der berühmten Villa Wesendonck gegenüber

I basically said that: "In ancient Greece, one
presented locations at which one descended to
the underworld. Sites with outstanding topological
characteristics were declared to be the manifestation of the veneration of a specific deity. At
such points where topos and mythology merged,
altars were erected . . . The structures with their
manifold overlaid structural principles that were
inserted into the natural context embodied the
reconciliation of ancient man with nature."

Twenty years later, the design for the Museum
Rietberg in Zurich, which I drafted with Alfred
Grazioli, took up precisely this theme and realized
it in a new form, predicated in a completely
different way.

Mönchengladbach was already one premise for
the fact that Alfred Grazioli and I were able to
envisage the underground positioning in the first
place. But we wanted to realize measures that
equalized the below and the above to a certain
extent. Integrated into the network of paths in
Rieterpark, the new museum district presented
itself as a grouping of structures spread out as a
sequence of spaces—from nature to the buildings
and back again.
The glass pavilion there responds to the entrance
hall of the famous Villa Wesendonck and signifies
entry into the museum world. The diaphanous
threshold in front of the woody slope signalizes
the transition and, with the stairs leading downward, also makes it possible to recognize the
submerged space below.

Museum Rietberg, Zurich

When approaching via the ascending paths of the
magnificent park, one first sees the villa from the

0213
Museum Rietberg
Baugrube für die unterirdische
Erweiterung / Excavation for
subterranean extension, 2007

Die Lage des Museums im
Rieterpark / Museum location
in Rieterpark

S. / pp. 68/69

Das ursprüngliche Holzstöckelpflaster des Platzbodens wurde
später aus technischen Gründen
durch diagonal verlegte Steinplatten
ersetzt. / The original wooden cube
pavement of the square was later
replaced with diagonally laid stone
panels for technical reasons.

und ist das Zeichen für den Eintritt in die Muse-
umswelt. Vor dem bewaldeten Hang signalisiert die
diaphane Schwelle den Übergang und lässt mit der
nach unten führenden Treppe auch die Tiefe des
darunter abgesenkten Raumes erkennen.

Museum Rietberg, Zürich

Beim Näherkommen über die ansteigenden Wege
des prachtvollen Parks sieht man zuerst die Villa von
der Seite, von ihrer Südseite, und dann, überraschend
nahe schon, gegenüber am Hangfuß den gläsernen
Portikus und man wird sich damit sofort auch der
neuen Mitte bewusst, dem Platz zwischen Villa,
Glasportikus und Ökonomiegebäude im Hintergrund. Der Platzboden ist Holzstöckelpflaster, nicht
Stein oder Kies, wie man erwarten würde. Eine
andere Qualität, die unterschwellig wirkt, aber
bewusst gesetzt wurde ...

Unser Entwurfsansatz – in meiner Arbeit generell
und beim Museum Rietberg sowie im Team mit
dem noch an der Hochschule für Gestaltung Ulm
ausgebildeten Grazioli besonders angebracht – war
nicht ein objekthaft auftretender Zubau, sondern
eine raumstrategische, szenografische Intervention.
Wir dachten an die Schaffung einer neuen Ge-
samtfigur, die sowohl die Eigenständigkeit der
Villa als auch die Dominanz der Naturräumlich-
keit des Ensembles erhält. Da ist auf der einen
Seite der denkmalgeschützte Bau mit seiner Geschichte als Bekrönung des Parks, und gegenüber
ist der naturgeschützte Hang, ein Stück eiszeit-
licher Endmoräne mit ganz spezieller Flora.
In dem Szenario entwickelten wir eine Dezentralisierung der Villa in den Umraum hinaus und eine
Erweiterung nach unten, indem die Museumsge-
schosse als neues Souterrain, als gemeinsame Basis
von Villa, Ökonomietrakt und Eingangsportikus

side, from its southern side, and then, already surprisingly close-by, opposite the villa at the foot of the
slope, the glass pavilion. One therefore also immediately becomes aware of the new center, the square
between the villa, the glass pavilion, and the former
outbuilding in the background. The square has a
wooden cube pavement, not stone or gravel, as one
would expect. Another quality that seems subliminal,
it but was intentionally used ...

Our design approach—laid out in my work in
general and specifically in the case of the Museum
Rietberg and in the team collaborating with
Grazioli, who was trained at the Hochschule für
Gestaltung Ulm (Ulm School of Design)—entailed
creating a scenographic intervention with a spatial
strategy instead of an addition with an object-
like appearance. We kept in mind the idea of
establishing a new overall character, retaining both
the autonomy of the villa and the dominance of
the natural spatial impression of the ensemble. To
one side is the listed historical building with
its history as a crowning element in the park;
situated opposite is the environmentally protected
hillside, an Ice Age terminal moraine with very
unique flora.

In the scenario, we developed a decentralization
of the villa into the surrounding space and an
extension underneath in which the museum
floors were designed as a new basement level, as
a basis shared by the villa, the outbuilding tract,
and the entrance pavilion. The main entrance
was, however, shifted to the foot of the hillside
to create a new distributor hinge, a center in the
open air—the square between the villa and the
glass pavilion. And this square was designed
with wooden cube paving: a wooden carpet
outdoors—as a contrast to the gravel paths and
the stone ascent to the villa, as a synonym, as a

konzipiert wurden. Der Haupteingang ist aber zum Hangfuß verlegt worden, sodass ein neues Verteiler-Gelenk entstand, eine Mitte im Freien – der Platz zwischen Villa und Glasportikus. Und dieser Platz wurde mit Holzstöckelboden gefasst: ein Holzteppich im Außenraum – als Differenz zu den Kieswegen und zum Steinaufgang der Villa, als Synonym, als Andeutung für ein Interieur im Außen und als Resonanz auf das Darunter, auf die mit Holzböden, Holztreppen versehenen Ausstellungshallen direkt darunter.

Du nennst diese Entwurfshaltung »raumstrategisch«. Ist das nicht analog zu unserer vorhin angesprochenen Erfahrung mit Malerei, Skulptur, Concept Art, Minimal Art? Die moderne, reflexive Kunst hat doch ihr Interesse von der Form, von der objekthaften Expression, von der gegenständlichen Repräsentation abgewendet und verlagert auf die phänomenologische Dynamik zwischen Formen, zwischen Farben, auf die Syntax von Wahrnehmung generell.

Lass uns das später diskutieren. Zuvor noch ein paar Ergänzungen zu den Details und weiteren Qualitäten von Rietberg: »Baldachine von Smaragd« war eine der Assoziationen für den Glasportikus. Er wirkt tatsächlich wie ein gläserner Vorhang, ein entmaterialisierter Portikus vor dem Berghang. In seinen Proportionen korrespondiert er mit dem westseitig dem Villenkorpus vorgelagerten alten Eingangstrakt, doch ansonsten steht er in größtmöglichem Kontrast zum Altbau und auch zur Naturkulisse.
Dieser »Baldachin« war ursprünglich noch nicht ornamentiert gedacht, erst mit den in mehrere Glasschichten integrierten, farbigen Rautenmustern entstand die irisierende Wirkung: Die kristallin-homogenen, spiegelnden Flächen erzeugen zugleich eine poröse, textilhafte Wirkung, wirken aber auch wie ein Echo des Blattwerks der umgebenden Baumkronen.

Wie kam es zu dieser Ornamentierung der Glasflächen? Sie ist geometrisch, das Muster könnte man floral »lesen« oder kristallin, es ist aber letztlich weder noch.

Das hat sich stufenweise ergeben, mit Bedacht auf mehrere messbare und weniger messbare Kriterien. Es gab den Aspekt der thermischen Dämmung, der Beschattung der Glasflächen, dann die Vermeidung des ungebrochenen Spiegeleffekts gegenüber dem Altbau, wichtig war auch der Aspekt des Vogelschutzes usw. Das Rautenmuster haben wir Schritt für Schritt entwickelt, es hat eine Ver-

suggestion of an interior outdoors, and as a resonance of what is below, namely, the exhibition halls with wooden floors and wooden staircases directly underneath.

You referred to this design concept as having a "spatial strategy." Isn't that analogous to our experience with painting, sculpture, Conceptual Art, and Minimal Art, which we already spoke about? Modern, reflective art has turned its interest away from form, away from object-like expression, away from figurative representation, and shifted it to the phenomenological dynamics between forms, between colors, to the syntax of perception in general.

Let's discuss that a bit later. First, just a few more words about the details and other qualities of Rietberg: "Baldachine von Smaragd" (canopies of emerald) was one of the associations for the glass pavilion. It actually seems like a glass curtain, a dematerialized portico against the hillside. In its proportions, it corresponds with the old entrance tract positioned in front of the west side of the villa structure. But it otherwise has the greatest possible contrast to the old building, as well as to the natural backdrop.

Originally, this "baldachin" was not designed with ornamentation. The iridescent effect was first created with the colored lozenge patterns integrated into the multiple layers of glass: the crystalline, homogeneous, reflecting surfaces produce a porous, textile-like effect and also seem to echo the foliage of the crowns of the surrounding trees.

How did this ornamentation of the glass surfaces come about? It is geometric and the pattern can be "read" as floral or crystalline, but it's ultimately "neither/nor."

It came about gradually, by taking numerous measurable and less measurable criteria into account. There was the thermal installation factor, the shading of the glass surfaces, then avoidance of an unrefracted mirror effect with respect to the old building. But the bird protection aspect and so on were also important. We developed the lozenge pattern step by step, and it alludes to the rhomboids in the villa's cast-iron balustrade banister, to the textile-like metal forms of the iron canopy at the old entrance. And last but not least, it also alludes to the "emerald" spoken of in the poem by Mathilde Wesendonck.

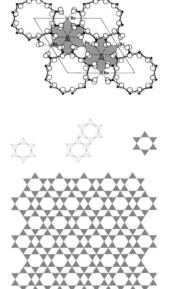

0213
Museum Rietberg
Entwicklung der Geometrie der Ornamentschicht des Glasportikus aus der hexagonalen Struktur von Smaragd-Molekülen / Geometric design development process for the glass portico's ornamentation based on the hexagonal structure of emerald molecules

S. / pp. 70/71

Jean Cocteau,
Orphée (Orpheus), 1950
Orpheus (Jean Marais) an der
Schwelle zur Unterwelt / on the
threshold to the underworld

wandtschaft mit den Rauten des gusseisernen Brüstungsgeländers der Villa, mit den textil wirkenden Metallformen des eisernen Vordaches am alten Portal, aber auch mit dem im Gedicht von Mathilde Wesendonck angesprochenen »Smaragd«.

Die gläserne Pforte

Wenn wir von Baldachin sprechen, meinen wir auch eine Sonderform des Pavillons, eine zeremonielle und zugleich private Würdeform des Pavillons: den tragbaren »Himmel«, den Bett- oder Thron-Himmel. Und das Spannende daran ist, wohin uns der Begriff etymologisch weiterführt. Denn *baldacca* war das italienische Wort für die Stadt Bagdad und stand synonym für die von Bagdad, von der Seidenstraße kommenden, golddurchwirkten Seidenstoffe, die zum Beispiel für Betthimmel oder Zeremonialbaldachine verwendet wurden. Damit wären wir dann beim Textilen …

Ja, es ist eine Art Stoffwechsel im Sinne Sempers, mit dem sich der gläserne Vorhang, der kristalline Baldachin an die Struktur seines Ursprungs erinnert und weiter zurückverweist auf geflochtenes Blattwerk, das Joseph Rykwert als die eigentliche Urhütte beschrieben hat.

Zum Eintritt ins Museum durch den gläsernen Vorhang hast du einmal eine Anspielung auf eine Szene aus einem Film von Jean Cocteau gemacht.

Es ist der Film *Orphée*, Cocteaus Bearbeitung des Mythos von Orpheus und Eurydike, die Szene, in der Jean Marais als Dichter Orphée vor dem Tor zur Unterwelt steht – ein Spiegel in der Wand. Er blickt hinein, hebt die Hände, berührt mit den Fingerspitzen die Spiegelfläche, taucht langsam die Hände in den Spiegel, der plötzlich flüssig wie aufrecht stehendes Wasser erscheint, und tritt dann ganz durch den Spiegel in die andere Welt: Spiegel – Wasser – Unterbewusstsein – »das Andere«, auch im Sinne von Jacques Lacan.

Um dem Glasportikus diese Anmutung zu geben, waren konstruktiv und formal einige Probleme zu lösen.

Die Glaskonstruktion ist selbsttragend – sie besteht aus laminierten Verbundgläsern mit sechs senkrechten Glasschwertern zur Aussteifung. Wir wollten da dezidiert eine gewichtslose und konstruktionslose Anmutung. Der erste Techniker, den wir konsultierten, berechnete die doppelte Mate-

The Glass Portal

When we speak of a "baldachin," we also mean a special form of pavilion, a ceremonial and simultaneously private, dignified form of the pavilion: a portable "sky," a bed or throne canopy. And what's exciting about this is where the term takes us etymologically. Since baldacca was the Italian word for the city of Baghdad and stood synonymously for the silk cloth woven through with gold threads coming from Baghdad over the Silk Road, which was used, for instance, for bed canopies or canopies of state. This brings us to the textile …

Yes, it's a type of metabolism in the sense of [Gottfried] Semper, with which the glass curtain, the crystalline baldachin, calls to mind the structure of its origin and refers back further to the plaited foliage that Joseph Rykwert has described as the true primitive hut.

In entering the museum through the glass curtain, you suddenly made an allusion to a scene in one of Jean Cocteau's films.

It's the film *Orpheus*, Cocteau's handling of the myth of Orpheus and Eurydice, the scene in which Jean Marais as a poet stands before the gate to the underworld—a mirror in the wall. He looks into it, raises his hands, touches the surface of the mirror with his fingertips, slowly dips his hands into the mirror, which suddenly seems fluid like water standing upright, and then steps completely through the mirror into the other world: mirror—water—the subconscious—"the other," also in the sense of Jacques Lacan.

To give the glass pavilion this impression, you had to solve various problems in terms of both construction and form.

The glass construction is self-supporting—it consists of laminated panes of glass with six vertical glass fins for reinforcement. We definitely wanted a weightless and structureless impression there. The first technicians we consulted calculated double the material thickness, which, for many reasons, was too much for us. We finally consulted Ludwig + Weiler from Augsburg, and they reduced the glass dimensions to half the amount. That likewise halved the material and cost expenditures, which was then also decisive, since we had strict cost limits.

The door in the glass wall reminds me of the gates of Japanese temples. I presume that this association

rialstärke, was uns aus mehreren Gründen zu viel war. Wir befragten schließlich Ludwig + Weiler aus Augsburg, und die verringerten die Glasdimensionen auf die Hälfte. Das halbierte auch den Material- und Kostenaufwand, was dann mitentscheidend war, denn wir hatten strenge Kostenlimits.

Die Tür in der Glaswand erinnert mich an japanische Tempeltore. Ich vermute, dass diese Assoziation nicht beabsichtigt war, sondern technische Gründe die Form bedingten.

Im Sinne der Übernahme einer universalistisch sublimierten Wirkung eines alten Formgedankens war es durchaus gewollt.

Komposition und Zufall

Auf den in Glas gehüllten Vorraum folgt die Halle mit einem lichtgrauem Steinboden und einer Decke aus hinterleuchteten Steinplatten. Naturmaterial folgt auf künstliches Material, Naturmuster auf geometrische Ornamentik. Die Eingangssequenz mündet in das mit Helmut Federle gestaltete Betonrelief der Rückwand: Es ist das Kontra zum Portikus aus Glas – eine Umformung, eine Fassung der Endmoräne, die uns hier entgegentritt, als von den Besucherinnen und Besuchern mit individuell setzbaren Goldplättchen mitgestaltbare, berührbare Schnittstelle zwischen Architektur und Natur.

Kannst du über diese zwischen Natur (Zufall) und Architektur (Ordnung) vermittelnde Szene und speziell über die Decke aus hinterleuchteten Onyxplatten etwas mehr sagen?

Wir haben die Platten für die Onyxdecke in Steinbrüchen in Ostanatolien ausgesucht. Sie wurden dort geschnitten, sind durchscheinend, geädert und haben farbige Zeichnungen. Wir erprobten zuerst eine klassische Anordnung, wo benachbarte Schnitte gestürzt aneinandergefügt werden und wechselnde Spiegeleffekte und Symmetrien entstehen – bekannt von Furnierflächen, Steinplattenmustern. Dies überzeugte uns gar nicht. Ich versuchte dann etwas völlig Unorthodoxes. Ich ließ die Steinmetze ähnlich gemusterte Platten in mehrere Stöße sortieren und den Rapport in einem Probefeld so auflegen, dass die nächste Platte immer vom jeweils am weitesten entfernten Stoß genommen wurde und immer die unterschiedlichsten Zeichnungen aufeinanderfolgten.

was not intentional and that technical reasons determined the form instead.

In the sense of taking over a universally sublimated effect of old ideas of form, it was definitely deliberate.

Composition and Coincidence

After the foyer wrapped in glass comes the hall with its light-gray stone floor and a ceiling of stone panels illuminated from behind. Natural material follows artificial material, and natural patterns follow geometric ornamentation. The entrance sequence flows into the concrete relief of the back wall designed in cooperation with Helmut Federle: it's the contra to the portico made of glass—a recasting, a version of the terminal moraine that confronts us here, as a touchable interface between architecture and nature that can be designed with the help of visitors using gold lamella that can be set individually.

Could you say a bit more about this scene that mediates between nature (coincidence) and architecture (order), and in particular about the ceiling of onyx panels lit from behind?

We picked out the panels for the onyx ceiling in stone quarries in eastern Anatolia. They were cut there and are translucent, veined, with colored markings. We first tried out a classical arrangement, where the adjacent sections are joined in a pitched manner, creating varying mirror effects and symmetries—as is familiar from veneer surfaces and stone-panel patterns. But this didn't convince us at all. I then tried something completely unorthodox. I had the stone masons sort similar panels into several stacks to display repeating patterns in a trial area in such a way that the next panel was always taken from the stack that was the farthest away respectively, with the most varied markings following one another. And this "gently" steered, random pattern, without symmetries or progressions, fit perfectly and required very few corrections.

You have also worked on urban planning concepts with similar random patterns, with rules of the game that circumvent classical principles of order. In the case of the settlement in Hadersdorf near Vienna, the parcels were divided among the planners by lottery. You also tend to go about creating patterns for laying parquet floors in a similar way.

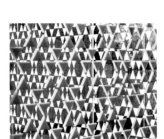

0213
Museum Rietberg
Glasornament Eingangspavillon
(Detail) / Glass ornamentation in
entry pavilion (detail)

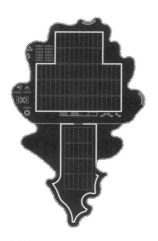

0604
Museum Liaunig, Neuhaus
Wettbewerbsprojekt 2004,
Grundriss / Competition project,
2004, floor plan

0213
Museum Rietberg
Treppe vom Portikus ins erste
Tiefgeschoss / Stairs from the
portico to the first lower level

»Das Rietberg-Museum ist das
einzige oder zumindest eines der
wenigen Museen, das seine
Besucher nicht einfach wie Hades
in unterirdische Löcher hinabreisst,
sondern vielmehr, darin an Eleusis
erinnernd, einen geregelten
Abgang in das *telesterion* anbietet
und den Gang in die Unterwelt
damit zu einem Erlebnis macht.«

Elisabeth von Samsonow,
in: *Museum Rietberg.
Die Erweiterung,*
Zürich 2007

Und diese mit wenigen Korrekturen »sanft« ge-steuerten Zufallsmuster, ohne Symmetrien und Verläufe, passten perfekt.

Mit ähnlichen Zufallsmustern, mit Spielregeln, welche klassische Ordnungsprinzipien unterlaufen, hast du auch bei städtebaulichen Konzepten gearbeitet. Bei der Siedlung in Wien-Hadersdorf wurden den Planern die Parzellen durch Verlosung zugeteilt. Ähnlich gehst du auch beim Verlegemuster von Parkettböden vor.

Für den Wettbewerbsentwurf für das Privatmu-seum von Herbert Liaunig auf einem Hügel in Kärnten inspirierte mich ein Eichenblatt, das ich auf dem Grundstück gefunden hatte. Sein Umriss ergab die Schablone für den Grundriss. Eine Ge-staltung »nach der Natur« wäre im Bau aber nicht mehr unmittelbar ablesbar gewesen. Die Matrize war floral, ihre Transformation dann geometrisch, Raumkonzept und Raumerleben eine offene Spannung zwischen Frei und Geordnet, Gekurvt und Orthogonal.

Zurück nach Zürich: Das Weitergehen in die Tief-ebenen des Museums wird von den meisten als Überraschung erlebt, als eine Art Inversion des Erwarteten. Wie erklärt sich das?

Die aus der Halle hinunterführende Holztreppe bildet einen eigenen Raum, eine in Material und Farbe von Glas, Stein und Beton klar unterschie-dene Passage, eine Holz-Licht-Passage in massiver Eiche, sehr taktil, klingend, zugleich optisch sehr porös. Beim Erreichen der ersten unteren Ebene erlebt man eine Transformierung der Licht-stimmung, ein Eintauchen in ein schattenloses, milchig-zartes, zugleich fast greifbares Licht, wie es etwa auch die klassischen japanischen Papierwände geben.

Wie habt ihr diesen Unterschied der Lichtqualität zu vielen ähnlich gestalteten Museumsräumen erreicht?

Die Lichtdecke ist nicht eben, nicht flach, sondern aus gefalteten Polycarbonat-Platten gegliedert. Die Faltung steift die dünnen, milchig-opaken Platten statisch aus. Sie gibt diesem feinen Relief eine eigene Wirkung. Die Faltung und die darüber-hängende Beleuchtung sind so ausgelegt, dass weder ein Eigenschatten noch ein Schlagschatten in der Decke entsteht. Wir unternahmen da viele Versuche mit 1:1-Modellen. Primär haben wir nach einem optimalen Licht für die Exponate aus außereuropäischen Kulturen gesucht und das

In the competition design for Herbert Liaunig's private museum on a hill in Carinthia, an oak leaf that I had found on the property served as inspiration. Its outline yielded the template for the layout. But it would no longer have been possible to discern a design "based on nature" in the building. The matrix was floral, but its trans-formation was geometric, and the spatial concept and experience then gave rise to an overt tension between free and ordered aspects, between the curved and the orthogonal.

But back to Zurich: most people experience con-tinuing on to the underground levels of the museum as a surprise, as a type of inversion of what they anticipate. How would you explain this?

The wooden staircase descending from the hall forms its own space, a space clearly distinct in material and color of glass, stone, and concrete, a wood-light passageway in solid oak, very tactile, sonorous, and at the same time optically quite porous. Upon reaching the first underground level, one experiences a transformation of the lighting atmosphere, immersion in a shadowless, delicate light that is milky, yet nearly palpable at the same time—as is, for instance, also provided by classic Japanese paper walls.

How did you achieve this difference in light quality for many similarly designed museum spaces?

The illuminated ceiling is not smooth, not flat, but structured in folded polycarbonate panels. The folding reinforces the thin, milky-opaque panels structurally. It gives this fine relief its own effect. The folding and the lighting hanging above it are designed in such a way that there are neither inherent nor cast shadows on the ceiling. To create this effect, we did various tests with 1:1 models. We were primarily looking for an optimal light for the exhibits from non-European cultures, which was tested and developed in a room specially equipped for us at the former Toni dairy complex in Zurich.

Inner Transparency

On the lowest level of the museum, the spatial character changes again.

Yes, resulting from three factors: the ceiling there is the highest, and there are also no fixed, load-bearing dividing walls. In contrast to the floor

in einem eigens dafür ausgerüsteten Raum im ehemaligen Zürcher Toni-Areal getestet und entwickelt.

Innere Transparenz

Auf der untersten Museumsebene gibt es nochmals einen Wechsel im Raumcharakter.

Ja, und zwar durch drei Faktoren: Die Raumhöhe ist dort am größten, es gibt auch keine fixen, tragenden Trennwände. Es ist im Unterschied zur darüberliegenden Etage ein durchgehender Raum, dezentriert, mit offener Mitte; die Treppe ist etwas länger, ihr oberer Abschluss ist im Unterschied zum darüberliegenden Lauf, wo die helle Onyxdecke der Halle mitwirkt, nun die hölzerne Untersicht des ersten Laufes.

Kannst du etwas über die Konstruktion sagen, mit der diese freie Dimension auf der tiefsten Ebene erreicht wird? Ist es nicht eine Art Einstülpung über dem untersten Boden, ein Zurückziehen der Traglasten in ein Stahlbeton-Raumfachwerk über der Lichtdecke, das sich in dieser Decke nur mehr in einer linearen Flächenteilung mitteilt? Die bündigste Formulierung dazu hat ja Aita Flury in einem Text für *werk, bauen + wohnen* gefunden. Sie schrieb: »Die nach unten gesteigerte Raumdimension ist Resultat eines Tragwerkskonzepts, das als geschossübergreifend wirksames und komplementäres Tragsystem von Decken und Wänden funktioniert, dessen Prinzipien aus dem Brückenbau abgeleitet sind. Die enormen technischen Anstrengungen im Schnitt bleiben aber hintergründig. Es ist nicht die Absicht, ein Prinzip sichtbar werden zu lassen, noch es eindeutig erfahrbar zu machen. Es ist die lichte Weiträumigkeit der kalkulierten Lichtmaschine, der künstliche, die Räume miteinander verspannende Himmel, in der sich die Leistung der Struktur widerspiegelt«.

Das ist es, genau das.

Einzelne Kommentare vermerkten, dass man in den tief gelegten Museumsräumen den Kontakt zur Außenwelt verliere und dass das Heraufkommen, das Auftauchen über die zweite Treppe in die alte Villa dann neuerlich unerwartet und überraschend sei.

Museen allgemein und speziell dieses sind eigene Welten. Wir sind mit einer krassen Künstlichkeit der Situation konfrontiert, und es gibt keinen »zu verortenden« Kontext für die Objekte, ganz besonders hier nicht. Das Museum Rietberg ist

above, it is a continuous space, decentralized, with an open center; the staircase is somewhat longer, and its upper end, in contrast to the staircase above it, where the light-hued onyx ceiling of the halls also plays a part, is now the wood-filled view of the first staircase from below.

Can you say something about the construction with which you achieved this free dimension on the lowest level? Isn't it a type of insertion over the lowermost floor, a shifting of the capacity loads to a reinforced concrete framework above the illuminated ceiling, which only divides the plane of this ceiling linearly? Aita Flury came up with what is perhaps the most concise way of putting this in a text for *werk, bauen + wohnen*. She wrote: "The increasing spatial dimension toward the bottom results from a structural design concept that functions as a complementary load-bearing system of ceilings and walls throughout all the levels and whose principles are derived from bridge construction. But the huge technical efforts generally remain hidden. The intention is not to make a principle become visible, nor to make it possible for it to be clearly experienced. It is the light spaciousness of the calculated dynamo, the artificial sky bracing together the spaces in which the achievement of the structure is reflected."

That's it, precisely that.

Some reviews mentioned that one loses contact with the outside world in the museum spaces located deep underground, and that coming up, surfacing via the two staircases in the old villa is then again unexpected and surprising.

Museums in general, and this one in particular, are worlds of their own. We are confronted with the glaring artificiality of the situation, and it's not possible to "localize" a context for the objects, especially not here. Historically, the Museum Rietberg is an art collection and not an ethnological museum. The inspiration for collecting the objects originally used mostly for rituals and cultish practices was primarily their artistic character. The artificiality of the spaces responds to this, their distinct exterritoriality, their introverted character as a stage, on which the elemental value of the objects is concentrated, as it were. All these artifacts have been dislocated from their genuine context once and for all, and we use and view them now primarily with an aesthetic gaze and interest.

In the villa "above," however, it is quite different. In it, there seem to be certain local landmarks,

»The completely symmetrical spatial order of the two exhibition levels in plan is overlaid in section by a structural concept whose principles are derived from bridge building. In accordance with the basic principle of the project the enormous technical effort involved remains in the background; the achievement of the structure is reflected in the calculated light machine of an artificial sky that spans the spaces, brings them together and generates a light expansiveness.«

Aita Flury,
»Elected affinity. The extension to the Museum Rietberg by Adolf Krischanitz and Alfred Grazioli«,
in: *werk, bauen + wohnen*, 5, 2007

S. / pp. 74/75

»Seit seiner Gründung im Jahr 1952 bezeichnet sich das Museum Rietberg als ein Kunstmuseum. Es zeigt Kunst aus Asien, Afrika, Ozeanien und Alt-Amerika. Der Gründungsdirektor des Museums, der Künstler, Bauhausgründer und Pädagoge Johannes Itten (1888–1967), hat als Erster die Sammlung van der Heydt in der Villa Wesendonck eingerichtet.«

Albert Lutz,
in: *Museum Rietberg. Die Erweiterung*, Zürich 2007

0213
Museum Rietberg
Helmut Federle,
Betonrelief in der Eingangshalle /
Concrete relief in the entry
hall, 2007

geschichtlich eine Kunstsammlung und kein Völkerkundemuseum. Im Vordergrund des Sammelns stand primär der Kunstcharakter der ursprünglich meist rituell und kultisch gebrauchten Objekte. Hierauf antwortet die Künstlichkeit der Räume, ihre eindeutige Exterritorialität, ihr introvertierter Charakter als Bühne, auf der sich die gleichsam elementaren Werte der Objekte konzentrieren. All diese Artefakte sind ein für allemal aus ihrem genuinen Kontext disloziert worden, und wir benutzen, betrachten sie nun mit einem primär ästhetischen Blick und Interesse.

In der Villa »oben« ist es doch deutlich anders. Dort gibt es scheinbare lokale Orientierungshilfen, die Blicke hinaus in den Park, die Farbqualitäten und Texturen der alten Räume, die Lichtstimmungen im Tagesverlauf. In Wahrheit, im Hinblick auf die »eigentliche« Welt der Objekte ist all das auf seine Weise ebenso hoch artifiziell und »entfremdet«.

Eine besondere Erfahrung war für mich die Farbigkeit der Kastenfenster in der Villa. Innen- und Außenseiten sind farbig extrem verschieden. Außen weiß und innen fast schwarz. In der Moderne hat sich das umgekehrt, und nicht nur das. Auch bei der denkmalpflegerischen Erneuerung der in dunklen Tönen gehaltenen Wände konnten wir nicht nur technisch, sondern auch im Hinblick auf Farb- und Lichtwirkungen ein Raffinement studieren und kennenlernen, das in der Moderne verloren gegangen ist.

Hattet ihr eine bestimmte Atmosphäre vor Augen, die diese Räume für die fernöstlichen Kultgegenstände bieten sollten? Gab es für dich oder Alfred Anregungen durch vergleichbare Museumsräume?

views out onto the park, the color qualities and textures of the old rooms, the changing ambience of light over the course of the day. In reality, in terms of the "actual" world of the objects, all of this is just as highly artificial and "alienated" in its own way.

For me, a special experience was the color of the casement windows in the villa. The interior and exterior sides are extremely different in terms of color—outside white and inside nearly black. In the modern era, this has been reversed, and not only this. When renewing walls painted in dark hues based on historical conservation criteria, we were able to study and become familiar with a refinement that has been lost in the modern era, not only in terms of technology, but also with respect to the effects of color and light.

Did you envisage a particular atmosphere which these spaces for displaying Far Eastern ritual objects were supposed to offer? Were you or Alfred able to find inspiration in comparable museum spaces?

In very few. What is unique about this museum is the huge spectrum of artifacts from very different cultures, which are represented by objects of the highest quality throughout. In the field of East Asian artifacts, it is one of the two best museums in the world. This therefore presented us with the difficult task of placing these different cultures within one framework, without compromises and without playing favorites. We did not try to do so by means of total neutralization, a kind of zero program, with an equal distance to all conceivable artifacts from the cultures of the world. We were instead looking for a design and a materiality that—as it seemed to us—functions transculturally and avoids anything contemporary, anything in love with detail or any structural verve, without this becoming noticeably compulsive.

The most difficult part was, however, the artwork on the back wall by Helmut Federle, who cannot be thanked enough for his work. It became clear to us quite early on that this back wall could not remain empty and needed to be supercharged with culture. Federle, as an authority on the Asian, African, American, and European art scenes, then inscribed this "universal" dimension into his concrete relief in a way that was hardly imaginable beforehand.

The ability to perform all of this "open-heart surgery"—at the beginning, we risked a frighteningly

Nur wenige. Das Singuläre an diesem Museum ist die enorme Bandbreite an Artefakten ganz unterschiedlicher Kulturen, die durchwegs mit Objekten höchster Qualität vertreten sind. Im Bereich der Ostasiatika zählt es zu den zwei besten Museen weltweit. So stellte sich uns die nicht einfache Aufgabe, all diese unterschiedlichen Kulturen in einen Rahmen zu setzen, ohne Abstriche und ohne sich anzubiedern. Wir versuchten es nicht mit totaler Neutralisierung, mit einer Art Nullprogramm, mit äquivalenten Distanzen zu allen erdenklichen Artefakten aus den Weltkulturen, sondern wir suchten eine Gestaltung und eine Materialität, die – wie uns schien – transkulturell funktioniert und alles Zeitgeistige, alle Detailverliebtheit oder konstruktive Verve vermeidet, ohne dass das wiederum zwanghaft spürbar wäre.

Das schwierigste Kapitel war aber das Kunstwerk an der Rückwand der Halle von Helmut Federle, dem dafür nicht genug gedankt werden kann. Sehr früh war uns klar, dass diese Rückwand nicht leer sein kann und einer kulturellen Aufladung bedarf. Federle hat nun als exzellenter Kenner der asiatischen, afrikanischen, amerikanischen und europäischen Kunstszene in sein Betonrelief diese »universelle« Dimension eingetragen, wie es vorher kaum denkbar war.

Die Durchführung all dieser »Operationen am offenen Herzen« – wir riskierten eine am Anfang erschreckend riesige Baugrube und die teilweise Unterfangung der Villa! – war natürlich der Leitung des Museums zu verdanken. Von der Ausschreibung des Wettbewerbs über das Raumprogramm bis hin zur schwierigen, jedoch im Großen und Ganzen friktionsfreien Abwicklung war dieser gewaltige Prozess vor allem in der Hand des Direktors Albert Lutz. Nur gemeinsam waren der »Bauherr« und die Architekten in der Lage, so eine Aufgabe zu stemmen. Die erste Ausstellung über Japan, die ich gemeinsam mit Katharina Epprecht gestalten durfte, war gewissermaßen noch eine schöne Draufgabe.

In der alten Tabakfabrik, neben dem Gefängnis

In Zürich war es ein gärtnerisch prachtvolles, anspruchsvolles Grundstück mit wertvollen Bestandsbauten für eine große, neue Intervention. Einige Jahre zuvor hattest du den Wettbewerb für die neue Kunsthalle in Krems in Niederösterreich gewonnen. Auch dort gibt es einen denkmalgeschützten Bestandsbau, zur Straße, zur Donau hin, die ehemalige

huge excavation pit and the partial underpinning of the foundation of the villa!—was naturally thanks to the management of the museum. This daunting process was, above all, in the hands of director Albert Lutz: from the competition announcement, to the planning process, to the difficult realization, which nonetheless ran smoothly on the whole. Only together were the "client" and the architects in a position to realize such a task. The first exhibition, which I had the opportunity to design in cooperation with Katharina Epprecht, focused on Japan and was, to a certain extent, simply a wonderful bonus.

In the Old Tobacco Factory next to the Prison

This was a challenging property with valuable existing buildings and magnificent horticulture earmarked for a large, new intervention in Zurich. Some years before, you won the competition for the new Kunsthalle in Krems in Lower Austria. There are also listed historical buildings there. Toward the Danube is the former tobacco factory, yet directly next to it is one of the largest prison complexes in Austria, both legendary and infamous and with a genius loci that is correspondingly distinctive. Adjusting to the old buildings present there was also quite tricky. What especially struck me as an issue was the fact that, in moving from the quite rural-seeming old building with old vaults and incident light from the south, one arrived at a canyon-like ramp structure of exposed concrete, which connects the various new levels with the level of old buildings and leads along a wide glass wall with a view into the new hall. And with the large skylight, the rhythm of the roof girders, and the masonry of the old windows on the south wall being left visible, the central exhibition hall, wreathed by the system of paths and spaces, produces a core space that is in no way neutral but instead very laden with tension. This tension already develops like a jolt in the dark impact of the ramp after the orderly vaults of the foyer, shifting visitors to another level of perception. A concentrated sequence of sharp spatial contrasts leads from the everyday world into the realm of art, certainly not an "unproblematic" or pleasant promenade. Looking back, how do you see it in comparison to the Museum Rietberg in Zurich or the Kunsthalle at Karlsplatz?

For, me, the Kunsthalle in Krems is a key building in terms of dealing with old substance. Naturally, the existing structure is not a nineteenth-century villa but instead an early industrial building from the empire period, and on the wall of a prison to

S. / p. 76

S. / p. 77

9206
Kunsthalle Krems, 1992–1996
Eingang über die Betonrampe /
Concrete ramp entrance

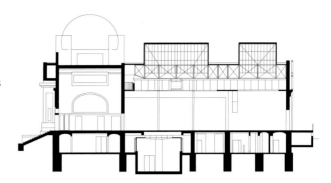

Tabakfabrik, doch direkt daneben liegt eines der größten Gefängnisareale Österreichs, legendär und berüchtigt, mit einem entsprechend ausgeprägten Genius loci. Dort war es ebenfalls eine knifflige Einpassung in alten Baubestand. Was mir dort speziell als Thema auffiel: Man gelangt aus dem mit alten Gewölben, mit dem von Süden einfallenden Licht so ländlich anmutenden Altbau in eine schluchtartige Rampenanlage aus nacktem Beton, welche die verschiedenen neuen Ebenen mit den Niveaus der Altbauten verbindet und an einer breiten Glaswand mit Einblick in den neuen Saal entlangführt. Und die zentrale Ausstellungshalle, rundum vom Raum- und Wegsystem umflochten, erzeugt mit großem Oberlicht, mit den Rhythmen der Dachträger und den sichtbar gelassenen Vermauerungen alter Fenster an der Südwand einen keineswegs neutralen, vielmehr sehr spannungsreichen Kernraum. Diese Spannung hat sich nach den friedlichen Vorraumgewölben schon in der dunklen Wucht der Rampe schockartig aufgetan und versetzt die Besucherinnen und Besucher in eine andere Wahrnehmungsebene. Eine dichte Folge scharfer Raumkontraste leitet aus dem Alltag in die Kunstsphäre, gewiss keine »unproblematische« oder gefällige Promenade. Wie siehst du das rückblickend im Vergleich etwa zum Museum Rietberg in Zürich oder auch zur Kunsthalle am Karlsplatz?

Für mich ist die Kunsthalle Krems ein Schlüsselbau, was den Umgang mit alter Substanz angeht. Natürlich ist der Bestand keine Villa des 19. Jahrhunderts, sondern ein frühindustrieller Bau aus dem Kaiserreich, noch dazu an einer Gefängnismauer. Darüber hinaus ist zu bemerken, dass der große Kernraum im Wettbewerb nicht im Raumprogramm war und sich erst aus der Anordnung der ursprünglich bestellten Räume ergab. Ich denke, diese größte Halle der Anlage hat sich dann zigfach bestätigt und generiert – wahrscheinlich die überraschendste räumliche Wirkung an diesem Ort.

Die enge Randlage der Rampen, die den winkelförmigen Altbau neu erschließen, die von dir erwähnten starken Kontraste in der Lichtsituation, im Wechsel von forcierter Enge und überraschender innerer Weite, erzeugen diese unheimliche Passage von da nach dort, deren Zeichenhaftigkeit der Polarität von Kunst und Alltag und der lokalen Dramatik des Ortes wohl zukommt.

Sowohl bei der Wiener Secession als auch bei der Renovierung des 20er Hauses gab es diesen Aspekt: Tiefgeschosse wurden unter die alten Pavillons geschoben, als technische und vor allem funktionale Basis des neuen Ganzen. In der Secession war es der

boot. What should also be mentioned is the fact that the large core space was not included in the competition and first arose from the arrangement of the spaces originally commissioned. I think that this space, the largest hall of the complex, has proved itself many times and generates perhaps the most surprising spatial effect on this site.

The narrow peripheral situation of the ramps, which open up the angled old building anew, the stark contrasts in the lighting situation, as you've already mentioned, and the change from forced closeness to surprising interior vastness—all this engenders an uncanny passage from here to there, produces its metaphoric character of polarity between art and everyday life, and perhaps corresponds to the local drama of the site.

This aspect was present in the case of both the Vienna Secession and the renovation of the 20er Haus: underground floors were slid under the old pavilion as a technical and, above all, functional basis for the new whole. In the case of the Secession, it was the space for the Klimt frieze, the new gallery under the entrance hall. In the 20er Haus, a great deal more . . .

The Second Molting of Karl Schwanzer's Expo Pavilion

One principal theme in the case of the 21er Haus (21st House), as it's now called, was upgrading the pavilion—originally a minimally engineered, raw skin-and-bones building with four main supports and a twelve-meter overhang of the upper floor— with lots of newer building technology: heating, ventilation, cooling system, and so on, integrating a huge number of new arteries and veins into the old, fragile skeleton that is visible all around. Upgrading it for current earthquake safety and thermal, technical fire protection standards gave us quite a few nuts to crack. The competition

Raum für den Klimt-Fries, die neue Galerie unter der Eingangshalle. Im 20er Haus dann noch viel mehr …

Die zweite Häutung von Karl Schwanzers Expo-Pavillon

Ein Hauptthema beim 21er Haus, wie es jetzt heißt, war die Nachrüstung des Pavillons – der ja ursprünglich ein minimal technisierter, roher Haut-und-Knochen-Bau mit vier Hauptstützen und 12 Metern Auskragung des Obergeschosses war – mit sehr viel neuer Haustechnik: Heizung, Lüftung, Kühlung usw., die jede Menge an neuen Arterien und Venen in das alte, fragile, überall sichtbare Skelett integrierten. Die Nachrüstung für Erdbebensicherheit und aktuelle thermische, brandschutztechnische Normen gab uns etliche Nüsse zu knacken. Schon im Wettbewerbsprogramm war eine wesentliche Erweiterung für Nebenräume, Büros, Lager und anderes verlangt worden, die unterirdisch integriert werden mussten, damit die offene Position des Pavillons zum begleitenden Skulpturengarten im Gelände erhalten blieb.

Nach der Wettbewerbsentscheidung und einer Pause, als das Projekt auf Eis lag, kamen dann mit der Zuweisung der Fritz-Wotruba-Sammlung und der Artothek, der Kunstsammlung des Bundes, noch Flächen hinzu. Das hat zum einen das Projekt überhaupt wieder in Gang gebracht, weil damit neue Budgetquellen zur Verfügung standen. Zum anderen musste ich noch ein Geschoss im Souterrain vorsehen und dabei sicherstellen, dass all diese Substruktionen natürlichen Lichteinfall und Sichtkontakt zum Außenraum haben. Die Systematik der Erschließung, der Raum- und Lichthofsequenzen im Sockel des Pavillons bei aller Enge klar und stringent zu halten, war keine leichte Sache.

Umstritten war dein Umgang mit den alten Treppen vom Parterre ins Obergeschoss. Einige Rezensenten haben sich total darauf fokussiert. Es gab aber mindestens vier triftige Gründe, die zum Abbruch und Neubau der Vertikalerschließung führten.

Die alten Treppen waren Elemente der ersten Nutzung des Hauses als Österreich-Pavillon bei der Expo 58 in Brüssel. Es waren echte Freitreppen, die in asymmetrischer Anordnung vom ebenerdigen, offenen Ausstellungsgelände in das »schwebende«, introvertierte Obergeschoss führten. Bei der Adaptierung zum Einraum-Museum im Wiener Schweizergarten 1964 blieben die

0307
Umbau und Erweiterung /
Renovation and Extension
20er / 21er Haus, Wien,
Ansicht vom Garten / view
from the garden

1958 als Österreich-Pavillon
nach Entwurf von Karl Schwanzer
auf der Expo Brüssel errichtet;
1964 in Wien wiederaufgebaut
und erweitert zum Museum des
20. Jahrhunderts; allgemein als
»20er Haus« bezeichnet

1958 Austrian Pavilion at the
Expo in Brussels, designed by
Karl Schwanzer;
1964 rebuilt in Vienna, adapted
and extended as the Museum des
20. Jahrhunderts, commonly called
the "20er Haus"

program already called for a substantial extension to accommodate ancillary rooms, offices, storage space, and other things, which had to be integrated underground so that the open position of the pavilion toward the accompanying sculpture garden on the grounds was retained.

After the competition decision and a pause when the project was on hold, other areas were then added with the allocating of the Fritz Wotruba Collection and the Artothek, the State Art Collection, to the Kunsthalle. On the one hand, this got the project going again in the first place, because with the additions, new budget resources became available. On the other, I had to design yet another floor underground and, in doing so, ensure that all these substructions receive natural light and have visual contact with the outdoors. Keeping the systematics of the development and the sequence of spaces and atria in the base of the pavilion clear and stringent despite the constrictions was not easy.

How you dealt with the old steps from the ground floor to the upper floor was controversial. Some critics focused completely on this. There were, however, at least four good reasons for demolishing the vertical access and building it anew.

The old staircase was an element connected with the original use of the building as the Austrian Pavilion at Expo 58 in Brussels. It was a true flight of stairs leading in an asymmetrical arrangement from the open exhibition area at ground level to the "floating," introverted upper story. When adapting the building to become a one-room museum in the Schweizer Garten (Swiss Garden) in Vienna in 1964, the staircase was retained, but it was then positioned symmetrically in the interior space. The competition in 2003 called for dealing

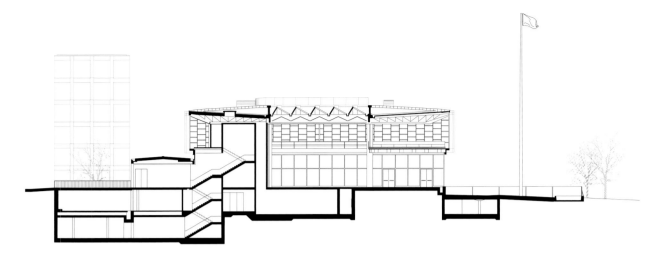

0307
21er Haus, Schnitt / Section

Treppen erhalten, waren allerdings nun symmetrisch im Innenraum positioniert. Im Wettbewerb 2003 war verlangt, die beiden Hauptetagen als getrennte Veranstaltungsorte und getrennte Brandabschnitte zu behandeln, weiters die Erschließung für die zusätzlichen Hausetagen und im Hinblick auf Barrierefreiheit des Hauses zu ergänzen.

Ziemlich rigide und komplexe Forderungen. Was war die Lösung?

Damit konnten die alten, offenen Treppen nicht mehr erhalten werden. Es ging nun darum, mit zwei neuen brandsicheren Stiegen vier Ebenen zu verbinden (beziehungsweise als Brandabschnitte zu trennen), Lifte einzubauen, zusätzliche Aussteifungen zur Erdbebensicherheit vorzusehen, die Schächte für Technik und Lüftungen zu nutzen, nachdem die diesbezügliche Nutzung der vier hohlen Hauptstützen allein für das ganze Haus nicht ausreichte – und bei all dem die zwei alten Deckenöffnungen nicht zu vergrößern.

Meine Lösung, schon in der Wettbewerbsjury von allen Experten als die raumschonendste akzeptiert, konzentrierte sich dann in der Detailplanung darauf, mit den neuen Elementen – wie auch in der ganzen Charakteristik der neuen Sockeletagen – keine Konkurrenz zur Leichtigkeit und Transparenz der Originalsubstanz zu bilden oder irgendeine subjektive, zweifelhafte Note einzuführen, sondern mit einer, nicht zuletzt auch budgetär bedingten, minimalen »Alltäglichkeit« Karl Schwanzers originäre Qualität mit meinen Ergänzungen eher noch zu unterstreichen.

Es kommt für mich eines hinzu: Die neue, sehr einfache und simpel »eingehauste« Treppe bietet wohl eine funktionell vielfältige Aufrüstung und Komplet-

with the two main floors as separate event locations and separate fire sections, and also supplementing access to the additional floors of the building, also with respect to making the building accessible for people with disabilities.

Quite rigid and complex requirements. What was the solution?

This meant that it was no longer possible to retain the open stairways. It was a question of connecting four floors with two new fireproof staircases (and/or dividing them as fire sections), installing elevators, planning additional reinforcements for earthquake safety, using the ducts for technology and ventilation systems, since using the four hollow main supports to this effect was not sufficient for the whole building—and, despite all of this, not enlarging the two old ceiling openings in the process.

My solution, which was already accepted by all the experts on the competition jury, then concentrated, in terms of detailed planning, on not allowing the new elements—as also in the overall characteristics of the new underground floors—to foster competition with the lightness and transparency of the original substance or to introduce some subjective, dubious elements. The goal instead, if nothing else also for budget reasons, was to emphasize the minimal "prosaicness" of Karl Schwanzer's original quality with my additions.

For me, there is also one more thing: the new, very simply "enclosed" staircase arguably offers a functionally multifaceted upgrading and complementing of the intersections from everyday life into the freedom of art. At the same time, it is also a symbol of the ruptured continuity in the history of the building.

tierung der Schnittflächen vom Alltag in den Freiraum der Kunst, sie ist aber auch ein Zeichen der gebrochenen Kontinuität innerhalb der Geschichte des Hauses. Genauer betrachtet evoziert die neue, introvertierte Stiege eine Aura der Abwesenheit, sie hält Distanz zu einer positivistischen Illusion von Vollständigkeit, von ungebrochenem Weiterleben einer vergangenen Situation.

Im neuen 21er Haus braucht und gibt es keine theatralische Treppe mehr zwischen »Unten und Oben«. Was in der ursprünglichen Situierung mit dem offenen Erdgeschoss, mit der Einbindung in die Passantenströme des Brüsseler Weltausstellungsgeländes, mit der Präsentation eines Landes »vor aller Welt« von Karl Schwanzer in Szene gesetzt wurde – diese freitragende Treppe, eine Auftrittsbühne wie etwa die großen Hoteltreppen von Morris Lapidus –, das ist es jetzt absolut nicht mehr.

Nicht nur die Brandschutzauflagen und dergleichen, auch viele andere Kontexte haben sich verändert. Und das zeigt sich nun sehr konzentriert an dieser Stelle.

Diese neue Treppe ist eine entzauberte Schleuse, die innerhalb des weiträumigen Sogs zwischen der Halle und dem nun in ganzer Breite geöffneten Foyer einen »Vorhalt« einbringt, eher als partielle Verengung oder Verdichtung wirkt, als dass sie sich schön offenherzig darbietet. Das Programm »Kunst für alle« der 60er-Jahre, die damals forcierte Integration aller Facetten von Alltag und Technik im Kunstraum ist vorüber, und diese schweigende, hinter der äußerlichen »Banalität« wie vorhin skizziert ziemlich komplexe Treppe führt – in meinem Verständnis – wieder weg von der versuchten Transzendierung der Warenästhetik, weg von der Popularisierungseuphorie der Boom-Epoche. Sie führt die Benutzer und Benutzerinnen aber auch nicht wieder in eine neue Illusion, sondern lässt sie fürs Erste eher allein mit sich und ihren richtigen und / oder falschen Projektionen an diesem Übergang zwischen Sphären und Ebenen.

More particularly, the new, introverted staircase evokes an aura of absence, maintains a distance from a positivist illusion of completeness, of the continuing survival of a past situation.

In the new 21er Haus, there is no theatrical staircase between "below and above" anymore, nor is one necessary. What Karl Schwanzer staged with the open ground floor in the original situation, the integration within the streams of passersby on the Expo grounds in Brussels, the presentation of a country "to the whole world"—this free-standing staircase, or a stage like the large hotel staircase designed by Morris Lapidus, for example—is now definitely no longer present.

Not only the fire protection regulations and the like have changed, but also many other contexts. And this is now shown in a very concentrated way here.

This new staircase is a demystified passageway that introduces a "note of suspension" within the large-scale slipstream between the hall and the foyer, whose entire breadth is now opened up. It also takes effect more as a partial narrowing or concentration rather than offering itself as pleasantly openhearted. The "art for all" program of the nineteen-sixties—the forced integration of all facets of everyday life and technology within an artspace—is over. And, behind the external "banality," as already outlined, this quite complex staircase, which is silent, once again leads away—as I see it—from the attempt to transcend the commodity aesthetic, from the popularization euphoria of the boom epoch. At the same time, it does not lead users to a new illusion once again, either. For now, it leaves them alone with themselves and their correct and/or incorrect projections in this transition between spheres and levels.

0213
Umbau und Erweiterung / Conversion and Extension of Museum Rietberg, Zürich / Zurich, mit / with Alfred Grazioli

0213
Museum Rietberg, Stiegenhaus / staircase

0213
Museum Rietberg

0213
Museum Rietberg, Eingangshalle / Entrance hall
Wandrelief von / Mural relief by Helmut Federle

9206
Kunsthalle Krems
Rampe / Ramp

Zentraler Raum / Main hall >

9703
Tauernbahnmuseum, Schwarzach

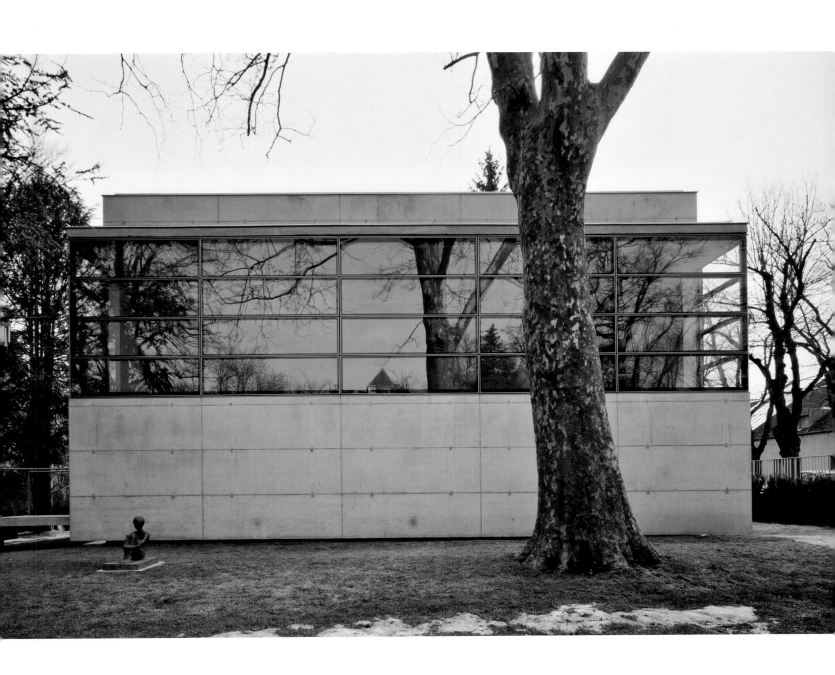

0304
Privatmuseum / Private Museum Gnad & Gawisch, Wien / Vienna

0304
Privatmuseum / Private Museum Gnad & Gawisch

0914
Umbau / Conversion Sammlung Friedrichshof, Zurndorf

1205
Ausstellungsgestaltung / Exhibition Design for *Penacho. Pracht & Passion*, Völkerkundemuseum, Wien / Vienna

8501
Umbau / Conversion Wiener Secession, Wien / Vienna
Installationsansicht / Installation view Dieter Roth, *Grosse Tischruine (Large Table Ruin),* Wiener Secession, 1995

0307
Umbau und Erweiterung / Conversion and Extension of the 20er / 21er Haus, Wien / Vienna

0307
Eingangsbereich mit Büroturm und neuem Tiefhof an der Straße /
Entrance with office tower and new sunken courtyard along the street

Gottfried Pirhofer

Städtebau am Prüfstand

Urbanism at Stake

Manchmal wird es besonders deutlich. Durch die Verlängerung einer U-Bahn-Linie rückt ein Gebiet, bisher »weit draußen«, in die schnelle Erreichbarkeit. Die Augen haben keine Zeit, sich gewöhnend umzustellen. Es ist nicht mehr »Peripherie«, aber die Differenz zur Stadt[1] ist unverrückt. Am U-Bahn-Ausgang der (vorläufigen) Endstation steht man nach zehn Minuten Fahrt in einem anderen Raumverhältnis, summarisch in der »Zwischenstadt«[2]. Man sieht förmlich, wie sie sich ausbreitet, verdichtet, transformiert, erkennt historische Schichten deutlicher als im »Zentrum«, das sich zunehmend collagiert und simuliert. Die Zwischenstadt ist naiver, kontrastreicher, unverblümter, auch wenn viele Straßen, die vielmehr Erschließungsstrecken sind, Blumennamen tragen. Dass sich hier das Städtebau-Feld der Zukunft zeigt, ist so sicher, wie große Rohstofflager im Recycling von obsoleten Bausubstanzen liegen. Und es zeigt sich noch schärfer, wenn man gezielt ein neu aufgeführtes Architekturstück aufsucht, ein Juwel des geförderten Wohnbaus mit eleganter Außenanmutung, eine Halle, wie sie der geförderte Wohnbau noch nicht sah, Loggiablick und Dachlandschaft für alle. Aber der Bau ist Singularität in einer Streuung, Statement in einem Geviert addierter Objekte, die von Stadt weit entfernt sind. »Wenn ich einschlafe, träume ich, dass ich aus dem Wohnblock auf die Straße gehe. Es ist keine Straße da.«[3]

Der Experte sagte, »die Zauberworte lauten Durchmischung, Dezentralisierung und Dichte. Das sind jene drei Regeln, die durch die zehn Jahrtausende, seitdem es Stadt gibt, konstant geblieben sind« und denen »in Zukunft mehr Aufmerksamkeit zu schenken« sei als »in der jüngeren Vergangenheit, wo jede Menge Fehlplanungen passiert sind«.[4] Dass Dezentralisierung seit Jahrtausenden die Regel war, bleibt ebenso dahingestellt, wie »in Zukunft« aus Zauberworten auch nur ein Stadtteil werden kann. Vielleicht muss man bescheidener fortfahren. Wenn ein Großteil der Stadtentwicklung des 20. Jahrhunderts als »Zwischenstadt« bezeichnet werden kann, mag der »Zwischenraum« von Bedeutung sein. In der historischen Stadt ergaben Zwischenräume sogar prägende Raumfiguren,[5] im urbanen Netz Stadt-Straßen, Gassen, Plätze, Parks, (Innen-)Höfe, Gärten (mit Gartenhaus); in der Zwischenstadt sind sie meist nur Diffusion, Abstandhalter, Vorläufigkeit, Unbeholfenheit[6]. Von der corbusierschen Moderne, der Emanzipation des Singulärobjekts freigestellt in

Sometimes it is really obvious. By extending a subway line, an area that was once "far away" becomes quickly assessable. The eyes do not have enough time to adjust. It is no longer the "periphery," yet the difference to the city[1] remains unchanged. At the exit of the (provisional) subway station at the end of the line, after a ten-minute trip, you find yourself in another kind of space, in short, the "intermediary city."[2] In a formal sense, you see how it expands outward, condenses, and transforms, and you recognize historic layers more clearly than in the "center," where things are increasingly collaged and simulated. The intermediary city is more naïve, has more contrasts, is more direct, even when many roads, which are really routes for development, are named after flowers. That the future of urban development is located here is as certain as the enormous raw material facilities engaged in the recycling of old building materials. And this becomes even more obvious when searching specifically for a newly completed work of architecture, a jewel of subsidized housing with an elegant exterior, a hall, never before seen in subsidized housing, with a balcony view and roofscape for all. But the structure is a singularity in an array, a statement in a district of additive objects far removed from the city. "When I fall asleep, I dream of entering the street from the residential complex. There is no street there."[3]

The expert said, "The magic words are mix, decentralization, and density. These are the three rules that have remained constant since the advent of the city ten millennia ago," and which "are to be heeded more in the future than they have been in the recent past, which has seen an abundance of bad planning."[4] That decentralization has been the rule for thousands of years remains open to question, just like whether "in the future" magic words will only lead to a city district.

Perhaps a more modest form of moving ahead is required. When a large part of twentieth-century urban development can be thought of as "intermediary city," then maybe "intermediary space" is relevant. In the historic city, intermediary spaces even gave rise to formative spatial forms,[5] city streets within the urban network, tiny alleys, squares, parks, (inner) courtyards, gardens (with garden houses); in the intermediary city these are mainly just diffusion, gaps, tentativeness, and awkwardness.[6] From Corbusian modernism, the emancipation of the singular object freely situated in light, air, and greenery,

1 Synonym für die dicht bebauten, im Wesentlichen gründerzeitlich geprägten Stadträume.
1 Here used as a synonym for densely built urban areas in primarily *Gründerzeit* style.

2 Thomas Sieverts, *Zwischenstadt. Zwischen Ort und Welt, Raum und Zeit, Stadt und Land*, Braunschweig 1997.
2 Thomas Sieverts, *Zwischenstadt: Zwischen Ort und Welt, Raum und Zeit, Stadt und Land* (Braunschweig, 1997).

3 Herta Müller, *Der Fuchs war damals schon der Jäger*, Reinbek bei Hamburg 1994.
3 Herta Müller, *Der Fuchs war damals schon der Jäger* (Reinbek bei Hamburg, 1994).

4 Vittorio Magnano Lampugnani, »Die Stadt ist kaputtgefahren«, in: *Der Standard*, 18. Mai 2012.
4 Vittorio Magnano Lampugnani, "Die Stadt ist kaputtgefahren," *Der Standard*, May 18, 2012.

5 In Wien u. a. Glacis / dann Ringstraße, Wienzeile, Linienwall / Gürtellinie, das Wassergeflecht der Donauauen.
5 In Vienna this includes Glacis / then Ringstraße, Wienzeile, Linienwall / Gürtellinie, the network of waterways of the Danube wetlands.

6 Wie die Endstation nach dem Charme, den Peripherie einmal hatte.
6 Like the station at the end of the line based on the charm the periphery once had.

Licht, Luft, Grün über die Wirtschaftsbanalrealisation der Funktionstrennungen (und gegenläufig: »Zentrums«-Bildungsversuche) in diversifizierten und geschmückten Kubaturen bis zum sich in die Hermetik des kleinen Privatfreiraums rettenden »verdichteten Flachbau« existiert keine Philosophie und noch weniger eine Praxis des Zwischenraums – als in der Moderne programmatisch geforderte Einheit von Funktion, Repräsentation, Anmutung und Gebrauch. Unbekümmert um die Drei- und Vierdimensionalität eines »Raumbildes«[7] errichtet Architektur »Blöcke« ohne sich um Kontingenzen zu kümmern,[8] zerlegt Stadtplanung das Feld in Verkehrsplanung, Flächenwidmungs- und Bebauungsplan, Freiraumplanung und »Stadtgestaltung«: in einer administrierbaren Sequenz, die keinen städtischen Raum erzeugt.[9]

Klimawandel, begrenzte Ressourcen und die Enttäuschung über die funktionalistische Moderne provozieren Überlegungen. Wenngleich das Leitbild der »nachhaltigen Entwicklung« deutlich angegriffen ist, reicht es noch für Paradigmen ressourceneffizienten Städtebaus. In einem unbekümmert technokratischen Ansatz, in dem »höhere Dichte« der Leitoperator[10] ist, entstehen drei- oder vierdimensionale Bilder, die zeigen, dass es mit »Passiv-« oder »Aktivhäusern« nicht getan ist. Beinahe könnte man an eine urbane Weiterentwicklung der Le-Corbusier-Stadt glauben: Hochhäuser in dichten Clustern, mit vertikalem Grün (und »vertikaler Landwirtschaft«), im Luftraum verknüpft, um »öffentliche Plätze, Parks, Wege und Straßen auf verschiedenen Ebenen« das »Hyperhäuser«-Ensemble durchziehen zu lassen. Was aber das Modell nicht anspricht, sind die realen Akteure des Städtebaus, die in der »Zwischenstadt« selbst »Nachverdichtung« zur Utopie machen. Auch der künftige Städtebau beruht auf den Akteuren, die den bisherigen Städtebau bewirkten.

Adolf Krischanitz agiert städtebaulich nicht mit Bildern,[11] zieht Schlüsse aus der historischen Produktion von Stadt. Nicht Planer, sondern Akteure produzieren Stadt. Da stadtprägende Räume nicht durch Addition entstehen und die Objektlogik das »Dazwischen« unbearbeitet lässt, müssen sich die Teilnehmer am Städtebau in einem Regelwerk bewegen. Mit wenigen, einfachen Regeln, wie im Vorbild der Bauordnung des 19. Jahrhunderts, in deren Rahmen nicht »Projekte«, sondern eine konkurrenzhaft-kollektive Praxis Großstadt, Stadt-Straßen, Plätze, Parks überformte und neu schuf. Allerdings offener, prozesshafter, dialektischer. Denn der Städtebau ist drei- und vierdimensional geworden. Im Bereich der Zwischenstadt und in großflächigen Implantaten in der historischen Stadt ist die Trennung von Verkehrs-, Transport-, Logistikebenen

to the economy-driven, banal manifestation of separated functions (and, in turn, "central" attempts at formation) in diversified and ornamented cubic forms, to the "compressed flat structure," redeemed in the hermeticism of the small, private open space, there exists neither a philosophy nor a practice of intermediary space—comparable to modernism's programmatically stipulated unity of function, representation, appearance, and use. Unconcerned with the three- and four-dimensionality of a "spatial image,"[7] architecture erected "blocks" without concerning itself about contingencies,[8] while urban planning carved up the field into traffic planning, zoning and development planning, spatial planning, and "urban design": in an administrable sequence that failed to give rise to urban space.[9]

Climate change, limited resources, and disenchantment with functionalist modernism provoke considerations. Although the model of "sustainable development" is clearly under attack, it is still sufficient for paradigms of resource-efficient urban development. In an unconcerned technocratic approach, in which "higher density" is the leading operative,[10] three- or four-dimensional images are created that demonstrate that "passive" or "active buildings" are not the solution. It is almost possible to believe in a further urban evolution of the Le Corbusier city: residential high-rises in dense clusters, featuring vertical areas of greenery (and "vertical farming"), linked to airspace so that "public squares, parks, routes, and streets" can cross through the "hyper-high-rise" ensemble. But what the model does not address are the real stakeholders of urban development who make a utopia out of "densification" in the "intermediary city" itself. Future urban development is also a function of the stakeholders who have effectuated urban development thus far.

Adolf Krischanitz's does not approach urban space with images;[11] instead he draws conclusions from the production of cities historically. Stakeholders, not planners, are the ones who produce the city. Since formative city spaces are not a result of additive processes, and since the logic of the structure leaves the "in-between" untouched, those involved in urban development must operate within a set of regulations. With several simple rules, similar to the model of building codes of the nineteenth century, within whose framework a competitive-like, collective practice—rather than "projects"—reshaped and recreated the metropolis, city streets, squares, and parks. However, in a more open, process-based, dialectical fashion. This is because urban development has become three- and four-dimensional. In the intermediary city zone, and in large-scale implants within the historic city, the separation between

7 Detlev Ipsen, *Raumbilder. Kultur und Ökonomie räumlicher Entwicklung*, Pfaffenweiler 1997.
7 Detlev Ipsen, *Raumbilder: Kultur und Ökonomie räumlicher Entwicklung* (Pfaffenweiler, 1997).

8 Zu »Block« und Kontingenz siehe Gilles Deleuze und Félix Guattari, *Für eine kleine Literatur*, Frankfurt am Main 2002.
8 On "block" and contingency, see Gilles Deleuze and Félix Guattari, *Kafka: Toward a Minor Literature* (Minneapolis, 1986).

9 Statt »Städtebau am Prüfstand« wäre »Städtebau im Windkanal« angemessener, sagte Otto Kapfinger: Die Modelle werden in die Ernstfalltestanlage gestellt und von Luftwirbeln, die von Politik, Investment, Massenmedien kommen, geprüft, und was sich ergibt ist der Mainstream, von dem alle Ecken und Kanten entfernt oder hinweggerissen sind, aber unmotivierte Schrägen und Anthrazit als Signalfarbe der die Katastrophe überlebenden Zombies bleiben.
9 Instead of "Urbanism at Stake" perhaps "Urbanism in the Wind Tunnel" would be more appropriate, as Otto Kapfinger has stated: models are placed in the emergency test facility and are evaluated by the air vortices of politics, investment, and mass media, and what emerges is mainstream, removed or stripped of all burrs and sharp edges but retaining the uninspiring angles and identifying anthracite hues of the zombies that have survived the catastrophe.

10 Siehe als ein Beispiel die Entwürfe von Brian Cody.
10 See Brian Cody's designs as examples.

11 Seine Zurückhaltung gegenüber formalen Exzessen ist bemerkenswert.
11 His restraint toward formal excesses is noteworthy.

und sanfter Mobilität (Fußgänger, Radfahrer) ein möglicher Gegenzug gegen den Übergriff der Geschwindigkeit im Stadtraum.

Die Parzelle – diese Grundeinheit der historischen Stadt, nun gleichfalls dreidimensional – benötigt aufgrund veränderter Wirtschaftseinheiten ein neues Maß, und die Zeit, im 19. Jahrhundert eine pragmatisch-unbekümmerte Zeit des Fortschritts (der Durchsetzung des Marktkonformsten), wurde reflexiv und projektiv. Einem städtebaulichen Projekt – und es gibt fast nur noch Projekte – kann der Fortgang nicht mehr sich selbst überlassen werden – zu viel ist gescheitert –, vielmehr ist er, soweit es in offener Zukunft möglich ist, in Bandbreiten zu steuern. Mit Krischanitz in der Strenge und Heiterkeit und Ernsthaftigkeit des Spiels, entlang von Regeln, deren Interpretation und Einhaltung der Spielleiter, der klassische Stakeholder (der am Spiel interesseloses Wohlgefallen hat und nur für ein gutes Ende sorgt) überwacht oder – sanfter – moderiert. Das von der Planung gern strapazierte Hoffnungsfeld – Planung als Prozess – wird von Krischanitz fast spieltheoretisch präzisiert. Städtebau in der Tradition des Sprachspiels.

Wenige Regeln stellen sicher, dass der erste und zweite und nächste Investor im Rahmen der urbanen Figuration zwar Freiheit hat, jedoch der Zuerstkommende nicht dem nächsten die Chancen nimmt und es auf die Spieler ankommt, Spielzüge zu einem Gesamtergebnis zu führen. In diesem gewinnt – weder wie im Zentrum, in dem alles zugeund überbaut wird, noch in der Zwischenstadt, durch die der Wind geht – das »Dazwischen« größte Bedeutung. Emanzipation des Zwischenraums, der nicht ein Nullfeld zwischen Objekten ist, sondern die Kontingenz des Stadtraums, zwischen den »Blöcken« das Öffentliche, Urbane generiert.

In der Mainstream-Architektur und im Mainstream-Städtebau ist der Zwischenraum das Unterschätzteste und Vernachlässigste. Bereits die Bezeichnung signalisiert die falsche Wahrnehmung, und es hilft nicht, Grünfläche, Platz, Straße einzusetzen, Pseudokonkretheiten, leere Versprechungen des heutigen Städtebaus. Unter derzeitigen Verhältnissen ist der urbane Raum kaum durch Planung oder Widmung, eher im Kampf oder im »Spiel« zu schaffen. Aber nach der Gründerzeit in einem neuen Spiel. Diese kannte zwar Straße, Platz und Park, jedoch war die Bebauung dicht für eine dichte Gesellschaft – Hygienenormen und Feuermauer –, der »Block« mit wenig Zwischenraum (Lichthof) für Klassen, Schichten, Individuen. Der Luxus des Freiraums, die Freiheit von Gruppen und Einzelnen in Aufenthalt und Bewegung im urbanen Raum, das brachliegende

traffic, transportation, and logistics layers and soft mobility (pedestrians, cyclists) is a potential countermove against the assault of speed in urban space.

The plot, which was the basic unit of the historic city, now equally three-dimensional, requires a new scale due to a change in economic units. And time—in the nineteenth-century the pragmatic carefree time of progress (the implementation of market requirements)—has become reflexive and projective. Progress itself can no longer be left up to an urban development project—and there are almost only ever projects—for too much has failed. Instead, it is a question of navigating bandwidths, as much as this is possible in an open future. Navigating in the rigorousness, exhilaration, and seriousness of the game with Krischanitz, along with rules whose interpretation and compliance are overseen or—more gently—moderated by the master of ceremony, the classic stakeholder (who is indifferent to the pleasures of the game and ensures only a positive outcome). Krischanitz almost stipulates the field of hope gladly strained by planning—planning as process—in game-theory-like fashion. Urban development in the tradition of linguistic games.

A few rules ensure that the first, second, and subsequent investors in the framework of urban figuration have freedom, but that the first on the scene does not take the opportunity away from the next who follows; and it is up to the players to transform the moves into an overall result. In this case, the "in-between" gains the most importance—unlike in the center, where everything is built up and overbuilt, or in the intermediary city, blown through by the wind. The emancipation of intermediary space, not a non-field between structures but the contingency of urban space that generates what is public and urban in between the "blocks."

In mainstream architecture and mainstream urban development, intermediary space is the most undervalued and neglected aspect. Even the term signalizes the wrong perception, and inserting parks, squares, and streets does not help things—pseudoconcreteness, the empty promises of urban development today. Under current conditions, the creation of urban space is nearly impossible through planning or dedication; instead it is produced through battles or in the "game." But in a new game post-*Gründerzeit*. At that time, streets, squares, and parks were the norm, but building density was high because of high social density—hygiene standards and fire walls—the "block" with only a small amount of intermediary space (light wells) for classes, social layers, and individuals. The luxury of free space, the freedom of groups and individuals residing in or

Potenzial der Moderne, das ist der Ausgangspunkt der städtebaulichen Projekte von Krischanitz. Wie wird Zwischenraum urban? Städtebau beginnt mit zwei Objekten, die sich gegenüberstehen. Aber die Spielfläche ist – reflektierter als in der Gründerzeit – nicht die Tabula rasa einer planierten Ebene, sondern die Oberfläche einer gekerbten Stadtlandschaft, auf der Städtebau stattfindet. In diesem Spiel werden die Glücksfälle lokalspezifischer Qualitäten und Potenziale, für die es keine allgemeine Regel gibt, die Zufälle des Zeitkerns, in dem ein Projekt zum Thema wird, und die momentanen »idees fixes« von Akteuren abgearbeitet und neu vereinbart, in einem gemeinsamen Handlungsraum, der Zeit braucht und Zeit schafft, gezeigt.[12] In Fortführung der Ansätze der klassischen Moderne deduziert / definiert Krischanitz für das »freie Spiel der Architektur« begrenzende Regeln, die sich im Spiel bewähren müssen. Nur das Spiel erweist die Qualität (Brauchbarkeit) der Regeln. Es braucht regelwillige Akteure und eine (sehr) gute Moderation / Mediation, Planung als Prozess.

Wenn die Moderne nach Walter Benjamin die dünne Schicht über dem Uralten ist, kann – wie von den Pariser Surrealisten, Situationisten, diesen vorläufig letzten Spielern des urbanen Spiels – davon ausgegangen werden, dass trotz überflutendem Kommerz und betonierter Stadtgeschichte ein »Basic« jeder Stadt auch in der Geschäftsstraße ein Jahrtausend altes Recht auf Gehen ist, im Glücksfall entlang von Bäumen und in einer Geraden zwischen Sonnenauf- und Sonnenuntergang als den Enden der Parabel. Der Gewährleistung der Zukunft der Wiener Mariahilfer Straße als Geschäftsstraße, bedrängt von Shopping-Citys, diente die Ausschreibung ihrer Erneuerung in den 1980er-Jahren. In Krischanitz' Blick war (ist) sie auch und vor allem eine normale Stadt-Straße, Teil der Urbanität und die ökonomische Funktion eine von vielen. »Der Weg durch die Straße ist die Perzeption von Raum und Zeit. Ordnungsmuster, aber auch ihre Negation, verdichten sich zum Wahrnehmungsmuster Stadt. In ihrer räumlichen Abfolge ist die Straße die Synopse aller erdenklichen stadttypischen Ausschnitte«.[13] Keine Ontologisierung, keine Wahrnehmungsreduktion auf Raum, keine Suche nach harmonischem Stadtbild als Vorwand für architektonische Gestaltung. Die Stadt-Straße ist Teil des konkreten Raums der Stadt, in dem die Stadt-Zeit stattfindet, die in historischer Kontinuität (und Brüchen) über funktionale Ausdifferenzierungen und Spezialisierungen hinweg eine »Einheit der Differenz«, ein Bild und eine Praxis der Gesellschaft immer noch bietet: ein sozialer Ort, »an dem Unbekannte einander treffen, Handel miteinander treiben und ihren Leidenschaf-

moving around urban space, the untapped potential of modernity—this is the point of departure of Krischanitz's urban development projects.

How does intermediary space become urban? Urban development begins with two structures situated opposite one another. But the playing surface—more reflective than in the *Gründerzeit* era—is not the tabula rasa of a flattened level, but the surface of a crenellated urban landscape on which urban development takes place. In this game, the flukes of locally specific qualities and potentials, for which no general rules exist, the coincidences of the cultural paradigm in which a project becomes a central theme, and the momentary idées fixes are processed and stipulated anew by stakeholders in a common space of action that requires and fosters time.[12] Furthering the approaches of classical modernism, Krischanitz deduces/defines the rules demarcating the "open-ended game of architecture" that must be preserved in the game. Only the game manifests the quality (viability) of the rules. It requires stakeholders who are open to the rules and must be moderated/mediated (extremely) well, giving rise to planning as process.

If, according to Walter Benjamin, modernism is the thin layer over the archaic, it can be assumed—as did the Parisian Surrealists, the Situationists, these provisional last players of the urban game—that, despite an inundation of commerce and a concreted urban history, the right to walk is one of the "basics" in every city, even on the shopping street. In a lucky case, this takes place alongside trees and in a straight line between sunrise and sunset as the bookends of the parable. Guaranteeing the future of Vienna's Mariahilfer Straße as a shopping street, threatened by shopping cities, was the focus of the call for proposals for its renovation in the nineteen-eighties. In Krischanitz's view, it was (is) also a normal city street, part of urbanity and one of numerous economic functions. "The path through the street is the perception of space and time. Patterns of order, but also their negation, solidify in the perceptual pattern of the city as a whole. In its special sequence the street is the synopsis of all imaginable typical urban sections."[13] No ontologies, no reduction of perceptions down to space, no search for the harmonic city image as a pretense for architectural design. The city street is part of the concrete urban space in which "city time" takes place, which, in historical continuity (and ruptures), still offers a "unity of difference" beyond functional differentiations and specializations, an image and a practice of society. This is a social location, "where strangers encounter one another, conduct business, and pursue their passions without concerning themselves

12 Dieses Zeigen ist die Rolle der Bilder in den Entwürfen von Adolf Krischanitz, im Gegensatz zu Demonstrationsartistiken und Überredungsroutiniers.
12 This demonstration is the role of images in the designs of Adolf Krischanitz, in contrast to a pretense of artistry and routine persuasion.

13 Adolf Krischanitz, »Die Straße«, in: *Architektur ist der Unterschied zwischen Architektur,* Ostfildern 2010, S. 170.
13 Adolf Krischanitz, "The Street," in *Architecture Is the Difference between Architecture* (Ostfildern, 2010), p. 171.

14 Dirk Baecker, »Platon, oder die soziale Form der Stadt«, in: Polis. Zeitschrift für Architektur und Stadtentwicklung, 14, März 2002, S. 12–16.
14 Dirk Baecker, "Platon, oder die soziale Form der Stadt," in Polis: Zeitschrift für Architektur und Stadtentwicklung, March 14, 2002, pp. 12–16.

15 Adolf Krischanitz und Leopold Redl, Stadtraumgestaltung Mariahilfer Straße. Variantenanalyse – Verkehr, Leitprojekte. Im Auftrag des Magistrats der Stadt Wien, MA 19 – Stadtgestaltung, Wien 1987.
15 Adolf Krischanitz and Leopold Redl, Stadtraumgestaltung Mariahilfer Straße: Variantenanalyse – Verkehr, Leitprojekte; Im Auftrag des Magistrats der Stadt Wien, MA 19 – Stadtgestaltung (Vienna, 1987).

16 Angemessener als Learning from Las Vegas.
16 More relevant than Learning from Las Vegas.

17 Adolf Krischanitz im Gespräch mit dem Autor.
17 Adolf Krischanitz in conversation with the author.

18 Im Sinn von André Corboz, wenn städtebauliche Intervention zu einer Bedeutungsänderung führt.
18 According to André Corboz, when urban developmental interventions lead to a shift in meaning.

ten nachgehen, ohne sich um die Vorgaben einer traditionellen Ordnung zu kümmern und ohne deswegen außerhalb jeder Ordnung zu leben; an dem die Übergänge zwischen den Zuständen des Vertrautseins und des Unvertrautseins entwickelt und erprobt werden.«[14]

Die Vielschichtigkeit in (der) Stadt-Straße zu stärken, nachdem eine Funktion, die Geschäftsstraße, überhand genommen hatte, war 1987 der Ansatz von Krischanitz/Redl[15], den Georg Schöllhammer damals als »verblüffenden Planungstrick« bezeichnete. In der Wahrnehmung und Wertschätzung der Stadt-Straße als grundlegende »strukturelle Kopplung« (Niklas Luhmann) der Funktionssysteme der modernen Gesellschaft (von Wirtschaft bis Religion) und daher nicht einer Sonderbehandlung bestimmter Figurationen, sondern in der Betonung ihrer Durchgängigkeit, legte der Entwurf über die gesamte Länge der Mariahilfer Straße ein schmales, mit einer Allee bepflanztes Fußgängerband als »Mittelstreifen« (Zwischenraum), akzentuiert von den »Lichtbäumen« der Beleuchtungsmasten und Trägerelementen für Werbe- und Ankündigungsschilder.

In historischer Wiederfindung – im 19. Jahrhundert führte in der Mitte eine Allee und bis 1930 die Kandelaber der Straßenlaternen –, im Lernen von Barcelonas Promenade La Rambla[16] und – vor allem – als Gegenzug zur Verzweiflungsoffensive der (damals in die Krise geratenen) Ökonomie in der alten Stadt-Straße, sollte den Passanten die Möglichkeit gegeben werden, entlang dieses – sparsam möblierten – Mittelstreifens bequem zu flanieren, wobei der Blick auf die reich gegliederten Fassaden, auf den historischen Raum der Straße frei und unverstellt geblieben wäre. Emanzipation des Zwischenraums als Potenzial und zugleich seine Bewahrung als »stille Reserve«[17]. Entlang der Geschäfte hätten die Wirtschaftstreibenden Freiheit zur »Selbstdarstellung« gehabt. Ein Spiel von Öffentlichkeit und Eigennutz auf der Basis von Struktur und Regelwerk in einem Raum für Eigeninitiativen und nicht formal gerastert und gestaltet.

Diese Neugründung[18] der Wiener Stadt-Straße fand nicht statt. Im Wesentlichen wurden nur die Gehsteige entlang der Schaufenster verbreitert. Fast ein Vierteljahrhundert später schienen die in einer banalen Planung betonierten Reserven der Mariahilfer Straße wiederum erschöpft, und anstatt zu verstehen, plante man die weitere Entmündigung der Stadt-Straße, deren Segmentierung und Degradierung zu einer Teil-Fußgängerzone. Primär ging es nun um die Erhöhung der Radfahrerquote. Diese erforderte – in einem Symbolprojekt der Verkehrsberuhigung – die Desintegration und Zerteilung

with the demands of a traditional order and therefore without living outside of any order; where the transitions between the conditions of familiarity and strangeness are developed and tested out."[14]

Strengthening complexity in (the) city street, after the shopping street had been taken hold by a function, was the 1987 approach of Krischanitz/Redl,[15] which Georg Schöllhammer described at the time as an "astonishing trick of planning." In the perception and appreciation of the city street as a fundamental "structural coupling" (Niklas Luhmann) of the functional system of modern society (from economics to religion)—and therefore not a special treatment of specific figurations, but an emphasizing of their consistency—the design situated over the entire length of Mariahilfer Straße a narrow pedestrian path planted with a promenade as a "median strip" (intermediary space), accentuated by the "illuminated trees" of the lighting masts and by support elements for advertising and announcement signs.

In a historical reinvention, namely, a promenade filling the median strip in the nineteenth-century and street lamp candelabras up until the nineteen-thirties; in learning from Barcelona's promenade La Rambla;[16] and, primarily, in a countermove to the despair offensive of the economy (caught in crisis at the time) along the old city street, passersby were to have the opportunity to stroll comfortably along this—sparsely furnished—median strip, although the view of the richly articulated façades, of the historical space of the street would remain open and unobstructed. It was the emancipation of the intermediary space as potential and at the same time its preservation as "hidden reserve."[17] Alongside the shops, the businesses would have been at liberty to "express themselves." A game of publicity and self-interest based on structure and rules in a space for self-generated initiatives—one not formally mapped out and designed.

This remaking[18] of the Viennese city street did not take place. In essence, only the sidewalks along the shop windows were widened. Almost a quarter of a century later, Mariahilfer Straße's residual elements, concreted in a banal design, seemed, in turn, to be depleted. Instead of understanding this, the further disenfranchisement of the city street was planned, segmenting and degrading it into a semi-pedestrian zone. This time it was primarily about increasing the number of cyclists. This necessitated—in a symbolic project to alleviate traffic—the disintegration and fragmentation of the city street by means of zoning. In 2014, the median was unpaved into a pedestrian zone inspired by the image of the "beach" and flanked by "encounter zones." A social analysis of the term "encounter zones" could prove informative.

der Stadt-Straße in Form einer Zonierung. Im Bild der »Beach« wurde 2014 das Mittelstück in eine Fußgängerzone umgepflastert, die von »Begegnungszonen« flankiert wird. Man könnte über das Wort »Begegnungszonen« einen gesellschaftlichen Befund versuchen.

Die Gründung der Wiener Donau City erfolgte in den späten 1980er- und frühen 1990er-Jahren inmitten eines Städtebaudiskurses. Wien wuchs nach einem Jahrhundert wieder, und es ging nicht nur um Hochhäuser und neue Wirtschaftsstandorte, vielmehr schien die monozentrische Struktur des 19. Jahrhunderts für weitere Entwicklungen erschöpft und eine mit Budapest geplante Twin-City-Expo als Gelegenheit, den alten Traum von einem neuen Zentrum an und über der Donau zu befördern. Jedoch fand die Expo nicht statt, und am Ort des projizierten Flaggschiffs des künftigen Städtebaus an und über der Donau klaffte zwischen UNO-City, Internationalem Amtssitz- und Konferenzzentrum, Ufer der Neuen Donau, Reichsbrücke über die Donau und angrenzendem Donaupark eine 9 Meter tiefe großflächige Grube, die durch den Aushub einer Mülldeponie entstanden war: projektiert als gigantische Expo-Parkgarage, auf deren Überplattung die Expo-Bauten und der künftige Stadtteil vorgesehen waren. Nachdem sich Experten und Stars nach der Expo-Absage zum Layout der »vorgezogenen Nachnutzung« auf der Platte über der Riesentiefgarage Pläne geliefert, aber die Verwertungsgesellschaft nicht überzeugt hatten, entschloss sich diese zu einem konzeptiven Neubeginn.

Statt auf die Suche nach Symbolen und Zeichen gingen die beauftragten Heinz Neumann und Adolf Krischanitz einer Frage auf den Grund. Wenn ein Stadtteil niemals mit einem einzigen Projekt gebaut wird und eine Vielzahl von Interessenten, Investoren, Nutzern die unterschiedlichsten Ansprüche stellt, kann der Ausgangspunkt in pluralistischer Gesellschaft nicht eine riesige Parkgarage und deren Überplattung sein. »Destruction of the box«[19], ohne dekonstruktivistisch zu sein. Der freigelegte Mutterboden wurde – wie in der historischen Stadt – zur Grundlage für Parzellen, aber in von der Jetztzeit gefordertem Maß und aus Anlass des Ortes und den neuen Möglichkeiten in städtebaulicher Dreidimensionalität.[20] Die Basisebene enthielt Straßen, Zufahrten zu Garagen, Freiräume für künftige Nutzungen, »durchfließende« Grünräume. Ein öko-urbaner Raum, über die Hauptebene fortgesetzt und in »hängenden Gärten« fortgepflanzt. Die Hauptebene (über einem Kollektorbau für Versorgungsleitungen) war der Stadtraum für Fußgänger und Radfahrer, eine durchgängige Sequenz zur Ver-

The founding of Vienna's Donau City followed in the late eighties and early nineties in the midst of a debate on urban development. Vienna was growing for the first time in a century and this was not only about residential high-rises and new business locations. Indeed, the monocentric structure of the nineteenth-century no longer appeared capable of sustaining further developments, and a Twin-City Expo with Budapest seemed like an opportunity to promote the old dream of a new center along and above the Danube. However, the Expo never took place, and at the site of the projected flagship of future urban planning along and above the Danube—located between the international headquarters and conference center of UNO City, the riverbanks of the New Danube, the Reichsbrücke over the Danube, and the neighboring Donaupark—was a gaping, nine-meter-deep pit created by the excavation of a landfill. Planned had been a gigantic Expo parking garage; the Expo buildings and future city district were to be constructed on top of its decking. Following the cancellation of the Expo, experts and stars came up with a plan for an "anticipated follow-up use" on top of the massive underground garage's decking, but they failed to adequately convince the contracting agent, so instead elected to return to the drawing board.

Instead of searching for symbols and signs, the commissioned designers Heinz Neumann and Adolf Krischanitz decided to get the bottom of an essential question. If a city district never sees the construction of a single project, and a plethora of interested parties, investors, and users present a wide range of demands, couldn't the point of departure in a pluralist society be a massive parking garage and its decking? "Destruction of the box,"[19] without being deconstructivist. The exposed topsoil became—as in the historic city—the basis for lots, but in a present-day timescale, and contingent upon the location and new possibilities in urban development three-dimensionality.[20] The base level included streets, garage access ways, space for future uses, and "free-flowing" areas for greenery—an eco-urban space that continues on the main level and is propagated in "hanging gardens." The main level (over a centralized utilities building) was the urban space for pedestrians and cyclists, a continuous sequence for linking plots together, with its own ground floor level also located inside the building—*rues interieures* in the dimension of a city district.[21] The "high relief" formed an open system of building configurations, staggered in height (offering a view of the Danube). The set of rules specified a maximum use in cubage for each plot under the condition that public space be available on the main level. Actually

19 Baecker 2002 (wie Anm. 14).
19 Baecker 2002 (see note 14).

20 Quadratisch, von 42 Metern Seitenlänge und mit der Hauptebene 9 Meter über dem Mutterboden.
20 Quadratic, with a side-length of forty-two meters and the main floor located nine meters above the soil.

21 Denn auch im Objekt ist der »Zwischenraum« ebenso potenziell wie meist vernachlässigt: die Bedeutung der Erdgeschosszonen für urbane Nutzungen und Querungen, Höfe und Dachflächen für Gemeinschaften. Im Neubau meist nichts Neues, in den gründerzeitlichen Substanzen Vergabe und Vernichtung (Penthaus mit Hausgarage)
21 Because in the structure the "intermediary space" is also a potential neglected like most: the importance of ground-level zones for urban use and traversing, courtyards and roof levels for communities. In new construction usually nothing new, for *Gründerzeit* structures the awarding of contracts and demolition (penthouse with in-house garage).

22 Vgl. Lampugnani 2012 (wie Anm. 4).
22 See Lampugnani 2012 (see note 4).

23 Übereinkunft in einem Regelwerk war 1995 auch Rüdiger Lainers Konzept zur äußeren Stadterweiterung Wiens am Flugfeld Aspern, gleichfalls gescheitert, wenn auch oberflächlich aus anderen Gründen als der »Zwischenstadt«.
23 Agreement on a set of rules also failed in Rüdiger Lainer's 1995 concept for Vienna's outer expansion at Aspern Airport, albeit superficially due to reasons other than the "intermediary city."

24 Adolf Krischanitz, »Vision vom architektonischen Raum«, in: Krischanitz 2010 (wie Anm. 13), S. 178.
24 Adolf Krischanitz, "The Vision of Architectonic Space," in Krischanitz 2010 (see note 13), p. 179.

knüpfung der Parzellen, mit einer eigenen Geschossebene auch innerhalb der Gebäude – »rues interieures« in der Dimension eines Stadtviertels.[21] Das »Hochrelief« bildete ein offenes System von Gebäudekonfigurationen, höhengestaffelt (im Blick auf die Donau). Für jede Parzelle galt im Regelwerk eine maximale Ausnutzung in Kubaturen mit der Auflage, öffentlichen Raum auf der Hauptebene zur Verfügung zu stellen. Eigentlich eine Win-win-win-Situation: Den Investoren die Freiheit im Regelwerk, den Bewohnern / Benutzern (dieses hilflose Wort für Städter) urbane Durchgängigkeit, Gelassenheit und Spielraum, der Stadtpolitik der Realismus eines Werdens (nicht einfach: wird schon) unter den Zielen[22] von Dichte und Durchmischung[23] ermöglichen. Städtebau sei »ein Gesamtklang«, indem »kein Element wichtiger ist als das andere, nicht die forcierte Konstruktion, nicht die polierten technischen Installationen, nicht irgendein Materialfetischismus«; »ein Gleichgewicht der verschiedensten Elemente, die in einer größeren immateriellen, aber durchaus resistenten Wirkung aufgehen«; ein »Kontinuum, gleichsam als ein alle Sinne erfassendes Strömen«.[24] Die Ergebnisse der Umsetzung, die unter Missachtung einer Reihe der Regeln erfolgte? Zwischen Einzelobjekten ein undefinierter Zwischenraum geringer Anmutungsqualität, durch den der Wind geht.

Krischanitz' städtebauliche Grammatik für die Siedlung Am Horn in Weimar ergibt einen heiteren Klang. Produktiv vergessen, dass das Bauhaus in Weimar die Station einer Fluchtbewegung war und das Konzentrationslager Buchenwald in der Nähe lag. Die städtebauliche Herausforderung drehte sich hier um: Während im Zentrum von Städten das teure Pflaster hart umkämpft ist und für den Zwischenraum nichts bleibt, bildet Fläche im noch unbebauten Feld einen Überfluss. So geht man üblicherweise damit um. Wie in Karl Valentins *Orchesterprobe*. Alle bemühten sich, aber das Ergebnis ist ein Desaster. Ein sehr schöner Naturraum, ein Hang mit Blick auf Goethe war zu unterteilen und sollte erhalten bleiben.

Parzellen, kurz nach dem Ende der DDR im Privateigentum, wurden gegen Gleichmacherei verschieden groß gesetzt. Abgegrenzt durch einen Betonsockel, der eine Zuordnung von öffentlichen und privaten Bereichen ergab. Habermassche Dialektik. Ein Rahmen, innerhalb dessen die Eigner nach Bebauungs- und Dichteregeln ihre Refugien errichteten. Land Art, die den unfertigen Zustand des Entstehens und Fortgangs der Siedlung, des Siedelns ästhetisch macht, plastische Eingemeindung. Bänder, die die Objekte verknüpfen, wie eine Weiterführung des loosschen Konzeptes des »Hauses

a "win-win-win" situation: enabling freedom for investors in the set of rules; urban continuity, serenity, and latitude for the residents/users (this helpless word for city dwellers); and allowing city politics the realism of actual transformation (not just: it will happen) under the goals[22] of density and mixing.[23] Urban development is "a total sound" where "no element is more important than another, not the forced construction, not the polished technical installations, not some material fetishism"; "a counterweight to the most varied elements, which merge in a greater immaterial, but thoroughly resistant effect"; as a "continuum, and at the same time as a sense-encompassing flow."[24] What were the results of an implementation effected without regard to a set of rules? An undefined intermediary space between individual structures of low-quality appeal blown through by the wind.

Krischanitz's urban planning grammar for the Am Horn settlement in Weimar yields a cheerful tone. Productively forgotten was the fact that the Bauhaus in Weimar was the stop for a refugee movement and that the Buchenwald concentration camp was located nearby. The challenge of urban development was inverted here: while pricey terrain is hotly contested in the city center and nothing is left for intermediary space, space in the still undeveloped areas is in abundance. Thus one approaches this in the usual way. Like in Karl Valentin's *Orchesterprobe*. Everyone makes an effort, but the result is a disaster. A very beautiful natural area, a hillside overlooking Goethe, was to be divided up and preserved.

Privately owned plots, shortly after the end of the German Democratic Republic (GDR), were divided up into different sizes in opposition to egalitarianism. Demarcated by a concrete foundation that produced an apportionment of public and private areas. A Habermasian dialectic. A framework within which owners erected their retreats according to zoning rules of construction and density. Land Art that makes aesthetic the unfinished state of the emergence and progress of the settlement, of settling—sculptural incorporation. Bands linking the objects together like a continuation of the Loosian concept of the "house with one wall": applied here—under late modernist conditions—not to the house but to the intermediary space. This is also the house itself since "the confrontation with nature swaps an outside for an inside," although "the occupation by architecture provides the framework plot for the excluded and also incorporated potential of nature and vice versa."[25] An architectural elite had actively engaged in producing the set of rules.

Situated on the slope in the direction of Weimar is a residential community that is much more than a

mit einer Mauer«: hier – unter Verhältnissen der Spätmoderne – nicht auf das Haus, sondern auf den Zwischenraum angewendet. Der auch das Haus selbst ist, da »die Auseinandersetzung mit der Natur ein Draußen mit einem Drinnen« tauscht,[25] wobei »die Besetzung durch Architektur die Rahmenhandlung für das exkludierte und auch inkorporierte Potenzial Natur und umgekehrt« bildet. Eine Elite von Architekten wurde im Regelwerk tätig. Am Abhang zu Weimar liegt eine Wohnanlage, die weit mehr ist als ein Patchwork von Familienhäusern. Hochgradig ästhetisch in einer Einheit aus Ähnlichkeit und Differenz, die dem besten Klassizismus Paroli bietet. Kurz nach der Abschaffung der Gesetze der DDR, die anders streng als die Bauordnung des 19. Jahrhunderts waren, hatte Krischanitz erneut das Spiel in Gang gesetzt. Jenseits der Antagonismen von Kapitalismus und Kommunismus ersuchte er die Damen und Herren Spieler um den Einsatz für ein schönes Wohnen, mit großen Freiheitsgraden entlang einer »flexiblen Regulierung«. Zuerkennung produktiver Differenz. Wer eine kleinere Parzellengröße hat, bekommt eine höhere Geschossflächenzahl, deren Ausnutzung / Ausformung jedoch nicht zur Verschattung der anderen führen darf: architektonischer Sozialausgleich.

Eine urbanere und ökologischere Raumprägung von Standorten wird, falls man das »europäische Stadtmodell«[26] nicht aufgeben, sondern weiterentwickeln will, die Ausbildung der einzelnen Architekturen funktionell stärker motivieren und deren Wirkung im stadträumlichen Zusammenhang erst zur Geltung bringen. Ökologisch, sozial und kulturell dauerhafte Stadträume von hoher Wohnqualität, Urbanität und Standortqualität für Gewerbe erfordern eine detaillierte Arbeit an Konfigurationen, die zudem entlang der Klimaveränderung sowie ökonomischer und sozialer Veränderungen anspruchsvollere und robustere[27] Konzeptionen bedingen werden. Die Vorleistung – Städtebau auf dem Prüfstand mit diversen Akteuren, ohne technokratischen Glauben – hat Krischanitz erbracht: spieltheoretisch und strategisch / taktisch spielerisch. Noch sind die Regelwerke für den Städtebau weit entfernt von Instrumenten, welche – als Ersatz der Bauordnungen des 19. Jahrhunderts – Urbanität außerhalb der historischen Stadträume erzeugen. Auf der Hand liegt, dass es nicht genügen wird, Ressourceneffizienz zu exekutieren, sondern Stadtraum wie Landschaft als Wert zu achten, der wieder und über uns kommen wird, die Naturbasis der Stadt, und (mit offenen Karten) einen neuen Gesellschafts- und Naturvertrag zu verhandeln. Es wird gut sein, das Regelwerk- / Spielkonzept von Adolf Krischanitz breiter und intensiver zu diskutieren und weiterzuführen.

patchwork of family dwellings. It is a highly aesthetic entity consisting of similarity and difference, which can compete with the best that classicism has to offer. Shortly after the laws of the GDR were abolished, which were of a different order than the building regulations of the nineteenth-century, Krischanitz had set the game in motion once again. Beyond the antagonisms of capitalism and communism, he solicited the commitment of female and male players to beautiful living with a high degree of freedom along "flexible regulations." The conferring of productive difference. Those with smaller plots have more floor area, however their utilization/form may not cast shadows on the others: social compensation in architectural terms.

A far more urban and simultaneously ecological spatial determination of locations, in case one does not abandon the "European urban model"[26] but wants to develop it further, will functionally motivate the formation of individual architectural designs in a more significant way and first showcase their impact in an urban spatial context. Environmentally, socially, and culturally enduring urban spaces with an exceptionally high quality of life, urbanity, and locational benefits for businesses of varying sizes require detailed work on configurations that also determine, in terms of climate change as well as far-reaching economic and social changes, more challenging and robust[27] designs. Krischanitz has already laid the foundation—urban development on the test bench with diverse stakeholders, without technocratic beliefs: in a fashion recalling game theory and playful in a strategic/tactical way. The rules for urban development are still far removed from the instruments that—as a substitute for the building codes of the nineteenth-century—produce urbanity outside the historic spaces of the city. It is obvious that executing an efficient use of resources is not enough, but that urban space must be respected, like landscape, as a valuable entity that will come back to and over us, the natural basis of the city, and that a new contract with society and nature must be negotiated (with cards on the table). It will be good to discuss Adolf Krischanitz's set of rules and game plan in a more comprehensive and intensive way, applying and carrying them forward.

25 Ders., »Architektur und Natur«, in ebd., S. 144.
25 Adolf Krischanitz, "Architecture and Nature," in ibid., p. 145.

26 Vgl. Hartmut Häussermann und Walter Siebel, *Neue Urbanität*, Frankfurt am Main 1987.
26 See Hartmut Häussermann and Walter Siebel, *Neue Urbanität* (Frankfurt am Main, 1987).

27 Die ehemaligen Avantgarden der Nachhaltigkeit.
27 The former avant-gardists of sustainability now speak of resilience.

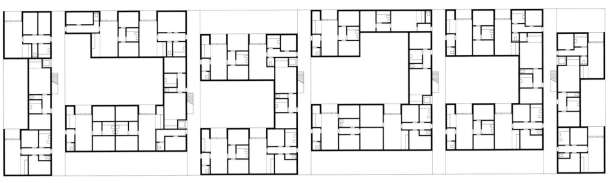

9405
Absberggasse, 0 ↘

1106 gswb Wohnen in Salzburg, +3 ⟨

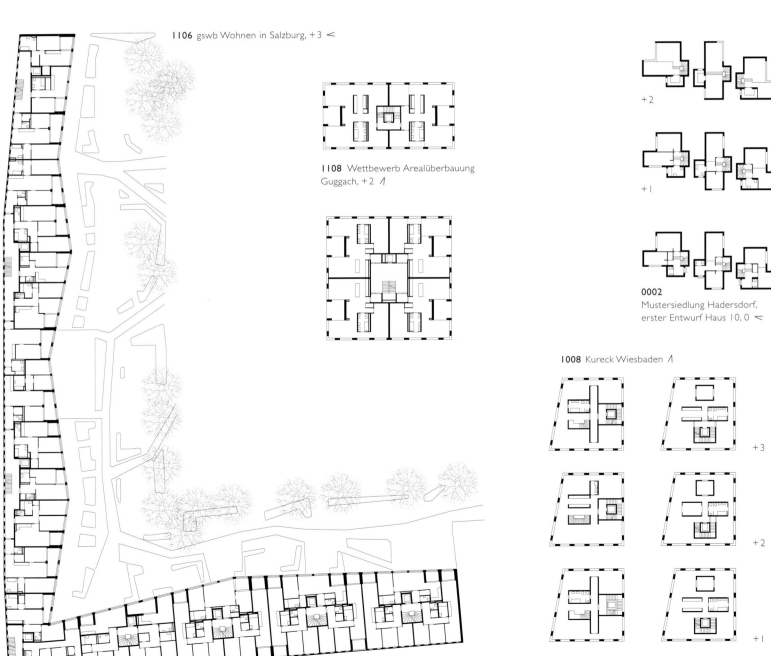

1108 Wettbewerb Arealüberbauung
Guggach, +2 ⟋

+2

+1

0002
Mustersiedlung Hadersdorf,
erster Entwurf Haus 10, 0 ⟨

1008 Kureck Wiesbaden ⟋

+3

+2

+1

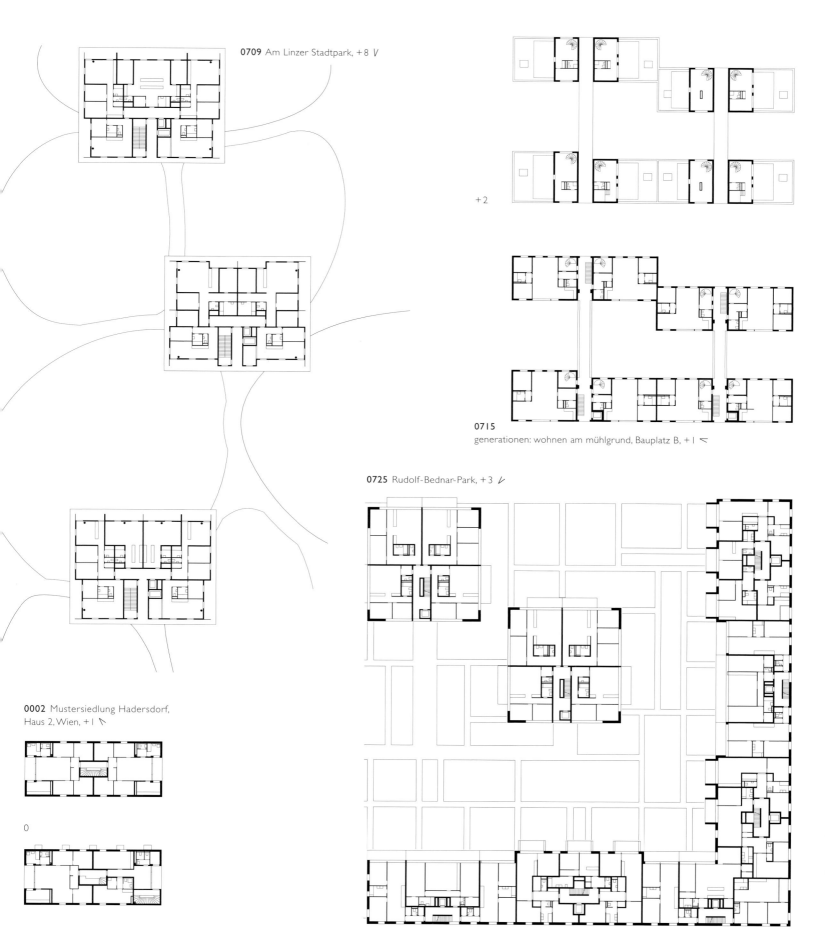

0709 Am Linzer Stadtpark, + 8 ⋁

+ 2

0715
generationen: wohnen am mühlgrund, Bauplatz B, + 1 ↖

0725 Rudolf-Bednar-Park, + 3 ⋁

0002 Mustersiedlung Hadersdorf,
Haus 2, Wien, + 1 ↖

0

WOHN-STADTRAUM

Otto Kapfinger: In der Mitte des Buches kommen wir zum zentralen Thema der klassischen Moderne und ihres Anspruchs auf grundlegende gesellschaftliche Innovation.

Adolf Krischanitz: Ja, und zugleich liegt da das Waterloo dieser Avantgarde. Denn nirgends zeigt sich die Kluft zwischen Vision und Wirklichkeit krasser, nirgends steht der Berufsstand pauschal so sehr am Pranger wie in der Kritik am Zustand von Städtebau und Siedlungswesen.

Es war aber überhaupt nicht allein die »Schuld« der Architektur, allein das Versagen der urbanistischen Theoretiker und Praktiker. Solche Pauschalkritik verfiel im Nachhinein denselben Kurzschlüssen wie die ursprünglich aufgestellten Intentionen – bloß mit umgekehrten Vorzeichen.

Leopold Redl, *Stadt im Durchschnitt. Texte zur Stadtplanung*, Wien, Köln und Weimar 1994 Coverdesign Oskar Putz

Gottfried Pirhofer hat in seinem Textbeitrag das Dilemma gut beschrieben. Auch einer meiner wichtigen früheren Diskussions- und Planungspartner, der Raumplaner und Stadtforscher Leopold Redl, hat dieses Schisma zwischen urbanistischen Theorien und siedlungspolitischem Alltag luzide analysiert – und er hat dennoch auf dem Weiterführen einer kritischen, dem Gemeinwohl und der subjektiven Autonomie verpflichteten Praxis bestanden. Das war allerdings im Übergang von den 80er- zu den 90er-Jahren, noch vor dem Durchbruch des Neoliberalismus, vor den Immobilienblasen und Finanzkrisen.

Markus Grob, *Gründe, dass es eine Stadt nicht mehr geben kann. Architektur im repräsentierten Gelände*, Wien-Hombroich 2005

Ein anderer deiner Mitarbeiter der späteren 90er-Jahre, Markus Grob, hat vor einiger Zeit in einer eigenen Publikation die Ursachen dieses Sinnzerfalls der städtebaulichen Disziplin grundsätzlich ausgelotet.

Den kompaktesten Befund dazu hatte Kenneth Frampton Mitte der 80er-Jahre geliefert. Sein Text »Die Industrialisierung und die Krisen der Architektur« bildete mit Manfredo Tafuris »Realismus und Architektur« den Angelpunkt im Katalog zur legendären Berliner Ausstellung *Das Abenteuer der Ideen*: eine bis heute gültige Diagnose, letztlich ohne praktikables Therapieangebot – nicht anders als die von Rem Koolhaas parallel entwickelten, zynisch-brillanten und letztlich auch gescheiterten Volten auf der Grundlage von: If you can't beat them – join them …

Wir müssen mit dem Begriff des Urbanen vorsichtig umgehen. Städtebau ist ein unreflektierter Begriff

DWELLING

Otto Kapfinger: Nearing the middle of the book now, we come to the central theme of classic modernism and its call for fundamental social innovation.

Adolf Krischanitz: Yes, and at the same time, this is where the Waterloo of this avant-garde lies. Indeed, nowhere is the gap between vision and reality shown more glaringly; nowhere is the profession as pilloried as in the common criticism of the state of urban planning and housing settlements.

But it's not only the "fault" of architecture, not only the failure of urban-planning theorists and practitioners. In retrospect, such blanket criticism also short-circuited in the same way as the intentions originally expressed—only from the opposite perspective.

Gottfried Pirhofer described the dilemma quite well in his text. The development planner and urban researcher Leopold Redl, who was one of my important partners in planning and discussions earlier on, also provided clear analyses of this schism between urban planning theories and everyday housing policy—and he nevertheless insisted on pursuing a critical practice committed to the common good and subjective autonomy. But that was in the transition from the nineteen-eighties to the nineties, still before the breakthrough of neoliberalism, before the real-estate bubbles and financial crises.

Markus Grob, another one of your employees in the late nineties, recently categorically addressed in one of his publications the reasons why urban-planning principles gradually lost meaning.

Kenneth Frampton provided the most concrete findings on this question in the mid-eighties. Along with Manfredo Tafuri's "Realismus und Architektur" (Realism and Architecture), Frampton's text "Industrialization and the Crises in Architecture" formed the pivot in the catalogue for the legendary *Das Abenteuer der Ideen* (The Adventure of Ideas) exhibition in Berlin: a diagnosis that still applies today but ultimately fails to offer any kind of feasible therapy—no different from the cynical, brilliant, and ultimately also failed turnabout that Rem Koolhaas devised in parallel along the lines of: if you can't beat them, join them …

von gestern. Man beschreibt damit Zusammenhänge, die es heute nicht mehr gibt und die nur in flachster Äußerlichkeit weiterleben, um den Status quo der Gewohnheit und der populären Nostalgie zu bedienen. Die genannten Texte haben es mit unterschiedlichen Sichtachsen erläutert: Bis zum Ende des 18. Jahrhunderts, bis zum Durchgreifen der Aufklärung und zur Französischen Revolution, war Stadtgestalt in Europa als hierarchisches Gefüge architektonischer Glieder, als Syntax der räumlichen Elemente bis zu den Details ein Ausdruck von spirituell begründeten und feudal durchstrukturierten Gesellschaften.

Das ist ein entscheidender Punkt. Und aus dieser Sicht: Der Städtebau als fachliche Disziplin kam erst auf, als die Kohärenz zwischen Mythos und Gesellschaft, zwischen Festtag, Alltag und Baukunst zerrissen war, oder anders gesagt: als – vergleichbar der romantischen Auffassung von Natur und Landschaft – der naive Status dieser Wirklichkeit aufbrach und als Verlust, als nun bewusst wiederherzustellender Zustand wahrgenommen wurde.

Seine Blüte erreichte der Städtebau im Historismus und in der Bewegung City Beautiful im späten 19. Jahrhundert – eigentlich als eine Kompensationsleistung, als das Großbürgertum sich in industrialisierter Form die Ausdrucksmittel der Aristokratie, der mythisch oder klerikal konstituierten Feudalwelten vor Augen führte. Architektur als Bühne für Plätze, Straßen und Parks erreichte in Paris und vor allem in der Wiener Ringstraße monumentale Ausmaße. All das wurde von den hellsichtigen Außenseitern dieser Ära wiederum als Potemkinsches Dorf abgelehnt. Wir müssen aber dazusagen, dass diese epochale und in vielen Aspekten kreative Anpassungsleistung – in Wien vor allem des jüdischen Großbürgertums – auch in allen geistigen und funktionalen Facetten gelebt und öffentlich ausagiert wurde.

Wir können diese immer noch nicht ganz verstandene Geschichte, die zudem durch die Traumata der Weltkriege und der Shoa kompliziert wurde, hier nicht weiter verfolgen. Der Städtebau der Moderne des 20. Jahrhunderts jedenfalls hatte mit Stadt oder Großstadt nur mehr die Worthülse gemein. Man definierte, trotz formaler und wissenschaftlicher Anstrengungen, ein unlösbares Dilemma, eine im Prinzip konträr zur Natur der überkommenen Stadt ausgerichtete Konzeption, die nie mehr im gesellschaftlichen Alltag – oder dem, was sich die Erfinder darunter vorstellten – ankommen konnte.

We have to deal with the concept of the urban very carefully. It's an unreflected concept from yesterday and is used to describe contexts that no longer exist today and survive only in the shallowest formality in order to serve the status quo of habit and popular nostalgia. The texts we've named have explained it from various points of view: until the end of the eighteenth century, until the drastic measures of the Enlightenment and up to the French Revolution, townscapes in Europe—as hierarchical frameworks of architectural structures, as syntax of spatial elements—were an expression of a spiritually predicated and entirely feudally structured society, down to the very details.

That's a very important point. And from this perspective, urban planning as a specialist discipline first came about when the coherence between myth and society, between feast days, everyday life, and architecture was ruptured. In other words, when—comparable to the Romantic understanding of nature and landscape—the naïve status of this reality broke apart and was perceived as a loss, as a state that now had to be deliberately reestablished.

Urban planning reached its heyday in historicism and in the City Beautiful movement of the late nineteenth century—in reality as a form of compensation, as the upper middle class began to appreciate, in industrial form, the aristocracy's means of expression, their mythically or clerically constituted feudal worlds. Architecture as a stage for squares, streets, and parks attained monumental proportions in Paris and particularly on the Ringstrasse in Vienna. The clear-sighted outsiders of this era then rejected all of this in turn as a Potemkin village. We should, however, add that this epochal and in many ways creative adaptive achievement—in Vienna, above all of the Jewish upper middle classes—was also lived and acted out publicly in all of its intellectual and functional facets.

Unfortunately, it's not possible for us to further pursue this still not completely understood history here—a history that was further complicated by the traumata of the World Wars and the Holocaust. In any case, the urban planning of twentieth-century modernism was related only tangentially to the city or the large city. Despite formal and academic efforts, what was defined was an irresolvable dilemma, a concept oriented, in principle, against the nature of the traditional city, which could never become a day-to-day reality in social life—or what the inventors imagined with the concept.

Kenneth Frampton,
»Die Industrialisierung und die Krisen der Architektur«,
in: *Das Abenteuer der Ideen*,
Berlin 1987

Ich denke, wir haben uns, noch in Missing-Link-Zeiten, schon Mitte der 70er-Jahre mit dem Thema befasst.

Es war in der Zeit, als nach den Utopien und den sozialen Umbrüchen der späten 60er-Jahre und dann nochmals durch den Ölschock von 1973 ein Paradigmenwechsel stattfand: die Abkehr von der autogerechten Stadt, die Besinnung auf alternative Siedlungs- und Wohnbaumodelle. Die Stadtstraße – bei Le Corbusier und Gleichgesinnten als überholte Form abgetan und verteufelt – wurde plötzlich als architektonisch gefasster, funktional vielseitiger Lebensraum wiederentdeckt.

Revision urbaner Typologien

Im Auftrag von Alfred Schmeller erarbeiteten wir 1973 zu der aus den Niederlanden kommenden Wanderausstellung *Die Straße* einen Wiener Beitrag. 1975/76 kam dann unsere individuelle Entdeckungsreise in die Geschichte und Gegenwart der Wiener Urbanistik der Zwischenkriegszeit. Die Wiener Wohnhöfe der Jahre nach 1923 wurden damals auch in Italien und Deutschland rehabilitiert. Ich erinnere mich an die entsprechenden Arbeiten von Manfredo Tafuri, Liselotte Ungers und anderen. Leon und Rob Krier machten mit ihren stadtmorphologischen Retro-Entwürfen Furore. Ihre Diagnose dessen, was am funktionalistischen Städte- und Wohnungsbau nicht funktionierte, war polemisch, schlagend. Ihre Therapievorschläge waren aber viel zu kurz gedacht, zu simpel und formalistisch gestrickt – auch das dann Potemkinsche Dörfer, diesmal ohne greifbare Adressaten, ohne die gesamtheitliche Struktur, die noch der Wiener Ringstraße oder dem Bauprogramm des Roten Wien zum langfristigen Erfolg verholfen hatte.

Wir versuchten damals moderne Varianten der Wohnhof-Typologie innerhalb einer rasterförmigen Straßen- und Blockstruktur. Die hermetischen Wohnanlagen der Wagner-Schüler waren prinzipiell von den Innenhöfen aus erschlossen. Im Kontrast dazu wollten wir die Ecken der Blöcke öffnen und dort in den Obergeschossen Gemeinschaftseinrichtungen vorsehen.

In Deutschland, Italien, Spanien, Großbritannien gab es damals viele vergleichbare Ideen und Projekte. Unser Konzept war auch am Muster von Ildefons Cerdàs Blockstruktur für Barcelonas Eixample orientiert.

Noch ein Moment war wichtig. Anders als die volkstümliche Rhetorik der Krier'schen Entwürfe,

I believe we already dealt with this theme when we were involved with Missing Link in the mid-seventies.

After the utopias and social upheavals of the late sixties, and then once again as a result of the fuel crisis of 1973, it was a time when a paradigm shift was taking place: a turning away from the car-friendly city, a reflection on alternative models for housing settlements and residential construction. The urban roadway—dismissed and demonized by Le Corbusier and like-minded individuals as an obsolete form—was suddenly rediscovered as an architecturally composed, functionally versatile living space.

Revision of Urban Typologies

In 1973, by request of Alfred Schmeller, we developed a Viennese contribution to the touring exhibition from the Netherlands, *Die Straße* (The Street). Then, in 1975–76, our personal tour of discovery through the history and present of urban planning in Vienna during the interwar period played out. The courtyard developments in Vienna in the years after 1923 were also being rehabilitated in Italy and Germany at the time. I recall the corresponding works by Manfredo Tafuri, Liselotte Ungers, and others. Léon and Rob Krier caused a furor with their urban morphology retro-designs. Their diagnosis of what didn't function in functionalist urban planning and housing construction was polemically convincing and percussive. But their proposals for therapy were too short-sighted, and too simple and formalistic—therefore also Potemkin villages, but this time without concrete addressees, without the overall structure that had still helped the Ringstrasse in Vienna or the building program of Rotes Wien (Red Vienna) to achieve long-term success.

At the time, we tried our modern variants of the courtyard development typology within a grid-shaped structure of streets and blocks. The hermetic residential complexes of students of Otto Wagner were developed principally from the courtyards outward. We, in contrast, wanted to open up the corners of the blocks and envisioned community facilities there on the top floor.

In Germany, Italy, Spain, and Great Britain at the time, there were lots of comparable ideas and projects. Our concept was also oriented toward the pattern of Ildefons Cerdà's block structure for the Eixample district of Barcelona.

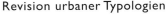

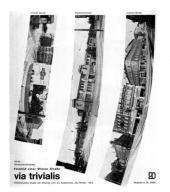

Die Straße. Form des Zusammenlebens, Ausst.-Kat. / exh. cat. Düsseldorf, Nürnberg und Wien 1973

Missing Link, *Via Trivialis. Feinbild einer Wiener Straße. Gürtel–Gumpendorferstraße,* Wien 1973

anders als die monumentalen Formen der Wagner-Schüler dachten wir den Ausdruck solcher Stadtquartiere als strukturell, gerüsthaft und »unfertig«. Wir imaginierten an Stelle von hübschen Fassaden – im Sinne von leicht konsumierbaren Bildern – eine Rhetorik der Produktion, also ein »Gesicht« der Straßen, das sich erst im Lauf der Aneignung und Überformung durch Nutzungen ausprägen sollte.

Es war eine ziemlich idealistische Vorstellung. Ein solches neues Hofsystem wurde aber weder in Wien noch anderswo gebaut. Auch die vielbeachtete, ehrgeizige IBA in Berlin hat nichts Vergleichbares hervorgebracht. Kennst du etwas Entsprechendes, in der Schweiz vielleicht, in Basel vielleicht, zu Beginn der 80er?

Es gab wohl innovative Einzelbauten, fragmentarische Ansätze, aber zu einer langfristigen und großräumigen Strategie ausgedehnt, zu einer allgemeinen Spielregel fortgesetzt, zum wirklichen Kraftschluss von Wohnen, Arbeiten, Handel und Freizeit geführt, von ruhiger Hofsphäre und lebhaft gemischten Straßenräumen – eigentlich nichts. Selbst eine Ikone der damaligen Stadt-Diskussion wie das Quartier Gallaratese in Mailand von Carlo Aymonino und Aldo Rossi war nur eine insuläre Zelle – ohne Netzwerkentwicklung zu einer Stadtstruktur: eine gebaute Bühne retrospektiv-urbaner Stimmung, eine gekonnte Inszenierung von Abwesenheit, fast wie die frühen Stadtbilder von de Chirico, melancholisch-schön ...

Maßstab Wiener Wohnbaupolitik

Die Qualität der sozialdemokratischen Wiener Wohnbaupolitik der 20er-Jahre kam aus der durchgängigen Erneuerung und Regelung aller Aspekte, von der Grundstücks- und Mietpreispolitik über die Bildungs- und Fürsorgeprogramme bis zum pragmatisch kalkulierten Maß leistbarer Standardanhebung des Wohnraums für breite, bedürftige Schichten, bei intensiver Nutzung billig vorhandener, handwerksintensiver Bautechnik. Und all das fußte eigentlich auf den noch grundsätzlicheren Motiven und Projekten der Wiener Siedlerbewegung – eine

One other moment was important. Unlike the folksy rhetoric of the Kriers' designs, unlike the monumental forms of the students of Wagner, we considered the expression of such city quarters to be structural, scaffold-like, and "unfinished." Instead of pretty façades—in the sense of easy-to-consume images—we imagined rhetoric of production, that is, a "face" for the street that was first supposed to find its expression over the course of being appropriated and transformed through use.

It was a relatively idealistic idea. But such a new courtyard system was built neither in Vienna nor anywhere else. The high-profile and ambitious IBA (International Architecture Exhibition) in Berlin didn't yield anything comparable. Can you think of anything relevant, in Switzerland perhaps, or maybe in Basel, at the beginning of the eighties?

Although there were indeed innovative individual buildings, fragmentary approaches, there was actually nothing that was expanded into a long-term and large-scale strategy, that became a general rule of the game, that resulted in real traction between living, working, commerce, and leisure time, between a serene courtyard sphere and vibrantly mixed street spaces. Even an icon of the city discussion at the time, such as the Quartier Gallaratese in Milan by Carlo Aymonino and Aldo Rossi, was only an insular cell—without network development on an urban structure: a built stage of retrospective urban atmosphere, a skillful staging of absence, almost like the early urban images of de Chirico, melancholic and beautiful . . .

Benchmark for Viennese Housing Policy

The quality of the social-democratic housing policy in Vienna in the nineteen-twenties resulted from continuously renewing and regulating all aspects, from property and rental fee policy, to the education and public welfare program, to the pragmatically calculated degree to which it was possible to raise standards for housing space for broad, needy population groups through intensively using cheap, existing, handcraft-intensive building techniques.

Klaus Novy und Günther Uhling,
*Die Wiener Siedlerbewegung
1918–1934* (ARCH+, Katalog 55),
Ausst.-Kat. / exh. cat., Aachen 1981

Adolf Krischanitz und
Otto Kapfinger,
*Die Wiener Werkbundsiedlung.
Dokumentation einer Erneuerung*,
Wien 1985

höchst bemerkenswerte Phase, die wir ebenfalls erst Mitte der 70er entdeckten und studierten.

Absurd war, dass es in Wien damals ja noch Zeitzeugen, direkte Beteiligte an diesen Siedlungsplanungen gab – Margarete Schütte-Lihotzky zum Beispiel, von der wir im Studium kaum etwas gehört hatten. Davon abgesehen haben wir um 1968 – als revolutionär Begeisterte – die Nachfahren der Gartenstadt-Verfechter, wie den als Akademie-Rektor sehr präsenten Roland Rainer, von vornherein als reaktionär, doktrinär und überholt abgelehnt.

Erst durch der Erweiterung des Blicks auf die Verflechtung der Wiener Siedlerarchitekten mit der sozialpolitischen Avantgarde – mit dem Wiener Kreis, mit Otto Neurath, mit der Pädagogik von Otto Glöckel –, erst damit wurden uns auch die Konzepte von Adolf Loos und Josef Frank zugänglich – die soziale Organisation als Vorform des Gebauten. Loos sprach von der kulturellen Autonomie und sozialen Emanzipation des Siedlerlebens, und eben nicht von autonomer Architektur.

Eine konkrete Vertiefung dessen brachte erst 1983 die Arbeit an der Renovierung der Wiener Werkbundsiedlung von 1932 – unter schwierigen Randbedingungen, technischen, finanziellen und organisatorischen Engpässen und mit der paradoxen Situation des Denkmalschutzes für eine ursprünglich konträr zu solcher Konservierung angelegte Modellpalette von 30 verschiedenen Typenhäusern.

In deinen Wettbewerbsentwurf für die Salzburger Forellenwegsiedlung von 1984 war einiges aus diesen Studien eingeflossen. In der Ausschreibung waren Reihenhäuser strikt verboten. Dennoch hast du – begründet durch die Lage zwischen Stadt und Flussraum – eine solche Typologie vorgeschlagen, topografisch aufgelockert und kombiniert mit dichter gesetzten Geschossbauten.

Das Siegerprojekt von Oswald Mathias Ungers propagierte das Gegenteil: eine streng geometrische, kastellhaft »städtische« Figur von Geschossbauten, was sofort öffentlich-medialen Aufruhr und hämische Fachkritik provozierte, letztlich aber, in der Aufteilung auf die individuellen »Handschriften« von sechs Teams, nicht so schlecht funktionierte, auch im Maßstab. Dennoch war auch das wieder nur eine Enklave, ein Sonderfall ohne Folgen, absolut keine urbane Zelle mit Rhizom-Potential.

And all of this was actually based on the still more fundamental motives and projects of the Vienna Settlement Movement—a quite remarkable phase that we also first discovered and studied in the mid-seventies.

What was absurd was that, in the seventies, there were still contemporary witnesses in Vienna, people who had been directly involved in the planning of these settlements—Margarete Schütte-Lihotzky, for example, about whom we had heard hardly anything while at university. Not to mention the fact that, as revolutionary enthusiasts in 1968, we rejected the descendants of proponents of the Garden City—such as Roland Rainer, who was very present as rector of the Master School for Architecture at the Academy of Fine Arts Vienna—as reactionary, doctrinaire, and outmoded from the start.

It was first by taking a broader view of the intertwining of Viennese settlement architects with the sociopolitical avant-garde—with the Vienna Circle, with Otto Neurath, with the education theory of Otto Glöckel—that concepts by Adolf Loos and Josef Frank also became accessible to us: social organization as an early form of the built structure. Loos spoke of the cultural autonomy and social emancipation of settler life, and not of autonomous architecture.

What first consolidated this in concrete terms was the renovation work started in 1983 at the Werkbundsiedlung in Vienna, or Werkbund settlement, from 1932—under difficult constraints, with technical, financial, and organizational bottlenecks, and with the paradoxical situation of trying to impose historical preservation standards on a palette of models consisting of thirty different types of standard houses, a palette that was originally created contrary to such ideas of conservation.

Some facets of these studies also influenced your competition design for the Forellenweg settlement of 1984 in Salzburg. In the call for tenders, row houses were strictly forbidden. However, in justifying your decision based on the site situated between city and river basin, you proposed just such a typology, topographically broken up and combined with densely positioned, multistory buildings.

The winning project by Oswald Mathias Ungers propagated the opposite concept: a strictly geometric, fortress-like "urban" figure of multistory

Als unsere letzte gemeinsame Arbeit habe ich da an der Planung des uns zugeteilten Randstückes im Ungers-Karree mitgewirkt: ein langer Trakt an der Kante zur Landschaft; an der Innenfront streng gerade, doch nach außen, zum Fluss, nach Nordwesten unregelmäßig ausschwingend. Wir haben diese irreguläre Figuration mit einem System offener Grundrisse gefüllt, wobei wir die wechselnde Trakttiefe mit entsprechend variierter Wohnungsbreite kompensierten. So entstanden (wie gefordert) gleich große Wohnungen unterschiedlicher Breite und Tiefe. Es war die Transponierung eines orthogonalen, nutzungsvariablen Raumsystems, wie es etwa Mies in seinem Block am Stuttgarter Weißenhof gebaut hatte.

In der Umsetzung mit der Wohnbaugenossenschaft traf uns die volle Wucht und Ignoranz des Bau-Alltags. Diese versuchte mit Brachialgewalt, unsere offenen Grundrisse in ihre Zimmer-Gang-Schemata umzupolen und vieles andere mehr. Es war grausam, an der Kippe zur Aufgabe, das Ganze ging irgendwie halbwegs gut aus, war aber eine sehr bittere Lektion.

Bei der mit Otto Steidle und Herzog & de Meuron entworfenen Siedlung Pilotengasse hast du ein solches Spiel von strenger Außenhülle und windradartig kreisenden, permutierenden Grundrissen weiterentwickelt. Gebaut aus sehr einfachen Elementen, mit einer Rotation der Stiegen in den Reihenhäusern um die Mittelmauern zu fünf unterschiedlichen Positionen. Auf den ersten Blick ergab das außen eine alltägliche, fast aufreizende Monotonie, innen aber eine Sequenz variabler Haus- und Raumcharaktere – bei der generellen Ost-West-Orientierung der Zeilen war das ja leicht zu machen; auch die Hauszugänge pendelten entlang der Zeile nach beiden Seiten.

Es gab dort bei meinen Häuserzeilen im Mikrokosmos ein wechselndes Gewebe von Längs und Quer, von Kette und Schuss, und erhielt eine analoge Systematik im übergeordneten Muster der Parzellen, der Wege und Baufelder der Anlage.

Konditionierte Felder, Planspiele

Ab 1990 gibt es eine neue Qualität in deinen städtebaulichen Konzepten und Wettbewerbsentwürfen.

Die Pilotengasse war so etwas wie eine unmögliche Transformierung des Gartenstadt- beziehungsweise Randstadtcharakters gewesen: ein Test, noch einmal über die überlebten Sozialutopien hinaus-

buildings, which immediately provoked a public and media uproar and derisive criticism from specialists. But in the end, when allocated to the individual "styles" of six teams, it didn't work that badly, also in terms of scale. Nevertheless, that was once again only an enclave, a special case without further consequences—definitely not urban cells with rhizome potential.

As in our last joint work, I also contributed to the planning for the border parcel on the periphery of Ungers's block of houses that was assigned to us: a long tract bordering the landscape, stringently straight on the inner front, but sweeping out irregularly toward the outside, toward the river, toward the northwest. We filled this irregular figuration with a system of open layouts and compensated for the varying depth of the tract with apartment widths that varied correspondingly. We therefore created (as stipulated) apartments of equal size but with different widths and depths. It was a transposition of an orthogonal spatial system adaptable for different uses, such as Mies van der Rohe built in his block at the Weissenhof settlement in Stuttgart.

In realizing the building with the cooperative housing association, we experienced the full force and ignorance of everyday construction work. The construction companies used brute force in trying to change our open layout so that it complied with their room-hallway schemata and many other things. It was terrible, with the project hanging in the balance—but the whole thing somehow worked out reasonably well, although it was a quite bitter lesson.

For the Pilotengasse settlement designed with Otto Steidle and Herzog & de Meuron, you further developed such a play of stringent outer shell and windmill-like circling, permuting layouts—using very simple elements, with the staircases rotating to five different positions around the central walls in the row houses. At first glance, that resulted in an everyday, almost obscene monotony from the outside, but inside a sequence of variable apartment and spatial characters. Since the rows were generally oriented east-west, that was easy to do; the entrances to the houses also faced toward both sides along the row in turn.

In my rows of houses within the microcosm, there was an alternating texture of lengthwise and crosswise, of warp and woof, and a system analogous to this was given in the overall pattern of the parcels, paths, and building lots on the site.

8603
Krischanitz / Kapfinger
Wohnbauten / Residential Complex Forellenweg, Salzburg, 1984
Vorentwurf der Mietwohnungen eines Trakts / Preliminary design for the rental apartments of one wing

zugehen, ein Stadtrandquartier zu bauen, sich aber von den üblichen Illusionen fernzuhalten; zu wissen, dass heute nicht das Haus, sondern Auto und Parkplatz die Mitte der durchschnittlichen Lebensentwürfe und Lebenserfahrung markieren; dass man also dementsprechend etwas baut, was wie eine Siedlung anmutet, sich zugleich aber von den gängigen Projektionen fernhält. Wenn du willst, war es ein Abschied vom Siedlungsgedanken in einer Pseudosiedlungs-Matrix, nicht als Ironie – daran wäre mit einem so »geerdeten« und erfahrenen Partner wie Otto Steidle nicht zu denken gewesen! – eher als eine Offenlegung, als dialektische Darstellung der Verhältnisse gedacht.

Und was war dann um 1990 ausschlaggebend für den Wechsel, weg von der Planung von Milieus, weg vom Phantasma des »stimmigen Ganzen« hin zum Anbieten von Planungs-, Spielstrategien?

Forellenweg, Pilotengasse und Werkbundsiedlung haben mir gezeigt: Als Architekten solcher Strukturen stülpen wir eine Maske von Klischees, von Wunschbildern und disziplinimmanenten Projektionen über die ganz anders gelagerte »unsichtbare Architektur« der behördlichen, finanztechnischen, infrastrukturellen, baurechtlichen und politischen Wirkkräfte. Und diese Strukturen sind viel mächtiger, bestimmender und absurderweise »wahrer«, als wir uns eingestehen wollen. Die Diskrepanz zwischen dieser Wirklichkeit und unseren Imaginationen zieht auch das Bestgemeinte in jene hoffnungslose Schizophrenie und Vereinzelung, von der schon Adorno sagte: »Es gibt kein richtiges Leben im falschen.«

Ich denke, es war dann weit weg, auf der Atlantikinsel Gomera, wo ich 1990 für den Immobilienzweig der Friedrichshof-Genossenschaft eine Bebauungsstudie für eine aufgelassene Plantage konzipierte, wo ich erstmals nicht mehr »das Spiel als Form gestaltete«, sondern nur Spielregeln für den Umgang mit Rahmenbedingungen entworfen habe. Es gab dort einen Hang mit alten Terrassen und hohen Stützmauern. Die verfügbaren Materialien waren Holzbalken, Mauersteine aus Tuff, Wellblech, Glas in beschränkten Formaten. Aus diesen Parametern generierte ich Szenarien für Bauweisen einfachster Art.

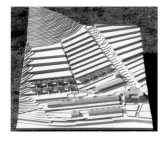

9006
El Cabrito, Bebauungsstudie Terrassenhäuser / Development Study for Houses on Terraces
La Gomera, 1990

Es war ein Katalog von Möglichkeiten, wie man in Abschnitten dort Gebäude errichten könnte – eben kein klassischer Vorentwurf mit Grundrissen, Ansichten, Schnitten, sondern eine Partitur für mögliche Handlungen, eine Gebrauchsanleitung,

Conditioned Fields, Planning Game

As of 1990, a new quality emerged in your urban-planning concepts and competition designs.

The Pilotengasse settlement was something like an impossible transformation of the Garden City and/or suburb character: a test to once again build a district on the edge of the city beyond the outlived social utopias, but to refrain from the usual illusions; to know that today it is not the house, but instead the car and parking space that denotes the center of average designs for daily life and life experience; that one therefore correspondingly builds something that appears to be a settlement, while keeping a distance from the conventional planning at the same time. If you will, it was a farewell to settlement concepts and a turning toward a pseudo-settlement matrix, not as irony—that would have been inconceivable with a partner as "grounded" and experienced as Otto Steidle!—but seen more as a disclosure than as a dialectical representation of the circumstances.

And what was then decisive around 1990 for the shift away from planning environments, away from phantasms of "coherent wholes," and toward the offering of planning, or game, strategies?

Forellenweg, Pilotengasse, and the Werkbund settlement showed me that, as architects, we put such structures over the quite differently superimposed "invisible architecture" of governmental, financial, infrastructural, building regulation, and political forces like a mask of clichés, of ideals, and discipline-immanent projections. And these structures are much more powerful, constitutive, and absurdly "truer" than we would like to admit. The discrepancy between this reality and the things we imagine also pulls even the best-intentioned into that hopeless schizophrenia and isolation of which [Theodor W.] Adorno already said: "There is no right life in the wrong one."

I believe it was then far away on the Atlantic island of Gomera, where I was designing a development study for an abandoned plantation for the real-estate arm of the Friedrichshof-Genossenschaft cooperative association in 1990, where, for the first time, I didn't "design the game as form" but instead only drew up rules of the game for dealing with basic conditions. There was a hillside with old terraces and high retaining walls on the property. The materials available were wooden beams, tuff building stones, corrugated sheet metal, and

eine Spielregel für variables Bauen unterschiedlicher Autorenschaft »in der Zeit« aus den lokalen Ressourcen.

Du hast dann bis 1995/96 diese Art von strukturellen Matrizen, von Spielplänen zur baulichen Entwicklung großer Stadtflächen, immer weiter zu einer eigenen »Marke« entwickelt: von den städtebaulichen Wettbewerben für Areale in Deutschland – Bottrop, Bühl, Eichstätt – über den internationalen Expo-Wettbewerb in Wien bis zum Masterplan für die Donau City und die Siedlung Am Horn in Weimar. Wie ist dieses Konzept dann mit deinen damaligen Mitarbeitern Markus Grob, Werner Neuwirth und Ingrid Dreer weiter ausgereift?

Es wurde immer klarer, dass es nach dem Wegfallen der historischen Konventionen für »Städtebau« Ansätze brauchte, um so etwas wie eine neue, eine andere Verbindlichkeit zu bekommen, um einen Kraftschluss zu finden zwischen den Strukturen unserer Gesellschaft und dem individuell-kollektiven Prozess des Bauens. Ich habe in diesem Sinn die ja massiv vorhandenen Regelungen etwa in Rechts- und Bauordnungen nicht mehr, wie im akademischen Genre üblich, als Gegner oder als irrelevante Hindernisse für immer nur subjektive urbane Visionen und »Würfe« gesehen, sondern als pragmatische Bausteine, als Spiel- und Sprachelemente, die man als solche benutzen und in ihren offensichtlichen wie auch latenten Möglichkeiten ausloten kann. Ich wollte damit zu Ergebnissen oder Strategien kommen, die nicht gegen diese Wirklichkeiten gedacht sind, sondern aus diesen heraus womöglich über sie hinausführen könnten.

Zweitens wurde immer klarer, dass alles Bauen, vor allem im größeren Maßstab, zuallererst mit den Konventionen der Grundverteilung, mit der Flächenteilung beginnt. Die Parzellierungen und die ihr zugeordneten Parameter sind entscheidende Grundlagen für das eigentliche Bauen. Und urbanistische Entwicklungspläne müssten auf dieser Ebene, mit der offensiven Interpretation dieser Grundlagen ansetzen.

Und drittens dachte ich, man könnte nach dem Wegfall der stilistischen oder morphologischen Konventionen in unserer offenen, postmodernen Verfassung anstelle des üblichen Nebeneinanders der Individualitäten doch so etwas wie eine produktive Kraft aus der Verschiedenheit gewinnen: also statt dem mehr oder weniger beliebigen Nebeneinander eine neue Qualität dadurch erreichen, dass verschiedene Planer und Planerinnen

glass in a small range of formats. Based on these parameters, I generated scenarios for construction methods of the simplest sort.

It was a catalogue of possibilities for how one might erect buildings there in phases—no classical preliminary design with layout, elevations, cross-sections, but instead a kind of musical score for possible actions, instructions for use, rules of the game for variable construction with varying authorship "over a period of time" and using local resources.

Until 1995 or 1996, you then developed this type of structural matrix further and further—from game plans to the structural development of large urban areas—to create your own personal "brand." This ranged from urban-planning competitions for sites in Germany—Bottrop, Bühl, Eichstätt—to the international Expo competition in Vienna, to the master plan for Donau City and the Am Horn settlement in Weimar. How did this concept then mature further with your employees at the time, Markus Grob, Werner Neuwirth, and Ingrid Dreer?

It became increasingly clear that, after getting rid of the historical conventions for "urban planning," other approaches were necessary in order to achieve something like a new and different way of engaging, so as to establish a strong connection between the structures of our society and the individual-collective process of building. In this sense, I no longer saw the dense amount of existing rules in legal and building regulations, for example—as is common in the academic genre— as an adversary or as irrelevant obstructions for urban visions and "castings of ideas" that are always only subjective. I instead saw these rules as pragmatic building blocks and as game and language elements that one should use as such and explore in both their apparent and latent possibilities. In doing so, I wanted to arrive at results or strategies that are not intended to counter these realities, but rather able to lead out and if possible overcome them.

Secondly, it was becoming increasingly clear that all construction, above all on a larger scale, begins first and foremost with the conventions regarding the division of the land, the allocation of the area. The subdivision of parcels and their assigned parameters are decisive foundations for the actual construction. And plans for urban development have to start on this level, with the offensive interpretation of these foundations.

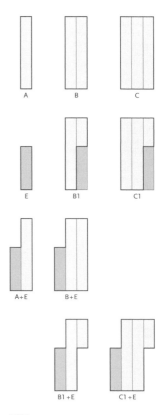

9611
neues bauen am horn
Weimar, 1996–1999
Parzellen-Module / Plot modules

»Das Grundmodul A, aus dem sich die unterschiedlichen Parzellen ergeben, ist an der Straße 7,5 Meter breit und je nach Lage zwischen 37 und 74 Meter lang; es kann bis zu dreimal nebeneinander angeordnet werden (C).
Zur Störung ist die kleine Parzelle E eingefügt, die ebenfalls 7,5 Meter breit, aber nur 30 bzw. 35 Meter tief ist. Um diese Parzelle können die anderen Parzellen verringert oder erweitert werden, sodass sich ein abwechslungsreicher ›Parzellenteppich‹ ergibt.«

aus / from:
Lars-Christian Uhlig und /and Walter Stamm-Teske (Hrsg./eds.), *Neues Bauen am Horn. Eine Mustersiedlung in Weimar*, Weimar 2004

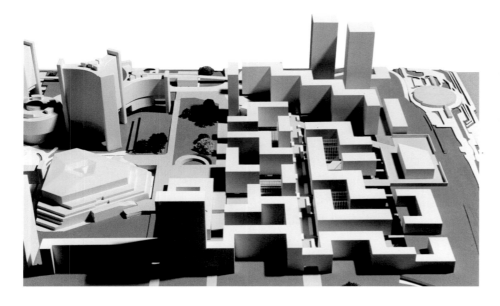

9201
Donau City, Wien, mit / with
Heinz Neumann
Entwicklungsstudie, Modell /
Development study, model, 1992

mit Hilfe des angebotenen Regelwerkes »in der Zeit« ein primär strukturell (und erst sekundär formal) integriertes Raumgefüge entwickeln, in dem der Zwischenraum von Baumassen – mit all den einschlägigen Vektoren für Belichtung, Erschließung, Grünraum etc. – genauso als gestaltete, als essenzielle Qualität behandelt wird.

Wenn ich mich recht erinnere, war bei der Wiener Donau City ein Hauptmotiv, das Spiel auf der neu geschaffenen Plattform am Flussufer so aufzusetzen, dass auch jene Investoren, die zuletzt kommen und normalerweise die hinteren Plätze am künftigen »Balkon« von Wien erhalten, die gleichen Chancen auf die »unique situation« erhalten wie die ersten.

Das Hauptanliegen der Auftraggeber war, die insgesamt genehmigten 1,5 Millionen Kubikmeter umbauten Raum so zu portionieren, dass auch der letzte Investor noch einen angemessenen Anteil an Baumasse erhalten konnte. Unsere Idee war nun, ein Spiel mit den Gebäudemassen und deren Positionierung zu betreiben, sodass dem einzelnen Investor größtmögliche Freiheit zugestanden wurde ohne den Prozess aus dem Ruder laufen zu lassen. Es wurden also »Parzellenmodule« von 42 x 42 Metern gebildet, die, abgestimmt auf die Wiener Bauordnung, als kleinste Grundeinheiten vorgesehen waren. Zudem war durch die vorhandene Baugrube für die nicht stattgefundene Weltausstellung eine Tiefebene als Vorgabe vorhanden. Wir haben das Spiel also nicht nur in der Fläche, sondern als dreidimensionale Versuchsanordnung konzipiert. Aufbauend auf der Grundstückteilung durch die Parzellenmodule entwickelten wir das Tiefrelief

And thirdly, I thought that, after doing away with stylistic or morphological conventions in our open, postmodern state, instead of the customary juxtaposition of individualities, one could obtain something like a productive power from the diversity. Therefore, instead of more or less arbitrary juxtaposition, the idea was to achieve a new quality in that different planners, "over a period of time" with the help of the set of rules offered, develop a spatial texture that is first structurally (and then formally) integrated, in which the interstitial space between building volumes—with all the relevant vectors for natural light, access, green space, etc.—is also dealt with as a designed, as an essential, quality.

If I remember correctly, one main motif in the case of Donau City in Vienna was drafting the rules of the game for the newly created platform on the bank of the river in such a way that the investors who come last and normally receive the rearmost positions on the future "balcony" of Vienna were also given the same chances to receive a "unique situation" as the first.

The client's main concern was apportioning the 1.5 million cubic meters of building space total, which had been approved in such a way that the last investor could also still receive an appropriate share of cubic capacity. Our idea now was to play with the volume of the buildings and how they were positioned, so that individual investors were given the greatest possible freedom without the process getting out of hand. This led to the creation of "parcel modules" of 42 x 42 meters, which, in alignment with Vienna's building code, were envisaged as the smallest basic units. In addition, as a result of the existing excavation pit for the unrealized World Expo, an underground level was also available as a default specification. We therefore conceptualized the game not only in terms of surface area, but instead as a three-dimensional experimental design.

Building on the partitioning of the land developed by means of the parcel modules, we developed the depth relief with the traffic level (– 9 m), above it the infrastructure level (media level), the pedestrian level on top of it (± 0 m), and above it the building pattern of the free height relief. The shaping of the individual layers was able to take place autonomously and resulted in a concept of city as a three-dimensional figuration that could develop over a longer period of time, but without impeding the overall progress of planning and construction.

mit der Verkehrsebene (– 9 m), darüber die Ebene der Infrastruktur (Medienebene), darauf die Fußgängerebene (± 0 m) und darüber das Bebauungsmuster des freien Hochreliefs. Die Ausformungen in den einzelnen Schichten konnten autonom erfolgen und mündeten in eine Vorstellung von Stadt als dreidimensionalem Gebilde, das sich über einen längeren Zeitraum entwickeln konnte, ohne den Planungs- und Baufortschritt insgesamt zu behindern.

Für dieses Konzept hast du mit Heinz Neumann viel Anerkennung eingeheimst. Die Donau City ist heute allerdings das abschreckende Beispiel einer beliebigen Ansammlung von Hochhäusern, mit einer Unwirtlichkeit der öffentlichen Räume, der immerhin autofreien Plätze und Passagen, die ihresgleichen sucht. Warum?

Die Entwicklungsgesellschaft verkürzte unser offenes Spiel zur reinen Willkür. De facto wurde dort jeder Neubau wieder konventionell als isoliertes Objekt gestaltet und behandelt und geriet auch der gemeinsame, öffentliche Raum dazwischen samt allen Übergängen aus dem Ruder. Die Träger der immensen planerischen Verantwortung hätten eben nicht nur ad hoc, sondern umsichtig und vorausschauend agieren müssen, was die auf Verwertung und Gewinn abzielende Entwicklungs- und Durchführungsgesellschaft konzeptuell und ethisch sichtlich überforderte. Schließlich kam es, und kommt es noch immer, zu hilflosen Identitätsgesten durch Errichten von Hochhäusern, die den Gedanken ihres urbanen Auftrags verloren zu haben scheinen.

Baukonzept Am Horn, Weimar

In der Wiener Donau City, wo dein städtebaulicher Ansatz ins Gegenteil gewendet wurde, hat man dir mit der Gestaltung von Infrastruktur-Aspekten und mit einer kleinen Feuerwehrstation ein bescheidenes Schmerzensgeld geboten. Im Gegensatz dazu Weimar: In der Siedlung neues bauen am horn hast du keinen einzigen Bau entwerfen können, dafür wurde dein städtebauliches Entwicklungskonzept von allen nur denkbaren Beteiligten bis ins kleinste Detail und über Jahre hinweg in verschiedenen kooperativen Verfahren exemplarisch angewendet und umgesetzt. Es gibt wohl in Europa kein vergleichbares Wohnquartier, und auch die abschließende Bewertung durch externe Fachleute und die Dokumentation waren vorbildlich, einzigartig. Was lief da so anders?

You and Heinz Neumann received many accolades for this concept. The Donau City is today, however, a dissuasive example of a random collection of high-rise buildings with inhospitable public spaces, which at the same time still seeks its match in car-free squares and passages. Why?

The development association reduced our open game to pure arbitrariness. De facto, every new building there was once again designed conventionally as an isolated object, and the shared public space between them, along with all transitions, got out of control. Those who bore the huge planning responsibility should have operated not only ad hoc, but also prudently and with foresight. But this was something that evidently overtaxed the development and realization company with its goals of exploitation and profit, both conceptually and ethically. What ultimately resulted and continues to result are helpless gestures of identity by erecting high-rise buildings that seem to have lost the idea of their urban mission.

Building Concept for Am Horn, Weimar

In Donau City in Vienna, where your urban planning approach turned out to be counterproductive, you were offered modest compensation for the opportunity to design infrastructure aspects and a small fire station. In contrast to that, Weimar: in the settlement neues bauen am horn (New Building on the Horn), you were not given the opportunity to design any individual buildings. But, in return, every conceivable participant used and realized your urban-planning development concept in an exemplary manner, down the smallest detail and in various cooperative processes over many years. There is perhaps no comparable residential area anywhere in Europe, and the final assessment by external specialists as well as the documentation was also exemplary, unique. What played out so differently there?

In contrast to Donau City, which, despite its failure, was nevertheless an important developmental step for me with respect to all my future urbanistic considerations and projects, Am Horn in Weimar presents itself as a positive urban-planning experiment whose further development has also been successful. The process publicly advertised by the City of Weimar along with Bauhaus University was originally tendered as a conventional competition with various focuses, such as living, university uses, et cetera. As part of a team that included Luigi Snozzi and Diener + Diener, who were more responsible for working on the central

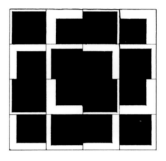

Oskar Putz, *ohne Titel 09*, 1979
Konzeptzeichnung / Conceptual drawing

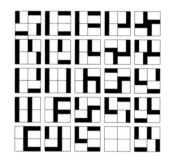

9201
Donau-City, Wien
Entwicklungsstudie / Development study, Masterplan, 1992

»Krischanitz's parcelling up of the site in urban projects exhibits subtle parallels with the abstract compositions of his painter friend Oskar Putz. In the 1980s Putz continued to develop the principles of concrete art, organizing the canvas surface as a structural field of geometric shapes and colours.«

aus /from:
Otto Kapfinger,
»Space-Text as Context«,
in: *Beyond the Minimal*,
Ausst.-Kat. / exh. cat. Architectural Association, London 1998

Im Gegensatz zur Donau City, die trotz ihres Scheiterns für mich ein wichtiger Entwicklungsschritt für alle weiteren stadträumlichen Überlegungen und Projekte war, stellt sich Am Horn in Weimar als positives, in seiner Weiterentwicklung gelungenes städtebauliches Experiment dar. Das von der Stadt Weimar mit der Bauhaus-Universität ausgeschriebene Verfahren war ursprünglich als konventioneller Wettbewerb mit unterschiedlichen Schwerpunkten wie Wohnen, universitäre Nutzungen etc. ausgeschrieben. Mein Beitrag im Team mit Luigi Snozzi und Diener + Diener, die eher die zentralen Areale der Kasernenbauten bearbeiteten, hatte die peripheren Bereiche mit dem Thema Wohnbau (Siedlungsbau) zum Inhalt. Wir gewannen schließlich den Wettbewerb, obwohl mein Entwurf nicht konkret die städtebauliche Planung einer Wohnsiedlung zum Inhalt hatte, sondern sich vertiefte mit dem Thema Grund und Boden auseinandersetzte.

Dies geschah mit einer solchen Konsequenz, dass unser Projekt keinen wie auch immer gearteten architektonischen Entwurf beinhaltete, aber entscheidende grund- und bodenrechtliche Voraussetzungen thematisierte. Unser Beitrag war, nicht eine bauliche Lösung vorzuschlagen, sondern die Anordnung von Grundstücksformen. Durch Richtlinien und Regeln, die auf der Thüringer Bauordnung fußten, diese verfeinerten und in gewissen Bereichen sogar ergänzten, wurden neue Voraussetzungen geschaffen.

Durch das bewusste Kombinieren von geschlossener, offener und halboffener Bauweise über das gesamte Bebauungsgebiet entstand eine neue Körnigkeit jenseits der »nach Bauordnung« gängigen Bebauungsmuster. Die Siedlung bildet sich aus regelgebundenen Einzelobjekten. Sie sind in einer für die Bauordnung »atypischen« Weise unmittelbar nebeneinander und sogar übereinander geschossweise differenziert kombiniert. Der Erwerb eines Grundstücks war vertraglich an diese Bebauungsregeln gekoppelt, und dies wurde meines Wissens die gesamte Zeit, bis zum letzten Bauantrag durchgehalten.

Wenn ich deine Siedlungs- und Wohnbauplanungen von 1994 bis 2014 Revue passieren lasse, fallen mir folgende Dinge auf. Das eine ist die sukzessive Differenzierung von unterschiedlichen städtebaulichen Typologien über die Jahre: flächig ausgebreitete, niedrige Bebauungsmuster, linear geschichtet wie das Friedrichshofkonzept oder netzartig gewebt wie beim Projekt Absberggasse oder bei der Muster-

9611
neues bauen am horn
Weimar, 1996–1999
Masterplan Wohnbebauung / Master plan for housing development

site with the barracks buildings, my contribution comprised the peripheral areas with the theme of residential building (settlement construction). We ultimately won the competition, although my design did not deal concretely with the urban planning of a housing settlement but instead examined the theme of land in-depth.

The consequent result of this was that our project did not include any certain kind of architectural design but rather decisively addressed building regulation prerequisites. Our contribution did not propose a construction solution but instead configured the shapes of plots of land. New prerequisites were established through using guidelines and rules based on the Thuringian building code and refining and even supplementing them in particular areas.

By intentionally combining closed, open, and half-open construction styles throughout the building area, a new granularity beyond conventional building patterns "according to the building code" was developed. The settlement consists of rule-bound individual objects. In a way that is "atypical" for the building code, they are combined in a differentiated way directly next to one another and even over one another in stories. Acquiring a plot of land was linked contractually with these building rules and—to my knowledge—this was maintained the whole time, until the last planning application.

When I review your settlement and housing development planning from 1994 to 2014, the following things catch my attention. One aspect is the successive differentiation of various urban-planning typologies over the years: low development models spread out two-dimensionally over an area, linearly layered like the Friedrichshof concept, or interwoven in a net-like way as in the Absberggasse project or the model settlement Hadersdorf; then compact, multistory, stand-alone building typologies—Karree St. Marx, Stadtpark Linz, and so on; furthermore, multistory buildings as rows, as in the case of Monte Laa or Eurogate; multistory buildings surrounding a courtyard or around meandering, open courtyards as on Tokiostrasse; and finally, clusters of individual buildings alternating between open and coupled design styles, as in Weimar, for example.

I would like to formulate the overarching quality of all these models roughly and impurely. In settlement and housing development, throughout rental apartments with limited construction costs and the other

siedlung Hadersdorf; dann kompakte, mehrgeschossige Punkthaustypologien – Karree St. Marx, Stadtpark Linz; weiters Geschossbauten als Zeilen wie bei Monte Laa oder Eurogate; Geschossbauten um Höfe beziehungsweise um mäandrierend geöffnete Höfe wie in der Tokiostraße; dann die zwischen offener und gekuppelter Bauweise pendelnden Einzelhaus-Cluster wie zum Beispiel in Weimar. Die alle diese Muster übergreifende Qualität formuliere ich einmal grob und ins Unreine: Im Siedlungs- und Wohnbau, durchwegs für Mietwohnungen mit limitierten Baukosten und den übrigen Restriktionen der Branche, verwendest du relativ konventionelle Konstruktionen und Standards bis zu den Details: durchwegs unaufgeregte Fassaden ohne alle Kunststücke.

Raumstrategien im Grundriss

Mein Bestreben war es, nicht durch Setzungen von »auffälligen« Gebäuden zu einem Städtebau als Summe von Einzelmaßnahmen zu kommen, vielmehr hatte die stadträumliche Figuration als urbane Geste das Primat. Die Arbeit mit der Gesamtform erlaubt es, verschiedene architektonische Ansätze und Handschriften zu integrieren, die per se den Gedanken des Städtischen als pluralistische Kulturleistung befördern. Man kann aber nicht sagen, dass so eine Haltung vom Einzelbauwerk gestalterisch nichts verlangt. Ich würde dies gar nicht so als Zurücknahme der gestalterischen Merkmale des Einzelgebäudes sehen. Vielmehr denke ich, dass sich das Hauptaugenmerk auf jene Bereiche verlagern sollte, die stadträumlich, also im Sinne eines städtebaulichen Gesamtereignisses wirksam werden. Umgekehrt muss jedes einzelne Gebäude auch selbst einen stadträumlichen Mehrwert produzieren, also bestimmte Wirkungen im Sinne einer allgemeinen, übergreifenden städtischen Nutzung und Ordnung liefern, die zur Identitätsbildung des Quartiers, des Stadtteils beitragen.

Die überraschende Qualität kommt aus meiner Sicht dann aus der inneren Organisation. Innerhalb des alltäglichen Rahmenwerks der Bauten gibt es eine variantenreiche, erst auf den zweiten Blick spürbare innere Dynamik, ein »Pulsieren« der Grundriss- und Raumfolgen um die ebenso variantenreich ausprobierten Kerne der hochinstallierten und vertikal organisierten Raumteile. Kannst du das näher erläutern und begründen?

Du hast schon am Pilotenweg die Spannung zwischen Hülle und Hauskern und rotierender

restrictions in this sector, you use relatively conventional structures and standards down to the smallest details: consistently calm façades without any ornamentation.

Spatial Strategies in Layout

My goal was not to arrive at a type of urban planning, as a sum of individual measures, by positioning "eye-catching" buildings. It was instead urban-planning figuration as an urban gesture that had priority. Work on the overall form makes it possible to integrate various architectural approaches and styles that advance the idea of the urban as a pluralistic cultural achievement per se. But it's not possible to say that such an approach doesn't demand anything creative from the individual building. I wouldn't see this as retracting the creative characteristics of the individual building at all. Rather, I think that the main focus should be shifted to those areas that take effect in terms of urban development, therefore in the sense of an overall urban-planning result. Conversely, each individual building must also produce an added urban-development value itself, must therefore deliver particular effects in the sense of general, overarching urban use and order, thus contributing to the formation of identity for the quarter or city district.

The surprising quality then comes, in my opinion, from the inner organization. Within the everyday framework of construction, there is, first at second glance, a perceptible inner dynamic with many variants, a "pulsing" of the layout and sequence of spaces tried out with just as many variants, of the highly specialized and vertically distributed segments of space, so that what then appears is the central and stable core. Could you explain and give some reasons for this in a bit more detail?

You've already touched on the tension between shell and building core, and the rotating spatial layout, at Pilotenweg. Later, I was able to take this a step further, most clearly in the case of multistory, stand-alone buildings. The most expensive aspects—beyond the façade—are the so-called functional spaces in an apartment: kitchen and bathroom. I try to keep them very compact, as standardized as possible, with cores of equal sizes, and to arrange them detached from one other, as focal points, as poles within the layout—with the definitions of other spaces around them remaining relatively free, variable, individual. The inner side

Mustersiedlung Hadersdorf.
Neues Wohnen in Wien,
Sulgen und Zürich 2009

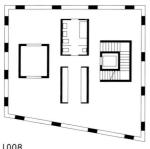

1008
Planstudie Wohnbebauung /
Housing Development Study
Kureck, Wiesbaden, 2010
Grundrissbeispiel / Sample
floor plan

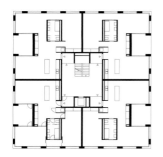

1108
Wettbewerb Wohnbau Areal-
überbauung / Competition
Housing Development Guggach
Zürich, 2011, Grundrissbeispiel /
Sample floor plan

Raumanordnung angesprochen. Am deutlichsten konnte ich das später bei den mehrgeschossigen Punkthäusern fortsetzen. Das Teuerste – neben der Fassade – sind die sogenannten Funktionsräume der Wohnung, Küche und Bad. Die versuche ich ganz kompakt zu halten, möglichst als standardisierte, gleich große Kerne, und voneinander gelöst anzuordnen, als Brennpunkte, als Pole innerhalb des Grundrisses – die weiteren Raumdefinitionen rundherum sind ziemlich frei, sind variabel, individuell. Die Innenseite der Gebäudehülle bleibt tendenziell frei, im Idealfall könnte der Wohnraum ungeteilt um die Kerne herumfließen und die ganze Innenseite der Außenwände erlebbar bleiben. So könnte – bei den limitierten Dimensionen des sozialen Wohnbaus! – doch eine räumliche Großzügigkeit erreicht werden.

Ein anderes Thema – bei Monte Laa noch rudimentär, bei Eurogate gelungen – war das schachbrettartige Versetzen der Freibereiche in den Wohnetagen, sodass mehr Sichtschutz, weniger gegenseitige Beeinträchtigung entsteht. Es klingt einfach, ist aber bei all den heutigen Zwängen ein logistischer Balanceakt. Bei Eurogate ist es so, dass die Decken der angesetzten Loggien die Bodenplatten der darüber liegenden Balkone bilden. Es sieht so simpel aus, im Rahmen unserer Wohnbaurichtlinien und Abwicklungsregeln müssen aber gleichsam Elefanten kreißen, damit solche »Mäuslein« geboren werden.

Ich versuche nochmals den Brückenschlag zu unseren Studien der 70er-Jahre. Uns faszinierte, dass sowohl im Geschosswohnbau als auch in den Siedlungen des Roten Wien und besonders dann in der Werkbundsiedlung die Qualität nicht aus konstruktiven Innovationen kam. Gerade in der Werkbundsiedlung hatte Josef Frank – zuvor noch Teilnehmer am experimentellen Manifest Stuttgarter Weißenhof – bewusst (auch durch die Umstände bestimmt) konventionelle, einfache Bautechnik eingesetzt, um mit alltäglichen Vokabeln eine ganz neue Geschichte zu erzählen: die erstaunliche raumtypologische Vielfalt und Differenzierung trotz bescheidener Maße und Dimensionen, mit 30 unterschiedlichsten Hauscharakteren in 70 Modellhäusern! Und trotz dieser Varianten zerfällt das Ganze nicht in Episoden, erzeugen die Varianten zusätzlich einen alles verbindenden Duktus.

Funktionsmischung – Normalstadt

Ein Stück Normalstadt zu erzeugen gehört wahrscheinlich zum Schwierigsten. Normalstadt ist

of the structural shell is generally free and, in the ideal case, the undivided living space is able to flow around the core, making it possible to experience the whole inner side of the outer walls. This makes it possible—in the limited dimensions of social housing!—to achieve a kind of spaciousness.

Another theme—still rudimentary in the case of Monte Laa, yet successful in the case of Eurogate—was the chessboard-like shifting of the free areas on the residential floors with an aim of fostering greater privacy protection and reducing mutual detriments. This sounds simple, but it is actually, with all the current constraints, a logistical balancing act. In the case of Eurogate, the ceilings of the recessed balconies form the floor slabs of the balconies situated above them. It looks so simple, but within the framework of our building regulations and procedures, you virtually have to fight elephants so that "little mice" can be born.

I'd once again like to build a bridge to our studies in the seventies. At the time, we were fascinated by the fact that quality did not arise from structural innovations, either in multistory residential buildings or in the settlements of Rotes Wien, or then in the Werkbund settlement in particular. Specifically in the Werkbund project, Josef Frank—who had already been a participant in the experimental Weissenhof manifesto in Stuttgart—intentionally (and also stipulated by circumstances) implemented simple, conventional building techniques to tell a completely new story using everyday vocabulary. He created astounding variety and differentiation in spatial typology through thirty extremely different building characters in a total of seventy model houses, in spite of the modest measures and dimensions! And despite all these variants, the whole doesn't fragment into episodes, and the variants also produce a style that connects everything.

Functional Mix—Normal City

Creating a piece of "normal city" is perhaps one of the most difficult things to pull off. Normal city is, however, necessary, for it serves to establish a standard of orientation and scale that shapes the sensory awareness for those buildings that require greater attention due to the degree to which they are public in nature or to other content-related criteria. The development of social housing that still exists (but is endangered) in Austria is still able to include this potential of

aber notwendig, weil dadurch ein Standard an Orientierung und Maßstäblichkeit geschaffen wird, der die Wahrnehmungsbereitschaft für jene Gebäude bildet, die auf Grund ihres Öffentlichkeitsgrades oder anderer inhaltlicher Kriterien größerer Aufmerksamkeit bedürfen. Der in Österreich immer noch existierende (aber gefährdete) soziale Wohnbau könnte dieses Potenzial an Normalstadt auf Grund eines durchgängigen Duktus immer noch enthalten und damit als baukulturelles Grundmuster dienen.

Offenbar schaffen das aber nur private Errichtergruppen oder Bauherrengemeinschaften, wie in Vorarlberg vor Jahrzehnten, dann auch in Wien bei ein paar Ausnahmebauten, und nicht die großen Bauträger.

Zum Abschluss ein Blick auf das schwierige Thema der urbanen Durchmischung solcher Anlagen. Die Mischung von Wohn- mit Arbeits- und Dienstleistungsbereichen bei solchen Anlagen wird immer gefordert, in Wettbewerben oft auch prämiert – und dann ganz selten gebaut. Warum? Und kannst du Gegenbeispiele, gelungene Beispiele, nennen und beschreiben?

Die Forderung der Durchmischung der Wohnanlagen mit anderen Nutzungen ist ebenso evident wie schwer umzusetzen. Diese Sonder- oder Folgenutzungen bedürfen einer besonderen Aufmerksamkeit hinsichtlich Standort, Flächenausmaß, Verkehrsanbindung, Raumhöhe, Emissionsarmut etc. Geht man nun davon aus, durch Wohngebäude Straßenräume zu bilden, also ein Stück Stadt zu wagen, ist ein Erdgeschoss zumindest straßenseitig kein Wohngeschoss, sondern eben eine Schicht mit Sondernutzungen, ob nun hausfremd wie Geschäfte, Dienstleistungs- und Gewerbebetriebe, oder hausintern wie Eingangshallen, Gemeinschaftsräume und anderes.

Organisationsformen wie vom Straßenniveau abgehobene Wohngeschosse, gekoppelt mit Hofgärten, stellen ebenso abschnittsweise Möglichkeiten dar. Jedenfalls sind all diese Maßnahmen Sonderlösungen, die abgesehen von den erhöhten Baukosten zusätzliche Anstrengungen bei der Vermietbarkeit dieser Flächen erfordern. Die Lindengasse als frei finanziertes Projekt in Wien-Neubau und mein Projekt am Limmatfeld bieten in der Hinsicht gelungene Beispiele.

Neben deinem Anteil am Limmatfeld in Dietikon nördlich von Zürich, der ja nur einen kleinen Part

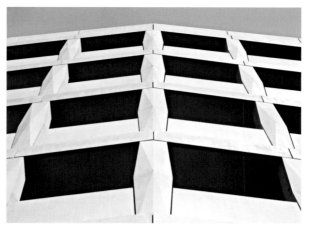

0412
Wohn- und Geschäftshaus / Residential and Commercial Building Lindengasse,
Wien, 2004–2008

normal city based on a universal style and therefore serve as a basic architectural pattern.

Apparently, however, only private groups of builders or associations of building owners manage this—as in Vorarlberg decades ago, and then also in Vienna in the case of a couple of exceptional buildings—but not the big property developers.

To conclude, let's a look at the difficult theme of the urban mix of such sites. The blend of residential areas with areas for work and the provision of services is always stipulated and often also awarded prizes in competitions—but then very rarely built. Why? And can you name and describe counterexamples, successful examples?

The call for intermingling other utilizations in residential complexes is as evident as it is difficult to realize. These special or subsequent uses require that special attention be given to location, surface area, transportation links, ceiling height, low emissions, et cetera. If we now assume that street spaces can be shaped through residential buildings, that a piece of city may be ventured, then a ground floor, at least to the street side, is not a residential level, but rather a level with special applications—whether now involving external parties, such as shops, service providers, and business establishments, or in-house spaces like entrance halls, community areas, and so forth.

Forms of organization like residential floors above street level, coupled with courtyard gardens, also present possibilities in some instances. But, in any case, all these measures are special solutions, which, apart from increased construction costs, also call for additional efforts with regard to making these areas rentable. Lindengasse, as an independ-

0724
Wohnbebauung Limmatfeld, Bau-
feld A / Residential Building
Limmatfeld, Plot A
Dietikon, 2007–2012
Wohnungen, Büros, Läden /
Apartments, offices, shops

Tibor Joanelly,
»Kleine Stadt in der Kleinstadt«,
in: *werk, bauen + wohnen*, 4, 2013

S. / pp. 130–133

eines großen, nach einem städtebaulichen Wettbewerb errichteten Ensembles an der Bahntrasse
ausmacht, zeigt sich aus meiner Sicht die Gratwan-
derung zwischen einem strukturellen, entwick-
lungsoffenen Bau- und Raumkonzept und dem
motivischen, objektzentrierten Gestaltungstrieb mo-
dellhaft bei den von verschiedenen Teams gestalteten
Nachbarbauten. Sie bieten eine »leicht konsumierbare Instant-Identität«, schwächen damit aber sofort
den angeblichen urbanen Charakter des Ganzen,
zerbröseln in subjektive Behauptungen. Es ergibt
sich dann nur ein »Abbild von Stadt in einem
zerbrochenen Spiegel«, wie ein Autor schrieb.

Das Projekt am Limmatfeld war wegen der vorhandenen Immissionen eine ziemliche Herausforderung: Im Süden die sehr verkehrsreiche Straße,
die unmittelbar nach dem Areal unter der Bahn
durchtaucht; im Westen die enorme Gleisanlage
des Bahnhofs mit Durchfahrts- und Verschubver-
kehr. Allerdings ermöglichen diese dem Lärm aus-
gesetzten Gebäudeseiten auch schöne Ausblicke,
einerseits zur Stadt hin und anderseits über die
gigantische Gleisanlage hinweg. Beide Seiten des
Bauareals mussten also vom Lärm abgekoppelt
werden, und die Frischluftzufuhr musste ohne
Belüftung durch Fenster gewährleistet sein. Neben
den technischen Anpassungen war es aber wichtig,
auch in Grundriss und Fassadenrelief städtebauliche Stützungsmaßnahmen durchzuführen. Dies

ently financed project in the Neubau district
of Vienna, and my project at Limmatfeld offer
successful examples in this respect.

Besides your part in Limmatfeld in Dietikon to the
north of Zurich, which indeed makes up only a small
part of a large ensemble on the train route that
was erected following an urban-planning competition,
the balancing act, from my point of view, between
a structural and spatial concept that is open to
development and a motivic, object-centered design
impulse is demonstrated exemplarily in the neighboring buildings designed by various teams. They
offer an "easily consumable instant identity," but
in doing so they immediately weaken the ostensibly
urban character of the whole, crumbling into subjective statements. What then results, as one author
wrote, is only a "reflection of city in a broken
mirror."

The project at Limmatfeld was quite a challenge
due to the emissions present there: to the south,
the quite congested street that ducks under the
train tracks just after the site; to the west, the huge
track system of the train station with its transiting
and shunting trains. At the same time, the sides
of the buildings exposed to the noise also offer
beautiful views, on the one hand toward the city
and, on the other, out over the gigantic track
system. Both sides of the building site therefore
had to be decoupled from the noise, and a supply
of fresh air had to be provided without ventilation
through windows. Besides the technical adapta-
tions, it was, however, also important to realize
supporting urban-development measures in the
floor plan and façade relief. In connection with
the floor plan, this led to a building layout that is
closed toward the south and, to the north, breaks
up into finger-like tracts that each open up to the
west and east again by means of setbacks. Based
on the inner spatial structure, the south façade
then has this rhythmic, undulating relief effect
along the street. The sloping at the edge of the
street directly follows only the ground level
business floor and the penthouse floor at the
very top.

The building accompanies and decisively creates
street spaces, yet it is not a conventional bloc
perimeter structure. It is a structurally open spatial
framework over the entire parcel, resembling a loft
structure, something that is also shown in the
external form, in the laconic rhythms of the façades.
The whole is then divided vertically and horizontally
and stratified based on the transformation of the

führte in Bezug auf den Grundriss zu einer Baufigur, welche sich nach Süden schließt und nach Norden in fingerartige Trakte auflöst, die sich jeweils durch Rücksprünge wieder nach Westen und Osten öffnen. Die Südfassade kommt dann, aus der inneren Raumstruktur heraus, entlang der Straßenkante zu dieser rhythmischen, gewellten Reliefierung. Der Schräge der Straßenkante folgen direkt nur das ebenerdige Geschäftsgeschoss und ganz oben das Staffelgeschoss.

Das Gebäude begleitet, schafft dezidiert Straßenräume, ist dann doch keine konventionelle Blockrandstruktur. Es ist ein strukturell offenes Raumgerüst über die ganze Parzelle, einer Loftstruktur ähnlich, was sich auch in der äußeren Gestalt, in den lakonischen Fassadenrhythmen zeigt. Das Ganze ist dann vertikal und horizontal geteilt und geschichtet aus der Geometrie und den Bedingungen des Grundstücks für Sicht- und Belichtungsqualitäten, für mehr öffentliche und mehr private Nutzungen.

Daraus entsteht trotz der relativ monotonen, großflächigen Architektursprache die raumplastische Spannung zwischen der gewellten Südzeile und den in Hofbereiche aufgelösten Trakten – über dem gemeinsamen, kommerziell genutzten Basisgeschoss. Das allein gut durchzuarbeiten scheint mir zu genügen, um ein Stück Normalstadt herzustellen – und ist vielleicht eine größere Herausforderung und nachhaltigere Lösung als ein noch so virtuoses Forcieren äußerlicher Komplexität mittels kleinteilig fixierter Innenwelten.

9908
Wohn- und Geschäftshaus / Residential and Commercial Building Theresienhöhe
München, 1999–2002
Bebauung für gemischte urbane Nutzung, in Struktur und Form polyvalent, robust, mehrdeutig / Mixed-use urban development, polyvalent, robust, and equivocal in structure and form

geometry and the plot conditions to foster visual and lighting qualities, to create more public and more private uses.

In spite of the relatively monotonous, large-scale architectural language, this engenders a tension of spatial relief between the undulating southern line and the dispersed tracts in the courtyard area—over the shared, commercially used ground level. To me, even just working this out seems sufficient to produce a piece of normal city—and it is perhaps a greater challenge and more sustainable solution than a forced outer complexity by means of inner worlds established on a small scale, however masterfully this is achieved.

0806
Wohnbau / Residential Building on Raxstraße, Wien, 2008–2013

9611
neues bauen am horn, Weimar

versiegelte Fläche

Wassergebundene Decke

Sandspielplatz

Wiese

Immergrüne Heckenkirsche

Hartriegel

Efeu

Bartblume

Robinie

vertiefter Rasenweg

Baufluchtlinie

Originalplan von / Plan by Anna Detzlhofer

0002
Mustersiedlung / Model Housing Settlement Hadersdorf, Wien / Vienna
mit / with Hermann Czech, Roger Diener, Max Dudler, Hans Kollhoff,
Peter Märkli, Meili & Peter, Otto Steidle, Heinz Tesar
Landschaftsplanung / Landscaping: Anna Detzlhofer

0715
generationen: wohnen am mühlgrund, Wien / Vienna, mit / with Hermann Czech, Werner Neuwirth

8705
Siedlung / Housing Settlement on Pilotengasse, Wien / Vienna
mit / with Herzog & de Meuron, Otto Steidle
Farbkonzepte / Color designs: Helmut Federle, Oskar Putz

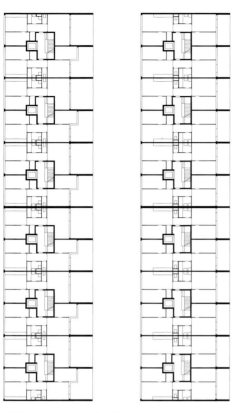

9609 Dernjacgasse, +2 / +1 <

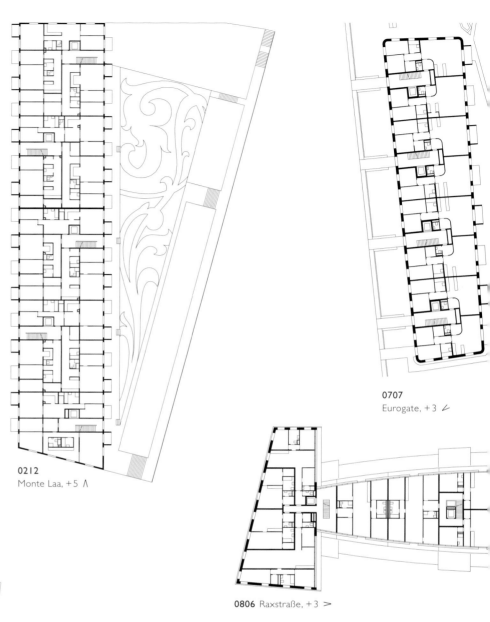

0212
Monte Laa, +5 Λ

0707
Eurogate, +3 ∠

0806 Raxstraße, +3 >

0306 Mandalahof, Wien, +6 ∠

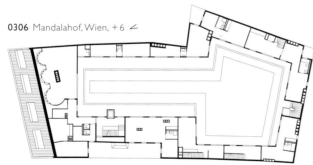

+5

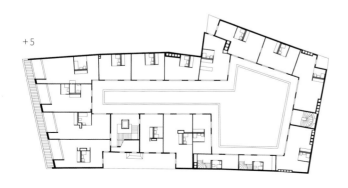

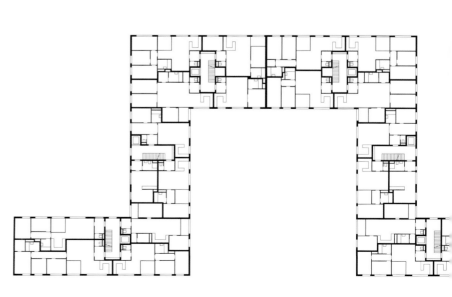

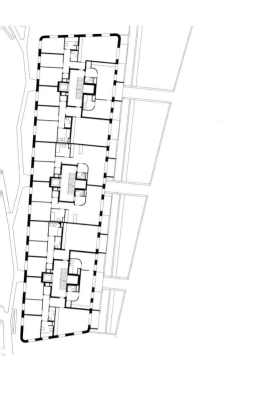

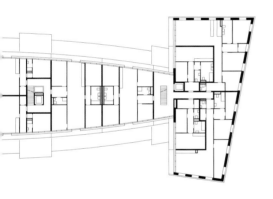

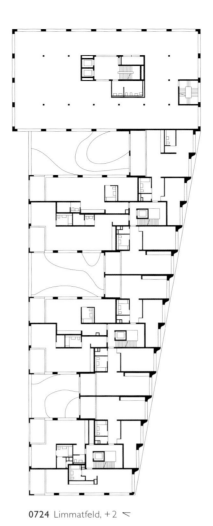

0724 Limmatfeld, +2 ⬑

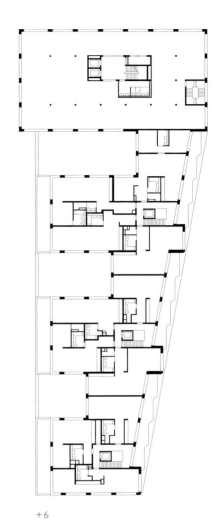

+6

9909 Tokiostraße, +3 ◁

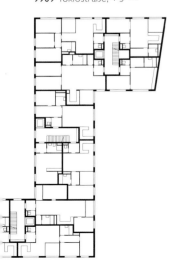

0412 Lindengasse, +1 ⬈

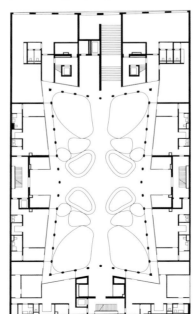

+3

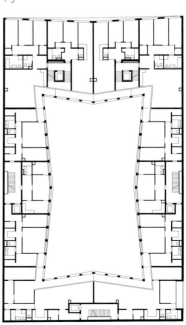

123

0707
Passivwohnbau / Passive Residential Building Eurogate, Wien / Vienna

0707
Passivwohnbau / Passive Residential Building Eurogate

0806
Wohnbau / Residential Building on Raxstraße, Wien / Vienna

0806
Wohnbau / Residential Building on Raxstraße

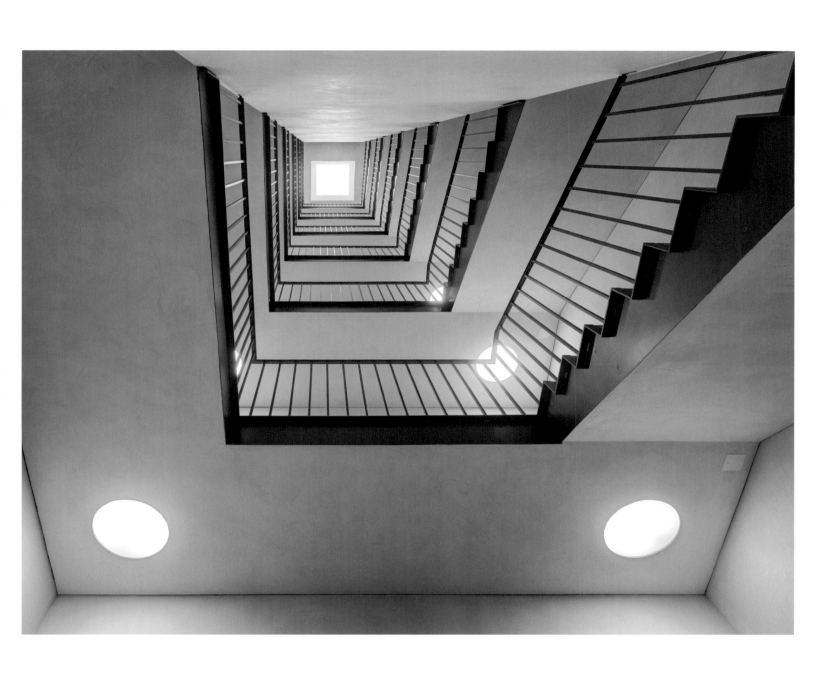

0724
Wohnbebauung / Residential Buildings at Limmatfeld, Dietikon

Südansicht / View from the south   >

0212
Wohnbau / Residential Building Monte Laa, Wien / Vienna

0412
Wohn- und Geschäftshaus / Residential and Commercial Building on Lindengasse, Wien / Vienna, mit / with Birgit Frank

0412
Wohn- und Geschäftshaus / Residential and Commercial Building on Lindengasse

0306
Buddhistisches Wohnheim / Buddhist Hostel Mandalahof, Wien / Vienna

Otto Kapfinger: Im Frühjahr 2013 konnte ich mit dir einen Vormittag lang den Novartis-Campus in Basel besichtigen. Wenn man einmal die hochgesicherte gläserne Pforte passiert hat – wir waren ja angemeldet – kann man sich dort frei bewegen. Wir haben nicht nur deinen Bau, sondern auch alle anderen durchwandert: Diener & Diener, Saana, Moneo, Gehry, Chipperfield, Ando, Taniguchi, Märkli. Es ist der Hauptsitz eines weltweit agierenden Pharmakonzerns. Derzeit arbeiten dort etwa 8000 Menschen aus aller Welt.

Adolf Krischanitz: Dieser Campus in Basel zählt in Europa, wenn nicht global, zu den ehrgeizigsten Architekturprojekten der letzten Jahrzehnte. Auf dem 30 Hektar großen Gelände entstand seit 2002 nach dem Masterplan von Vittorio Magnago Lampugnani, und wächst immer noch weiter, ein »Zentrum des Wissens«: Bauten für Forschung, Entwicklung und Verwaltung in ebenso hochwertig gestalteten Freiräumen. Jeder neue Bauabschnitt im Rahmen des Masterplans wird nach spezifischen Vorgaben entwickelt. Man hat hier wohl am nur fünf Kilometer entfernten Campus von Vitra in Weil auf der anderen Seite des Rheins Maß genommen – und hat das allein quantitativ längst weit überboten.

Das Ganze erinnert mich an das legendäre Engagement des Olivetti-Konzerns in Ivrea zwischen Turin und Mailand, wo von den 1930er- bis zu den 1970er-Jahren eine modellhafte Produktions- und Wohnstadt entstand, ein Pantheon der zeitgenössischen Baukunst mit den damals besten italienischen und internationalen Architekten. Dein Bau in Basel, mit Birgit Frank konzipiert, war eine einzigartige Gelegenheit, eine Herausforderung. Wie kam es dazu?

Es war nach den zuvor errichteten Verwaltungs- und Bürotrakten das erste Labor- und Entwicklungsgebäude dort. Novartis wünschte sich ein Haus, das besonders die Kommunikation von Forschern und Forscherinnen erlaubt, diese geradezu fördert. Ich wurde mit vier weiteren Büros zu einem Wettbewerb eingeladen.

Netzwerk der Raumbildung

Dem Portfolio deiner Wettbewerbspräsentation hast du eine Grundsatzerklärung vorangestellt: »Poetik einer Arbeitsstätte«. Du verweist, fast in faustischer Manier, auf das Ineinander von apollinischen und

Otto Kapfinger: In the spring of 2013, you and I had the opportunity to spend a whole morning exploring the Novartis Campus in Basel. After having passed through the high-security, glass entrance gate—we were already registered—it is possible to move around the campus freely. We wandered through your building, as well as those of all the others: Diener & Diener, Saana, Moneo, Gehry, Chipperfield, Ando, Taniguchi, and Märkli. The campus is the headquarters of a globally active pharmaceutical company. At the time, some eight thousand people from around the world were working there.

Adolf Krischanitz: This campus in Basel is one of the most ambitious architecture projects in Europe, if not globally, of recent decades. Based on the master plan by Vittorio Magnago Lampugnani, a "center of knowledge" has been created on the thirty-hectare-large site since 2002 and is still growing. This center of knowledge consists of buildings for research, development, and administration positioned in open spaces designed with equally high quality. Each new building phase within the framework of the master plan is developed according to specific guidelines. The Vitra Campus located only five kilometers away in Weil on the other side of the Rhine perhaps served as a yardstick—and the Novartis Campus has long since outdone it alone in terms of quantity.

The whole thing reminds me of the legendary commitment of the Olivetti group in Ivrea, between Turin and Milan, where, from the nineteen-thirties to the seventies, an exemplary production and residential city was created, a pantheon of contemporary architecture with the best Italian and international architects of the time. Your building in Basel, drafted with Birgit Frank, was a unique opportunity, a challenge. How did it come about?

After the already established administration and office structures, it was the first laboratory and development building there. Novartis wanted a building that allowed, and even specifically facilitated, communication between researchers. I was invited along with four other architectural offices to take part in the competition.

Network of Creating Space

You prepended a declaration of principle to your presentation portfolio for the competition: "Poetics

dionysischen Motiven, von rationalen und transrationalen Vorgängen in so einem Forschungslabor. Und dann kommt eine große Reverenz an die Schriften von Gottfried Semper, der am Zürcher Polytechnikum lehrte und ein wissenschaftliches Werk über die Entwicklung von Kunst und Baukunst aus den sozialen, technischen und regionalen Vektoren der Kulturen verfasste.

Ja – und im Zentrum seines Buches steht das Kapitel über die Kunstwerdung des Technischen durch den Wechsel der Formstrukturen von einem Material in ein anderes, meist ein dauerhafteres. Und beide Aspekte, das Textile als Sempers archetypische »techne« und der erwähnte »Stoffwechsel« haben mich bei diesem Entwurf inspiriert.

Auf der ersten Seite des Portfolios zeigtest du Abbildungen aus Sempers Buch – verschiedene Knotenbildungen aus Fäden, Seilen oder Stäben, Flechtwerke, Gewebestrukturen, der Flächenaufbau durch Webmuster. Diese Hinweise sind in den Publikationen und Kommentaren über den Laborbau aufgegriffen worden. Der »Faltenrock« der Glasfassaden wurde intensiv analysiert, ein wenig auch die Bodenmuster von Gilbert Bretterbauer. Ich möchte aber noch eine andere, ergänzende Lesart des Hauses und dieser Aspekte vorschlagen.

Da bin ich aber gespannt, und was wäre das?

Kommunikation ist Netzwerkbildung, Verwebung von Einzelfäden zum immer weiterwachsenden Teppich des einschlägigen Firmen-Knowhows. Man sagt ja, dass mehr als drei Viertel der Erkenntnisse der Grundlagen- und Produktforschung aus der Kommunikation der Beteiligten entstehen. Ich sehe die von dir zitierten Knoten Sempers als Kürzel für die Raum-, die Trag- und Fassadenstruktur des Gebäudes. Es ist eben nicht der klassische Büro- oder Laborbau mit minimiertem Trag- und Versorgungsskelett, mit den klassischen Raumzellen, ummantelt von einer homogenen Curtain Wall, sondern etwas ganz anderes.

Es fing tatsächlich bei dieser Grundfrage an, wie man für ein extrem hochinstalliertes Gebäude, dessen Etagen flexibel teilbar und nutzbar sein sollen, die Infrastruktur der Versorgung und Entsorgung mit allen Medien – Strom, Wasser, Licht, Chemikalien, Datenleitungen, Lüftung, Heizung, Kühlung usw. – als offenes, polyvalentes Netzwerk anlegen könnte, und zwar in einem Raumgitter, das zugleich die leichte Kommunikation anbietet – zwischen den Labors und den Büros wie auch zwischen den Einzellabors und den allge-

of a Workplace." You make reference in an almost Faustian manner to the intertwining of Apollonian and Dionysian motifs, of rational and transrational processes in such a research laboratory. And then comes great reverence for the writings of Gottfried Semper, who taught at the Polytechnikum in Zurich and wrote a scientific work about the development of art and architecture from the social, technical, and regional vectors of cultures.

Yes, and in the center of his book is the chapter about the technical becoming art through the change of form structures from one material into another, generally more enduring material. And both aspects, the textile as Semper's archetypal *techne* and the *Stoffwechsel* (metabolism) mentioned, inspired me in the case of this design.

On the first page of the portfolio, you showed pictures from Semper's book—various images of knot formations of threads, ropes, or rods, wickerwork, textile structures, of creating surfaces using woven patterns. These references were taken up in the publications and commentaries on the laboratory building. The "pleated skirt" of the glass façades has been intensively analyzed, and Gilbert Bretterbauer's floor pattern quite a bit as well. But I would like to propose yet another, supplementary way of reading the building and these aspects.

Well, I'm very curious, and what would that be?

Communication is about building networks, about weaving individual threads into a carpet of relevant company know-how that continues growing. It's said that more than three quarters of the insights of basic and product development research arise from communication among the participants. I see the knots of Semper that you cite as a shorthand symbol for the building's spatial, load-bearing, and façade structure. It is not a classic office or laboratory building with a minimized load-bearing and supply skeleton, with classic room modules, enclosed by a homogeneous curtain wall, but something quite different.

It did in fact start with the fundamental question of how, in a very highly specialized building with floors that are supposed to be capable of being divided up and used flexibly, one might lay out the infrastructure for supplying and disposing of all media—electricity, water, light, chemicals, data cables, ventilation, heating, air-conditioning, and so on—as an open, polyvalent network. The idea was to do so within a spatial lattice that simulta-

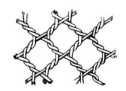

Beispiele von Knoten aus: / Sample knots from: Gottfried Semper, *Der Stil in den technischen und tektonischen Künsten, oder Praktische Ästhetik*, Frankfurt am Main und München 1860–1863; Reprint 1977

meinen Flächen für Seminare, Workshops, Konferenzen und den informellen Austausch.

Wie hast du dieses Raumgitter dann letztlich gefunden?

Wenn du den Grundriss betrachtest, siehst du im Kern eine breit gefächerte Verteilung von massiven, fixen Elementen. Das sind sozusagen die Hauptknoten. Wir teilten die Stränge der Ver- und Entsorgung auf zwölf Einheiten auf, die auch die vertikale Tragstruktur des Ganzen bilden. Dann führten wir die horizontale Verteilung aller Medien immer von den Etagendecken herab. So blieben die Bodenflächen frei, völlig flexibel. Durch die weitmaschige Stellung der Vertikalschächte ist einerseits die Versorgung der Grundfläche dicht und polyvalent, und andererseits reduzierten wir so die Querschnitte der luftführenden Horizontalschächte. Was wir durch die Verteilung der Kerne über die Geschossfläche gegenüber Standardlösungen im Grundriss an Fläche einbüßten, konnten wir in der Höhe beziehungsweise durch geringere Deckenstärken und die gleichmäßige mediale Versorgung mehr als wettmachen. Das ergab – im vorbestimmten Gebäudeumriss! – einen Qualitätsgewinn aller Etagen durch größere Raumhöhen als üblich: 280 Zentimeter; weiters viel Einsparungen an Deckenkonstruktionen und die Flexibilität des Gesamtsystems.

Flechtwerk der Dimensionen

Noch bevor ich den Bau sehen konnte, faszinierten mich die fast ornamentalen, digitalen Grundrisspläne der Laboretagen. Ist es nicht so wie bei den Flechtwerk-Beispielen Sempers, dass da abwechselnd enge und weite Maschen generiert werden – größere Öffnungen als Zentren und kleinteiligere Verknüpfungen an den Rändern?

Es geht noch weiter! In den einseitig offenen, in sich steifen Hohlkästen der Primärstruktur aus Stahlbeton ist die vertikale Durchlässigkeit des gesamten Raumes und im Speziellen des zentralen Atriums schon angelegt – struktiv und formal. An den äußeren Rändern benötigte dieses Raumwerk dann nur mehr punktuelle Stützung, die stählernen Pendelstützen hinter der Glashaut, die nur Normalkräfte abtragen müssen, daher sehr zart sein können und so die durchgängige Transparenz und Freiheit der Fassade eröffnen.

Wir haben in der skizzenhaften Beschreibung des Baugefüges Sempers Netzformeln von Raumbildung

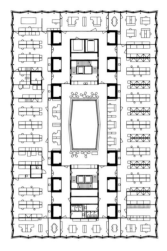

0301
Laborgebäude / Laboratory Building Novartis Campus, Basel, 2003–2007
Grundriss 3. OG / Floor plan, 4th floor

S. / pp. 160/161

neously facilitates easy communication—between the labs and the offices, as well as between the individual labs and the general areas for seminars, workshops, conferences, and informal exchange.

How did you then ultimately arrive at this spatial lattice?

When you look at the layout, you see a diversified arrangement of solid, fixed elements in the core. These are, so to say, the main nodes. We divided the supply and waste disposal lines into twelve units that also form the vertical load-bearing structure of the whole. We then always conducted the horizontal distribution of all the media down from the ceiling of each floor. This allows the floor surfaces to remain free and completely flexible. As a result of the wide-meshed position of the vertical shafts, on the one hand, the supply of the floor area is concentrated and polyvalent and, on the other, we also reduced the cross-sections of the horizontal shaft with the air supply. What we forfeited in terms of area, as a result of distributing the cores over the floor area in comparison to laying them out using standard solutions, we were able to more than make up for in the height and/or by means of smaller slab thicknesses and the consistent supply of media. This served—in the predetermined building structure!—to enhance quality for all the floors as a result of room heights that, at 280 centimeters, are greater than usual. And, in addition, it resulted in significant savings on ceiling structures and the flexibility of the overall system.

Interwoven Structure of Dimensions

Even before I had the chance to see the building, I was fascinated by the nearly ornamental, digital floor plans for the laboratory floors. Isn't it similar to the case of Semper's examples of interwoven structures in that alternating close and wide meshes are generated in them—larger openings as centers and smaller-format links on the edges?

It goes even further! The vertical permeability of the whole space, especially of the central atrium, is already established—structurally as well as formally—in the inherently stiff, hollow box sections of the reinforced-steel primary structure that are open to one side. On the outer edges, this spatial structure then only required selective supports, the steel pendulum supports behind the glass skin,

erwähnt. Und das ist der Punkt, wo sich – die Assoziation von Textilem oder Kristallinem übersteigend – eine andere Semantik anzeigt. Nimm' einmal die Glasfassaden: Ich sehe da weniger den Faltenrock oder das Thema expressiver, kristalliner Glasästhetik. Es ist nicht einfach eine plissierte, gefältelte Vorhangfassade, ich sehe sie eher als eine große Stapelung – ein »Tafelwerk« von Paravents!

Du meinst die früher in Ostasien und auch bei uns gebräuchlichen faltbaren Raumteiler, die tragbaren Faltwände.

Ja. Diese in leichter Knickung ihrer klappbaren Teile aufgestellten Wandschirme dienten als transitorische Gliederung, als leichte Teilung von Räumen. Sie ziehen gewisse Grenzen, doch ist die Kontinuität der Räume weiter spürbar, sichtbar. Und diese Elastizität, das wellenartige Ineinander von Grenze und Öffnung, ist auch der Grundzug deines Laborgebäudes, der Raumstruktur wie ihrer Hülle. Solche Elastizität zeigt sich – abgewandelt, gleichsam in anderer Tonart – auch an bisher wenig rezipierten Details der Fassade. Obwohl auf den ersten Blick so homogen, ist sie geometrisch fein differenziert.

Die Fassade des Erdgeschosses hat generell flachere Knickungen als die oberen Etagen; auch variieren die Höhen der Einzelteile: Das Sockelgeschoss ist am höchsten (mit einer inneren Raumhöhe von 6 Metern!), der erste Stock ist höher als der zweite und dritte und etwas niedriger als der oberste Stock.

Und wer noch genauer hinsieht, wird auch spüren: Die Rhythmen, die Achsmaße der Schmal- und Längsfassaden sind verschieden. Und um das im Rundherum zu verbinden, hast du die äußeren Felder der Längsseiten jeweils sukzessive etwas breiter gemacht, damit über Eck die Symmetrie gegeben ist.

Knicklinien, Flächenfaltung

Die Differenz bei den Obergeschossen, die im Rauminneren ja gleich hoch sind, kommt aus den konstruktiven Fakten beim unteren und oberen Rand und ist anhand der Schnittpläne gut nachzuvollziehen. Diese Paravent-Geschichte ist interessant. Ich sehe nur, dass da genauso die Analogie zum Textilen gegeben ist. Denn üblicherweise waren das filigrane Rahmen, die mit Stoffen oder mit Flechtwerken bespannt waren, aus pflanzlichem Material, aus Bast, aus Rohr oder Spänen usw., später erst mit opaken Flächen – die japanischen

which only have to deal with axial forces and can therefore be very delicate and thus open up the consistent transparency and freedom of the façade.

In the description of Semper's building structures that we outlined, we only mentioned mesh formulas for creating space. And that is the point at which—going beyond the associations with the textile or the crystalline—a different semantics is shown. Take, for example, the glass façade: what I see there is not so much the pleated skirt or the theme of an expressive, crystalline glass aesthetics. It isn't simply a pleated, folded curtain wall. I see it more as a large act of stacking—a *Tafelwerk*, a "latticework" of screens!

You mean the room dividers, the portable folding wall panels commonly used in earlier times, both in East Asia and in Europe.

Yes. These folding screens, erected by slightly bending their hinged partitions, serve as transitory structures, as an easy way to divide spaces. They draw particular boundaries, but the continuity of the spaces continues to be visible. And this elasticity, the wave-like interplay of boundary and opening, is also the essential feature in your laboratory building, in both the spatial structure and its shell. Such elasticity is also shown—in a modified manner, quasi in another tonality—in the details of the façade, which have up to now remained little discussed. Although it seems quite homogeneous at first glance, it is actually finely differentiated in terms of geometry.

The façade of the ground floor has generally flatter bends than the upper floors; the heights of the individual sections also vary: the ground floor is the highest (with an interior room height of six meters!), while the first floor is higher than the second and third and a bit lower than the top floor.

And people who take a closer look also notice that the rhythms, the axial dimensions of the narrow and longitudinal façades are different. In order to connect this all around, you made the outer fields of the long sides successively wider so that there is symmetry at the corners.

Bending Lines, Surface Folding

The difference in the case of the upper floors, which are indeed of equal height in the interior of the space, results from the constructional facts connected with the upper and lower edge and can easily be comprehended based on the sectional

0301
Laborgebäude / Laboratory
Building Novartis Campus
Atrium

S. / pp. 164/165

Eileen Gray, Paravent, 1926
Perforiertes Metall / Perforated
metal

S. / pp. 162/163

Lackschirme! Denk' an die wunderbaren Paravents von Eileen Gray.

Sicher, und die Knicklinien dieser hybriden, mobilen Gebilde, die abschirmen und doch nicht trennen – wellenartige Gesten im Raum –, setzen sich bei Novartis in der Figuration des Atriums fort. Man erwartet das beim Eintreten in das Haus ja überhaupt nicht, diesen schwebenden, Licht fassenden, textilhaften Vertikalraum. Du hast das »Lampion« genannt, sehr treffend: Lampions sind mit durchscheinendem Material bespannte, minimale Gerüste, die Licht und Raum definieren. Vor Gebrauch sind sie flach zusammengefaltet, und im auseinandergezogenen Zustand sind immer noch die Horizontalknicke der Papieroder Stoffschirme sichtbar. Und das Atrium hier – gleichsam das Innere eines Lampions – hat ebenfalls solche Knickungen im Grundriss, im Schnitt der Parapete und schließlich im aufgedruckten Linienmuster der inneren Brüstungspaneele.

In Spannung zur Technosphäre der Labors sollte das Atrium – als zentrale Erschließungs- und Verbindungseinheit des kollektiven Raumangebots mit den spezialisierten Laboretagen – eine visionäre, festliche und lichtstrahlende Aura haben. Die Gangbrüstungen haben als äußere Schicht eine Verkleidung aus Polykarbonat-Platten. Diese sind mit cremeweißer Farbe bedruckt, und zwar die Flächen; die dünnen Lineamente sind unbedruckt, durchsichtig. Hinter diese Platten sind unzählige LED-Elemente montiert, sodass die Brüstungen morgens und abends oder anlassbezogen als Ganzes leuchten und die Lineamente wie Lichtadern darüber hinwegziehen. Die Knickungen erzeugen auch beim reinen Tageslichteinfall durch das Oberlicht wechselnde Reflexionen, eine starke Modulation der Helligkeit der »Lampionhülle«. Schon die historischen Kronleuchter hatten das Prinzip, das von der Lichtquelle erzeugte Licht weiter zu zerlegen, in tausende Lichtquanten zu zerstreuen. Und diesen Effekt haben wir ebenfalls angestrebt. In anderer Form – mit den großen Glas-Eprouvetten an den Decken – ist dieses Prinzip in den Sitzungsräumen weitergeführt.

Knicklinien und grafische Netze mit Knoten verwendete auch Gilbert Bretterbauer für die Gestaltung der Böden in den gemeinschaftlichen Räumen. Im Erdgeschoss gliederte er damit die mittlere Fläche. Der Teppichboden in Moosgrün und Mittelgrau und deine drehbaren Lederfauteuils, Hocker und Beistelltischchen bieten mitsamt den Durchblicken zu den Konferenz- und Workshop-Räumen eine Atmosphäre, die jeder noblen Hotellobby, jedem Konzerthaus-

plans. This paravent story is interesting. To me it seems that the exact same analogy to the textile is present here. Indeed, filigree frames were normally spanned with fabric or with woven work, made of vegetal matter, of raffia, cane, or shavings, and so on, and not with opaque surfaces until later—the Japanese lacquered screens! Just think of the wonderful ones by Eileen Gray.

Of course, and in the case of the Novartis building, the bending lines of these hybrid, mobile structures that screen and yet don't separate—wave-like gestures in space—are continued in the design of the atrium. When one enters the building, one does not at all expect this floating, light-catching, textile-like vertical space. You quite aptly named it the "Lampion," since lampions are minimal frameworks spanned with translucent material that define the light and space. Before being used, they are folded flat, and when they are their unfolded state, the horizontal folds in the paper or fabric shades are still visible. And the atrium here—the inside of a lampion, as it were—also has such folds in the horizontal section, in the pattern of the parapets, and finally in the line pattern imprinted on the inner panels of the balustrade.

In the interplay with the techosphere of the labs, the atrium—as a central access and connection unit of the overall space available on the specialized laboratory floors—was supposed to have a visionary, festive, and luminous aura. The passageway balustrades have a cladding of polycarbonate panels as an outer layer. These are printed in a creamy-white shade, but only the surfaces; the thin line elements are unprinted, transparent. Innumerable LED elements are mounted behind these panels so that the balustrades can be illuminated in the morning and evening or as a whole depending on the occasion, and the lines run across them like arteries of light. The folds also produce changing reflections in the natural daylight coming from the roof light, a powerful modulation of the luminosity of the "shell of the lampion." Historical chandeliers already worked with the principle of further dispersing or scattering the light generated by the light source into thousands of photons. And this is the effect that we were also striving for. This principle is also taken up in another form—with the large glass test tubes on the ceiling—in the meeting rooms.

Gilbert Bretterbauer also used bending lines and graphic networks with nodes for the design of the floors in the communal spaces. On the ground floor,

Foyer gut anstehen würde. Das Muster, das Analogien zu Molekularstrukturen andeutet, wiederholt sich dann auf den Galeriegängen im Atrium, dort aber in hellen Tönen und in geschliffenem Terrazzo: eine Art Stoffwechsel, gewiss. Du hast mit Bretterbauer unter anderem bei den Innenräumen der Swiss Re in Zürich kooperiert. Wie war das hier? Sprecht ihr euch ab? Wie kommt er auf die Muster?

Zuvor noch ein Wort zu den Biologie- und Chemie-Labors: Wir haben mit Konsulenten da jede Menge neuer Dinge entwickeln können, von der Haustechnik- und Lichtdecke bis zu den Glastüren und Glaswänden und dem gesamten Mobiliar. Farbige Akzente und Unterstützung der Orientierung bringen die Böden in Kautschuk, wobei jede Etage eine andere Farbe hat – blau, gelb, rot, grün – und diese sich, vor allem abends oder morgens bei eingeschalteter Beleuchtung, auch in den Reflexionen an Decken und Schrankwänden bemerkbar macht.

Gottfried Semper

Ich komme auf Semper und seine Schriften zurück. Du erinnerst dich, *Der Stil* war eines der ersten Bücher, das wir für unsere damals noch gemeinsame Atelierbibliothek gekauft haben.

Wir hatten erstmals ein wenig Überschuss auf dem Konto, haben das Atelier am Getreidemarkt günstig mieten können. Es war 1977, das Buch erschien im Reprint. Semper war uns wohl als Architekt der pompösen Wiener Hofburg-Erweiterung und der großen Museen bekannt, aber überhaupt nicht weiter interessant.

Als ich das Buch in der damals einzigen einschlägigen Buchhandlung Wiens sah, griff ich sofort zu. Es war, wie man so sagt, eine Primärerfahrung. In den Studienjahren hatte man nichts davon gehört. Und nun entdeckte man ein Kompendium an technischer, künstlerischer und anthropologischer Recherche. Für mich war damals unfassbar, wie ein praktizierender Architekt diese Masse an historischem, technischem und sozialem Wissen erarbeiten konnte – und in eine kulturgeschichtliche Evolutionstheorie fassen konnte!

Wobei sekundär ist, ob er in allem Recht hatte. Allein die methodische Leistung, die Schönheit und Prägnanz der geistigen Durchdringung so vieler Grundfragen der Kultur faszinierte uns einfach. Nicht zu vergessen seine interessanten

he used them to structure the central area. The wall-to-wall carpet in moss green and medium gray and your rotating leather armchairs, stools, and side tables, along with the view through to the conference and workshop room, have an atmosphere that would fit wonderfully into any classy hotel lobby and any concert-house foyer. The pattern, which suggests analogies to molecular structures, is then repeated on the balcony passageways in the atrium, but here in bright shades and in a polished terrazzo: a type of metabolism, certainly. You cooperated with Bretterbauer on the interiors of the Swiss Re building in Zurich, among other projects. How did it work here? Did you discuss things with each other? How did he come up with the pattern?

Before answering that, I'd like to say another word about the biology and chemistry labs: we were able to develop quite a few new things in cooperation with the consultants, from the building technology and illuminated ceiling to the glass doors and walls, and all of the furnishings. The rubber floors bring in color accents and serve as orientation aids, since every floor has a different color—blue, yellow, red, green—and this also becomes perceptible in the reflections on the ceilings and wall units, above all in the evening or the morning when the lights are turned on.

Gottfried Semper

I'd like to return to Semper and his book. You'll remember that *Practical Aesthetics* was one of the first books that we bought for the library of the studio that we shared at the time.

We had a bit of extra money in the account for the first time, since we'd been able to rent the studio on Getreidemarkt quite inexpensively. It was 1977, and a reprint of the book was published. We were familiar with Semper as the architect of the pompous extension to the Vienna Hofburg and the big museums, but he was otherwise of no interest.

When I saw a copy in the only bookshop in Vienna that sold such books at the time, I grabbed it immediately. It was, as one says, a primary experience. We hadn't heard anything about it when we were studying. And now there was this compendium of technical, artistic, and anthropological research. At the time, I found it inconceivable that a practicing architect could process such a mass of historical, technical, and social knowledge—and summarize it in a historico-cultural theory of evolution!

Gottfried Semper, *Der Stil*, Titelseite Band I / Title page, vol. I, 1860

0301
Laborgebäude Novartis Campus
Längsschnitt / Longitudinal section

»Im Gebäude spannt sich der Raum wie in einem Stickrahmen auf. Die einzelnen Geschosstableaus, von den Säulenschächten und den filigranen Fassadenstücken auf Abstand gehalten, tragen die Funktionsgeflechte der Laborebene. Auch die Fassade, eine in Falten gelegte Glaskonstruktion, weist in ihrer filigranen Anmutung, ihrer oszillierenden Innen-Außen-Wirkung auf das Textile.«

Adolf Krischanitz,
Rede zur Eröffnung des Novartis-Laborgebäudes, 2008

Kontroversen mit Karl Bötticher, die vor allem Heinz Quitzsch in seinen Studien erläutert hat.

Und dann wurde auch klar und nachvollziehbar, wie und warum Semper einen so großen Einfluss auf Otto Wagner und Adolf Loos hatte. Im selben Jahr entdeckten wir auch, vom Atelier gleich um die Ecke, sein damals leer stehendes, vom Abbruch bedrohtes Kulissendepot für die Wiener Oper – eigentlich sein Hauptwerk in Wien, viel wichtiger und »moderner« als seine Ringstraßenbauten.

1977 gab es in Wien eine Ausstellung über die Möglichkeiten der Neunutzung dieses riesigen Werkstatt- und Depotgebäudes, typischerweise nicht von Wien aus, sondern vom Münchner Lehrstuhl von Friedrich Kurrent erarbeitet. Es dauerte dann mehr als zehn Jahre, bis diese grandiosen Räume nach der Adaptierung als Atelierhaus der Akademie durch Carl Pruscha wieder vollständig nutzbar wurden.

Gehen wir nochmals zu den Knoten zurück, zu deinen Ideen, das »wie aus Papier oder weißem Stoff gefaltete« Atrium des Novartis-Labors in eine »Stimmung von Damast« zu bringen. Wir könnten noch einen Schritt weitergehen und die ornamentale Welt des Textilen, des Webens und Flechtens im Sinne der Cultural Studies verstehen. Da steht das Textile, als archetypisch weibliche Domäne, für eine subversive Textualität jenseits beziehungsweise innerhalb der offiziellen Sprache. Und darin spiegelte sich ein Großteil der Ornamentphobie der klassischen, patriarchalen Law-and-Order-Modernität, nicht nur in der Architektur. Vermutlich führt uns das jetzt in vages Terrain. Oder? Aber mit dem Hinweis auf

Whether he was right about everything is actually secondary. We were simply fascinated by the methodological achievement alone; the beauty and conciseness of intellectually penetrating so many fundamental cultural questions simply fascinated us. Not to forget his interesting controversies with Karl Bötticher, which, above all, Heinz Quitzsch elucidated in his studies.

And then it became clear and understandable how and why Semper had such a big influence on Otto Wagner and Adolf Loos. The same year, just around the corner from the studio, we also discovered his scenery warehouse for the Vienna Opera, which was standing empty and in danger of being torn down at the time—it was actually his main work in Vienna and much more significant and "modern" than all of his buildings on Ringstrasse.

In 1977, there was an exhibition in Vienna about the possibilities of a new use for this huge workshop and warehouse building, however, as was typical, not organized starting in Vienna but instead by Friedrich Kurrent's professorship in Munich. It then took more than ten years before these magnificent spaces were usable as a whole after Carl Pruscha converted it into a studio building for the Akademie.

Let's go back once again to the knots or nodes, to your ideas for making the atrium "folded as if made of paper or white fabric," for giving the Novartis laboratories an "ambiance of damask." We might go yet a step further and comprehend the ornamental world of the textile, of weaving and braiding, in the sense of cultural studies. There, the textile stands for an archetypal female domain, for a subversive textuality beyond and/or within official language. And reflected in this is a large part of the ornament phobia of classical, patriarchal law-and-order modernity, not only in architecture. This presumably now leads us into vague terrain. Or not? But, as I mentioned earlier, you did also address this—if only peripherally—with your reference to Apollo and Dionysus in the Novartis portfolio . . .

For me this reference is quite noteworthy. A research laboratory is not simply a place of applied knowledge. In addition to the virtues of applying knowledge rationally and scientifically, which I euphemistically referred to as "Apollonian" in the competition phase—usually with a male connotation—there are also "Dionysian" insights, which generally have a female connotation and are to be found more in repressed and under-

Apollo / Dionysos im Novartis-Portfolio hast du das doch, wie eingangs erwähnt, auch angesprochen – wie peripher auch immer …

Für mich ist dieser Hinweis durchaus bemerkenswert. Ein Forschungslabor ist eben nicht ausschließlich ein Ort angewandten Wissens. Neben den Tugenden einer rationalen wissenschaftlichen Anwendung von Erkenntnissen, die ich in der Wettbewerbsphase euphemistisch als »apollinisch« bezeichnet habe – und die in der Regel männlich konnotiert sind –, gibt es auch »dionysische«, im Allgemeinen eher weiblich konnotierte Erkenntnisse, die eher in den verdrängten und unterschätzten Schichten menschlichen Seins zu finden sind. Zur Verbesserung der menschlichen Konstitution als Zielvorstellung jeder Wissenschaft bedarf es der Erkenntnisse aus der männlichen und aus der weiblichen Lebens- und Denksphäre.

Autobahn-Zentrale Wien

Die Novartis-Labors waren nicht dein erstes gewerbliches Projekt, aber sicher das bisher komplexeste und in den Randbedingungen am besten ausgestattete. Zuvor konntest du in Wien die Rechner- und Informationszentrale der österreichischen Autobahngesellschaft ASFINAG realisieren. Das Grundstück war – wieder einmal – eine Extremlage: ein Dreieck zwischen den am meisten befahrenen Straßenstücken im Süden der Stadt, ein Zwickel, an dem zwei Autobahnen im spitzen Winkel zusammentreffen.

Ich habe das in Zusammenarbeit mit der Freiraumplanerin Anna Detzlhofer als »Landschaftsersatzteil« interpretiert: an diesem Un-Ort ein Stück künstlich geschaffener »Natur« als widerständige Insel zwischen den Straßenschneisen. Es macht ja Sinn, dass sich das technische Autobahnmanagement mitten ins Geschehen setzt und nicht irgendwo in einen lauschigen Park. Wir haben das Grundstück mit einem geschosshohen begrünten Zaun umgeben, die Bepflanzung weiter unters Gebäude gezogen und auch das Hauptgeschoss intensiv bewachsen lassen. Zaun und Gebäude und Baumgruppen ergeben zusammen einen grünen Keil. Und aus dieser »Kunstnatur« auftauchend befindet sich »on top« ein Observatoriumsgeschoss aus Glas, das bereits über den Autobahnniveaus liegt und sowohl Aussichtsplattform ist als auch – für die von Süden darauf zufahrenden, hier in die Stadt eintauchenden Fahrzeuge – als leuchtender Signalkörper wirkt.

estimated layers of human existence. Improving the human constitution as an objective of all science requires insights from both male and female spheres of life and thought.

Autobahn Center in Vienna

The Novartis laboratories were not your first commercial project, but surely the most complex and best equipped with respect to the basic conditions up to now. Before that project, you had the opportunity to realize the central computer and information offices of the Austrian autobahn corporation ASFINAG in Vienna. The property was—once again—an extreme location: a triangle between the most congested sections of road in the south of the city, a point at which two autobahns come together at an acute angle.

Working with the spatial planner Anna Detzlhofer, I interpreted it as a "spare piece of landscape": a piece of artificially fashioned "nature" at this non-place as a resistant island between the lanes of road. It indeed makes sense to situate the technical management of the autobahn in the middle of the action and not somewhere in a secluded park. We surrounded the property with a story-high greened fence, pulled the planting further beneath the building, and also allowed the main story to become intensively greened. Together, the fence and building and groups of trees result in a green wedge. And emerging from this "art-nature," situated "on top," is a glass observatory that already lies above the level of the autobahn and is a viewing platform while also serving as a luminescent signal device for vehicles approaching it from the south and entering the city here.

Atrium on Company Grounds

For a leading global producer of citric acid, you recently realized a company headquarters to the north of Vienna. It is also an atrium building, but much smaller and simpler. At this point, I have to ask a tangential question: What do people use citric acid for?

Citric acid is a water-soluble preservative obtained through fermenting corn, and trace amounts of it are added to industrially produced foodstuffs and beverages around the world. In the idyllic agricultural landscape at the Austrian-Czech border is a factory with its own rail siding, its own routing

S. / pp. 180–183

0108
Verkehrsrechenzentrale / Traffic Computer Center ASFINAG, Wien-Inzersdorf, 2001–2003 Im Zwickel zweier Autobahn-Trassen am Südrand von Wien / At the junction of two highway routes along Vienna's southern border

Atrium im Werksgelände

Für einen global führenden Hersteller von Zitronensäure hast du kürzlich einen Konzernsitz nördlich von Wien realisiert. Es ist ebenfalls ein Atriumhaus, doch viel kleiner und einfacher. Bei dieser Gelegenheit muss ich eine Nebenfrage stellen: Wozu braucht man Zitronensäure?

Zitronensäure ist ein wasserlösliches, aus der Fermentierung von Mais gewonnenes Konservierungsmittel, das weltweit bei industriell hergestellten Nahrungsmitteln und Getränken in Spuren zugemengt wird. In idyllischer Agrarlandschaft an der österreichisch-tschechischen Grenze steht da eine Fabrik mit eigenem Gleisanschluss, eigener Trasse der Hochspannungsleitung und riesigen Kläranlagen – eine von mehreren Produktionsstätten der Firma Jungbunzlauer. Diese expandiert beständig, ist aus einem bescheidenen Familienunternehmen kontinuierlich gewachsen.

Die Produktionshallen sind sehr groß und konsequent in Weiß gehalten, sie sind durch ihre Fassaden introvertiert, geschlossen, funktionieren mit Oberlichten, Sheddächern. Die Konzernleitung wollte dort ein neues Büro- und Konferenzzentrum errichten lassen, auch für die Meetings ihrer Topleute aus aller Welt. Das Volumen für diese Funktion ist neben den bestehenden Werkshallen relativ klein. Es kann in Zukunft vielleicht wachsen, weshalb der Bau auch für die spätere Aufstockung mit zwei weiteren Etagen konzipiert ist. Aber im Moment sind es lediglich drei Etagen.

Du hast dort eine quadratische Grundfigur mit quadratischem Hof entworfen, überdacht, innere Galeriegänge, die Außenfassaden verglast, die vier Ecken leicht gerundet. Dort befinden sich, diagonal gegenüberliegend, spezielle Räume: die Sanitärbereiche (mit Mattverglasung) beziehungsweise die Stiegen und Lifte (klar verglast); und dann umgürtet das Ganze außen ein Rahmenwerk aus Sichtbeton, das vom gerundeten Quadrat in eine kontinuierliche Ringform übergeht, fast ein Kreis wird. Warum?

Die neue Werkszentrale muss sich maßstäblich und formal gegenüber den benachbarten Hallen klar behaupten können. Sie hat aus diesem Grund eine rundum ausstrahlende und fokussierende Wirkung. Das erzielt ein zentripetaler, an den Kreis angenäherter Körper besser als ein prismatischer, wobei die reine Kreisform schon wieder zu statisch, zu »ruhig« sein würde. Das ist ein Aspekt. Der andere: Für die Büros ist der orthogonale

0910
Büroneubau / Office Building
Jungbunzlauer, Niederösterreich /
Lower Austria, 2009–2012

S. / pp. 167–175

of power lines, and huge wastewater treatment plants—one of several production sites belonging to the Jungbunzlauer company. It is constantly expanding, continually growing from its origins as a modest family business.

The production halls are extremely large and painted white throughout. As a result of their façades, they are introverted, closed, and have transom windows and shed roofs. The company management wanted to have a new office and conference center erected there, also designed to accommodate meetings with their top people from around the world. For this function, the volume is relatively small in comparison to the existing work halls. It might grow in the future, which is why the building is also designed to allow two additional floors to be added later. But at the moment, there are only three stories.

You created a basic square form there with a square courtyard, roofed over, inner balcony passageways, glass outer façades, and the four corners slightly rounded. Situated diagonally opposite are special spaces: the sanitary areas (with matte glazing) or the stairways and elevators (clear glazed); and the whole thing is then girded on the outside by a framework of exposed concrete, which devolves from the rounded square into a continuous ring shape, nearly becoming a circle. Why?

The corporate headquarters has to be able to clearly assert itself in scale and form with respect to the neighboring halls. This is the reason why it has an all-around radiating and focusing effect. This aims at a centripetal corpus approximating a circle more than a prismatic one, whereby a pure circle shape would already again be too static, too "calm." That is one factor.

The other: for the offices, the orthogonal perimeter is simpler and much more practical. Indeed, here the offices are closed toward the atrium and instead open up on one side toward the exterior—as desired by the company. And the consequence here was realizing the shading of the room-high glass surfaces by means of broad, circumferential, fixed sunshades. At the same time, such an external spatial framework offers a visual framing and expansion of the offices from the viewpoint of the users—in surroundings where, as mentioned earlier, the large-format and hermetically sealed halls are extremely present. The autonomous, thermally separated latticework of concrete elements, which only touches the

Perimeter einfacher, viel praktischer. Nachdem hier – wie intern gewünscht – die Büros zum Atrium hin geschlossen sind, öffnen sie sich einseitig nach außen. Und da war die Konsequenz, die Verschattung der raumhohen Glasflächen durch breit umlaufende, fixe Sonnenbrecher zu erzielen. Zugleich bietet ein solches äußeres Raumfachwerk eine optische Fassung und Erweiterung der Büros aus der Sicht der Benutzer – in einem Umfeld, in dem, wie gesagt, großflächige und hermetisch abgeschlossene Hallen sehr präsent sind. So gibt das autonome, thermisch getrennte, nur punktweise den Baukörper berührende Gitterwerk aus Betonteilen dem Glaskörper eine schattenbildende, raumgreifende und tiefenwirksame Fassung.

Was auffällt sind die schlanken Proportionen der Bürotüren, die allein schon den Umgängen im Atrium eine gewisse Extravaganz verleihen. Diese Türen sind drei Meter hoch, und die Räume dahinter fast dreieinhalb Meter, was den Maßen der Wiener Ringstraßenpalais entspricht; weiters fallen die sorgfältigen Details der Zargen auf, der Wand- und Bodenanschlüsse, der Beschläge von Türen und Schrankwänden. In den Decken und ihren Wandanschlüssen sind die technischen Komponenten der kontrollierten Be- und Entlüftung perfekt integriert; beim Mobiliar wird nicht mit den bekannten Klassikern aufgetrumpft; schließlich gibt es am Empfang als unterschwelligen Blickfang eine Wandarbeit von Sol LeWitt, einem erstklassigen internationalen Künstler. Da wird doch eine besondere Distinktion der Bauherrschaft spürbar. Wie kam es zu dem Projekt?

Diesen Auftrag verdankten wir dem sehr baukunst- und kunstaffinen Aufsichtsratsvorsitzenden Alexander Kahane und dem gesamten Vorstandsteam, die uns einluden, einen Vorentwurf und dann die Planung für dieses Gebäude zu erstellen. Schließlich war die gemeinsame Arbeit eine, wie ich glaube, sehr beglückende Erfahrung für alle Beteiligten – bis zu den tagtäglichen Nutzern und Nutzerinnen.

Werkskantine erster Güte

Gleich daneben kam jetzt ein zweistöckiger Neubau für die Betriebsmensa und weitere Büroräume.

Die Kantine ist funktional, konstruktiv ganz anders. Sie muss sich ebenso wie die Werkszentrale gegen die Dimensionen der Umgebung behaupten und sehr unterschiedliche Funktionen – Betriebsküche und Speisesaal unten, Büroräume und Tech-

building structure at points, thus lends the glass structure a silhouetting, expansive, and deeply penetrating framing.

The slender proportions of the office doors are particularly striking and already give the tribunes in the atrium a certain extravagance. These doors are three meters high and the rooms behind them nearly 3.5, which corresponds to the measurements of the Ringstrassenpalais in Vienna; furthermore, the meticulous details of the doorframes, the wall and floor connections, the fittings on the doors and wall units also catch the eye. The technical components for aeration and ventilation are perfectly integrated in the ceilings and at the point where they meet the walls; in the case of the furnishings, there is no showing off with the well-known classics; then, at the reception desk, as a subliminal eye-catcher, is a wall work by Sol LeWitt, a first-class international artist. So, a special cachet of the client becomes perceptible. How did the project come about?

For this commission, we need to thank the great affinity for architecture and art of the Chairman of the Supervisory Board, Alexander Kahane, and the entire management board team, who invited us to create a preliminary design and then do the planning for this building. In the end, working together was, I believe, a very rewarding experience for all those involved—including the everyday occupants.

First-Class Company Cafeteria

Just recently, a new two-story building for the company cafeteria and additional office space was erected next door.

The cafeteria is functionally and structurally quite different. Like the company headquarters, it also has to hold its ground against the dimensions of the surroundings and unite quite diverse functions—company kitchen and dining hall below, office spaces and technology above them. It's a modern wooden structure and certainly unusual in proportions, with five-meter-high windows and expanses of glass. The mighty chestnut tree standing on the narrow side of the building is therefore presented in a format-filling manner from the interior. The effect is that of a simple pavilion, which, however, is not inferior to the nobility of the central office building in terms of dimensions and details.

0910
Büroneubau / Office Building
Jungbunzlauer

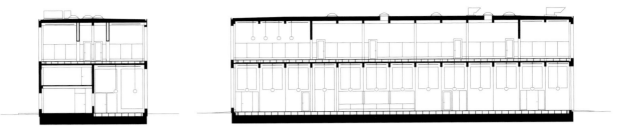

1202
Jungbunzlauer Werkskantine /
Canteen, Niederösterreich /
Lower Austria, 2012/13,
Querschnitt und Längsschnitt /
Cross section, longitudinal section

nik darüber – vereinen. Es ist ein moderner Holzbau, in den Proportionen freilich ungewöhnlich, mit 5 Meter hohen Fenster- und Glasflächen. So präsentiert sich der mächtige, an der Schmalseite des Gebäudes stehende Kastanienbaum im Innenraum formatfüllend. Die Wirkung ist die eines einfachen Pavillons, der jedoch im Maßstab und den Details der Noblesse der Bürozentrale nicht nachsteht.

Die Fotos des Speisesaals sehen sehr »aufgeräumt« aus, neben der ungewöhnlichen Raumhöhe und den großen Glasscheiben gibt es absolut nichts Spektakuläres zu sehen …

Bevor man hier an irgendetwas Optisches denken kann, haben in so einem Raum viele andere Dinge Vorrang: Akustik, Klima, Lichtstimmung, Olfaktorisches, Pflege-Logistik.

Fangen wir beim Licht an?

Nein, besser mit dem Schall. In einem Speisesaal, wo 100 und mehr Leute gleichzeitig essen und in Stoßzeiten viel Bewegung herrscht, darf es nicht zu laut werden. Deshalb gibt es in den Deckenfeldern und an der Mittelwand spezielle Elemente, von der Decke abgehängte, perforierte Metallkassetten, die den Schall schlucken. Die Wandplatten sind etwas anders konstruiert und dämpfen andere, tiefere Frequenzen. Und noch etwas: Auch die Sessel, aus meiner für Braun Lockenhaus entworfenen Kollektion, sind eigens schallgedämpft, indem die Stützrohre mit leichtem Dämmstoff gefüllt wurden. So reduziert sich auch das notorische Sesselklappern.

S. / p. 180

Die Decken- und Wandelemente, ihr nennt sie Hybridsegel, können aber auch noch mehr, wie mir dein Projektleiter berichtete.

Allerdings! Von den Decken kommt auch noch eine mögliche Beschallung aus kleinen, integrierten Lautsprechern, aber viel wichtiger noch: Diese Elemente sind auch für das Raumklima zuständig. Sie enthalten in Vlies gebettete Rohre, mit Wasser

In the photos, the dining hall looks very "tidied up," and besides the unusual height of the room and the large panes of glass, there is absolutely nothing spectacular to see …

Before it is possible to think here about anything visual, many other things take precedence in such a space: acoustics, climate, lighting atmosphere, olfactory considerations, service logistics.

Shall we start with light?

No, preferably with sound. In a dining hall where one hundred people eat at the same time and there's a lot of movement at peak times, it can't be too loud. That's why there are special elements in the ceiling panels and on the middle wall, as well as perforated metal cartridges suspended from the ceiling, to absorb noise. The wall panels are constructed somewhat differently and absorb other, deeper frequencies. And something else: the easy chairs from the collection I designed for Braun Lockenhaus are also inherently sound-damping since the support tubes are filled with a lightweight insulating material. This therefore also reduces the notorious clattering of chairs.

As your project manager has told me, the ceiling and wall elements, you call them *Hybridsegel* (hybrid sails), are also able to do even more.

Certainly! Possible acoustic irradiation also comes from the ceiling from small, integrated loudspeakers, but what is much more important is that these elements are also responsible for the indoor climate. They contain tubes that are embedded in fleece, filled with water, and connected to the main climate control system, emitting either coolness or warmth. Last but not least, these elements also contain covertly mounted lighting strips that reflect indirect light downward.

Simple spherical luminaires supplement the basic lighting with their anti-glare, uniform light and also structure the whole room.

gefüllt und mit der Klimazentrale verbunden, die entweder Kühle oder Wärme abstrahlen. Last but not least enthalten diese Elemente noch verdeckt montierte Leuchtbänder, die indirektes Licht nach unten reflektieren.

Einfache Kugelleuchten ergänzen die Grundbeleuchtung mit ihrem blendfreien, gleichmäßigen Licht und gliedern nebenbei den ganzen Raum.

Es sind die von Hermann Czech entwickelten Varianten der Standardkugeln. Zum Klima ist noch nachzutragen: In den senkrechten Wandelementen sind unsichtbar große Absaugöffnungen für den Luftkreislauf integriert. Die Einblasöffnungen liegen zwischen Sockelband und Fensterrahmen unter den großen Glasflächen.

Du hast schon bei der Werkszentrale erwähnt, dass in einer Fabrik, die täglich 1000 Tonnen Mais fermentiert, trotz höchster Umweltstandards Geruchsemissionen auftreten können und man nicht nur die Büros, sondern auch einen Speisesaal mit entsprechenden Luftfiltern ausstatten muss.

Wir haben in diesem Kantinenpavillon, wie auch in der Werkszentrale gegenüber, eine automatische Vollklimatisierung und Filter, durch die auch die Luftfeuchtigkeit fortlaufend optimiert wird, vergleichbar einem Museumsinterieur – in diesem spezifischen Produktionsareal eben unumgänglich.

Zum Schluss noch was zum Boden und über die Haustechnik?

Der Linoleumboden ist rundum mit einer Hohlkehle 26 Zentimeter an den Wänden hochgezogen, für die leichte Reinigung. Darunter sind Hohlböden – wie generell im Haus –, die alle Infrastrukturen verteilen.

Über der Küche, zwischen Speisesaal und Büroetage, wurde ein Technikgeschoss eingezogen. Wofür?

Es versorgt die Küche (und den Saal) von oben und die Büros von unten mit allen nötigen Medien, mit Luft, Wärme, Strom, Wasser usw. Der Vorteil ist, dass wir zum Beispiel für die Luftführungen minimale Wege haben und alles von dieser Techniketage aus sehr praktikabel regeln oder warten können. Die Tragkonstruktion besteht aus massiven, vorgefertigten Holzelementen mit durchgehendem Modulraster. Allerdings erhielten wir nicht die ursprünglich geplante Sichtqualität

1202
Jungbunzlauer Werkskantine /
Company cafeteria
Blick zum Bürogebäude / View of
the office building

They are a variant on the standard spheres developed by Hermann Czech. Regarding climate, it should also be added that large, concealed exhaust ports are integrated within the vertical wall elements for air circulation. The vents for blowing in air are located between the skirting band and window frame under the large expanse of glass.

In connection with the company headquarters, you've already mentioned that in a factory in which one thousand tons of corn are fermented every day, emissions of smells can occur despite the highest environmental standards, and that it is therefore necessary to equip not only offices but also a dining hall with commensurate air filters.

In this cafeteria pavilion, as well as in the headquarters opposite, we also have automatic full-climate control and filters for continuously optimizing humidity, comparable with the interior of a museum—absolutely essential for this specific production site.

To conclude, perhaps a bit of information about the flooring and the building technology?

The linoleum flooring is raised up twenty-six centimeters along the walls all around with a chamfer to make cleaning easy. Under it are cavity floors—as in general in the building—for distributing all the infrastructure.

A technical level was installed above the kitchen, between the dining hall and the office floor. Why?

It supplies the kitchen (via the hall) from above and the offices from below with all the necessary media, with air, warmth, electricity, water, and so on. The advantage is that we have minimal routes, for instance for the airflow, and are able to regulate

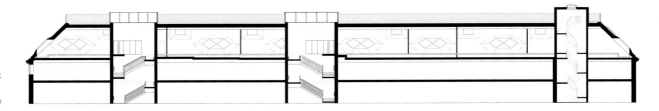

0801
Dachausbau / Roof Conversion
Oesterreichische Kontrollbank
Wien, 2008–2012
Längsschnitt / Longitudinal section

S. / pp. 192–199

für die Oberflächen. Deshalb mussten wir innen noch Dreischichtplatten aufbringen; außen gibt es einen leichten Holzschirm, hinterlüftet, über den gedämmten Konstruktionen.

Dachtransformation Wien, Innere Stadt

Schon überraschend, dass hinter einer scheinbar simplen, minimalistisch-eleganten Optik eine so komplexe Technik und Planung steht, die jenen Raumfaktoren dient, die man zwar nicht sieht, doch mit den vier anderen Sinnen wesentlich fühlt ...

Für die Oesterreichische Kontrollbank hast du im Wiener Stadtkern einige Umbauten und den Ausbau des riesigen Dachraumes geplant. Die Überformung der alten Dachlandschaft im Zuge der »Nachverdichtung« erfuhr in der Innenstadt von Wien zuletzt einen regelrechten Hype. Die Ergebnisse waren meist gestalterisch problematisch und funktional spekulativ. Wie bist du mit dem schwierigen Thema umgegangen?

Ich sehe beim Dachausbau zwei Aspekte. Der eine: Es wurde Mode, diese alte Schicht der Stadt abzuräumen und durch kontrastierende neue Aufbauten zu ersetzen, sozusagen die Altsubstanz zu deklassieren und als Plattform zu nutzen für pittoreske neue »Hüte« oder »Flieger«, die da oben eine autonome neue Welt spielen. Dem steht mein Ansatz diametral entgegen, auch bedingt durch die strengen behördlichen Auflagen, die anderswo in der Wiener Innenstadt offenbar viel »lockerer« waren.

Der andere Aspekt: Ob man nun in einen alten Dachstuhl neue Räume integriert oder dem alten Haus ein ganz neues »Top« aufsetzt – es kommt jedes Mal zu einer Transformation, zu einer räumlich und atmosphärisch besonderen Raumqualität. Und die wenigsten neuen Lösungen haben es vermocht, im Sinne von »Weiterbauen«, diese alte Dachboden-Raumreserve in eine »konsonante« neue Raumschicht vergleichbarer Kraft zu verwandeln.

Auf den ersten Blick sehe ich: Die Homogenität der steilen Dachhaut und all ihrer Konturen ist trotz

or maintain everything very practically from this technical level. The load-bearing structure consists of solid, prefabricated wooden elements with a uniform modular grid. We did not, however, achieve the visual quality for the surfaces that was originally planned. That's why we also had to mount triple-layer panels inside; outside, there is a light, back-ventilated, wooden screen over the insulated structures.

Roof Transformation in Vienna, City Center

It's quite surprising that such complex technology and planning is behind a seemingly simple, minimalist-elegant look, which serves spatial factors that may not be visible but can be fundamentally experienced with the four other senses ...

For the Oesterreichische Kontrollbank, you planned some conversions and the development of the huge roof space in the center of Vienna. The molding of the old roof landscape during the course of "densification" in the downtown Vienna recently received quite a bit of hype. The results were generally problematic in terms of design and also functionally speculative. How did you deal with this difficult topic?

When developing roofs, I see two aspects. First, it became fashionable to clear away this old layer of the city and replace it with contrasting new additions, so to say, to whitewash the old substance and use it as a platform for new, picturesque "hats" or "topsails" that feign an autonomous new world up there. My approach is diametrically opposite, also due to the strict official regulations, which were apparently much "looser" at other sites in downtown Vienna.

Second, whether one now integrates new spaces within an old attic or puts a completely new "top" on a old building—it's a transformation in any case, a spatially and atmospherically special ambient quality. And, in the sense of "further development," only very few new solutions have managed to transform these old reserves of space in attics into a "consonant" new spatial stratum.

großer neuer Öffnungen erhalten geblieben. Die Fenster sind große liegende Sechsecke und darüber kleinere Quadrate, beide wurden in ihrer Geometrie und im Formverlauf exakt in das Netz der rautenförmigen Dachplatten integriert. Und nach innen öffnen sich dann diese Fensterflächen zu breiten Trichtern. Ich empfinde es wie ein dosiertes »Atmen« der neuen Dachhaut.

Es gibt einerseits diese starke Licht-Raum-Schicht, diese Raumteile zwischen außenliegenden Glasflächen und Innenraum. Andererseits entsteht innen durch die ungewöhnlichen Raumhöhen, durch die homogene Verkleidung in Holz und die »gefaltete« Geometrie des zentralen Ganges eine Erinnerung an die Merkmale, die großen alten Dachbodenräumen generell eigentümlich waren und sind. Ich suchte nach einer solchen Umformung, nach einer Neufassung der in alten Dachstühlen immer präsenten Latenz – nach einer schwer definierbaren, irgendwie entrückten und zeitenthobenen Offenheit. Analoges versuchte ich da in einer durchgängigen Transparenz, nicht im Sinne von platter Durchsichtigkeit, sondern in der Gestaltung eines eigenständigen Raumzusammenhangs, der aber nicht ganz durchschaubar ist und gerade von der Spannung, von dieser Ambivalenz lebt.

Mir fällt auf, dass diese hexagonalen Fenster weder die üblichen Gauben oder Mansarden noch die auch oft benutzten, tiefen Terrassen-Einschnitte sind, und auch nicht das großflächige Aufschlitzen mit horizontalen oder schief geschnittenen Fensterbändern, wie es auch Mode ist.

Ich wollte den Zustand der »irregulären« Dachzone über dem mehrfach geknickten Grundriss beibehalten und dennoch in eine andere Kondition überführen. In den alten Dächern gab es verschiedene Elemente zur Einfügung von Öffnungen in die Sonderform der Dachschräge: Mansarden, Gauben, Ädikulen und dergleichen. Es gab dann auch modernistische Lösungen dieses Themas. Ich versuchte hier eine Verräumlichung innerhalb der gegebenen Schräglage mit einer Neudefinition der Syntax von Öffnung, Sturz, Laibung, Parapet – nicht im Kontrast, sondern im Einklang mit der alten Geometrie und Morphologie.

Diese liegenden Sechsecke erscheinen in der Außenhaut als leichte Auswölbung innerhalb der großen Flächen, innerhalb ihrer geometrischen Textur. Innen sind es dann kristallhafte, diamantförmige Raumausschnitte innerhalb der mit dem

At first glance, I see that the homogeneity of the steep roof cladding and all its contours has been retained despite the sizeable new openings. The windows are large, reclining hexagons and above them smaller squares, both of which were integrated precisely into the network of rhomboid roofing slabs in their geometry and form. And toward the inside, these window surfaces then open up into broad funnels. I see this as a controlled "breathing" of the new roof membrane.

On the one hand, there's this intense light-dark layer, the parts of the space between the external glass surfaces and the interior. On the other, as a result of the unusual room height, as a result of the homogeneous cladding in wood and the "folded" geometry of the central passageway, a memory of the special features that were and are generally specific to large old attic spaces arises on the inside. I sought such a transformation, a new version of the latency always present in old attics—an openness that is difficult to define, quite enraptured and timeless. Analogously, I sought a general transparency there, not in the sense of commonplace transparency, but rather in the design of a self-contained spatial context, which, however, is not completely transparent and thrives specifically on the tension, on this ambivalence.

What strikes me is that these hexagonal windows are neither the customary dormers or mansards, nor the deep terrace incisions that are frequently used, and not even the large-scale slits with horizontal or obliquely imperforated bands of windows, as are likewise fashionable.

I wanted to retain the "irregular" roof zone over the layout with its multiple bends and nevertheless transform it into another state. In the old roofs, there were various elements for inserting openings in the special shape of the pitch of the roof: mansards, dormers, aediculae, and the like. There were then also modernist solutions for this theme. Here, I tried a spatialization within the given pitch situation by redefining the syntax of opening, lintel, soffit, parapet—not in contrast to, but rather in harmony with, the old geometry and morphology.

These reclining hexagons in the exterior skin appear to be slight curvatures within the large surface, within its geometric texture. Inside, they are then crystalline, diamond-shaped spatial cutouts within the layer thickness of the pitch of the roof given by the new wall structure. The form reaches all the way downward, integrates the horizontal of the ground

0801
Dachausbau / Roof Conversion
Oesterreichische Kontrollbank

0801
Dachausbau / Roof Conversion
Oesterreichische Kontrollbank
Fensterdetail / Window detail

S. / p. 196

neuen Wandaufbau gegebenen Schichtstärke der Dachschräge. Die Form greift ganz nach unten, integriert die Horizontale des Bodens und die Schrägen von Wand und Sturz; die Öffnung hat breite umlaufende Laibungen, eigentlich ohne eigenständiges Parapet. Man kann in diese großen Nischen eintreten und aus einer intakten Dachschicht die Wiener Innenstadt und ihre Dachlandschaft wie ein Panorama überblicken; man ist eindeutig in einem Dach und zugleich an hervorgehobener Stelle über den Dächern rundum.

Kontinuum des Heterotopen

Die neuen Büroräume haben diese großen »Augen« nach draußen. Sie entstehen als Folge einer innenräumlichen Maßnahme. Die Glasflächen sind gar nicht so groß, durch die Trichterwirkung der Laibungen ist die Lichtwirkung – wie bei alten Fensternischen – aber sehr großzügig, sie ist mit Reflexionsflächen sogar verstärkt worden und erscheint auch plastisch. All das verbindet die Glasebene mit der Wandebene zu einem Kontinuum, wobei die Schattenmarkisen innen fast bündig geführt sind.

Kontinuität spüre ich auch in der Behandlung des neuen Bodens. Der geht als horizontale Holztextur durch die gesamte Etage, unter den Trennwänden und diversen Öffnungen durch, wirkt auch als gemeinsame »Festplatte« der infrastrukturellen Versorgung aller Räume, zeigt sich auch in der Ausbildung der Schwellen, Tür- und Wandanschlüsse. Als Betonung des Kontinuums sehe ich auch die Reduktion aller Details der Gangwände zugunsten der ungebrochenen Materialwirkung der ein- und ausschwingenden Paravents, das Entfallen der üblichen Elemente von Zarge und Sturz bei den als satinierte Schiebeflächen ausgebildeten Türen.

Das Gebäude ist ein Konglomerat von Zeitschichten. Es war ursprünglich ein fürstliches Palais aus der ersten Phase der Ringstraßen-Epoche, wurde noch vor der Wiener Weltausstellung von 1873 an die Anglo-Österreichische Bank verkauft, erlebte vor 1914 Umbauten, Aufstockungen nach den 1970er-Jahren, Erweiterungen in die viel älteren Häuser der Naglergasse. Wir sind hier am Steilrand der ältesten Siedlungsterrasse der Stadt. Der Dachausbau musste nicht nur die Vertikalerschließungen nachziehen und aus Gründen der Erdbebensicherheit die Statik des gesamten Gefüges ertüchtigen. Die Kontrollbank wollte von Anfang an auch die Energiebilanz verbessern. Trotz des großen Ausbaus

and the inclines of wall and lintel; the opening has broad circumferential soffits, actually without a self-contained parapet. It is possible to enter these large niches and look out over the center of Vienna and its roof landscape from an intact roof layer; one is clearly on a roof and simultaneously at an elevated position above the surrounding roofscape.

Continuum of Heterotopes

The new office rooms have these big "eyes" toward the outside, arising as a result of interior-design decisions. The glass surfaces are not really that large, but as a result of the funneling effect of the soffits, the light effect—as in the case of old window niches—is very generous, and it is even amplified with reflection surfaces and also seems sculptural. All of this connects the glass level with the wall level to create a continuum, whereby the sun blinds on the inside are nearly flush.

I also sense continuity in the treatment of the new floor. It runs as a horizontal wood texture throughout the story, under the partition walls and through diverse openings, but it also seems to be a shared "hard drive" for providing infrastructure to all the rooms and is also evident through a continuous blending of details in the thresholds, the door and wall connections. I also see the reduction of all the details in the walls of the corridor in favor of the unbroken material effect of the screens that swing in and out, the omission of the customary elements of frame and lintel in the doors formed as satined sliding surfaces as an emphasis of the continuum.

The building is a conglomerate of temporal strata. It was originally a princely palace from the first phase of the Ringstrasse epoch, was sold to the Anglo-Austrian Bank still before the Vienna World Expo of 1873, underwent conversions prior to 1914, had extra floors added to it after the nineteen-seventies, as well as additions to connect it to the many older buildings on Naglergasse. Here we are on the edge of the oldest terrace wall in the city. The rooftop development not only had to trace the vertical connecting elements and shore up the statics of the entire structure for reasons of earthquake safety; from the very beginning, the Kontrollbank also wanted to improve energy consumption. Despite the large expansion, no more operating energy than prior to the conversion was to be necessary. The entire roof zone therefore satisfies the conditions for passive buildings.

sollte nicht mehr Betriebsenergie nötig sein als vor dem Umbau. Die ganze Dachzone erfüllt deshalb Passivhaus-Konditionen.

Im Hintergrund gibt es also eine Vielzahl zusätzlicher technischer Aspekte. Ohne Details zu kennen, vermute ich, dass aus Platzmangel sehr viel der neuen Haus- und Energietechnik ebenfalls aufs Dach musste beziehungsweise in die Dachkontur einzubinden war.

Und diese Dinge blieben nicht ausgeblendet, sie wurden im Gebäude spürbar gemacht. Wie in einem alten Dachboden die Kamine und ihre Armaturen, Schachttüren, Servicetreppen etc. präsent waren, so gibt es hier im ausgebauten Dach eine optische Präsenz der Lüftungsführungen, der Stege und Brücken in den einzelnen Licht- beziehungsweise Luft-Höfen – über innere Glaswände in die Gangzonen hinein und bis in einzelne Büros spürbar. In der obersten Dachlandschaft sind diese Infrastruktur und viel Photovoltaik dann besonders exponiert. Die gesamte Silhouette wurde deshalb mit Gitterflächen und Stegstrukturen sorgfältig gestaltet – vergleichbar der Revitalisierung beim Museum 20er (heute 21er) Haus, wo die komplexe Überformung des Daches innerhalb der denkmalpflegerischen Auflagen eine neue technische und gestalterische Brisanz erhielt.

Zurich Insurance Company

Wir sind jetzt mit dem Büro- und Gewerbebau auf ein für dieses Genre untypisches Terrain komplizierter Bestands-Interventionen gelangt. In noch größerem Maßstab war das auch beim Wettbewerb für den Erweiterungsbau der Zurich Insurance Company der Fall.

Das ist ein denkmalgeschützter Bestand am Zürcher Mythenquai mit unterschiedlichen Bauhöhen, unterschiedlicher Geschossanzahl und exklusiver Lage südlich des Zentrums, am See. Dort hat die Versicherung ihr altes Stammhaus, das sie auf 1300 Arbeitsplätze samt attraktiven Konferenzbereichen und allem Drum und Dran erweitern möchte.
Bevor man überhaupt an Architektur denken kann, muss man sich da viele elementare Fragen stellen: Was vom Bestand soll wirklich erhalten bleiben, was kann ich wegnehmen, wo wird es zum Konflikt mit dem Denkmalamt kommen, was sind dann meine Argumente? Und parallel dazu: Wo ist der neue Haupteingang in diesem großen, bisher fast labyrinthischen Baublock? Wo liegt

There are therefore a large number of additional technical aspects in the background. Without knowing the details, I presume that, due to lack of space, much of the new building and energy technology also had to be integrated into the roof and/or the roof contour.

And these things do not remain hidden. They were made palpable in the building. Like in an old attic, the fireplaces and their fittings, shaft doors, service staircases, et cetera, were present. So here in the developed attic there is a visual presence of the ventilation pipes, the catwalks and bridges to the individual atria or air wells—noticeable through interior glass walls in the corridors and in some individual offices. So on the uppermost roof landscape, this infrastructure and many photovoltaic panels are particularly exposed. The whole silhouette was therefore carefully designed with grille surfaces and catwalk structures—comparable with the revitalization of the 20er (today 21er) Haus, where the complex transformation of the roof received new technical and design brisance within the historic preservation requirements.

Zurich Insurance Company

With the office and commercial buildings, we have now come to terrain that is untypical for this genre, that of complicated interventions in existing buildings. This was also the case on a still larger scale in the competition for the extension at the Zurich Insurance Company.

It is a listed complex at Mythenquai in Zurich with various building heights, different numbers of floors, and an exclusive location to the south of the city center, along the lake. The insurance company has its original, old company building there and wanted to expand it to include 1,300 workplaces along with attractive conference areas and all the trimmings.
Before it was possible to think about architecture at all, it was first necessary to ask many fundamental questions: What of the old substance should really be retained? What can be removed? Where will this lead to conflict with the authority responsible for listed historical buildings? What arguments do I then have? And in parallel: Where should the new main entrance into this large, nearly labyrinthine block of buildings be placed? Where should the new foyer be situated so that it can be connected with the conference and presentation rooms? Where then would the new

1114
Quai Zurich, Headquarters
Zurich Insurance Company Ltd
Zürich
Wettbewerb / Competition 2012
Ansicht vom Mythenquai /
View from Mythenquai

155

damit dann das neue Foyer, das mit den wichtigen Konferenz- und Präsentationsräumen verbunden sein muss? Wo kommt die neue Einfahrt zur Tiefgarage hin, wo das große, vermutlich mit spezieller Raumhöhe ausgestattete Auditorium, wo dann eine zuschaltbare Cafeteria? Wie schaffe ich eine absolut übersichtliche Orientierung von diesem neuen, vermutlich mehrere Etagen übergreifenden Foyer mit klar einsichtigen Wegen nach allen Seiten, vor allem auch zum Stammhaus am See?

Als nächstes – ganz wichtig: Wo platziere ich in diesem vermutlich immer noch etwas zerfurchten neuen Gefüge die Küche und das Restaurant – für über 1000 Leute?! Lässt sich das vielleicht aufteilen? Welche Freiraumbeziehungen kann ich schaffen für die großen Kommunikationszonen und -räume – in der gegebenen Situation? Wie hoch kann ich werden, um mit den Auflagen der Behörden zu korrelieren oder auch nicht?

Du hast vorgeschlagen, mehr als ein Drittel der Altbauten – die West- und Nordtrakte – abzubrechen und die drei absolut geschützten Trakte mit einem kammartigen Neubau von der Westseite her neu zu fassen und zu verbinden. Damit das auch zum See hinaus wirksam wird, hast du im Spalt zwischen den alten Ufertrakten einen schmalen, turmartigen Trakt hervorlugen lassen, eingekleidet in eine Glashülle mit »Diamantschliff« in Form von Rauten.

entrance to the underground garage be located, and how about the large auditorium presumably equipped with a special ceiling height or a cafeteria connected to it? How do I create absolutely clear orientation from this new foyer that will presumably span multiple stories, with clearly discernible paths to all sides, above all to the original company building at the lake?

And next, something very important: Where do I position the kitchen and restaurant—for over one thousand people!—in this presumably still somewhat furrowed new framework? Could it perhaps be split up? What connections to open space can I create for the extensive communication zones and spaces in the given situation? How high can I go in order to meet the requirements of the authorities or not?

You proposed tearing down one third of the old buildings—the west and north tracts—and framing and connecting the three absolutely protected tracts with a comb-shaped new building from the west site. So that this would also be effective toward the lake, you made a narrow, tower-like tract peek out, clad in a glass shell with a "diamond cut" in the form of rhomboids—in the gap between the old tract.

The complex analysis of the building site was essentially shaped by numerous measures, which

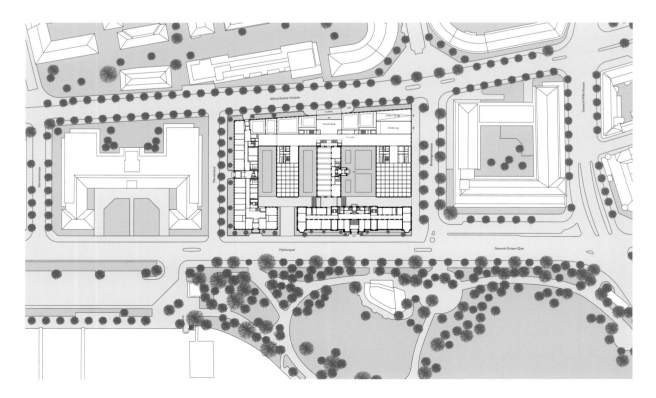

1114
Quai Zurich, Headquarters
Zurich Insurance Company Ltd
Lageplan / Situation

Die konfliktträchtige Auseinandersetzung mit dem Bauplatz war im Grunde geprägt durch mehrere Maßnahmen, die erst gemeinsam zu einem ansprechenden Ergebnis führten. Eine davon war die Verschlankung der bestehenden Gebäude auf die jeweils ursprüngliche Bautiefe und die Entkernung der bestehenden Höfe. Erst diese Maßnahmen befreiten das im Altbestand nur latent vorhandene Potenzial und ermöglichte die Setzung eines einfachen U-förmigen Baukörpers mit den erforderlichen Primär- und Komplementärtugenden, die dann zum See hin im turmartigen Bauteil des Mitteltraktes kulminieren und dort dem Areal gleichsam »aus der zweiten Reihe heraus« eine neue ikonografische Mitte, ein neues Zentrum geben.

Das Motto »in Ketten tanzen« gebrauchte Friedrich Nietzsche, um ein wesentliches Merkmal von Kunst zu beschreiben: »Es sich schwer machen und dann die Täuschung der Leichtigkeit darüberbreiten, das ist das Kunstwerk.« In deinem Œuvre gibt es eindeutig diesen Hang zum Es-sich-schwer-Machen oder das Phänomen, dass die Auseinandersetzung mit schwierigen Randbedingungen zum eigentlichen Agens der Projektfindung wurde.

Ich sehe es absolut so: Nicht das Sich-Behaupten einer autonomen neuen Idee steht im Vordergrund, sondern die Konfrontation, der ganz pragmatische Infight mit dem oft banalen, aber gesellschaftlich wirkmächtigen Gordischen Knoten der Projektkontexte. Es geht darum, diesen dann aufzulösen in ein raum-zeitliches Gewebe, das optisch nicht gleich spektakulär erscheint, doch eine Nutzungs-Matrix erzeugt, die jenseits von optisch auffälligen architektonischen Gegenständen etwas anderes, Nachhaltigeres bietet: den architektonischen Zustand.

first together led to a satisfactory outcome. One of them was streamlining the existing buildings to the respective original building depth and gutting the existing courtyards. It was first these measures that freed the potential that was only latent in the old buildings and made it possible to position a simple U-shaped building structure with the necessary primary and complementary virtues, which then culminate in the tower-like building section of the middle tract toward the lake, and there, so to speak, give the site a new iconographic middle, a new center, so to say, "from the second row."

Friedrich Nietzsche used the phrase "dancing in chains" to describe a fundamental characteristic of art: "To make things difficult for oneself but then cover it over with the illusion of ease and facility—that is the artifice they want to demonstrate for us." In your oeuvre there is also clearly this tendency toward making things difficult for yourself, or the appearance that your analysis of difficult conditions becomes the real medium for developing projects.

I see it absolutely the same way: what stands in the foreground is not the self-assertion of an autonomous new idea, but rather the confrontation, the very pragmatic infighting with the often banal, but socially influential, Gordian knot of the project contexts. What's important is then resolving it in a spatiotemporal texture that does not appear spectacular right away but nonetheless yields a utilization matrix that offers something different, something sustainable beyond visually striking architectural objects: the architectural condition.

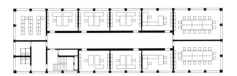

1202
Werkskantine Jungbunzlauer, +1 ↗

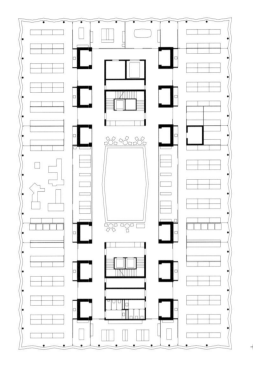

+2

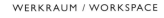

0301
Laborgebäude Novartis
Campus, 0 ↘

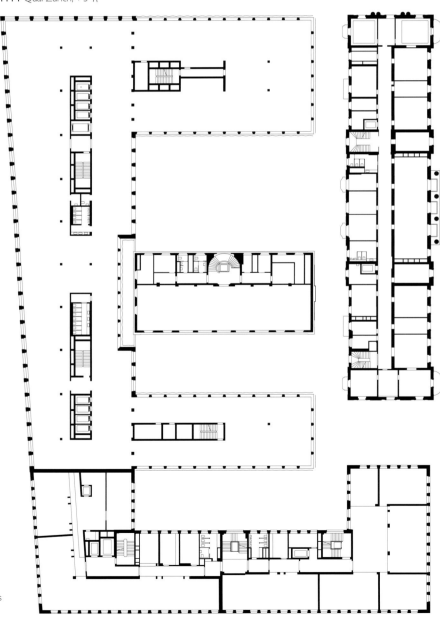

0801
Dachausbau Oesterreichische
Kontrollbank, +6 ↗

1114 Quai Zurich, +3 ⋀

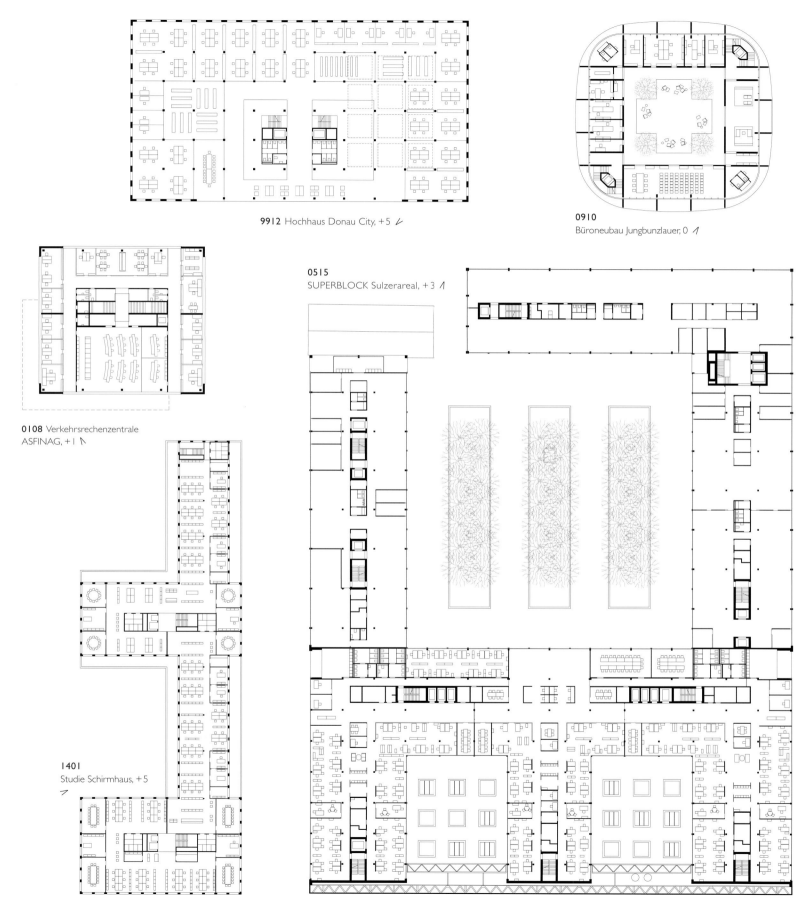

9912 Hochhaus Donau City, +5 ∠

0910
Büroneubau Jungbunzlauer, 0 ↗

0108 Verkehrsrechenzentrale
ASFINAG, +1 ↖

0515
SUPERBLOCK Sulzerareal, +3 ↗

1401
Studie Schirmhaus, +5
↗

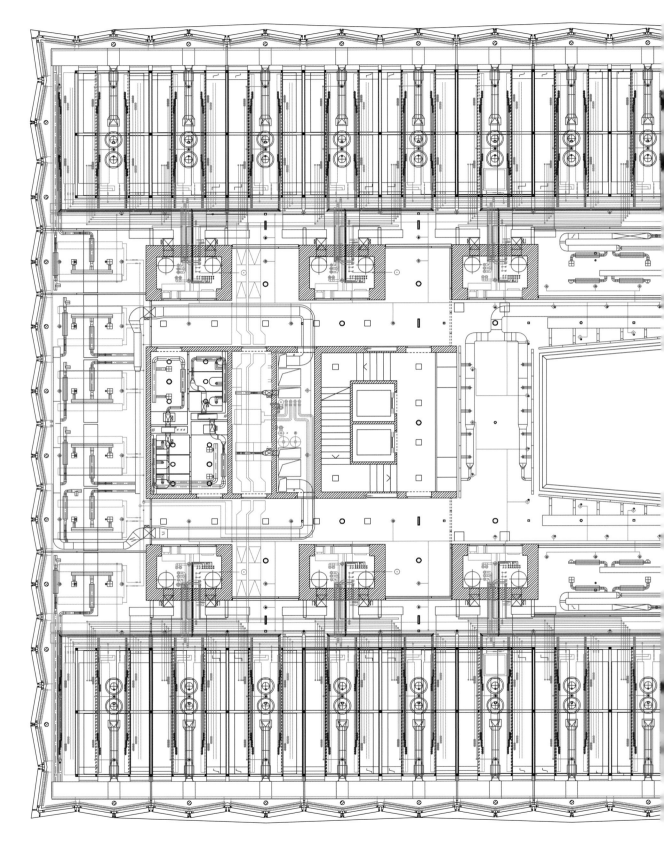

0301
Laborgebäude / Laboratory Building, Novartis Campus, Basel, mit / with Birgit Frank

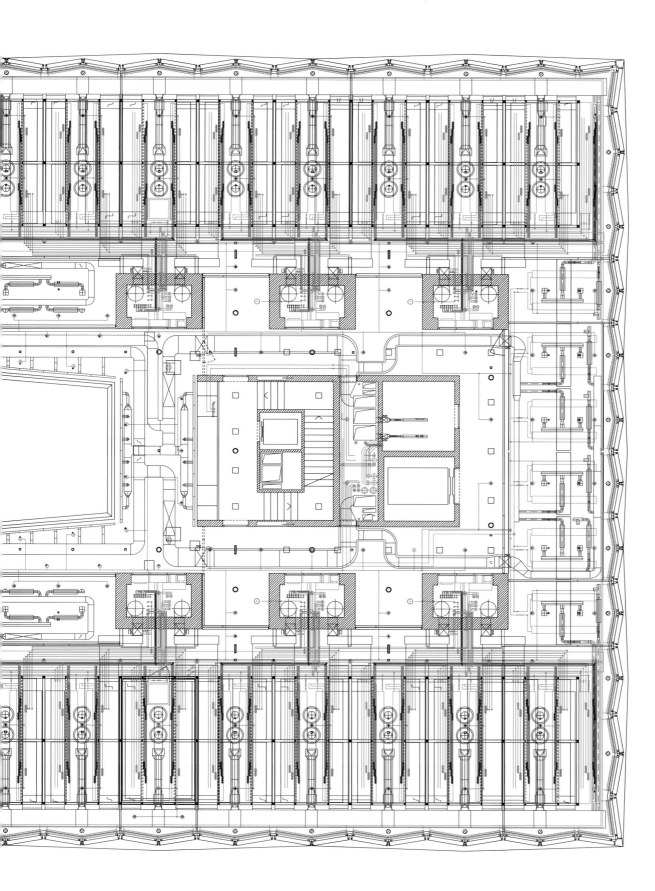

161

0301
Laborgebäude / Laboratory Building, Novartis Campus
Teppichboden / Floor pattern: Gilbert Bretterbauer

Nordostseite / Northeast side   >

0301
Laborgebäude / Laboratory Building, Novartis Campus

0910
Büroneubau / New Office Building for Jungbunzlauer, Niederösterreich / Lower Austria
Eingangshalle mit Wandbild von / Entrance hall with mural by Sol LeWitt

0910
Büroneubau / New Office Building for
Jungbunzlauer

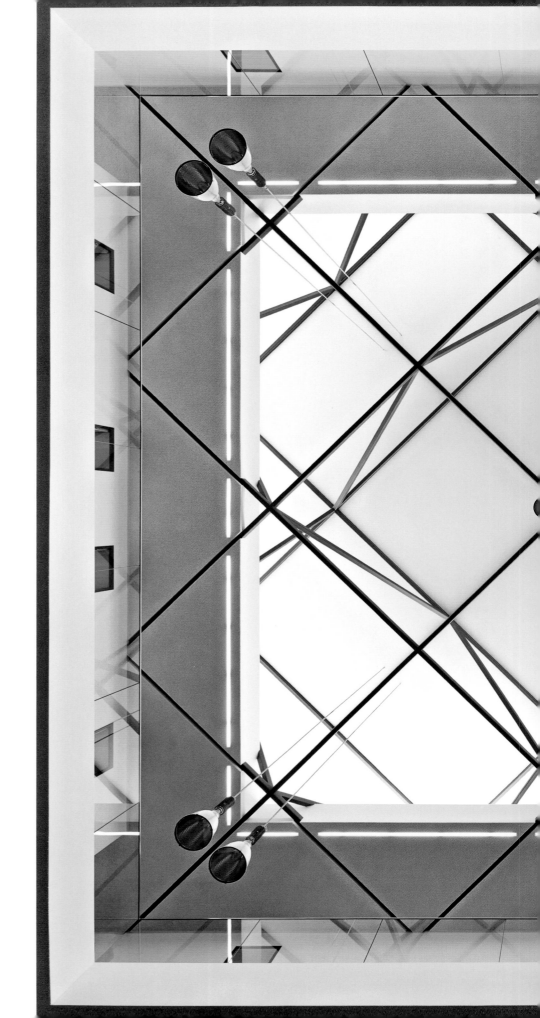

0910
Büroneubau / New Office Building for
Jungbunzlauer

0910
Büroneubau / New Office Building for Jungbunzlauer

1202
Werkskantine / Company Cafeteria for Jungbunzlauer, Niederösterreich / Lower Austria

1202
Werkskantine / Company Cafeteria for Jungbunzlauer, Nordseite / view from the north

1202
Werkskantine / Company Cafeteria for Jungbunzlauer

0108
Verkehrsrechenzentrale / Traffic Computer Center ASFINAG, Wien / Vienna

0108
Verkehrsrechenzentrale / Traffic Computer Center ASFINAG

0515
SUPERBLOCK Sulzerareal, Winterthur

0515
SUPERBLOCK Sulzerareal
Bereich der denkmalgeschützten Fassade / Part of protected façade

186

0515
SUPERBLOCK Sulzerareal

0515
SUPERBLOCK Sulzerareal

0801
Dachausbau / Roof Conversion for the Oesterreichische Kontrollbank, Wien / Vienna

0514
Oesterreichische Kontrollbank, Eingangsbereich / foyer   >

0801
Dachausbau / Roof Conversion for the Oesterreichische Kontrollbank

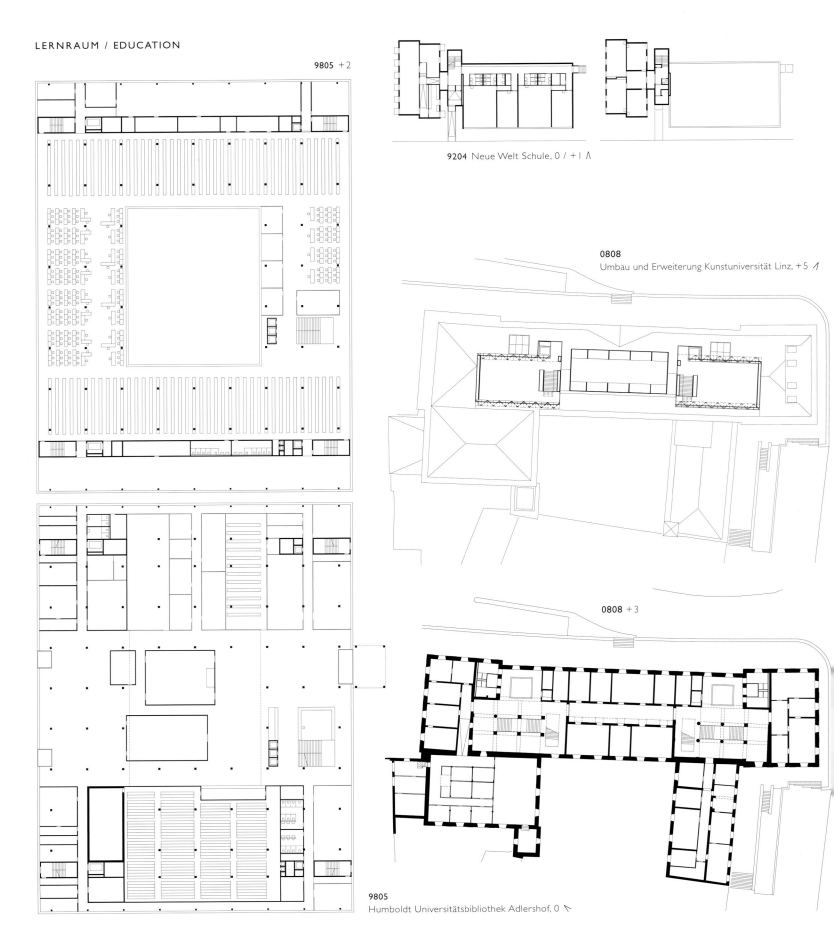

9805 +2

9204 Neue Welt Schule, 0 / +1 ∧

0808
Umbau und Erweiterung Kunstuniversität Linz, +5 ∕

0808 +3

9805
Humboldt Universitätsbibliothek Adlershof, 0 ∧

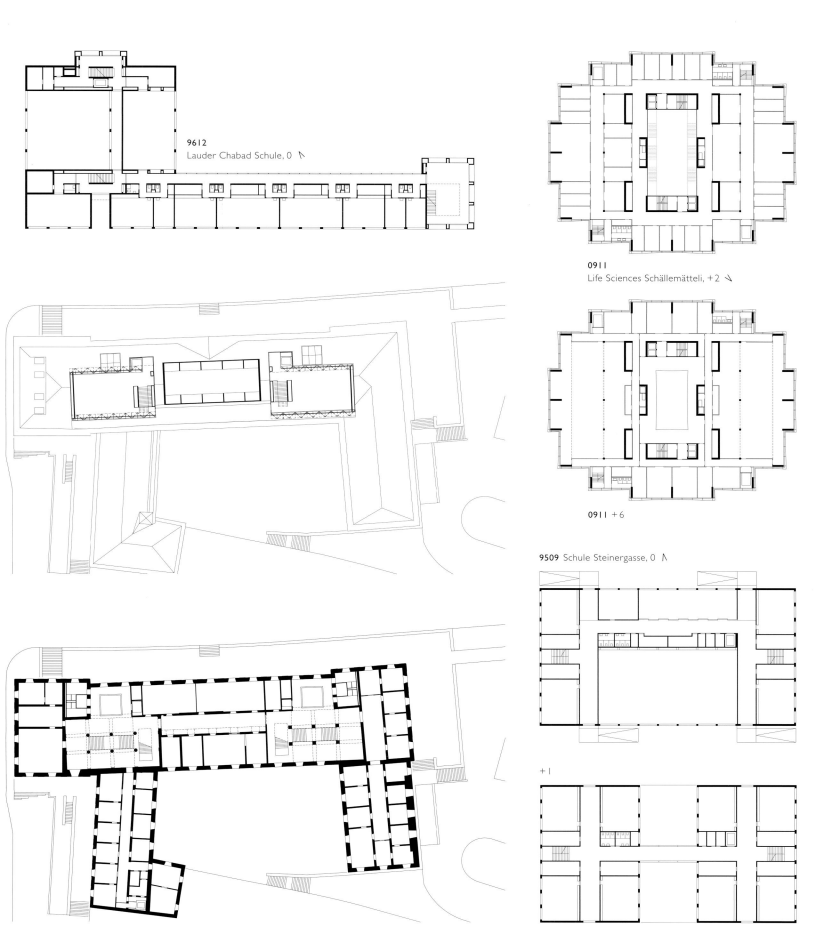

9612
Lauder Chabad Schule, 0 ⋏

0911
Life Sciences Schällemätteli, +2 ⋎

0911 +6

9509 Schule Steinergasse, 0 ⋏

+1

LERNRAUM

Otto Kapfinger: Bei deinen Projekten für Bildungsinstitutionen, die ja auch Arbeitsstätten sind, gab und gibt es wieder die typische Häufung der Kontroversen: um die Standorte, um die Formen, um die Haltung zur Geschichte …

Adolf Krischanitz: Es begann mit der Kindertagesstätte Neue Welt Schule für jüdische Kinder der Gemeinde Wien unter der Leitung des Rabbiners Jacob Bidermann — einem kleinen, aber sorgfältig geplanten Volumen in der Praterau neben älteren Kindergartenpavillons der Stadtgemeinde. Durch die strenge Form und die Farbgestaltung in dunklem Anthrazit nach einem Material- und Farbkonzept von Helmut Federle gab es aus nichtjüdischen Kreisen harsche Kritik, bis hin zu Kommentaren in den TV-Nachrichten im Abendprogramm. Die Nutzer der Schule, der Spender der Bausumme, Alexander Kahane, und alle, die sich niveauvoll mit zeitgenössischem Bauen auseinandersetzen, haben das Konzept massiv unterstützt. Es ist uns gelungen, etwas Alltägliches und Zurückhaltendes innerhalb der üppigen Natur der Praterau zu entwickeln. Eine wichtige Komplementärstrategie war der Einsatz der Material- und Farbpalette als Resonanz auf die mächtigen, dunklen Stämme der Schwarzpappeln auf dem Grundstück. Der anthrazitfarbene Verputz geht mit der — je nach Jahreszeit wechselnden — farbigen Grunddisposition der Umgebung einher, manchmal in integrativer, manchmal in kontrastierender Weise.

Bald danach kam der Auftrag für ein Schulgebäude für die Jüdische Gemeinde Wiens.

Anlässlich der Renovierung der Secession hatte ich den als US-Botschafter in Österreich wirkenden Kunstmäzen Ronald S. Lauder kennengelernt. Er hatte die Rekonstruktion der goldenen Secessionskuppel großzügig unterstützt. Schließlich wurde er auch Finanzier der Lauder Chabad Schule.

Fast absurd war, dass das einzige passende Grundstück im traditionellen jüdischen Wiener Bezirk Leopoldstadt ein Streifen am Rand des Augartens war — direkt neben einem in der NS-Zeit errichteten riesigen Flak-Turm.

Ja, und noch dazu neben jenem der sechs Wiener Flak-Türme, der groteskerweise nach dem Krieg mit Marmor verkleidet und so zu einem Monument für Adolf Hitler »nobilitiert« werden sollte. Es war sowohl für die Schulgemeinde als Bauherr-

EDUCATION

Otto Kapfinger: In the case of your projects for educational institutions, which are indeed also workplaces, the typical controversies have and continue to accumulate: regarding the locations, the forms, the approach to history …

Adolf Krischanitz: It began with the Neue Welt Schule (New World School) daycare center for Jewish children of the city of Vienna under the direction of Rabbi Jacob Bidermann—a small, but carefully planned structure on the Prater River meadow near older kindergarten pavilions belonging to the municipality. The austere form and color design in dark anthracite, as based on a material and color concept by Helmut Federle, resulted in harsh criticism from non-Jewish circles, culminating in commentaries on the evening television news. The users of the school, the donor of the construction sum, Alexander Kahane, and everyone who deals with contemporary architecture in a sophisticated way gave the concept their solid support. We succeeded in developing something prosaic and reserved within the luxuriant natural environment of the Prater River meadow. An important complementary strategy was to use the material and color palette as a response to the mighty, dark trunks of the black poplars on site. The anthracite-colored roughcast goes hand in hand—changing according to the season—with the colorful basic disposition of the surroundings, sometimes integrative, sometimes in a contrasting manner.

Soon afterward came the commission for a school building for the Jewish community of Vienna.

In connection with the renovation of the Secession, I got to know the patron of the arts Ronald S. Lauder, who was posted as U.S. Ambassador to Austria. He provided generous support for the reconstruction of the Secession's golden dome. He was later also the person who provided the financing for the school called Lauder Chabad Schule.

What was almost absurd was that the only suitable property in the traditionally Jewish Leopoldstadt district of Vienna was a strip on the edge of the Augarten—directly next to a huge flak tower erected during the National Socialist era.

Yes, and for good measure, next to that was one of the six flak towers in Vienna that was grotesquely clad with marble after the war and was therefore

---

»Anders als mit seiner ›Neuen Welt Schule‹ wird Krischanitz mit diesem Bau kaum jemand vor den Kopf stoßen. Trotzdem: Hinter der freundlich hellen Putzhaut und der beinahe klassischen Erscheinung verbirgt sich ein autonomes Objekt, das es mit seinem unmittelbaren Nachbarn, der mächtigen Betonskulptur des Flakturms, aufnehmen kann. Damit hat er einen bei dieser Bauaufgabe an diesem Ort zentralen Auftrag erfüllt: ein Haus für eine andere, bessere Ewigkeit zu bauen.«

Christian Kühn,
in: *Die Presse, Spectrum*
23. Oktober 1999

S. / pp. 212/213

S. / pp. 208–211

9612
Lauder Chabad Schule
Wien / Vienna, 1996–1999,
erweitert / expanded 2007
Erbaut neben einem der sechs
1942–1945 nach Plänen von
Friedrich Tamms errichteten
Flaktürme / Hochbunker mit
Flugabwehrgeschützen und
Feuerleitanlagen / Built alongside
one of six flak towers / elevated
bunkers constructed between
1942–45 based on designs by
Friedrich Tamms and featuring
anti-aircraft guns and fire-control
systems

schaft als auch für mich als Entwerfer eine klare
Herausforderung, an diesem Ort die Konfrontation anzunehmen. Meine Architektur setzt dem
monolithisch aufragenden Turm eine sehr kräftige
Horizontale entgegen. Die Entwicklung der
Raumorganisation aus der Modulierung mehr-
stöckiger Raumfiguren erwies sich als sehr
effiziente Wirkungsform. Wegen der Nachfrage
nach Schulplätzen musste das Haus nach wenigen
Jahren um eine Etage aufgestockt werden.

Kunstuniversität Linz

**Dein größter Bildungsbau wird die Erweiterung
der Kunstuniversität Linz sein. Wieder war ein
Konflikt mit der lokalen NS-Vergangenheit Stein
des Anstoßes.**

Anfang 2009 konnte ich das europaweit ausgelobte
Bewerbungsverfahren für diese Erweiterung gewinnen. Es ging um die Adaptierung jener beiden
Trakte, die den Linzer Hauptplatz zur Donau hin
abgrenzen und als »Brückenkopf« den zentralen
Übergang über die Donau zum Stadtteil Urfahr
fassen und rahmen. Diese Trakte sind der einzige
realisierte Teil des Prachtboulevards, den Adolf
Hitler in Linz errichten wollte. Architekt war
Roderich Fick, doch Hitler selbst hatte als Leitbild einen monumentalen »Heimatstil Münchner
Prägung« vorgegeben. Die Bauten wurden übrigens
innen erst nach dem Krieg fertiggestellt!

supposed to become ennobled as a monument to
Adolf Hitler. It was a clear challenge both for the
school community as client and for me as designer
to take on the confrontation at this location. My
architecture counters the monolithic tall tower
with a powerful horizontal. The development
of the spatial organization based on modulating
multistory spatial figures in space turned out to be
a very efficient type of effect. Due to the demand
for schools, another story had to be added to the
building after just a few years.

Art University in Linz

**Your biggest education building would be the exten-
sion to the art university in Linz. A conflict with the
local National Socialist past once again became a
stumbling block.**

At the beginning of 2009, I succeeded in winning
the application process for this extension, which
was praised throughout Europe. The competition
concerned adapting the two tracts delimiting
the Hauptplatz in Linz toward the Danube and
making the central crossing over the Danube to
the city district of Urfahr into, and framing it as,
a "bridgehead." These tracts are the only realized
part of the stately boulevard that Adolf Hitler
wanted to construct in Linz. The architect had
been Roderich Fick, but Hitler himself decided
on the monumental "Heimat-style with a

0808
Umbau und Erweiterung /
Renovation and Extension
Kunstuniversität Linz
Planungsstand 2014, Blick vom
Hauptplatz Richtung Donau:
verglaste Dachaufbauten auf den
in der NS-Zeit errichteten
Brückenkopfgebäuden; Skulpturen
von Stefan Wewerka / Current
state of planning 2014, view from
Hauptplatz toward the Danube:
glazed roof structures on the
bridgehead buildings erected
during the National Socialist era;
sculptures by Stefan Wewerka

Seit ihrer Gründung in den 1970er-Jahren nutzte die Kunstuniversität Linz den westlichen Trakt, der östliche diente dem Finanzamt. Nach dessen Umzug in den 90er-Jahren stand er leer. Noch während des Wettbewerbsverfahrens mit acht erstrangigen Büros aus dem In- und Ausland bekräftigte das Bundesdenkmalamt in einem ausführlichen Gutachten explizit den vorher für einen Bundesbau nur generell geltenden Denkmalschutz.

Die Denkmalbehörde war in die Vorbereitung und Abwicklung des Wettbewerbs voll eingebunden. Sie vertrat schon damals den sehr eigenartigen, akademischen Standpunkt, dass keinerlei Änderung des Erscheinungsbildes der NS-Trakte genehmigt werde.

Die Universität dagegen forderte in der Ausschreibung, dass »Zu-, An-, Auf- und Überbauten angedacht werden, um einerseits das Raumprogramm erfüllen zu können, andererseits aber auch, um das Image einer Kunstuniversität architektonisch zu manifestieren«.

Im Protokoll der Jury, die einstimmig meinen Entwurf prämierte, heißt es: »Die wesentlichen Elemente des Gebäudes bleiben erhalten, die historischen Fassaden praktisch unverändert; mit Absicht kontrastieren die eigenständigen, gläsernen Stiegenaufsätze zum Bestand. Die Zeichenhaftigkeit dieser Aufsätze geben jenes Signal, das von einer Kunstuniversität erwartet wird.«

Es waren diese geplanten Aufbauten über den Attikageschossen des Bestandes, gegen die das Denkmal-

Munich character" as a model. The insides of the buildings were, incidentally, first completed after the war!

Since it was established in the nineteen-seventies, the art university in Linz had been using the western tract, while the tax authority used the eastern tract. After it moved in the nineties, the tract stood empty. During the competition process along with eight first-class offices from Austria and abroad, the Federal Monuments Office already explicitly confirmed its (previously only generally applicable) historical protection status as a federal building in an extensive expert assessment.

The monument office was completely involved in preparing and conducting the competition. At that time, it already took the very peculiar, academic view that no change to the appearance of the National Socialist tracts would be approved.

The university, on the other hand, had stated in the call for tenders that "extensions, additions, developments, and structures on top should be considered in order to, on the one hand, fulfill the spatial program and, on the other, also manifest the image of an art university architecturally."

The transcripts of the jury, which unanimously selected my design, included the following: "The essential features of the building are retained, the historical façade practically unchanged; the self-contained, glazed staircase additions to the building provide an intentional contrast. The metaphoric

amt vehement opponierte und an denen sich auch die öffentliche Kritik entzündete.

Noch in der Wettbewerbsphase hatten der Bürgermeister von Linz und sein Planungsstadtrat mit fundierten Aussagen Einspruch gegen den Denkmalbescheid erhoben. Dieses Verfahren dauerte etliche Monate. In dieser Zeit wurde das Thema in den Medien begierig aufgegriffen, breitgetreten, ein fachlich eindeutiger Juryspruch bagatellisiert.

Die Haltung der Denkmalbehörde, in der Öffentlichkeit nochmals verkürzt kolportiert, war insofern richtig, als dass es darum ging, eben auch »unbequeme Dokumente als Zeitzeugen« zu erhalten. Doch in der Art der Begründung und der Verfechtung dieser Haltung war die Behörde so undifferenziert, so apodiktisch, dass daraus wieder nur die hierzulande oft gepflegte, populäre Mischung aus fortgesetzter Verdrängung von Geschichte durch restaurative Überkompensation herauskam.

In den Medien wurde eine Umfrage publiziert, nach der die Mehrheit der Bevölkerung die NS-Trakte pur und durch meine Planung »ungestört« erhalten wollte. Zu diesem Zeitpunkt war in der Stadt völlig unbekannt oder zumindest ein Tabu, dass diese Bauten mit Material aus dem berüchtigten Steinbruch des Konzentrationslagers Mauthausen – es liegt 20 Kilometer östlich von Linz – errichtet wurden und dass am Bau selbst Zwangsarbeiter aus ganz Europa tätig waren! Für mich wie für die Bauherrschaft konnte der Umgang mit diesen architektonischen Zeitzeugen nur glaubwürdig sein, indem man eben nicht eine Haltung »absoluter Denkmalwerdung« vertrat – ein »nur nicht Anrühren« –, sondern indem man ganz im Gegenteil die Auseinandersetzung eröffnete.

character of these attached structures gives the signal that is expected from an art university."

It was these planned additions above the attic floor of the existing building that the historical monument agency vehemently opposed and that also ignited public criticism.

The mayor of Linz and his city planning council had already submitted an appeal with well-founded statements to the monument office during the competition phase. These proceedings took several months. During this time, the topic was eagerly picked up in the media, widely discussed, and the unanimous expert jury trivialized.

The stance of the monument office, once again circulated in an abridged form in public, was correct to the extent that it involved also preserving "uncomfortable documents as contemporary witnesses." However, the office was so undifferentiated, so apodictic in the way it justified and advocated this stance that what resulted was once again only the continued avoidance of dealing with history by means of restorative repression that is often cultivated in Austria.

A survey was published in the media, according to which the majority of the population wanted the National Socialist tracts to be preserved purely, "unmolested" by my planning. At this point in time, the fact that these buildings had been constructed using material from the infamous stone quarry of the Mauthausen concentration camp— situated only twenty kilometers to the east of Linz—and that forced laborers from all over Europe were involved in the construction was completely unknown or at least taboo in the city. For both the client and myself, dealing with this

»Die Linzer Brückenkopfbauten sind architektonische Zeitzeugen, denen man eine gewisse städtebauliche Qualität nicht absprechen kann. Aber es handelt sich nicht um architekturgeschichtliche Schlüsselbauten, schon gar nicht der österreichischen Architekturgeschichte. Selbstverständlich kann man solche Bauten adaptieren und ergänzen.«

Friedrich Achleitner,
in: *Oberösterreichische Nachrichten*,
24. Februar 2009

0808
Umbau und Erweiterung /
Renovation and Extension
Kunstuniversität Linz
Stiegenhaus / Stairwell
Revitalisierung mit Raumerweiterungen, 1. OG / Refurbishment
with room extensions, 2nd floor
Neubau im Bestand, 2. und 3. OG /
Existing new construction, 3rd
and 4th floors

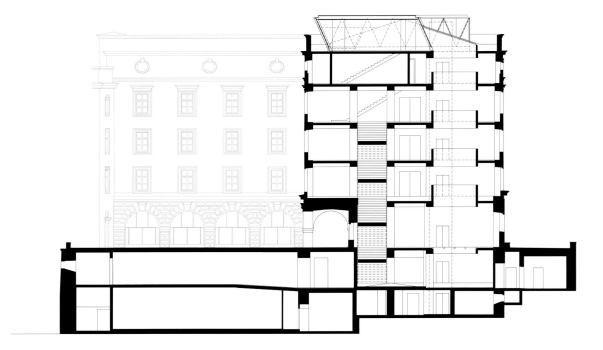

0808
Umbau und Erweiterung /
Renovation and Extension
Kunstuniversität Linz
Querschnitt Brückenkopfgebäude,
Planungsstand 2014 / Bridgehead
buildings cross section, current
state of planning 2014

Die gläsernen Aufbauten sind ja äußeres Zeichen der geplanten Neuordnung der inneren Raumsubstanz beider Trakte.

Im Bestand gibt es vier großzügige Stiegenhäuser, die aber nur ins erste Obergeschoss führen, dort völlig verebben und auch nicht gut zugänglich sind. Mein Vorschlag: diese vier Stiegenhäuser restaurieren, verlängern, als System über alle Etagen weiter hochziehen, mit Liften ergänzen und mit weiten Lichtschächten, die das ganze Haus bis übers Dach hinaus vertikal öffnen und auch Licht bis ins erste Untergeschoss leiten. Die Dachaufbauten bringen diese Transformation des Bestandes, die innere Durchlichtung und durchgängige Öffnung der Kern- und Erschließungszonen als »Protuberanzen« auch außen im Stadtbild zum Ausdruck. Dort oben sollten dann Veranstaltungsbereiche untergebracht werden, der große Aktsaal, Sitzungsräume.

Genau diese innere Öffnung, diese Neudefinition des Rückgrats der Trakte und ihr im Äußeren manifester Ausdruck als Zeichen der Neunutzung und der Resonanz auf die benachbarten neuen Kulturbauten – Lentos-Museum, Ars Electronica Center, Schlossmuseum –, hatte die Jury einhellig überzeugt.

Das Projekt ruhte nach der ersten Diskussionswelle jahrelang. Der Einspruch der Stadt gegen das Denkmalamt wurde abgewiesen. Es gab kein Budget, nur ein Weiterarbeiten an der Planung, am Vorentwurf,

contemporary architectural witness could only be credible by specifically not taking a position of "absolute creation of a monument"—a "do not touch" approach—but instead, quite to contrary, by opening up the debate.

The glass additions are indeed an outward sign of the planned rearrangement of the inner spatial substance of the two tracts.

In the existing building, there are four large stairwells, but they only lead to the first floor, completely end there, and are also not easily accessible. My proposal was to restore these four stairwells, extend them, raise them up further as a system over all the floors, supplement them with elevators and with wide light wells that open the entire building vertically up over the roof, and also channel light all the way down to the first underground floor. The roof structures also express this transformation of the existing building, the penetration of light into the interior, and the overall opening up of the core and access zones as "protuberances," to the outside in the cityscape. Up there, event areas were to be situated, such as a large hall for drawing and painting, meeting rooms.

It was specifically this opening up of the interior, this redefinition of the backbone of the tract and its outwardly manifest expression as a sign of the new utilization and a response to the new neighboring cultural buildings—the Lentos Art

auf kleinster Sparflamme. Vier Jahre nach dem Jury-entscheid zeichnet sich im Frühjahr 2014 nun eine Wende ab.

Ich sagte immer, dass die Dachaufbauten ja noch modifiziert werden können, niedriger werden können, wehrte mich aber vehement dagegen, dass die Kunstuniversität in äußerlich intakte NS-Bauten einziehen sollte. Stadtpolitik und Fachwelt haben meinen Standpunkt immer unterstützt. Wir simulierten dann mit Gerüststangen die Umrisse der neuen Dachkonturen.

Nach einer weiteren, diesmal schriftlichen Ab-lehnung der Aufbauten durch das Denkmalamt reduzierten wir in einem weiteren Versuch die Höhe um fast die Hälfte und änderten die Nei-gungsrichtung der Stahl-Glas-Konstruktion so, dass sie vom Hauptplatz wegfluchtet, von dort gesehen die Kontur noch etwas niedriger erscheint, jedoch zur Donau noch die unbedingt nötige Höhe behält.

Nach dem weiteren Beharren der Denkmalbehörde drohte ich ernsthaft damit, den Auftrag nieder-zulegen, und appellierte zusätzlich an das über-geordnete Ministerium. Und plötzlich gab es eine reduzierte, aber aussichtsreiche Budgetierung. Als Ausgleich für die geringere Höhe schlug ich für das Dach periodisch wechselnde Skulpturen vor, beginnend mit zwei Entwürfen des genialen Stefan Wewerka, dessen Karriere in Österreich, in der Wiener Galerie nächst St. Stephan be-gonnen hat.

Museum, the Ars Electronica Center, and the Schlossmuseum (Castle Museum)—that had unanimously convinced the jury.

After the first wave of discussions, the project remained dormant for years. The city's appeal to the monument office was denied. There was no budget, only further work on the planning, on the prelimi-nary design, all placed on the smallest back burner. Four years after the jury decision, a turning point then became visible in the spring of 2014.

I always said that the roof structures could still be modified, could be lower, but was vehemently opposed to the idea that the art university should move into externally intact National Socialist buildings. City politics and the specialist world always supported my viewpoint. We then simu-lated the outlines of the new roof contours with scaffolding poles.

After the monument office once again rejected the additions, this time in writing, in another attempt we reduced the height by nearly half and altered the direction of the incline of the steel and glass structure in such a way that it is aligned away from the Hauptplatz. Seen from there, the contour appears somewhat lower, but toward the Danube it still retains the absolutely necessary height.

After the further insistence of the monument office, I seriously threatened to resign the com-mission and also appealed to the higher-level ministry. And suddenly there was a reduced but promising budget. As a trade-off for the lower height, I proposed periodically alternating sculp-tures for the roof, beginning with two designs by the brilliant Stefan Wewerka, whose career in Austria began in the Galerie nächst St. Stephan in Vienna.

9612
Lauder Chabad Schule / School, Wien / Vienna

9612 / 0513
Lauder Chabad Schule / School, Erweiterung / Extension

9204
Neue Welt Schule, Wien / Vienna
Farbkonzept / Color concept: Helmut Federle

0902
Archiv der Zeitgenossen, Krems
Tiefspeicher, Markierung im Gelände / Underground storage, Marking on site

0902
Archiv der Zeitgenossen
Vier Räume, vier verschiedene Hölzer / Four rooms, four different types of wood

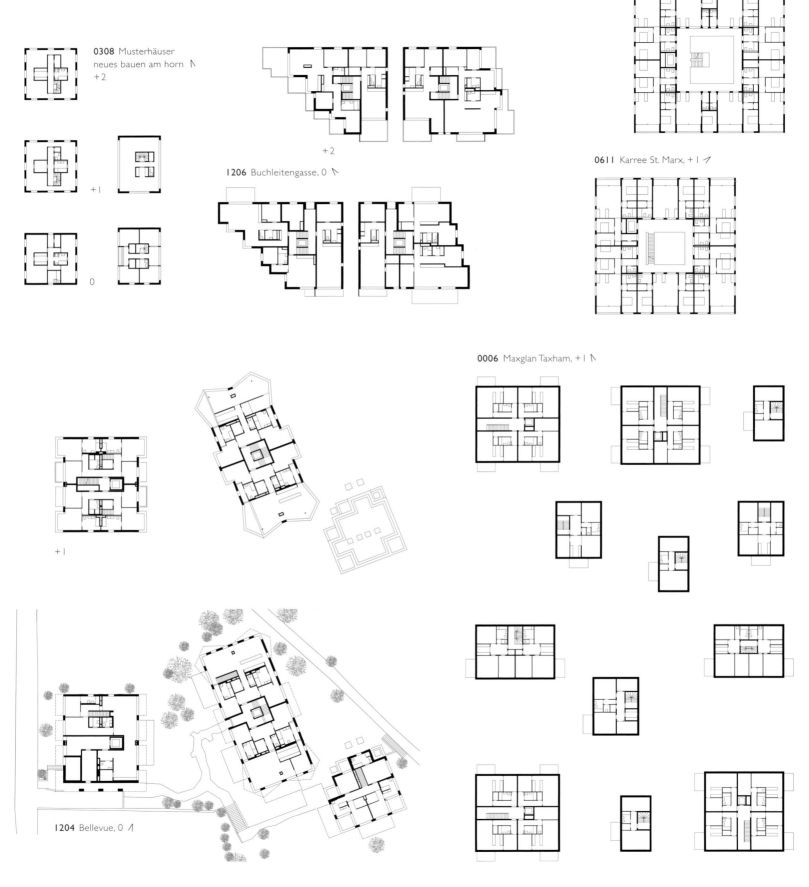

0308 Musterhäuser
neues bauen am horn Ṅ
+2

+1

0

+2

1206 Buchleitengasse, 0 Ṅ

+1

1204 Bellevue, 0 ↗

0611 Karree St. Marx, +1 ↗

0006 Maxglan Taxham, +1 Ṅ

INTERIEUR

Otto Kapfinger: Das schmucke Einfamilienhaus im Grünen mit seinen Inszenierungen und Illusionen, seinen ökonomischen und ökologischen Fragwürdigkeiten, steht im Zentrum alltäglicher Lebensentwürfe. In deinem Werk gab es anfangs, wie oft bei jungen Büros, einige kleine anspruchsvolle Häuser. Es waren Aufträge, zum Teil noch Gemeinschaftsarbeiten, in denen wir Klischees von Identität und Komfort, vom Umgang mit Wohn- und Bautradition abgearbeitet und mit ironischen Untertönen gewürzt haben. Wir hatten beide keinen einschlägigen, »kultivierten« biografischen Hintergrund – und auch diese Bauherren damals nicht. Danach spielte das Thema bei dir keine Rolle mehr. Du zeigst hier nur drei oder vier Häuser. Und die sind wenig glamourös oder schick, eher Sonderfälle, untypisch für das Genre wie etwa das extrem schmale Hofhaus.

Adolf Krischanitz: Noch im Auftrag der Baugenossenschaft der damaligen Mühl-Kommune in Friedrichshof entwarf ich den 1980er-Jahren den Strukturplan für eine Siedlung im Nordburgenland. Das liegt 30 Autominuten östlich von Wien, knapp vor der Grenze, man spürt schon die ungarische Tiefebene. Vorbild war die im pannonischen Klima traditionelle Typologie aneinandergebauter schmaler Hofhäuser: ein System von Mauern, Dächern und Wegen, von gedeckten und offenen Räumen – innerhalb der früher überall mit kleinen Schwankungen üblichen Parzellenbreite von 7,5 Metern – das sind 4 Klafter beziehungsweise 24 Fuß und kommt von den Ziegelmaßen, von den unseren Körpermaßen entsprechenden Einheiten.

Die typologische und städtebauliche Plausibilität war offensichtlich nicht stark genug, um diese intelligente, aber auch rigide Siedlungsform als verbindliche Matrix durchzuhalten. Später hinzukommende Bauwerber wählten entgegen dem Bebauungsplan die Positionierung ihrer Häuser eher nach dem Prinzip des zufällig gefallenen Tropfens – das Haus als Einzelobjekt auf einem Baufeld innerhalb von möglichst viel Umland auf allen Seiten. Diese Art der Bebauung konsumiert pro Haus ein Maximum an einsehbarer Fläche, ohne jemals so etwas wie eine sinnvolle Dichte und Struktur zu erzeugen.

Das Haus unseres vorbildlichen Klienten in Friedrichshof wurde im Sinn des gültigen Bebauungsplans konzipiert und gebaut – mit einfacher Außenform ohne jegliche Verzierung, mit mas-

INTERIORS

Otto Kapfinger: The ornamental one-family house in the country with its displays and illusions, its economic and ecological questionability, stands in the center of everyday life plans. In your early work, there were, as is often the case for young offices, some small ambitious houses. They were commissions, in part still joint efforts, in which we executed clichés of identity and comfort, addressing living and building traditions, and spiced them up with ironic undertones. Neither of us had any pertinent, "cultivated" biographical background experience—nor did these clients at the time either. Afterward, the theme no longer played a role in your work. You present only three or four houses here. And they are not so much glamorous or stylish, but rather special cases, untypical for the genre, such as for instance the extremely narrow courtyard house.

Adolf Krischanitz: In the nineteen-eighties, still on behalf of the Mühl commune's building cooperative in Friedrichshof at the time, I created the structural plan for a settlement in Northern Burgenland. It's thirty minutes away from Vienna by car, just this side of the border, and one already senses the Hungarian lowland plain. The model was the typology traditional in the Pannonian climate of narrow attached courtyard houses: a system of walls, roofs, and paths, of covered and open spaces—within the small parcel widths of 7.5 meters with slight variations that were previously found everywhere—which is four sazhens, or fathoms, or twenty-four feet, and comes from brick dimensions, from units corresponding to our body measurements.

9410
Masterplan Friedrichshof
Modell zu einem Haustyp der Siedlungsstruktur / Settlement structure model home
Zurndorf, Burgenland, 1994

The typological and urban-planning plausibility was apparently not strong enough for this intelligent but also rigid form of settlement to endure as a binding matrix. Building promoters who came later instead chose, contrary to the land-use plan, to position their houses more according to the principle of a randomly fallen raindrop—the house as a single object in a building area with as much surrounding countryside on all sides as possible. This type of development consumes a maximum of open area per house without ever producing anything like sensible concentration and structure.

9507
Haus Sperl, Zurndorf, Burgenland, 1995/96, Innenhof / Interior courtyard

The house of our model clients in Friedrichshof was designed and built according to the land-use plan that was in effect at the time—with a simple outer form without any ornamentation, with

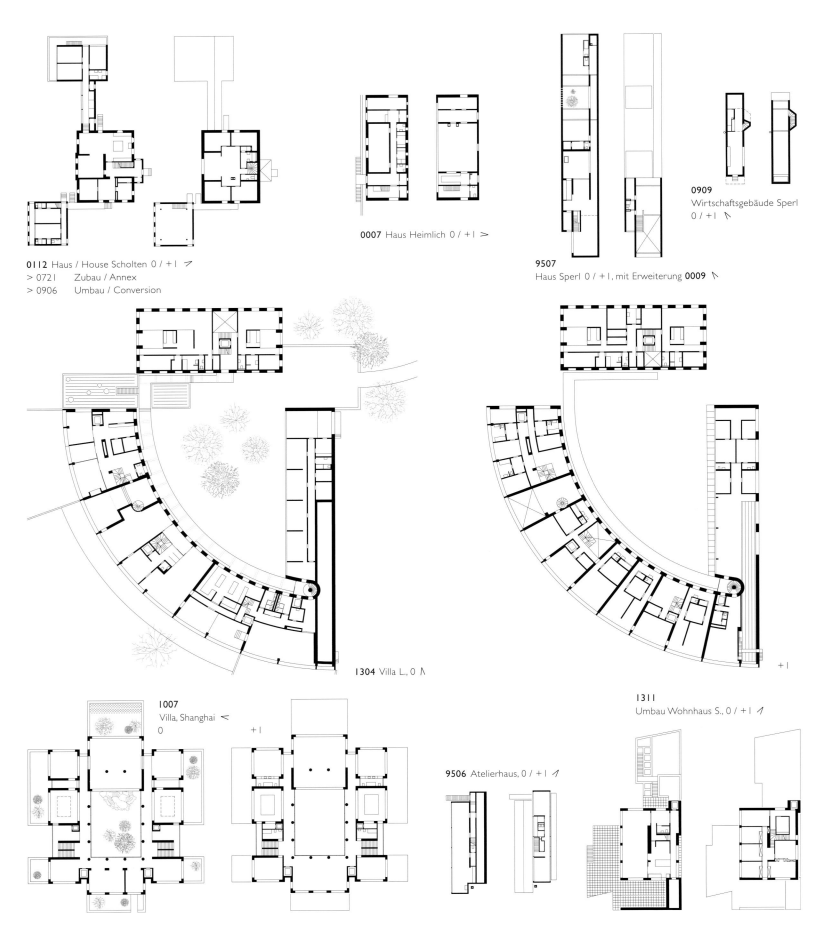

0112 Haus / House Scholten 0 / +1 ↗
> 0721   Zubau / Annex
> 0906   Umbau / Conversion

0007 Haus Heimlich 0 / +1 ⟩

9507
Haus Sperl 0 / +1, mit Erweiterung 0009 ⟍

0909
Wirtschaftsgebäude Sperl
0 / +1 ⟍

1304 Villa L., 0 ⟍

+1

1007
Villa, Shanghai ⟨
0   +1

1311
Umbau Wohnhaus S., 0 / +1 ↗

9506 Atelierhaus, 0 / +1 ↗

218

siven hermetischen Mauern, mit seiner klimatisch bedingten Introvertiertheit, alles Merkmale einer mehrere Jahrhunderte alten Tradition. Die Struktur folgt einem Mäander, dem Wechsel von geschlossenen und geöffneten Abschnitten. Das Wichtigste sind die von Mauern umfassten Höfe: sonnen- und windgeschützte Plätze mit Pflanzen, die auch im Herbst noch gut für einen Aufenthalt im Freien nutzbar sind.

Jahre nach diesem ersten Haus hat der Bauherr ein zweites und drittes errichtet, auf der nördlich anschließenden Parzelle, diesmal frei stehend und immer parallel zum ersten Gebäude.

Das dritte ist ein Studiohaus, in dem hauptsächlich gearbeitet wird, sehr klein, ein »Einraumhaus«. Aus der Trennschicht zwischen Gebäude und Außenraum, durch ihre zweifach formgebende Wirkung, entsteht eine Spannung zwischen Innen- und Außenform – so wie bei einem Salettl, wo die Licht- und Farbstimmungen das Wichtigste sind, kein Detail sich aufdrängt und die Fassade nur Struktur ist. Die Landschaft hier ist karg, weitläufig, einschichtig. Der riesige Himmel, die Sonne, der ständige Wind, das besondere Licht dominieren. Und das muss ein Haus reflektieren, nicht mehr und nicht weniger.

Du hattest eine zweite Bauherrschaft mit ähnlichem Temperament, für die du zuerst einen Dachboden im Zentrum von Wien adaptiert hast und dann Um- und Anbauten an altem Baubestand planen konntest, zwei Autostunden nördlich von Wien.

Da gab es Ähnlichkeiten, denn auch dieser Grundbesitz liegt abgeschieden, ist eine Waldlichtung auf der Böhmischen Platte, nahe der Grenze zur Tschechischen Republik. Auf ihm standen ein altes Verwalterhaus mit Walmdächern und Giebel, daneben ein schlichtes Gesindehaus. Für die schnell wachsende Familie gab es zuerst ein kompaktes zweites Haus mit Steildächern, Holzfassade und polyvalentem Grundriss, mit dem Altbau durch ein Gelenk verbunden – ein Duett in sich zentrierter, in sich »kompletter« Typen, die sich nur über Eck an der Hand fassen.

War dieser Anbau ursprünglich nicht für die beiden Töchter, damals noch kaum Teenager?

Ja, und die Mädchen wuchsen heran, schließlich brauchten sie mehr Raum, da zu guter Letzt eine dritte Tochter geboren wurde. So entstand Jahre später der zweite Zubau mit drei Kinderzimmern

solid, hermetic walls, with its climate-dependent introverted quality, all characteristics of a tradition going back many centuries. The structure meanders, following the alternating of closed and open sections. The courtyards surrounded by walls are the most important element: places with plants sheltered from the sun and wind that can also be used to spend time outdoors in the fall.

Years after this first house, the client erected a second and a third on the parcel adjoining to the north, this time free-standing but always parallel to the first building.

The third is a studio house used mainly for work, very small, a "one-room house." The separating layer between building and outdoor space, due to its dually formative effect, generates tension between inner and outer form—as in the case of a gazebo, where the light and color moods are the most important aspect, with no detail intruding, and the façade is only structure. The landscape here is austere, extensive, single-layered. The huge sky, the sun, the constant wind, and the special light dominate. And a house has to reflect this, not more and not less.

You had a second client with a similar temperament, for whom you first adapted an attic in the center of Vienna and were then able to plan modifications and extensions to an old existing building two hours to the north of Vienna.

There were some similarities, since this property is also quite isolated, being in a clearing in the woods on the Bohemian plain, near the border to the Czech Republic. On the property stood an old administrator's house with hipped roofs and gables, and next to it a simple servant's house. For the quickly growing family, there was first a second compact house with pitched roofs, a wooden façade, and a polyvalent layout, connected to the old building by a joint—an inwardly centered duet of types "complete" in themselves, which only touch each other over a corner.

Wasn't this addition originally intended for the two daughters, who were at that time still barely teenagers?

Yes, and the girls grew up and then needed more space, since a third daughter was actually born later. This led, some years later, to the building of the second addition with three children's rooms on the other side, which, with its simple structure,

0906
Ausbau Obergeschoss / 2nd Floor
Conversion Haus Scholten
Pengers, 2009–2011

auf der anderen Seite, der in sehr einfacher Konstruktion über dem Terrain »schwebt« und damit zugleich einen überdachten Freiraum erzeugt, der im Sommer intensiv genutzt wird.

Du hast dort auch im Altbau einiges verändert. Auffallend sind diese turmartigen Dachaufbauten.

Das sind Lichtfänger; sie bringen von oben gebündeltes Licht in die adaptierten Dachetagen. Nicht der Ausblick wird naiv inszeniert – das romantische Klischee – oder die hohe Dachfläche mit Verglasungen durchlöchert. Es wird vielmehr eine innenräumliche Konzentration erzeugt mit einem Lichteinfall, der, sagen wir einmal, viel intensiver, viel transzendenter und stimulierender ist als jedes Panoramafenster.

Die Uneindeutigkeit des Privaten

Bei den Häusern und auch bei vielen deiner Interieurs und Möbelentwürfen fällt auf, dass wohl alles sehr sorgfältig gemacht ist, dass aber nirgends eine auf den ersten Blick eindeutige, einladende oder wie auch immer gemütliche Stimmung oder ein pittoresker Eindruck entsteht. Die Interieurs sind aber auch nicht pointiert asketisch oder minimalistisch gestylt.

Was du ansprichst, betrifft generell meine Einstellung zum Raumschaffen. Meine persönliche Entwicklung ging vom Studium über die politische Aktion, die konsum- und funktionskritische Missing-Link-Zeit und das Spiel mit der Postmoderne zu einer letztlich skeptischen Äquidistanz zu all diesen rezepthaften Ansprüchen des Raumschaffens als Bühnen für unser Leben, das doch inzwischen jede funktionale oder soziale oder biografische Eindeutigkeit hinter sich gelassen hat.

m31
Kleiner Fauteuil / Small Armchair
1989

"floats" over the terrain and thus simultaneously creates a roofed-over open space that is used intensively in the summertime.

You also changed a number of things in the old building there. These roof structures are striking.

They're light catchers; they bring concentrated light from above into the converted attic floor. It was not about staging a view—the romantic cliché—or perforating the high roof surface with glass. It's more of a spatial concentration inside, produced with an incidence of light that is, let's say, more intensive, more transcendent and stimulating that any panorama window.

The Ambiguity of the Private

In the case of the houses, as well as many of your interiors and furniture designs, what stands out is that arguably everything is very carefully done, but that, at first glance, no clear, inviting, or, whatever the case may be, cozy atmosphere or picturesque impression arises. Yet the interiors are not styled to be pointedly ascetic or minimalist, either.

What you're talking about pertains in general to my approach to creating space. My personal development went from studying to political action, the consumption- and function-critical Missing Link period and the play with postmodernism, to an ultimately skeptical equidistance to all those recipe-like demands to create space as a stage for our lives, which has in the meantime left any functional or social or biographical unambiguousness behind.

In an interview in Berlin, you mentioned a formative spatial experience from your childhood.

Yes: I grew up in alternately rural and urban surroundings with a very sensory characteristic style and materials. My first building was a pile of wood belonging to my grandfather. I found a hollow space in it and interpreted it accordingly. It was a huge amount of material, and the rooms were actually created through the contrived absence of material at various points. The material therefore fascinated me less than the nothing in between, the space in itself.

In the city I come from, I had a nearly identical experience. A classmate from my time at elementary school came from a family of carpenters and coopers.

In einem Interview in Berlin hast du eine prägende Raumerfahrung aus der Kindheit erwähnt.

Ja: Ich bin in einer in Duktus und Materialien sehr sinnlichen, abwechselnd ländlichen und städtischen Umgebung aufgewachsen. Mein erstes Gebäude war ein Holzstoß meines Großvaters. Ich habe einen Hohlraum darin gefunden und entsprechend interpretiert. Es war eine Unmenge an Material, und die Räume entstanden eigentlich durch das arrangierte Fehlen des Materials an vielen Stellen. Mich hat dabei weniger das Material fasziniert als das Nichts dazwischen, der Raum an sich.

Ich hatte in der Stadt, aus der ich komme, ein fast identisches Erlebnis. Ein Mitschüler aus der Volksschulzeit stammte aus einer Zimmerer- und Fassbinderfamilie. Neben der Werkstatt gab es Stapel von Holzlatten beziehungsweise Fassdauben, polygonal aufgeschichtet wie hohe Iglus. Wir konnten von unten hineinschlüpfen und von drinnen alles rundum bestens beobachten, ohne von außen gesehen zu werden.

Genauso – wie bei den traditionellen Balkon- und Fenstergeflechten: ambivalente, einseitig poröse Räume mit vielfach gestreutem, gefiltertem Licht ...

Bei solchen zum Ausschwemmen und Trocknen gesetzten Holzstapeln entsteht der Raum nebenbei, ohne Absicht. Das Muster der Wand entsteht zufällig und zugleich logisch aus dem Stapelvorgang mit regelmäßigen Luftschlitzen zwischen den Schichten. Was diese Räume so besonders macht, ist vermutlich ihre heimelige un-heimliche Anonymität.

Jedenfalls erscheint mir genau diese Stimmung – jenseits von allen Klischees, weder schön noch hässlich, eigentlich nicht-schön – als probates Leitmotiv, mit dem ich meine Architektur und speziell solche Innenräume durch die Stromschnellen der Moden und ideologischen Kurzschlüsse hindurchsteuern kann. Wir befinden uns im postmodernen Zustand. Jeder Hang zum Gesamtkunstwerk ist da pure Nostalgie, jede avantgardistische Behauptung eine Privatmythologie. Hat nicht Theodor W. Adorno formuliert: »Was als Utopie sich fühlt, bleibt ein Negatives gegen das Bestehende, und diesem hörig«? Und in diese Richtung weist, denke ich, auch die Beobachtung, das Haus sei heute »eine Ansammlung von Objekten und Stimuli, jenseits aller architektonischen Komposition«. Das hat eben Josef Frank

9508
Schreibstube für / Scriptorium for
Robert Menasse
Wien, 1995/96

Next to the workshop, there were stacks of wooden slats or barrel staves, stacked in the shape of tall, polygon-like igloos. We were able to slip in from below and observe everything all around really easily without being seen from the outside.

Exactly—just like in the case of traditional Arab balconies and window meshes: ambivalent, one-sided, porous spaces with lots of scattered and filtered light ...

In stacks of wood subjected to such washing out and drying, the space is created incidentally, unintentionally. The pattern of the wall results by accident and at the same time logically due to the process of building such stacks with regular air slots between the layers. What makes these spaces so special is presumably their cozy, overt anonymity.

In any case, it is precisely this atmosphere that seems to me—beyond all clichés, neither beautiful nor ugly, actually non-beautiful—to be an appropriate leitmotif with which I can navigate my architecture, and especially such interior spaces, through the rapids of fashions and short-circuited ideologies. We find ourselves in a postmodern state. Every penchant for the Gesamtkunstwerk is pure nostalgia here, and every avant-gardist claim a private mythology. Didn't Theodor W. Adorno say: "What feels like a utopia remains a negative

Theoder W. Adorno,
Ästhetische Theorie,
Frankfurt am Main 1973

schon früh verdeutlicht, als er sich von den Form-
doktrinen der klassischen Moderne distanzierte
und auch den von Adolf Loos geprägten Typus des
introspektiven Futterals – das nach Innen gestülpte
Drama der Loos'schen Raumplan-Häuser – hinter
sich ließ.

Bei unseren gemeinsamen Hausprojekten haben wir
um 1980 wohl versucht, etwas von diesen Loos'schen
und Frank'schen Qualitäten in die Gegenwart zu
lotsen; auch deine erste Möbelserie für die Secession
1984/85 brachte Assoziationen zu Hoffmann, Frank,
Haerdtl. Es waren letztlich Sackgassen, obwohl der
extrem kleine und herrlich robuste »Mickey-Maus-
Sessel« aus der Secessionsserie sich vielfach
bewährte und es demnächst eine Neuauflage dieser
Bugholzminiatur geben wird.

Danach hast du mit Schichtholzplatten in leuchten-
den Oskar-Putz-Farben experimentiert. Ab Mitte der
90er-Jahre mündete das, oder entspannte beziehungsweise konzentrierte es sich, ins raffinierte Understatement der Möbel für die Kunsthalle Krems,
die Swiss Re in Zürich und aktuell für den ostöster-
reichischen Bugholz-Produzenten Braun Lockenhaus.

Möbel ohne Etikett

Die Befreiung vom Retro-Touch sowohl der
Secessionsmöbel als auch der Schichtholz-Bunt-
heiten begann mit dem Armlehnstuhl für die
Kunsthalle Krems. Das ist ein vielseitig verwend-
barer Stapelstuhl mit klarer Trennung zwischen
dem schlichten Gestell – hier einfach zu klappen
für das Stapeln – und dem eingehängten Polster-
sitz, einem präzise der Sitzhaltung angeformten
Polsterkörper. Das Modell kam auch erfolgreich
beim Pavillon der Frankfurter Buchmesse zum

compared to what exists, and a slave to it?" And it
is in this direction, I think, that the observation of
the house today being a "collection of objects and
stimuli, beyond any architectural composition" also
points. This is something that Josef Frank illus-
trated early on, when he distanced himself from the
doctrines of form of classical modernism and also
left behind the type of the introspective sheath
coined by Adolf Loos—the inverted drama of
Loos's spatial-plan buildings.

In the house projects we worked on together, around
1980, we did try to bring something of Loos's and
Frank's qualities into the present; your first series of
furniture for the Secession in 1984–85 also brought
connotations of Frank, Josef Hoffmann, and Oswald
Haerdtl. In the end, they were blind alleys, although
the extremely small and wonderfully robust "Mickey
Mouse Easy Chair" from the Secession series has
proven itself many times, and a new edition of this
bentwood miniature is coming soon.

Afterward, you experimented with plywood layers in
bright Oskar Putz colors. Starting in the mid-nineties,
this culminated, or became relaxed and/or concentrated, in the refined understatement of the furniture
for the Kunsthalle Krems, the Swiss Re in Zurich,
and currently for Braun Lockenhaus, the bentwood
producers in eastern Austria.

Furniture without Labels

The liberation from the retro-touch as well as the
Secession furniture and also plywood variegations
started with the armchair for the Kunsthalle Krems.
This is a versatile stacking chair with a clear
separation between the plain frame—here simple
to fold for stacking—and the mounted upholstered

Einsatz, dann beim Swiss Re Centre for Global Dialogue, beim Archiv der Zeitgenossen in Krems usw. Auf dieser Dualität von Traggestell und Sitzschale aufbauend, konnte ich eine ganze Palette von Sesseln entwickeln, zuletzt für Braun Lockenhaus, für die ich Liegen, Betten und Liegesessel in der Kombination von Bugholzrahmen mit Gurtgeflechten entwarf.

Mit Hermann Czech wurdest du eingeladen, für den Neubau des Swiss Re Centre die gesamte Innenausstattung zu entwerfen. War das nicht auch eine Wegmarke für deine Vision von Möblierungen, die mit dem Raumgefüge »mitgehen«, die weder besonders gestylt noch allzu bürokratisch-neutral auftreten?

Die Arbeit für Swiss Re – auf Vorschlag der Architekten Marcel Meili und Markus Peter – war in vieler Hinsicht eine Pionierphase, zum Teil auch wirklich skurril und abenteuerlich. Es war überhaupt nicht klar, dass wir dort »alles« machen würden. Da das Gebäude ja gerade erst von Meili & Peter gebaut wurde, hatten wir keine konkreten räumlichen Vorgaben. Wir mussten alle Räume anhand von Modellen (von 1:10 bis 1:1) simulieren, um danach die Innenraumkonzepte entwickeln zu können.

Kommen wir in diesem Thema nochmals auf eine allgemeine Fragestellung. Du sagst ja vom Möbel, dass es für dich erst dann die Nagelprobe besteht, wenn es eben keinen allzu objekthaften Eigenwert mehr ausstrahlt, wenn es sich nicht als auffällige Physiognomie in den Vordergrund spielt, sondern seine Alltagstauglichkeit mit ausgetüfteltem, hintergründigem Understatement erfüllt.

Ich denke, hier gilt noch mehr, was Theodor W. Adorno und andere generell am Fetischismus un-

cushion, a padded element that precisely forms itself to the sitting posture. The model also came to be used successfully in the pavilion at the Frankfurt Book Fair, then at the Swiss Re Centre for Global Dialogue, in the Archiv der Zeitgenossen (Archive of Contemporaries) in Krems, and so on. Building on this duality of bearer frame and seat pan, I have been able to develop an entire palette of armchairs, most recently for Braun Lockenhaus, for which I also designed daybeds, beds, and chairbeds in a combination of bentwood frames with meshwork.

With Hermann Czech, you were invited to do all the interior design for the new Swiss Re Centre building. Wasn't that also a milestone for your vision of furnishings that "go along" with the spatial structure, that appear neither particularly styled nor overly bureaucratic and neutral?

The work for Swiss Re—at the suggestion of the architects Marcel Meili and Markus Peter—was a pioneering phase in many ways, and also sometimes really bizarre and adventurous. It was in no way clear that we would make "everything" there. Since the building was then first being built by Meili & Peter, we had no concrete spatial guidelines. We had to simulate all of the rooms based on models (from 1:10 to 1:1) in order to then be able to develop the concepts for the interior afterward.

On this topic, we come once again to a general question. You say that, for you, furniture has first passed the acid test when it specifically no longer emanates an overly object-like intrinsic value, when it no longer stands in the foreground as an eye-catching physiognomy but instead fulfills its suitability for daily use with subtle, enigmatic understatement.

m38
Seminarstuhl / Seminar Chair
1998

m60
Easychair
2012

S. / p. 246

9803
Interieur Swiss Re
Centre for Global Dialogue
Interieur einer Suite / Suite interior
mit / with Hermann Czech

1308
Liska Pelzmoden am Flughafen /
Airport Shop, Wien-Schwechat

serer Konsumgesellschaft diagnostizierten, was die Postmoderne als Stilbewegung, speziell aus Italien, an sinnlichem Überschuss in der Objektwelt dann paradox übersteigert zur Schau stellte, ohne das Grundproblem lösen zu können.

Meine Haltung dazu ist, dass nicht der äußerliche Sinn, die »Stimmigkeit« der Sache, des Raumes, des Möbels entscheidend ist – aber auch nicht ein wie auch immer formal befreiter oder destruierter Un-Sinn. Ich suche nach einem Zustand des Nicht-Sinns, nach jener Dimension des Gestalteten, die uns im Umgang damit, im Gebrauch, in der Ver-Formung des gestalteten Angebots möglichst wenig bevormundet, möglichst viel Freiheit lässt.

Zwischen den Ismen

Kari Jormakka,
Geschichte der Architekturtheorie,
Wien 2003

Am Ende seines Buches Geschichte der Architektur-theorie nannte Kari Jormakka – nach der kritischen Durchleuchtung aller modernen und postmodernen Ideologien – eine Handvoll Teams, denen er eine Unabhängigkeit von den gängigen pseudo-strukturalistischen oder neo-biomorphen Haltungen zugesteht. Zu diesen zählte er Toyo Ito, Herzog & de Meuron, Peter Zumthor, noch einige andere und auch dich. Und er fasste das unter dem Begriff Neo-Minimalismus zusammen, der sich weniger für Raum und Konstruktion interessiere, aber mehr für Material, Farben, Textur und Licht, die unproblematische Alltagsdimension.

In unseren Gesprächen für dein 1994 bei Artemis publiziertes Buch haben wir in dieser Richtung eine Positionsbestimmung versucht, und wir haben uns damals mit dem Begriff des »Dazwischen« beholfen …

Adolf Krischanitz, mit Beiträgen von Friedrich Achleitner, Otto Kapfinger und Walter Zschokke, Zürich, München und London 1994

I think that what still applies here is what Adorno and others generally diagnosed as the fetishism of our consumer society, what postmodernism as a style movement, especially from Italy, then paradoxically flaunted in an exaggerated way, in a sensual excess, in the world of objects, but without succeeding in solving the basic problem.

My position on this is that it is not the outward meaning, the "coherence" of the thing, the space, the furniture, that is decisive—but also not meaninglessness, however formally liberated or destroyed. I am searching for a state of non-meaning, for that dimension of the designed object that patronizes us as little as possible, gives us as much freedom as possible in dealing with it, in use, in de-forming the designed goods being offered.

Between the Isms

At the end of his book Geschichte der Architektur-theorie (History of Architectural Theory), Kari Jormakka—after critically scrutinizing all modern and postmodern ideologies—named a handful of teams to which he concedes independence from the conventional pseudo-structuralist or neo-biomorphic positions. He ranked Toyo Ito, Herzog & de Meuron, Peter Zumthor, and a few others, with you among them as well. And under the term neo-minimalism, he subsumed those who are less interested in space and structure, but more in material, colors, texture, and light, in the unproblematic dimensions of everyday life.

In our conversation for your 1994 book published by Artemis, we made attempts in this direction and we then made do with the term the "in-between" …

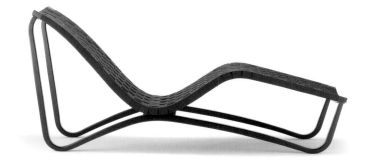

Es war eine Möglichkeit, dem unsäglichen Zwang zu entgehen, ein Schlagwort für eine »Richtung« zu prägen oder eine Kontinuität mit schon einmal formulierten »Ismen« herzuleiten. Wie gesagt misstraue ich solchen Zuordnungen, so interessant sie auch sein mögen. Interessanter als alle aktuelle Architekturtheorie waren und sind für mich gedankliche Positionen der zeitgenössischen Kunst, die sich mit Grundfragen unserer Bilder von Wirklichkeit befassen, mit den Mustern unserer Wahrnehmung und Begrifflichkeit und der Handhabung von Raum, von Welt. Da konnte ich durch die Arbeit für die Secessions-Ausstellungen der 90er-Jahre eine weitere Schicht des Zugangs, der Begriffsschärfung gewinnen.

Du hast mir vor einem Jahr ein Buch über Gerhard Richter gegeben, mit dem Kommentar, das sei ein Konzeptkünstler, ein konzeptueller Forscher, der sich der Malerei, der Rauminstallation, des Objekthaften bediene, um in solchen und durch solche Medien eine Auseinandersetzung mit Konventionen des Bildhaften, der Repräsentation, des Verstehens und Sehens von »Wirklichkeit« zu führen.

Richter war eine Art Augenöffnung oder ein Wiedererkennen für mich. Denn in seiner Arbeit nimmt er seit Jahrzehnten immer neue Anläufe, all diese Klischees von Figuration oder Abstraktion, von Komplexität oder Transparenz, von Natur und Kunst und Authentizität zu untergraben. Stillosigkeit, Kompositionslosigkeit etwa sind für ihn Ausgangspunkte für die wirklich spannende, die Augen öffnende Durchdringung so vieler immer noch gültiger Konventionen der »Kultivierung« von Bewusstsein, von Zeitgenossenschaft usw.

Hat nicht auch Rem Koolhaas vor etlichen Jahren von der »Nichtigkeit« oder der »Nichtsheit«

It was a way of avoiding the unspeakable pressure to coin a catchword for a "direction" or to derive some kind of continuity with already formulated "isms." As I've mentioned, I mistrust such classifications, as interesting as they might also be. For me, what was and is more interesting than any current architectural theory are intellectual positions in contemporary art that deal with fundamental questions related to our images of reality, with the patterns of our perception and terminology, and with the handling of space, of the world. Through the work for the Secession exhibitions in the nineties, I was able to obtain a further layer of access, a whetting of concepts in this regard.

One year ago, you gave me a book about Gerhard Richter, with the comment that he is a Conceptual artist, an explorer of concepts who makes use of painting, installations, and the object-like in order to conduct an analysis of conventions of the pictorial, of representation, of understanding and seeing "reality" with such, and by means of such, media.

Richter was a kind of eye-opener or sense of recognition for me—since, for decades, he has continued to make new attempts in his work to undermine all these clichés of figuration or abstraction, of complexity or transparency, of nature and art and authenticity. Absence of style, absence of composition, for instance, are for him starting points for the truly exciting, the eye-opening penetration of so many conventions of the "cultivation" of awareness, of contemporaneity, and so on, that continue to be relevant.

Didn't Rem Koolhaas also speak some years ago about the "nullity" or "nothingness" of our everyday Western culture, about the death of architecture in

m63
Daybed
2012

m62
Chairbed
2012

unserer westlichen Alltagskultur gesprochen, vom Tod der Architektur im alten Sinn, worauf man nur mit apolitischem Pragmatismus reagieren könne, mit forschem Umsteigen beziehungsweise günstigenfalls mit einem leicht subversiven, illusionslosen Einsteigen in diese stillose, sinnlose Dynamik der dominierenden Ökonomie?

Ich glaube, Koolhaas hat diesen Anspruch durch seine eigene Praxis widerlegt – oder eben nicht bestätigt. Und es ist bei Richter doch anders. Er blieb, was in der freien Kunst leichter geht, im Konkreten immer identisch mit dem Gemeinten. Wenn er zum Beispiel mit dem Verwischen seiner »realistischen« Bilder diese Irritation leistet, weder gegenständlich noch abstrakt zu sein, dann hat das bleibende Brisanz. Und wenn er sagt, er halte alles für gleich wichtig und gleich unwichtig, und das in seinen Medien – die auch die Medien, Muster unserer optischen und haptischen Alltagswelt sind – tatsächlich erfahrbar, nachvollziehbar macht, dann beschäftigt mich das essenziell. Und es zeigt mir Markierungen, die ich seit einiger Zeit und auch in Zukunft im Auge zu behalten versuche, auch in meiner Arbeit fassbar machen möchte.

the old sense, to which one could only react with apolitical pragmatism, with a brisk transfer or at best with a slightly subversive climbing on-board without illusions to this dynamic of the prevailing economy devoid of style or meaning?

I believe that Koolhaas has disproved this claim— or at least not confirmed it—through his own practice. And it is nonetheless different in the case of Richter, who, in the concrete, has always remained identical with what is meant, which is easier in the fine arts. When, for instance, with the blurring of his "realistic" pictures, he achieves this irritation of being neither representational nor abstract, he actually attains lasting explosive power. And when he says that he takes everything as equally important and equally unimportant, and actually makes this experienceable, perceivable, in his media—which are also the media and patterns of our visual and haptic everyday world—then this fundamentally engages me. And it shows me markers that I have been attempting keep in view for some time and will also continue to attempt to keep in view in the future, and that I would also like to make palpable in my work.

m06
Barhocker / Barstool S3
1986

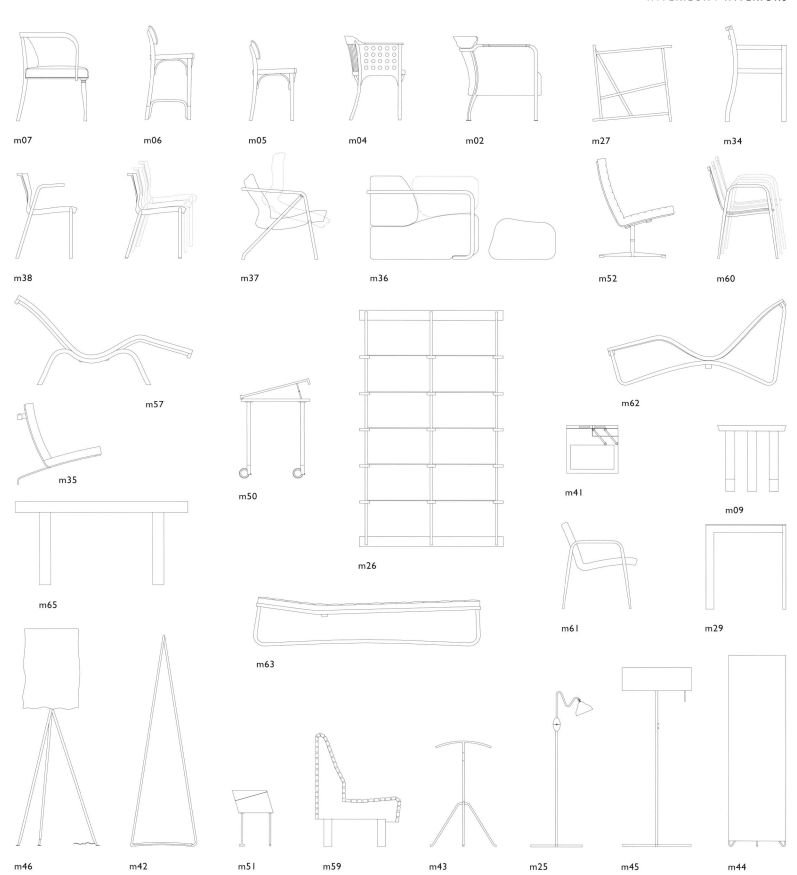

m07

m06

m05

m04

m02

m27

m34

m38

m37

m36

m52

m60

m57

m35

m50

m26

m62

m41

m09

m65

m63

m61

m29

m46

m42

m51

m59

m43

m25

m45

m44

9507
Haus / House Sperl, Zurndorf

9507
Haus / House Sperl

0009
Erweiterung / Extension

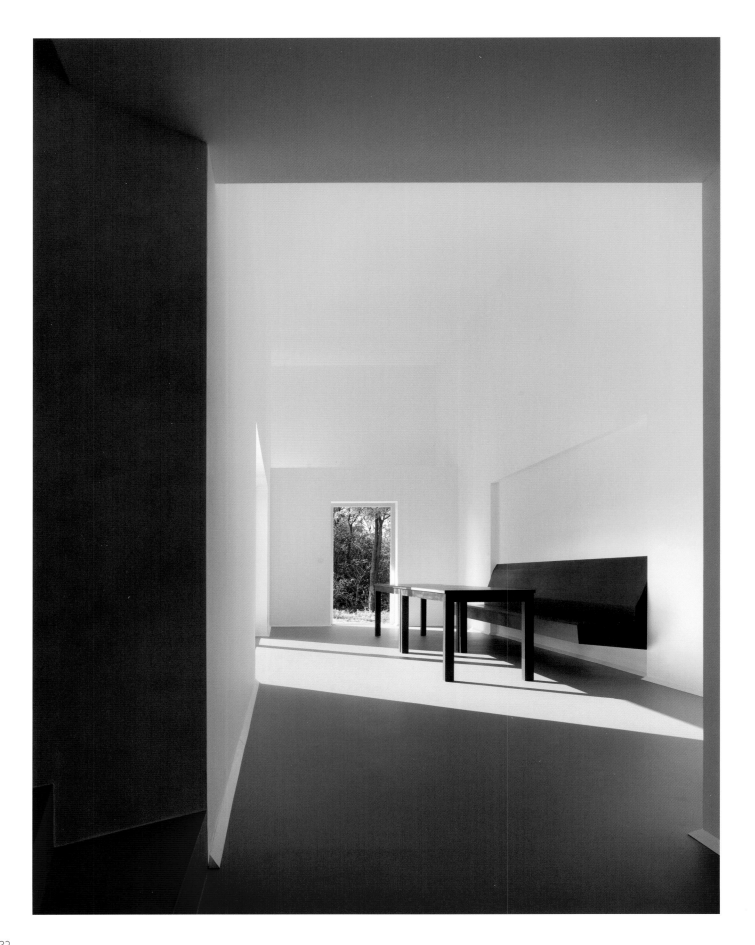

0112
Haus / House Scholten, Pengers

0112 / 0906
Haus / House Scholten, Ausbau Obergeschoss / Upgrading of 2nd Floor

0112
Haus / House Scholten, Ensemble

9506
Atelierhaus / Studio House, Furth-Steinaweg bei / near Göttweig

9506
Atelierhaus / Studio House

9506
Atelierhaus / Studio House

9114
Umbau Wohnung L. / Conversion of Apartment L., Wien / Vienna
Farbkonzept / Color concept: Oskar Putz

244

9114
Umbau Wohnung L. / Conversion of Apartment L.

9803
Interieur / Interior of Swiss Re – Center for Global Dialogue, Rüschlikon mit / with: Hermann Czech, Gilbert Bretterbauer

9102
Umbau Wohnung / Conversion of Apartment Scholten, Wien / Vienna
Farbkonzept / Color concept: Oskar Putz

1310
Wohnung K. / Apartment K., Hochhaus / High-Rise Building on Herrengasse, Wien / Vienna

1012
Umbau Wohnung A. / Conversion of Apartment A., Wien / Vienna

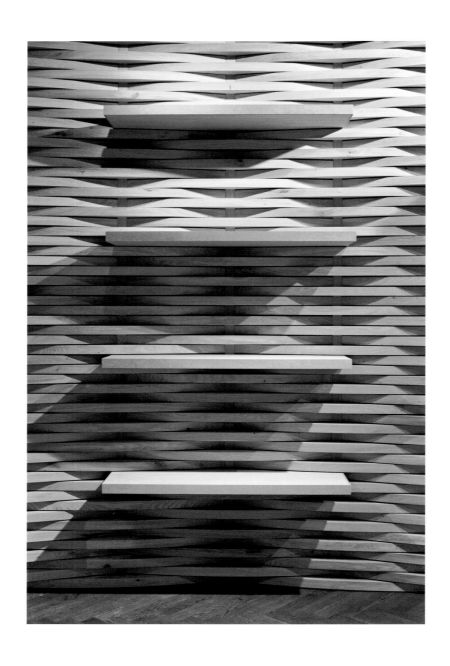

Die Physis von Gebäuden – Material, Technik, Funktion, und Form – verschwindet zugunsten des Sinns. Der Raum im nichtmateriellen Sinn bleibt bestehen. Das Verschwinden, besser Zurücktreten der Physis in unbewusste Alltäglichkeit oder Routine heißt aber nicht, dass man sie vernachlässigen kann – im Gegenteil. Es ist erst die sorgfältig gefügte Physis unserer Bauten, die jenes Vertrauen schafft, uns an einem Ort – über die physikalische Konditionierung hinaus – soweit geborgen zu fühlen, dass wir die Vorstellung von der zerstörerischen Zeit ertragen können.

The physical existence of buildings—materiality, technology, functionality, and form qualities—disappears in favor of meaning. The space in a nonmaterial sense remains intact. But the disappearance, or better, retreat of the physical existence in an unconscious day-to-day routine does not mean that one can neglect it—on the contrary. It is the carefully fitted physical existence of our buildings which creates that trust to feel sheltered enough at a location beyond the physical conditioning, so that we can bear the idea of a destructive time.

Adolf Krischanitz

Werkverzeichnis der Architektur / Catalogue Raisonné of Architecture

0000	Projektnummer / Project number
S. / p.	Seite / Page
P	Partner
K	Künstler / Artist
A	Auftraggeber / Client
I	Auslober / Initiator
AP	Ausführungsplanung / Detail planning
LP	Landschaftsplanung / Landscape planning
S	Statik / Statics
PL	Projektleiter / Project leader
W	Wettbewerb / Competition

8002 S. / pp. 12/13
Geschäftseinrichtung / Shop Design for Kuoni
Wien / Vienna (AT)
1980
P: Otto Kapfinger
A: Reisebüro Kuoni Ges.m.b.H.

8101
Haus / House N.
Perchtoldsdorf (AT)
1981
P: Otto Kapfinger
A: privat / private

8102
Haus / House H.
Schwarzach (AT)
1981/82
P: Otto Kapfinger
A: privat / private

8103
Studie Haus / Study House S.
Gröbming-Mitterberg (AT)
1981
P: Otto Kapfinger
A: privat / private

8201
Geschäftseinrichtung / Shop Design for
Lederwaren Delarue
Wien / Vienna (AT)
1982
P: Otto Kapfinger
A: Delarue Co.

8301 S. / pp. 102, 104, 110
Renovierung Wiener Werkbundsiedlung /
Renovation of the Vienna Werkbund Settlement
Wien / Vienna (AT)

1983–1985
P: Otto Kapfinger
A: Stadt Wien / City of Vienna

8501 S. / pp. 7/8, 11, 24/25, 50, 53/54, 64, 85, 202, 222, 225
Umbau / Conversion of the Wiener Secession
Wien / Vienna (AT)
1985/86
P: Otto Kapfinger
A: Vereinigung Bildender KünstlerInnen
Wiener Secession
PL: Jürg Meister, Werner Neuwirth, Gerhard Schlager
> 8601 Möbel / Furniture 1986
> 9017 Barpavillon / Bar Pavilion, 1992
> 9203 Vitrinen / Display Cases, 1992
> 9702 Eingangsbereich / Foyer, 1997
> 9702 Dokumentation *Beethovenfries* /
Documentation *Beethoven Frieze*, 1997
> 0410 Depot, 2007
Ausstellungen / Exhibitions:
> 8605 *Weltbilder*, 1986
> 9018 *Ludwig Wittgenstein. Das Spiel des Unsagbaren*, 1990
> 9108 *Bernhard Prinz*, 1991
> 9202 *Schullin – Seitner*, 1992
> 9305 *Brigitte Kowanz*, 1993
> 9306 *Ernst Caramelle*, 1993
> 9411 *Aura*, 1994
> 9514 *Dieter Roth*, 1995
> 9515 *Pierre Klossowski*, 1995

8502
Gutachterverfahren Bürogebäude / Expert Report
on Office Building Schömer
Klosterneuburg (AT)
1985
P: Otto Kapfinger
A: Fritz Schömer GmbH

8602
Haus / House R.
Wien-Salmannsdorf / Vienna-Salmannsdorf (AT)
1986
K: Oskar Putz
A: privat / private
PL: Jürg Meister

8603 S. / pp. 102–104
Wohnbauten / Residential Buildings
on Forellenweg
Salzburg (AT)
1986–1990
P: Otto Kapfinger
K: Oskar Putz
A: Gemeinnützige Salzburger Wohnbau-
gesellschaft m.b.H.
AP: Wolfgang Soyka
PL: Gerhard Schlager

8702
Studie U3 Oberflächengestaltung / Study for the
U3 Surface Design Mariahilferstraße
Wien / Vienna (AT)
1987/88
P: Leopold Redl
A: Stadt Wien / City of Vienna

8704
Winarsky-Hof, Aufzugseinbauten Bauteil / Elevator
Modules, Structural Component Josef Frank und /
and Oskar Wlach
Wien / Vienna (AT)
1987/88
A: Stadt Wien / City of Vienna
AP: Rudolf Lamprecht

8705 S. / pp. 103/104, 120
Siedlung / Housing Settlement on Pilotengasse
Wien / Vienna (AT)
1987–1992
P: Herzog & de Meuron, Otto Steidle
K: Helmut Federle, Oskar Putz
A: ÖSW Österreichisches Siedlungswerk
PL: Gerhard Schlager

8802 S. / p. 104
Fahrtenbüro / Tour Office El Cabrito
La Gomera, Kanarische Inseln / Canary Islands (ES)
1988–1990
A: Cooperation Friedrichshof, San Sebastian
PL: Markus Grob, Klaus W. Heinemann, Regula
Lüscher
> 9019 Depothalle / Warehouse Hall, 1990
> 9020 Bananenhalle / Banana Hall, 1990
> 9006 Bebauungsstudie Terrassenhäuser /
Development Study on Terraced Houses, 1990

8803
Haus / House in Pötzleinsdorf
Wien / Vienna (AT)
1988–1990
P: Otto Kapfinger
K: Oskar Putz
A: privat / private
PL: Jürg Meister

8804 S. / pp. 17–20, 28, 31, 42
Ausstellungspavillon an der Traisen /
Exhibition Pavilion on Traisen River
St. Pölten (AT)
1988/89
K: Oskar Putz
A: NÖ Landeshauptstadt Planungs-Ges.m.b.H.
S: Wolfdietrich Ziesel
PL: Jürg Meister

8901
Büro- und Geschäftshaus / Office and Commercial
Building Schillerpark
Linz (AT)
1989–1994
K: Oskar Putz
A: Die ERSTE Baumanagement Planungs- und
Errichtungsgesellschaft m.b.H.
AP: Hinterwirth Architekten
PL: Franz Meisterhofer

8902   S. / p. 18
Städtebaulicher Wettbewerb Regierungsviertel /
Urban Planning Competition for the Government
Quarter
St. Pölten (AT)
1989
K: Oskar Putz
I: NÖ Landeshauptstadt Planungsgesellschaft m.b.H.

9001
Büro- und Geschäftsgebäude / Office and
Commercial Building Steirerhof
Graz (AT)
1990–1994
P: Achammer-Tritthart-Partner
K: Oskar Putz
A: IVG Immobilienerwerbs- und Vermietungs-
gesellschaft m.b.H.
PL: Franz Meisterhofer

9002
Studie Wohngebäude / Study for Housing in
Urfahr, Projekt 1,2,3
Linz (AT)
1990
I: DIE ERSTE Baumanagement Planungs- und
Errichtungsgesellschaft m.b.H.

9003
Studie Bebauungsplan / Development Plan Study
Urfahr
Linz (AT)
1990
I: Stadt / City of Linz

9008   S. / pp. 22/23
Indoor-Halle / Indoor Hall
anlässlich der Ausstellung / in connection with
the exhibition *Von der Natur in der Kunst*
Messepalast, ehemalige Winterreitschule / at the
former Winter Riding School
Wien / Vienna (AT)
1990
A: Wiener Festwochen
PL: Stefan Rudolf

9010
Wettbewerb / Competition for Wiental-Brücke
Wien / Vienna (AT)
1990
K: Oskar Putz
I: HL-AG Eisenbahn-Hochleistungsstrecken AG
S: Wolfdietrich Ziesel

9011
Städtebaulicher Wettbewerb Zechengelände /
Urban-Planning Competition for the
Mine Premises Prosper III
Bottrop (DE)
1990
K: Oskar Putz
I: Stadt / City of Bottrop
S: Wolfdietrich Ziesel

9013
Städtebauliche Studie / Urban-Planning Study
Esplanade
Gmunden (AT)
1990
I: Land Oberösterreich / Province of Upper Austria;
Stadt / City of Gmunden

9016
Städtebaulicher Wettbewerb / Urban-Planning
Competition for Donauraum, EXPO '95
Wien / Vienna (AT)
1990
I: EXPO-VIENNA AG

9102   S. / p. 247
Umbau Wohnung / Conversion of
Apartment Scholten
Wien / Vienna (AT)
1991/92
K: Oskar Putz
A: privat / private
PL: Marco Fedier, Markus Grob

9110
Wettbewerb Ideenfindung / Competition for
Brainstorming Schönbrunn
Wien / Vienna (AT)
1991
I: Stadt Wien / City of Vienna

9114   S. / pp. 244/245
Umbau Wohnung / Conversion of Apartment L.
Wien / Vienna (AT)
1991
A: privat / private
PL: Franz Meisterhofer
> 0704   Interieur Wohnung / Interior of
Apartment L., 2007

9115
Innenausbau Hauptpost / Interior Construction of
the Central Post Office Fleischmarkt
Wien / Vienna (AT)
1991 (nicht erhalten / not preserved)
K: Oskar Putz
A: Post- und Telegraphendirektion für Wien
PL: Markus Grob

9116   S. / pp. 22–27, 31–33, 42, 64
Kunsthalle Karlsplatz
Wien / Vienna (AT)
1991/92 (abgebaut / dismantled in 2001)
K: Oskar Putz
Fassadengestaltungen Ausstellungsreihe / Façade
designs for the exhibition series *Großbild*,
museum in progress:
Ed Ruscha, *17th Century – 20th Century*, 1993
Walter Obholzer, *20 Fleck*, 1994/95
Gerhard Richter, *river*, 1995/96
Douglas Gordon, *raise the dead*, 1996
Ken Lum, *There is no place like home*, 2001
A: Stadt Wien / City of Vienna
PL: Stefan Rudolf, Wolfgang Tröger

9117
Städtebauliche Entwicklungsstudie 6. und 7. Bezirk /
Urban Planning Study for Districts 6 and 7
Wien / Vienna (AT)
1991
A: Stadt Wien / City of Vienna

9201   S. / pp. 11, 93, 105–108
Entwicklungsstudie / Development Study for
Donau City (Masterplan / Master Plan)
Wien / Vienna (AT)
1992
P: Heinz Neumann
A: WED Wiener Entwicklungsgesellschaft für den
Donauraum AG

9204   S. / pp. 46, 200, 202, 212/213
Neue Welt Schule
Wien / Vienna (AT)
1992–1994
K: Helmut Federle
A: NEUE WELT Fonds zur Unterstützung und Aus-
bildung von Jugendlichen
PL: Mark Gilbert, Eric Red

9205
Wohnhaus / House on Engilgasse
Wien / Vienna (AT)
1992–1995
K: Oskar Putz
A: DIE ERSTE Baumanagement Planungs- und Errich-
tungsgesellschaft m.b.H.
PL: Susanne Ostertag

9206   S. / pp. 48, 63/64, 77–79, 222
Kunsthalle Krems
Krems (AT)
1992–1996
A: Stadt / City of Krems
PL: Željko Ivošević, Jürg Meister, Gerhard Schlager
> 0113   Pavillon / Pavilion, 2001/02

9207
**Wettbewerb Österreichisches Kulturinstitut /
Competition for the Austrian Cultural Institute**
New York (US)
1992
K: Oskar Putz
I: Bundesministerium für auswärtige Angelegenheiten /
Austrian Federal Ministry for Foreign Affairs

9301   S. / p. 105
**Städtebaulicher Wettbewerb Bahnhofsgelände /
Urban-Planning Competition for the Railway
Station Grounds**
Eichstätt (DE)
1993
P: Thomeczek + Scherzer + Team, Sal 4
I: Stadtbauamt / Municipal Planning Office Eichstätt

9302
**Studie CI-Konzept, Innenausbau und Fassaden-
gestaltung / Study CI, Interior Construction
and Façade Design for Wein & Co.**
Wien / Vienna (AT)
1993
P: Alexander Kahane
I: WEIN & CO Handelsges.m.b.H.

9303
**Bauwerke der Infrastruktur / Infrastructure
Buildings for Donau City**
Wien / Vienna (AT)
1993
A: WED Wiener Entwicklungsgesellschaft für den
Donauraum AG
PL: Markus Grob (W), Ingrid Dreer

9304
**Wettbewerb Kongresshotel / Competition for
Hyatt Conference Hotel**
Zürich / Zurich (CH)
1993
K: Oskar Putz
I: Stadt Zürich / City of Zurich; Konsortium
Suter + Suter AG / Park Hyatt Hotel AG

9401
**Wettbewerb / Competition for Europark
Interspar**
Salzburg (AT)
1994
I: SPAR Österreichische Warenhandels-AG

9402
**Wettbewerb Amtsgebäude / Competition for
Official Building Stadtgraben**
Krems (AT)
1994
K: Oskar Putz
I: Magistrat der Stadt Krems, Stadtbauamt / Magis-
trate of the City of Krems, Municipal Planning Office

9404
**Wettbewerb Remise / Competition for Coach
House Ottakring**
Wien / Vienna (AT)
1994
I: GESIBA Gemeinnützige Siedlungs- und Bauaktien-
gesellschaft

9405   S. / pp. 96, 108
**Städtebaulicher Wettbewerb / Urban-Planning
Competition for Absberggasse**
Wien / Vienna (AT)
1994
I: ÖSW Österreichisches Siedlungswerk

9406   S. / pp. 26/27, 34, 42, 222
**Österreich-Pavillon auf der Frankfurter Buchmesse /
Austrian Pavilion at the Frankfurt Book Fair**
Frankfurt am Main (DE)
1994/95
A: Hauptverband des Österreichischen Buchhandels
PL: Eric Red

9407
**Wettbewerb Verwaltungsgebäude /
Competition for Administration Building
EA Generali**
Wien / Vienna (AT)
1994
I: Generali Holding Vienna AG

9408   S. / p. 26
**Wettbewerb Informationspavillon / Competition
for Information Pavilion Leipziger Platz**
Berlin (DE)
1994
I: Berlin, Senatsverwaltung für Bau- und Wohnungs-
wesen / Senate Administration of Building and
Housing

9409
**Städtebaulicher Wettbewerb Industriepark /
Urban-Planning Competition for the Industrial
Park Klotzsche IVG-AG**
Dresden (DE)
1994/95
A: IVG AG

9410   S. / pp. 108, 217
Masterplan Friedrichshof
Zurndorf (AT)
1994

A: Friedrichshof Wohnungsgenossenschaft
registrierte Genossenschaft m.b.H.
PL: Markus Grob

9413
Studie / Study for Paradeplatz (Parade 2000, SKA)
Zürich / Zurich (CH)
1994
I: Schweizerische Kreditanstalt

9501
**Wettbewerb Artistensporthalle / Competition for
Artiste Sports Hall**
Berlin (DE)
1995
I: Stadt / City of Berlin

9503
**Städtebaulicher Ideenwettbewerb /
Urban-Planning Idea Competition for
Stadtquartier Nordbahnhof**
Berlin (DE)
1995
I: Deutsche Bahn AG

9504
**Wettbewerb Leitprojekt / Competition for Pilot
Project Kagran-West**
Wien / Vienna (AT)
1995
P: Elsa Prochazka
I: Mischek Bauträger Service GmbH

9505
**Wettbewerb Torhäuser / Competition for
Gatehouses at Leipziger Platz**
Berlin (DE)
1995
I: Stadt / City of Berlin

9506   S. / pp. 218, 238–243
Atelierhaus / Studio House
Furth-Steinaweg bei / near Göttweig (AT)
1995–1998
A: privat / private
PL: Robert Felber

9507   S. / pp. 217/218, 228–232
Haus / House Sperl
Zurndorf, Burgenland (AT)
1995/96
A: privat / private
PL: Mark Gilbert, Dirk Haid, Karoline Mayer,
Wendy Wulff
> 0009   Erweiterung / Extension, 2000/01
> 0705   Gewächshaus / Greenhouse, 2007
> 0909   Wirtschaftsgebäude / Outbuilding, 2010

9508 S. / p. 221
Schreibstube für / Scriptorium for Robert Menasse
Wien / Vienna (AT)
1995/96
A: privat / private
PL: Anna Wickenhauser

9509 S. / p. 201
Wettbewerb Schule / Competition for School-
house Steinergasse
Wien / Vienna (AT)
1995/96, 2000
I: Stadt Wien / City of Vienna

9510
Feuerwache / Firehouse Donau City
Wien / Vienna (AT)
1995–2001
A: Stadt Wien / City of Vienna
PL: Frank Boehm, Wilfried Kühn

9511
Wettbewerb Jugendzentrum / Competition for
Youth Center Wolkenspange
Wien / Vienna (AT)
1995/96
I: Richard Lugner

9512
Bebauungsstudie / Development Study for
Fondachhof
Salzburg (AT)
1995
I: Fürst Developments

9513
Studie Straßenbeleuchtung / Study for Street
Lighting Donau City
Wien / Vienna (AT)
1995
I: WED Wiener Entwicklungsgesellschaft für den
Donauraum AG

9601
Wohnhaus / Residential Building Fondachhof
Salzburg (AT)
1996–1999
A: Fürst Developments
PL: Frank Boehm, Ingrid Dreer, Anna Wickenhauser

9602
Städtebaulicher Ideenwettbewerb / Urban-Planning
Idea Competition for EXPO Plaza
Hannover (DE)
1996
I: EXPO Grund GmbH / EXPO 2000 Hannover GmbH

9603
Wettbewerb Gemeindezentrum / Competition for
Community Center

Lech / Arlberg (AT)
1996
I: Gemeinde / Municipality of Lech am Arlberg

9604
Wettbewerb Hotel und Konferenzeinrichtungen /
Competition for Hotel and Conference Facilities
Adlershof
Berlin (DE)
1996
I: Arwobau GmbH Berlin

9609 S. / p. 122
Städtische Wohnhausanlage / Urban Residential
Complex Dernjacgasse
Wien / Vienna (AT)
1996–2000
P: Rudolf Prohazka, Albert Wimmer, NFOG Atelier
für Architektur, Ganahl-Ifsits-Larch
A: Gartenheim Gemeinnützige Genossenschaft
PL: Manfred Hasler, Wilfried Kühn,
Anna Wickenhauser

9610
Wettbewerb Brücke und Brückenköpfe /
Competition for Bridge and Bridgeheads
Kassel (DE)
1996/97
I: Projektentwicklungsgesellschaft Kassel-Unter-
neustadt; Konversion in Kassel mbH

9611 S. / pp. 11, 94, 105, 107/108, 114
Masterplan Wohnbebauung / Residential Buildings
neues bauen am horn
Weimar (DE)
1996–1999
I: Bauhaus-Universität Weimar, in Kooperation mit
der / in cooperation with the Landesentwicklungs-
gesellschaft (LEG) Thüringen / Thuringia und der
Stadt / and the City of Weimar
PL: Werner Neuwirth, Anna Wickenhauser

9612 S. / pp. 201–203, 208–211
Lauder Chabad Schule / School
Wien / Vienna (AT)
1996–1999
A: Ronald S. Lauder Verein zur Förderung der
Jugend in Österreich
PL: Frank Boehm, Annette Großkinsky, Wilfried Kühn
> 0513 Erweiterung / Extension, 2007
> 1403 Projektstudie Erweiterung / Project Study
Extension for Lauder Chabad Campus, 2014

9703 S. / pp. 42, 80
Tauernbahnmuseum
Schwarzach (AT)
1997–2001
P: Werner Neuwirth
A: Verein Museum Tauernbahn, ÖBB

9705
Studie / Study Bank Austria, Donau City
Wien / Vienna (AT)
1997
I: Bank Austria

9706
Wettbewerb Messestand o.tel.o / Competition for
o.tel.o Exhibition Stand at CeBIT '98
Hannover (DE)
1997
I: o.tel.o communication GmbH

9707
Städtebaulicher Wettbewerb Neugestaltung Messe-
platz und Service Center, Messe Basel / Urban-
Planning Competition for the Conversion of the
Exhibition Grounds and Service Center Messe Basel
Basel (CH)
1998
I: MCH Messe Basel
LP: Anna Detzlhofer

9801
Wettbewerb Abfertigungshalle / Competition for
Terminal Building of Swarovski Kristallwelten
Wattens (AT)
1998
I: D. Swarovski & Co. Kristallwelt

9802
Entwurf / Design for Max Weiler Museum
Innsbruck (AT)
1998
A: Max Weiler-Privatstiftung / Yvonne Weiler

9803 S. / pp. 13, 45, 145, 222–224, 246
Interieur / Interior of Swiss Re –
Center for Global Dialogue
Rüschlikon (CH)
1998–2000
P: Hermann Czech; Marcel Meili,
Markus Peter Architekten
A: Swiss Re
PL: Željko Ivošević, Werner Neuwirth

9804
Wettbewerb Pfarrzentrum / Competition for
Parish Center
Podersdorf am See (AT)
1998
I: Erzbischöfliches Ordinariat Eisenstadt

9805 S. / p. 200
Wettbewerb Informations- und Kommunikations-
zentrum / Competition for Information and
Communication Center at Adlershof (IKA)
Berlin (DE)
1998
I: Land Berlin und / and Wista Management GmbH

I: Schweizerische Eidgenossenschaft, Bundesamt für Bauten und Logistik / Swiss Confederation, Federal Office for Building and Logistics

0106
Wettbewerb Therme / Competition for Spa
Bad Hofgastein (AT)
2001
I: Gasteiner Thermen Errichtungs GmbH

0108 S. / pp. 147, 159, 181–183
Verkehrsrechenzentrale / Traffic Computer Center ASFINAG
Wien-Inzersdorf / Vienna-Inzersdorf (AT)
2001–2003
P: ARGE Axis Ingenieursdienstleistungen
A: ASFINAG Autobahnen- und Schnellstraßen-Finanzierungs AG
LP: Anna Detzlhofer
PL: Victoria von Gaudecker

0110
Liska Pelzmodengeschäft am Graben
Wien / Vienna (AT)
2001/02
A: M. Liska & Co GmbH
PL: Victoria von Gaudecker, Željko Ivošević

0111 S. / p. 42
Kunsthalle Wien, Project Space
Wien / Vienna (AT)
2001/02
A: Verein Kunsthalle Wien
PL: Manfred Hasler

0112 S. / pp. 218/219, 233–237
Haus / House Scholten
Pengers (AT)
2001/02
A: privat / private
PL: Robert Felber, Michael Flury, Dirk Haid, Željko Ivošević, Luciano Parodi, Harald Siemens, Daniel Sutovsky
> 0702   Försterhaus / Forester's House, 2007
> 0721   Zubau / Annex, 2007/08
> 0906   Umbau / Conversion, 2009–2001; Ausbau Obergeschoss / Upgrading of 2nd Floor, 2009–2011

0201
Städtebaulicher Wettbewerb Bahnhofsareal / Urban-Planning Competition for the Railway Station Grounds DB
Basel (CH)
2002
A: Kanton Basel-Stadt, Baudepartement / Canton of Basel-Stadt, Building Department

0202
Städtebaulicher Wettbewerb Kernzone / Urban-Planning Competition for Core Area of Donau City
Wien / Vienna (AT)
2002
I: Stadt Wien / City of Vienna

0203
Schwimmbad / Swimming Pool K.
Wien / Vienna (AT)
2002
A: privat / private
PL: Victoria von Gaudecker

0204
Studie Kunstmeile / Study for "Art Mile" Krems
Krems (AT)
2002
A: Magistrat der Stadt Krems, MAIV Planungsamt / Municipal Authority of the City of Krems, MAIV Planning Office
LP: Anna Detzlhofer
> 0903   Entwurf Platzgestaltung Kunstmeile / Plaza Design for "Art Mile" Krems, 2009–2011

0205
Wettbewerb Landeskrankenhaus / Competition for State Hospital
Steyr (AT)
2002
I: LKV Krankenhaus Errichtungs- und Vermietungs GmbH

0206
Städtebaulicher Wettbewerb / Urban-Planning Competition for Rapid-Areal
Dietikon (CH)
2002
P: Birgit Frank
I: Rapid Holding AG
LP: Anna Detzlhofer

0207
Wettbewerb / Competition for Hotel Savoy Baur en Ville
Zürich / Zurich (CH)
2002
I: Hotel Savoy Baur en Ville

0208
Städtebaulicher Wettbewerb / Urban-Planning Competition for St. Jakobsplatz
München / Munich (DE)
2002
I: Landeshauptstadt München / City of Munich

0210
Faltbarer Kinosaal / Folding Cinema Hall for MUMOK
Wien / Vienna (AT)

2002
A: MUMOK (Museum Moderner Kunst Stiftung Ludwig)
PL: Victoria von Gaudecker

0211 S. / p. 49
Umbau / Conversion of Kölnischer Kunstverein »Die Brücke«
Köln / Cologne (DE)
2002/03
A: Kölnischer Kunstverein »Die Brücke«
PL: Volker Spies, Karin Triendl

0212 S. / pp. 10, 108–110, 122, 134
Wohnbau / Residential Building Monte Laa, Bauplatz / Building Plot 7
Wien / Vienna (AT)
2002–2006
K: Maria Hahnenkamp
A: EBG Gemeinnützige Ein- und Mehrfamilienhäuser Baugenossenschaft
PL: Patrick Fessler, Henri Rochat

0213 S. / pp. 7/8, 46, 49, 55–64, 68–76
Umbau und Erweiterung / Conversion and Extension of Museum Rietberg
Zürich / Zurich (CH)
2002–2007
P: Alfred Grazioli
K: Gilbert Bretterbauer, Helmut Federle
A: Stadt Zürich / City of Zurich
PL: Birgit Frank (W), Elke Eichmann, Wieka Muthesius, Ralf Wilkening

0214
Wettbewerb / Competition for IKEA Berlin
Berlin (DE)
2002
I: IKEA Deutschland GmbH & Co. KG; Senatsverwaltung / Senate Administration Berlin

0301 S. / pp. 13/14, 46, 140–147, 156, 158, 160–166
Laborgebäude / Laboratory Building, Novartis Campus
Basel (CH)
2003–2008
P: Birgit Frank (W)
K: Gilbert Bretterbauer, Sigmar Polke
A: Novartis Pharma AG
PL: Henri Rochat

0303
Wettbewerb Brücke / Competition for Bridge at Alberner Hafen / Harbor
Wien / Vienna (AT)
2003
I: ÖBB Österreichische Bundesbahnen

0304 S. / pp. 42, 81/82
Privatmuseum / Private Museum Gnad & Gawisch
Wien / Vienna (AT)
2003–2006
A: privat / private
PL: Ole Ritzke

0305
Wohn- und Geschäftshaus Olympisches Dorf / Residential and Commercial Building for Olympic Village
Turin (IT)
2003–2005
P: Birgit Frank (W)
A: Agenzia Torino
PL: Ole Ritzke

0306 S. / pp. 122, 138/139
Buddhistisches Wohnheim / Buddhist Hostel
Mandalahof
Wien / Vienna (AT)
2003–2008
A: Univ. Prof. Dr. Peter Riedl
LP: Atelier Auböck + Kárász
PL: Karoline Mayer, Felix Siegrist, Karin Triendl

0307 S. / pp. 49–55, 64–66, 86/87, 155
Umbau und Erweiterung / Conversion and
Extension of the 20er/21er Haus
Wien / Vienna (AT)
2003–2012
A: Burghauptmannschaft Österreich in Vertretung
des BMWFJ (Phase 1), Österreichische Galerie
Belvedere (Phase 2)
PL: Florian Zierer (W), Karin Triendl, Luciano Parodi,
Jana Raudnitzky

0308 S. / p. 216
Studie Musterhäuser / Study of Model Houses for
neues bauen am horn
Weimar (DE)
2003/04
I: Bauhaus-Universität Weimar, in Kooperation mit
der / in cooperation with the Landesentwicklungs-
gesellschaft (LEG) Thüringen / Thuringia und der
Stadt / and the City of Weimar

0309
Zubau Pfadfinderheim / Annex for Scouts' Camp
Hollenstein (AT)
2003–2006
A: Gemeinde / Municipality of Hollenstein / Ybbs

0402
Wettbewerb für eine Villa / Villa Competition
St. Gilgen (AT)
2004
P: Birgit Frank
A: privat / private

0403
Gutachterverfahren / Peer Review of Gozzoburg
Krems (AT)
2004
I: Gozzoburg Immobilienverwaltungs GmbH

0404
Städtebauliche Studie / Urban-Planning Study for
the Raumortlabor Hombroich
Neuss (DE)
2004
P: Birgit Frank
A: Stiftung Insel Hombroich

0405
Städtebaulicher Wettbewerb / Urban-Planning
Competition for Köbis Dreieck
Berlin (DE)
2004
P: Birgit Frank
I: Freie Planungsgruppe Berlin GmbH

0409
Studie / Study Villa S.
Neusiedl (AT)
2004–2007
A: privat / private

0412 S. / pp. 46/47, 111, 123, 135–137
Wohn- und Geschäftshaus / Residential and
Commercial Building on Lindengasse
Wien / Vienna (AT)
2004–2008
P: Birgit Frank (W)
A: Palmers AG
PL: Marcella Ressegatti, Karin Triendl

0501
Wettbewerb Fachhochschule Wien / Competition
for the University of Applied Sciences Vienna,
Altes Landgut
Wien / Vienna (AT)
2005
I: FH Campus Wien

0502
Wettbewerb / Competition for Uniqa Tower
Wien / Vienna (AT)
2005
I: Uniqa Versicherung AG

0503
Studie Autobahnmeisterei / Study for Highway
Agency
Wien / Vienna (AT)
2005
A: ASFINAG Autobahnen- und Schnellstraßen-
Finanzierungs-AG

0504
Wettbewerb Luft- und Raumfahrtzentrum / Com-
petition for Aerospace Center Oberpfaffenhofen
Weißling (DE)
2005
A: Deutsches Zentrum für Luft- und Raumfahrt e.V.
(DLR)

0505
Wettbewerb Hochschule Film und Fernsehen +
Staatliches Museum Ägyptischer Kunst /
Competition for University of Television and Film
+ State Museum of Egyptian Art
München / Munich (D)
2005
I: Landeshauptstadt München, Kommunalreferat
Vermessungsamt / State Capital of Munich, Municipal
Department Surveying Office; Universitätsbauamt
München / University Building Authority Munich

0506
Studie / Study for Künstlerhaus
Wien / Vienna (AT)
2005
I: Kunsthalle Wien

0507
Wettbewerb / Competition for Niederösterreich-
Haus
Krems (AT)
2005
A: NÖ Landesimmobiliengesellschaft mbH

0510
Praxis / Medical Practice Scholten
Wien / Vienna (AT)
2005/06
A: Dr. Christine Scholten
PL: Anna Dabernig, Kate Lemmen
> 0706   Erweiterung / Extension 2007

0511
Wettbewerb Polizei- und Justizzentrum /
Competition for Police and Justice Center
Zürich / Zurich (CH)
2005/06
P: Alfred Grazioli
A: Baudirektion Kanton Zürich, Hochbauamt /
Building Department of the Canton of Zurich,
Construction Authority

0515 S. / pp. 159, 184–191
SUPERBLOCK Sulzerareal
Winterthur (CH)
seit / from 2005
P: Birgit Frank (W)
A: AXA Leben AG, vertreten durch / represented by
AXA Investment Managers Schweiz AG
AP: Allreal Generalunternehmung AG
PL: Roger Huwyler, Anne Marie Kristokat,
Manuela Schwab

0516
Wettbewerb Werkbundsiedlung / Competition for Werkbund Settlement Wiesenfeld
München / Munich (DE)
2005
I: Arbeitsgemeinschaft Werkbundsiedlung München GbR
LP: Anna Detzlhofer

0517   S. / p. 42
Pavillon / Pavilion Architekturgalerie Berlin
Berlin (DE)
2005
P + K: Gilbert Bretterbauer
A: Architekturgalerie Berlin, Ulrich Müller

0601
Studie / Study for Bank Gutmann
Wien / Vienna (AT)
2006
A: Bank Gutmann AG

0602
Treppe / Stairway in the Kreisky-Villa
Wien / Vienna (A)
2006
A: Bruno Kreisky Forum

0603
Ausstellungsgestaltung / Exhibition Design for
Why Pictures Now
Wien / Vienna (A)
2006
A: MUMOK (Museum Moderner Kunst Stiftung Ludwig)
PL: Karoline Mayer

0604   S. / pp. 49, 60
Wettbewerb / Competition for Museum Liaunig
Neuhaus (AT)
2006
I: Herbert Liaunig

0605
Studie Rinderhallen / Study for the Cattle Halls
St. Marx
Wien / Vienna (AT)
2006
A: MUMOK (Museum Moderner Kunst Stiftung Ludwig)

0607
Ausstellungsgestaltung / Exhibition Design
Die Tafelrunde. Egon Schiele und sein Kreis
Wien / Vienna (AT)
2006
A: Österreichische Galerie Belvedere
PL: Karin Triendl

0609
Wettbewerb Staatliche Ballettschule / Competition for State Ballet School
Berlin (DE)
2006
P: Birgit Frank
I: Senatsverwaltung für Stadtentwicklung / Senate Administration for Urban Development

0610   S. / p. 42
Pavillon / Pavilion Durchhaus
Zürich / Zurich (CH)
2006
P + K: Gilbert Bretterbauer
A: Museum für Gestaltung Zürich; Museum Bellerive
PL: Vadim Unger

0611   S. / pp. 108/109, 216
Wettbewerb Wohnbau / Competition for Residential Building Karree St. Marx
Wien / Vienna (AT)
2006
I: EBG Gemeinnützige Ein-und Mehrfamilienhäuser Baugenossenschaft

0612   S. / p. 201
Wettbewerb / Competition for ETH. Life Science Plattform
Zürich / Zurich (CH)
2006
P: Alfred Grazioli
I: ETH Zürich; Zürich Immobilien, Abteilung Bauten / Department of Building

0613
Wettbewerb Innenarchitektur / Competition for Interior Design of Deutsche Bank
Frankfurt am Main (DE)
2006
P: Hermann Czech, Werner Neuwirth
K: Otto Zitko
I: Deutsche Bank AG

0614
Bebauungsstudie für eine Hochhausgruppe / Development Study for a Group of High-Rise Buildings
Nowosibirsk / Novosibirsk (RU)
2006
P: Diener + Diener
A: Charles Butler

0616
Studie / Study for the Keltenmuseum am Glauberg
Glauburg (DE)
2006
A: Land Hessen / State of Hesse, vertreten durch / represented by Hessisches Baumanagement, Regionalniederlassung / Regional Office Mitte

0617
Foyergestaltung / Foyer Design Kunsthalle Wien im / in the Museumsquartier
Wien / Vienna (AT)
2006/07
A: Kunsthalle Wien
PL: Marcella Ressegatti

0703   S. / pp. 21/22, 26/27, 34–42, 46
Temporäre Kunsthalle Berlin
Berlin (DE)
2007/08 (abgebaut / dismantled in 2010)
K: Gerwald Rockenschaub
A: Stiftung Zukunft Berlin; cube Kunsthalle Berlin gGmbH
PL: Anke Hafner

0707   S. / pp. 108–110, 122–126
Passivwohnbau / Passive Residential Building Eurogate, Bauplatz / Building Plot 7
Wien / Vienna (AT)
2007–2012
A: ÖSW Österreichisches Siedlungswerk
PL: Luciano Parodi (W), Hartmut Lissak

0708
Studienauftrag / Study Contract for Weiherfeld
Rheinfelden (DE)
2007
P: Alfred Grazioli
A: Tersa AG Rheinfelden

0709   S. / pp. 97, 108/109
Wohnbaustudie / Residential Building Study for Am Linzer Stadtpark
Linz (AT)
2007/08
A: GLV Gruberstrasse Linz Verwertungsgesellschaft mbH

0712
Städtebaulicher Wettbewerb Projektentwicklung / Urban-Planning Competition for Project Development for Leopoldstraße
München / Munich (DE)
2007
P: Werner Neuwirth
I: Jost Hurler Beteiligungs- und Verwaltungsgesellschaft GmbH & Co KG; CM 00 Vermögensverwaltung 511 GmbH

0714
Wettbewerb Schweizer Botschaft / Competition for Swiss Embassy
Moskau / Moscow (RU)
2007
P: Alfred Grazioli
I: Bundesamt für Bauten und Logistik / Federal Office for Buildings and Logistics, Bern

1004
Wettbewerb / Competition for Seespange und /
and Seestadt
Bregenz (AT)
2009/10
P: CukrowiczNachbaur Architekten, Riegler Riewe
Architekten
I: Seestadt Bregenz, Besitz- und Verwaltungsges. m.b.H.

1005
Wettbewerb / Competition for Les Arts Gstaad
Gstaad (CH)
2009/10
P: Alfred Grazioli
I: Verein Les Arts Gstaad

1006
Wettbewerb Wohnbau / Competition for
Residential Building Mautner Markhof Gründe
Wien / Vienna (AT)
2010
P: triendl und fessler architekten ZT OG
K: Gilbert Bretterbauer
I: Wien Süd in Kooperation mit / in cooperation
with wohnfonds_wien, fonds für wohnbau und stadt-
erneuerung

1007   S. / p. 218
Studie für eine Villa / Study for a Villa
Shanghai (CN)
2010/11
A: privat / private
PL: Wei Cai

1008   S. / pp. 96, 110
Planstudie Wohnbebauung / Project Study for
Housing Kureck
Wiesbaden (DE)
2010
P: Max Dudler
A: IFM Immobilien AG

1009   S. / p. 48
Wettbewerb Museum der Weltkulturen /
Competition for Museum of World Cultures
Frankfurt am Main (DE)
2010
I: Stadt Frankfurt am Main, Dezernat VII
Kultur und Wissenschaft / City of Frankfurt,
Department VII Culture and Science

1012
Umbau Wohnung / Conversion of Apartment A.
Wien / Vienna (AT)
2010
A: privat / private

1014
Studie / Study for Künstlerhaus at Karlsplatz
Wien / Vienna (AT)
2010

P: Jabornegg & Pálffy Architekten
A: WINK Wirtschaftsinitiative Neues Künstlerhaus

1101
Liska Pelzmoden am Flughafen / Airport Shop
Wien-Schwechat (AT)
2011/12
A: M. Liska & Co GmbH
PL: Fabian Schütz

1104
Wettbewerb Erweiterung Universität für angewandte Kunst Wien / Competition for Extension
of the University of Applied Arts Vienna
Wien / Vienna (AT)
2011/12
I: BIG Bundesimmobiliengesellschaft m.b.H.

1106   S. / p. 96
gswb Wohnen in Salzburg
Salzburg (AT)
seit / from 2011
P: triendl und fessler architekten ZT OG
A: gswb Gemeinnützige Salzburger Wohnbaugesell-
schaft mbH
PL: Hartmut Lissak

1108   S. / pp. 96, 110
Wettbewerb Wohnbau Arealüberbauung /
Competition for Residential Building Complex
in Guggach
Zürich / Zurich (CH)
2011
I: Allreal Generalunternehmung AG, Zürich / Zurich

1113   S. / p. 49
Wettbewerb Erweiterung / Competition for
Extension of Bündner Kunstmuseum
Chur (CH)
2011/12
I: Hochbauamt / Building Department Graubünden

1114   S. / pp. 155–158
Quai Zurich, Headquarters for the Zurich
Insurance Company Ltd
Zürich / Zurich (CH)
seit / from 2011
A: Zurich Insurance Company Ltd
PL: Ralf Wilkening (W), Michael Konstanzer,
Achim Pietzcker

1202   S. / pp. 149–152, 158, 176–180
Werkskantine / Company Cafeteria for
Jungbunzlauer
Niederösterreich / Lower Austria (AT)
2012/13
A: Jungbunzlauer Austria AG
PL: Stefan Just

1204   S. / p. 216
Wohnbau / Residential Building Bellevue
Wien / Vienna (AT)
seit / from 2012
A: PRISMA Zentrum für Wohn- und Lebensraum-
entwicklung GmbH
PL: Fabian Schütz (W), Luciano Parodi, Tobias Weske

1205   S. / p. 84
Ausstellungsgestaltung / Exhibition Design for
Penacho. Pracht & Passion, Völkerkundemuseum
Wien / Vienna (AT)
2012
A: Kunsthistorisches Museum Wien mit / with MVK und
ÖTM Wissenschaftliche Anstalt Öffentlichen Rechts
PL: Luciano Parodi

1206   S. / p. 216
Wohnbau / Residential Building on
Buchleitengasse
Wien / Vienna (AT)
seit / from 2012
P: Hermann Czech
A: Palmers Immobilien Development AG
PL: Luciano Parodi, Jana Raudnitzky

1301
Dachausbau / Roof Conversion Scholten
Wien / Vienna (AT)
2013
A: privat / private
PL: Stefan Just

1304   S. / p. 218
Wettbewerb / Competition for Villa L.
Zürich / Zurich (CH)
2013/14
A: privat / private

1305
Vorprojekt / Preliminary Project for Liska
Pelzmodengeschäft am Hohen Markt
Wien / Vienna (AT)
2013/14
A: M. Liska & Co GmbH
PL: Jana Raudnitzky, Carola Tarmastin

1306
Studienauftrag / Study Contract for Oerlikon –
Südwest Mitte
Zürich / Zurich (CH)
2013/14
A: SBB Immobilien

1307
Kassabereich / Cash Point Area of Bank Gutmann
Wien / Vienna (AT)
2013
A: Bank Gutmann AG
PL: Fabian Schütz

1308 S. / pp. 224, 250
Liska Pelzmodengeschäft 2, Flughafen Wien / Vienna Airport
Wien-Schwechat / Vienna-Schwechat (AT)
2013
A: M. Liska & Co GmbH
PL: Fabian Schütz, Carola Tarmastin

1310 S. / p. 248
Wohnung K. / Apartment K., Hochhaus / High-Rise Building on Herrengasse
Wien / Vienna (AT)
2013
A: privat / private

1311 S. / p. 218
Umbau Wohnhaus / Conversion of Residential Building S.
Wien / Vienna (AT)
seit / from 2013
A: privat / private
PL: Stefan Just, Carola Tarmastin

1313
Verhandlungsverfahren Sanierung Parlament / Negotiation Procedure for Renovating the Parliament
Wien / Vienna (AT)
2013/14
P: Hermann Czech, Werner Neuwirth
I: Republik Österreich / Republic of Austria

1401 S. / p. 159
Studie / Study for Schirmhaus on Escher Wyss Platz
Zürich / Zurich (CH)
2014
A: Allreal West AG

1402
Wettbewerb Veranstaltungszentrum / Competition for Event Center Sinergia
Chur (CH)
2014
P: b+p baurealisation ag
A: Kanton / Canton of Graubünden, vertreten durch das Bau-, Verkehrs- und Forstdepartement bzw. das Hochbauamt / represented by the Building, Transportation, and Forestry Department and/or the Building Department

1404
Wettbewerb / Competition for Haus Niederösterreich
Krems (AT)
2014
A: Land Niederösterreich / Province of Lower Austria

Werkverzeichnis der Möbel / Catalogue Raisonné of Furniture

B   Breite / Width
H   Höhe / Height
L   Länge / Length
SH   Sitzhöhe / Seat height
T   Tiefe / Depth

SECESSION

m01
Fauteuil
1986
nicht ausgeführt / not produced

m02 S. / p. 227
Fauteuil F1
1986
Wiesner-Hager Möbel GmbH
B 60 / T 77 / H 76 / SH 46 cm

m03
Sprossen-Fauteuil / Runged Fauteuil F2
1986
Wiesner-Hager Möbel GmbH
B 65 / T 79 / H 77,5 / SH 45,5 cm

m04 S. / p. 227
Stuhl / Chair S1
1986
Wiesner-Hager Möbel GmbH
B 54 / T 52,5 / H 76 / SH 45,5 cm

m05 S. / pp. 222, 227
Stuhl / Chair S2
1986
Wiesner-Hager Möbel GmbH
B 40,5 / T 41,5 / H 72,5 / SH 47,5 cm

m06 S. / pp. 226/227
Barhocker / Barstool S3
1986
Wiesner-Hager Möbel GmbH
B 40,5 / T 41,5 / H 85 / SH 60 cm

m07 S. / pp. 222, 227
Sitzbank / Settee B1
1986
mit / with Otto Kapfinger
Wittmann Möbelwerkstätten GmbH
L 168 / T 73,5 / H 73,5 / SH 46 cm

m08
Konferenztisch / Conference Table T1
1986
Wiesner-Hager Möbel GmbH
L 272 / B 80 / H 73 cm

m09 S. / p. 227
Beistelltisch / Side Table T2
1986
Wiesner-Hager Möbel GmbH
L 60 / B 40 / H 60 cm

m10
Tisch / Table T3
1986
Wiesner-Hager Möbel GmbH
L 72 / B 72 / H 72 cm

m11 S. / p. 227
Buchschrein / Bookcase
seit / from 1986
verschiedene Hersteller und Maße / various producers and dimensions

---

MADERNA

m12
Tischleuchte / Table Lamp TL1
1987
Maderna Werkstätten
H 43 / B 33 / T 33 cm

m13
Tischleuchte / Table Lamp TL2
1987
Maderna Werkstätten
H 40 / B 25 / T 25 cm

m14
Tischleuchte / Table Lamp TL3
1987
Maderna Werkstätten
H 53 / B 20 / T 44 cm

m15
Wandleuchte / Wall Lamp WL1
1987
Maderna Werkstätten
L 73 / B 35 / T 33

m16
Wandleuchte / Wall Lamp WL2
1987
Maderna Werkstätten
L 50 / B 53 / T 50 cm

m17
Wandleuchte / Wall Lamp WL3
1987
Farbkonzept / Color concept by Oskar Putz
Maderna Werkstätten
L 70 / B 20 / T 13 cm

m18
Wandleuchte / Wall Lamp WL4
1987

Farbkonzept / Color concept by Oskar Putz
Maderna Werkstätten
L 70 / B 23 / T 15

m19
Deckenleuchte / Ceiling Lamp DL1
1987
Maderna Werkstätten
B 51 / T 51 / H mit Stab / with bar 147 cm

m20
Deckenleuchte / Ceiling Lamp DL2
1987
Maderna Werkstätten
L 45 / B 30 / H 22 cm

m21
Deckenleuchte / Ceiling Lamp DL3
1987
Maderna Werkstätten
L 71 / B 71 / H 9 cm

m22
Stehleuchte / Standing Lamp STL1
1987
Maderna Werkstätten
H 177 / B 90 / T 90 cm

m23
Stehleuchte / Standing Lamp STL2
1987
Maderna Werkstätten
H 190 / B 62 / T 138 cm

m24
Stehleuchte / Standing Lamp STL3
1987
Maderna Werkstätten
H 186 / B 71 / T 71 cm

m25   S. / pp. 227, 245
Stehleuchte / Standing Lamp STL 4
1987
Maderna Werkstätten
H 166 / B 33 / T 46 cm

WIEN MÖBEL

PL: Marina Hämmerle

Alle Möbel dieser Serie wurden für die Ausstellung
Wien Möbel, Wiener Secession, 1989, entworfen. /
All furniture in this series was designed for the
exhibition *Vienna Furniture*, Wiener Secession,
1989.

m26   S. / p. 227
Regal / Shelves Fonso
1989
Farbkonzept / Color concept by Oskar Putz

Tischlerei Moser
H 215 / B 125 / T 33 cm

m27   S. / p. 227
Fauteuil Capricorn
1989
Farbkonzept / Color concept by Oskar Putz
Wiesner-Hager Möbel GmbH
B 67 / T 69 / H 69 / SH 40 cm

m28
Einser Liege / One-Person Chaise Longue
1989
Farbkonzept / Color concept by Oskar Putz
Wittmann Möbelwerkstätten GmbH
L 210 / B 63–94 / H 60 cm

m29   S. / p. 227
Tisch / Table Quadrant
1989
Farbkonzept / Color concept by Oskar Putz
Wiesner-Hager Möbel GmbH
L 70 / B 70 / H 75 cm

m30
Umkehrtisch / Inversion Table
1989
Farbkonzept / Color concept by Oskar Putz
Tischlerei Moser
L 280 / B 80 / H 73 cm

m31   S. / p. 220
Kleiner Fauteuil / Small Fauteuil AK01
1989
Farbkonzept / Color concept by Oskar Putz
Wiesner-Hager Möbel GmbH
B 56 / T 54 / H 83 / SH 45 cm

---

m32   S. / p. 221
Lederliege / Leather Chaise Longue
seit / from 1992
Wittmann Möbelwerkstätten GmbH
verschiedene Maße / various dimensions

m33   S. / pp. 215, 232, 240, 248
Holztisch / Wooden Table
ab / as of 1992
verschiedene Hersteller und Maße / various
producers and dimensions

m34   S. / pp. 215, 227, 240
Holzstuhl / Wooden Chair AK07, AK08, AK09
ab / as of 1992
verschiedene Hersteller / various producers
B 49 / T 53 / H 86,6 / SH 48 cm

m35   S. / pp. 194, 227, 241, 249
Hängepolsterbank / Suspended Upholstered Bench
AK12
ab / as of 1992

Wittmann Möbelwerkstätten GmbH
L 190 oder / or 220 / T 70 / H 82 / SH 44 cm

m36   S. / p. 227
Polstersessel / Upholstered Chair AK04
1992
Wittmann Möbelwerkstätten GmbH
B 61 / T 98 / H 76 / SH 42
Der Fauteuil und ein dazugehöriger Hocker (B 56 /
T 56 / H 36) können zu einem kompakten Objekt
kombiniert werden. / The fauteuil and a matching
stool (B 56 / T 56 / H 36) can be combined to
create a compact object.

m37   S. / pp. 221, 227
Stapelbarer Polstersessel / Stackable Upholstered
Chair AK03
1992
Wittmann Möbelwerkstätten GmbH
B 60 / T 80 / H 80 / SH 44 cm

m38   S. / pp. 151, 177, 223, 227
Seminarstuhl / Seminar Chair AK05
1998
Braun Lockenhaus GmbH
B 41–55 / T 52,6 / H 76 / SH 46,6 cm
verschiedene Ausführungen / various models

m39
Stapelbarer Hocker / Stackable Stool AK06
1998
Braun Lockenhaus GmbH
B 53 / T 36 / H 46,6 cm

SWISS RE

m40
Arbeitstisch / Worktable
2008
Braun Lockenhaus GmbH
L 200 / B 80 / H 75 cm

m41   S. / p. 227
Nachttisch / Nightstand
2008
B 45 / T 45 / H 43,5 cm

m42   S. / p. 227
Kleiderständer / Coatrack
2008
7 Möbel AG
H 190 / B 78,2 / T 58,2 cm

m43   S. / p. 227
Stummer Diener / Valet Stand
1998
7 Möbel AG
H 94,7 / B 57,6 / T 42,8 cm

m44   S. / p. 227
Stehleuchte / Standing Lamp Zylinder
1998
H 171,4 / B 50 / T 50 cm;
oder / or H 171,4 / B 60 / T 60 cm

m45   S. / pp. 224, 227, 245
Stehleuchte / Standing Lamp Suite
1998
Thonet Karolinsky KG
H 167 / B 60 / T 60 cm

m46   S. / pp. 227, 246
Stehleuchte mit Stoffüberwurf / Standing Lamp with
Cloth Cover
1998
H 198 / B 50 / T 50 cm

m47   S. / p. 215
Bibliotheksleuchte / Library Lamp
ab / as of 1998
Helmut Krischanitz
B 30 / T 7 / H 32–37 cm

m48   S. / p. 232
Hängebank / Suspended Bench
ab / as of 1998
verschiedene Hersteller / various producers
L variiert / varied / T 73 / H 100 / SH 46 cm

m49   S. / p. 38
Bistrot-Tisch / Bistro Table
ab / as of 2001
verschiedene Hersteller und Maße / various producers and dimensions

---

ARCHIV DER ZEITGENOSSEN

m50   S. / p. 227
Lesepult / Lectern
2010
Karl WALTER GmbH
L 90 / B 47 / H 69,3–91 cm

m51   S. / p. 227
Vitrine / Display Case
2010
Karl WALTER GmbH
H 115 / L 298 / T 71 cm

NOVARTIS

m52   S. / pp. 162/163, 167–169, 227
Drehstuhl / Revolving Chair AK12
2007
Wittmann Möbelwerkstätten GmbH
B 74 / T 72 / H 81 / SH 45 cm

m53   S. / pp. 162/163, 168/169
Drehhocker / Revolving Stool AK12
2007
Wittmann Möbelwerkstätten GmbH
B 74 / T 49 / H 44 cm

m54
Bank / Bench AK12
2007
Wittmann Möbelwerkstätten GmbH
L 231 / T 49 / H 44 cm

m55
Kronleuchter / Chandelier
2008
Licht Kunst Licht AG
verschiedene Maße / various dimensions

m56   S. / pp. 162/163, 167–169
Loungetisch / Lounge Table
2008
GLAESER Baden AG
L 90 / B 40 / H 60 cm

---

m57   S. / p. 227
Liege / Chaise Longue
2008
Braun Lockenhaus GmbH
L 153,5 / B 51 / H 77,5 cm

m58
Stapelstuhl / Stackable Chair
2010
Braun Lockenhaus GmbH
B 58,5 / T 66,5 / H 62,6 / SH 41 cm

m59   S. / pp. 227, 238
Außenbank / Outdoor Bench
ab / as of 2011
Karl WALTER GmbH
L 220 / T 54 / H 102 / SH 45 cm und weitere Maße /
and other dimensions

BENTWOOD
Mitarbeit / Collaboration Martin Behrens

m60   S. / pp. 223, 227
Easychair
2012
Braun Lockenhaus GmbH
B 54,5 / T 62 / H 83 / SH 45,5 cm

m61   S. / p. 227
Armchair
2012
Braun Lockenhaus GmbH
B 58,5 / T 70,1 / H 98,7 / SH 54,5 cm

m62   S. / pp. 225, 227
Chairbed
2012
Braun Lockenhaus GmbH
L 156,5 / B 50,5 / H 78,1 cm

m63   S. / pp. 225, 227
Daybed
2012
Braun Lockenhaus GmbH
L 199,2 / B 61 / H 43,9 cm

m64   S. / p. 227
Nightbed
2012
Braun Lockenhaus GmbH
L 210 / B 140 / H 28 cm

Publikationen (Auswahl) / Publications (Selection)

Architektur ist der Unterschied zwischen Architektur
hrsg. von / ed. Uta Graff, Universität der Künste
Berlin, Stadterneuerung
Ostfildern: Hatje Cantz
2009

Mustersiedlung Hadersdorf. Neues Wohnen in Wien
Sulgen und Zürich / and Zurich: Niggli
2009

Novartis Campus. Fabrikstrasse 16
hrsg. von / ed. Ulrike Jehle-Schulte Strathaus
Basel: Merian
2008

Museum Rietberg. Die Erweiterung
hrsg. von der / ed. Stadt Zürich / Amt für Hochbauten
und dem / and Museum Rietberg
Zürich / Zurich: Museum Rietberg
2007

Kunst fürs 20er Haus. 20er Haus für die Kunst
hrsg. von / ed. Gerbert Frodl und / and
Adolf Krischanitz
Ausst.-Kat. / Exh. cat. Österreichische
Galerie Belvedere, Wien / Vienna
2006

*neues bauen am horn. Eine Mustersiedlung
in Weimar*
hrsg. von / ed. Lars-Christian Uhlig und / and
Walter Stamm-Teske
Weimar: Universitätsverlag
2005

*Mitten in Metropolen. Übungen zur Stadterneuerung
an der Universität der Künste Berlin*
hrsg. von der / ed. Universität der Künste Berlin
Berlin: Universität der Künste,
Fachbereich Architektur
2004

Secession. Die Architektur
hrsg. von der / ed. Vereinigung bildender KünstlerInnen
Wiener Secession
Wien / Vienna: Brandstätter
2003

9 = 12. Neues Wohnen in Wien (Hintergrund 16)
hrsg. vom / ed. Architekturzentrum Wien
Ausst.-Kat. / Exh. cat. Architekturzentrum Wien
2002

Swiss Re Rüschlikon. Centre For Global Dialogue
hrsg. vom / ed. Kunsthaus Bregenz
Ostfildern: Hatje Cantz
2001

Swiss Re Rüschlikon Essay
hrsg. vom / ed. Kunsthaus Bregenz
Ostfildern: Hatje Cantz
2000

*Adolf Krischanitz, Architect. Buildings and Projects
1986–1998*
Basel: Birkhäuser
1998

Beyond the Minimal
hrsg. von / ed. Peter Allison und / and
Pamela Johnston
Ausst.-Kat. / Exh. cat. AA – Architectural Association,
London: Architectural Association Publishers
1998

Adolf Krischanitz
Barcelona: Editorial Gustavo Gili
1997

Ideale Realitäten 1992–97
hrsg. von / ed. Designtransfer, Hochschule der
Künste Berlin
Ausst.-Kat. / Exh. cat. Designtransfer, Berlin
Berlin: Hochschule der Künste
1997

Krischanitz, Federle. Neue Welt Schule
hrsg. vom / ed. Kunsthaus Bregenz
Ostfildern: Hatje Cantz
1994

Adolf Krischanitz
Zürich u. a. / Zurich et al.: Artemis
1994

Siedlung Pilotengasse Wien
Zürich u. a. / Zurich et al.: Artemis & Winkler
1992

Bau-Werke Adolf Krischanitz
Ausst.-Kat / Exh. cat. Architekturgalerie Luzern
Luzern / Lucerne: Edition Architekturgalerie
1990

*Die Wiener Werkbundsiedlung, Dokumentation einer
Erneuerung*
Wien / Vienna: Böhlau
1985

Biografien

Adolf Krischanitz
(* 1946 in Schwarzach / Pongau) gründete 1970, gegen Ende seines Studiums an der Technischen Universität Wien, zusammen mit Angela Hareiter und Otto Kapfinger die Architektengruppe Missing Link. 1979 zählte er zu den Begründern der Zeitschrift *UmBau* der Österreichischen Gesellschaft für Architektur und übernahm 1982 den Vorsitz dieser Gesellschaft. Als Mitglied und schließlich Präsident der Wiener Secession (1991–1995) verantwortete er die Gestaltung und Organisation zahlreicher Ausstellungen zeitgenössischer Kunst. Als Gastprofessor war er 1989 an der Technischen Universität München sowie an den Sommerakademien in Karlsruhe (1990), Neapel (1994/95) und Wien (1996) tätig. 1992–2011 war er Professor für Stadterneuerung und Entwerfen an der Universität der Künste Berlin. Seit 1979 arbeitet Krischanitz als freischaffender Architekt mit Ateliers in Wien und Zürich.

Otto Kapfinger
(* 1949 in St. Pölten) studierte von 1968 bis 1972 Architektur an der Technischen Universität Wien und gründete 1970 zusammen mit Angela Hareiter und Adolf Krischanitz die Architektengruppe Missing Link. 1979 war er Mitbegründer der Zeitschrift *UmBau* der Österreichischen Gesellschaft für Architektur; bis 1982 realisierte er Bauten und Projekte mit Adolf Krischanitz. Danach verlagerte er seinen Schwerpunkt auf Architekturforschung und Publizistik: 1981–1990 veröffentlichte er eine wöchentliche Baukritik in der Tageszeitung *Die Presse* und publizierte zahlreiche Bücher und Artikel in europäischen Fachzeitschriften. Als Kurator gestaltete er 20 Ausstellungen zur Architektur des 20. Jahrhunderts und der Gegenwart in Österreich. 1997–1999 war er Gastprofessor an der Hochschule für Gestaltung Linz. Kapfinger lebt als freiberuflicher Architekturpublizist und Ausstellungskurator in Wien.

Ákos Moravánszky
(* 1950 in Székesfehérvár) erwarb 1974 sein Architekturdiplom an der TU Budapest und begann, in Budapest als Architekt zu arbeiten und gleichzeitig über die Architektur der Jahrhundertwende zu forschen. Mit einem Herder-Stipendium studierte er die Architekturgeschichte der Donaumonarchie, um 1980 an der TU Wien zu promovieren. 1986–1988 war er Gastforscher am Zentralinstitut für Kunstgeschichte in München, 1989–1991 Research Associate am Getty Center for the History of Art and the Humanities in Santa Monica und 1991–1996 Visiting

Biographies

Adolf Krischanitz
(* 1946 in Schwarzach / Pongau) co-founded the architectural firm Missing Link with Angela Hareiter and Otto Kapfinger in 1970, toward the end of his studies at the Vienna University of Technology. In 1979, he was one of the founders of the journal *UmBau* of the Austrian Society for Architecture (ÖGFA), and in 1982 he took over the society presidency. As a member and eventually president of the Vienna Secession (1991–95), he was responsible for the design and organization of numerous exhibitions of contemporary art. Krischanitz was a visiting professor in 1989 at the Technische Universität München and at the summer academies in Karlsruhe (1990), Naples (1994–95), and Vienna (1996). From 1992 to 2011, he was Professor of Urban Renewal and Design at the University of the Arts Berlin. Since 1979, Krischanitz has worked as a freelance architect with studios in Vienna and Zurich.

Otto Kapfinger
(* 1949 in St. Pölten) studied architecture from 1968 to 1972 at the Vienna University of Technology and, in 1970, co-founded the architectural firm Missing Link with Angela Hareiter and Adolf Krischanitz. In 1979, he was a co-founder of the journal *UmBau* of the Austrian Society for Architecture (ÖGFA); through 1982 he realized buildings and projects with Adolf Krischanitz. He then shifted his focus to architectural research and publishing: from 1981 to 1990 he wrote a weekly design review for the daily newspaper *Die Presse* and published numerous books and articles in European journals. As a curator, Kapfinger organized twenty exhibitions on twentieth-century and contemporary architecture in Austria. From 1997 to 1999, he was a visiting professor at the Hochschule für Gestaltung Linz. Kapfinger lives and works in Vienna as a freelance architectural journalist and exhibition curator.

Ákos Moravánszky
(* 1950 in Székesfehérvár) earned his degree in architecture in 1974 from Budapest University of Technology and began working as an architect in Budapest while also researching architecture from the turn of the twentieth century. With a Herder Scholarship he studied the architectural history of the Danube Monarchy, earning a PhD in 1980 from Vienna University of Technology. From 1986 to 1988, Moravánszky was a visiting researcher at the Zentralinstitut für Kunstgeschichte in Munich, from 1989 to 1991 Research Associate at the Getty Center for the History

Professor am Massachusetts Institute of Technology. Seit 1996 ist er Professor für Architekturtheorie an der ETH Zürich (Institut gta). 2003/04 war er als Szent-Györgyi Fellow Visiting Professor an der Moholy-Nagy Universität für Kunst in Budapest. Er ist in den Forschungskommissionen mehrerer deutscher Hochschulen und den Beiräten wissenschaftlicher Zeitschriften aktiv.

Gottfried Pirhofer

(* 1950 in Schwaz) studierte Architektur an der RWTH Aachen mit den Schwerpunkten Planungstheorie und Städtebau. Ab 1975 arbeitete er an Forschungsprojekten und Publikationen zur Theorie und Geschichte der Stadtentwicklung und Stadtplanung, zur Entwicklung des Wohnbaus, zum Österreichischen Werkbund und zu aktuellen Planungen der Stadt Wien. 1990–2007 verfasste er im Auftrag der Stadt Wien Beiträge zum Stadtentwicklungsplan und zum Strategieplan. 2013 erschien sein Stadtessay *Maria Hilf! Eine Straße geht ihren Weg.* Gottfried Pirhofer lebt als Stadtforscher und Schriftsteller in Wien.

Loys Egg

(* 1947 in Bern) studierte an der Akademie für angewandte Kunst und der Akademie der bildenden Künste in Wien; 1972–1986 lehrte er an der Akademie für angewandte Kunst. Er ist Mitglied der Wiener Secession und der Grazer Autorenversammlung. Seine Werke waren in vielen Ausstellungen zu sehen, unter anderem im Museum Moderner Kunst, Wien, im Landesmuseum Joanneum, Graz sowie in der Galerie Ulysses, Wien. 1978 gründete er mit Peter Weibel das Hotel Morphila Orchester (Konzerte unter anderem im Museum Moderner Kunst, Wien; Musée d'Art moderne et contemporain, Straßburg; 20er Haus, Wien; Flex, Wien, Städtische Galerie im Lenbachhaus, München). Zudem gestaltete Loys Egg zahlreiche Bücher und Kataloge für nationale und internationale Kunst- und Architekturbuchverlage wie Springer, Birkhäuser oder Hatje Cantz.

Elisabeth von Samsonow

(* 1956 in Raubling) ist Philosophin und Künstlerin. Nach Studien der Philosophie, Theologie und Germanistik unterrichtete sie an Hochschulen in München und Wien, bis sie 1996 zur Professorin für Philosophische und Historische Anthropologie der Kunst an die Akademie der bildenden Künste Wien berufen wurde. In ihrer Arbeit beschäftigt sie sich mit den Transformationen von Ontologie und Ästhetik in der Gegenwart am Beispiel der Begriffe Mädchen, Geosophie, Parageologie = Architektur, Zuständlichkeit / Sinnlichkeit und Leib. Samsonow lebt und arbeitet in Wien und Hadres / NÖ.

of Art and the Humanities in Santa Monica, and from 1991 to 1996 Visiting Professor at the Massachusetts Institute of Technology. Since 1996, he has been Professor of Architectural Theory at ETH Zurich (gta). From 2003 to 2004, he served as the Szent-Györgyi Fellow Visiting Professor at Moholy-Nagy University of Art and Design in Budapest. He serves on the research committees of several German universities and scientific journal advisory boards.

Gottfried Pirhofer

(* 1950 in Schwaz) studied architecture at the RWTH Aachen with a focus on planning theory and urban development. In 1975, he began working on research projects and publications about the theory and history of urban development and urban planning, the development of housing, the Österreichischer Werkbund, and on current plans for the City of Vienna. From 1990 to 2007, Pirhofer authored contributions to the city development plan and the strategic plan on behalf of the City of Vienna. In 2013, he published his essay on the city "Maria Hilf! Eine Straße geht ihren Weg." Gottfried Pirhofer lives and works as an urban researcher and writer in Vienna.

Loys Egg

(* 1947 in Bern) studied at the University of Applied Arts and the Academy of Fine Arts in Vienna; from 1972 to 1986, he taught at the University of Applied Arts. He is a member of the Vienna Secession and the Grazer Autorenversammlung. His works have been shown in many exhibitions, including the Museum Moderner Kunst, Vienna, the Landesmuseum Joanneum, Graz, and Galerie Ulysses, Vienna. In 1978, he co-founded the band Hotel Morphila Orchester with Peter Weibel (with performances at the Museum Moderner Kunst, Vienna, Musée d'Art moderne et contemporain, Strasbourg, 20er Haus, Vienna, Flex, Vienna, Städtische Galerie im Lenbachhaus, Munich). In addition, Loys Egg has designed numerous books and catalogues for national and international art and architecture book publishers such as Springer, Birkhauser, and Hatje Cantz.

Elisabeth von Samsonow

(* 1956 in Raubling) is a philosopher and artist. After studying philosophy, theology, and German, she taught at universities in Munich and Vienna, until she was appointed Professor of Philosophical and Historical Anthropology of Art at the Academy of Fine Arts Vienna in 1996. Her work deals with the transformation of ontology and aesthetics in the present, focusing specifically on the terms girl, geosophie, parageology = architecture, state of being / sensuality and body. Samsonow lives and works in Vienna and Hadres (Lower Austria).

Dank / Acknowledgments

Dank für die erfolgreiche Zusammenarbeit von
1979 bis 2014 geht an: / Thanks are extended
to the following individuals for successful
collaboration between 1979 and 2014:

Neda Afazel, Martin Ahner, Ludolf von Alvensleben,
Neslihan Aydogan
Nina Bachofner, Hilmar Bauer, Saskia Bechtel,
Martin Behrens, Ulrich Beringer, Irene Biswanger,
Frank Boehm, Benedikt Bogenberger, Maciej Boltryk,
Veronika Bonora, Eva Born, Miriam Brandstetter,
Sarah Breidert, Matthias Brücke, Andreas Bruer,
Simon Burko
Wei Cai, Margarethe Cufer
Katarina Dabac, Anna Dabernig, Ingrid Dreer
Elke Eichmann, Julia Ess
Marco Fedier, Hubert Feiglstorfer, Robert Felber,
Anne Femmer, Patrick Fessler, Michael Flury,
Matthias Forster, Birgit Frank, Nathalie Fritschi,
Andreas Fuchs
Thomas Gaiser, Thomas Garcia, Alejandra García
Sahelices, Victoria von Gaudecker, Janisch Gerald,
Mark Gilbert, Susanne Glöckner, Markus Grob,
Annette Großkinsky, Diana Gunkel
Philipp Hächler, Edin Hadžović, Anke Hafner,
Oliver Hagen, Charlotte Hager, Dirk Haid,
Naomi Hajnos, Marina Hämmerle, Benjamin Häni,
Peter Hanousek, Manfred Hasler, Gregor Hauke,
Christoph Hayn, Klaus W. Heinemann,
Sebastian Heinemeyer, Timm Helbach,
Angelika Hergovich, Tobias Hilbert, Sven Hinrichs,
Julia Hinterecker, Franziska Horn, Aniko Horvath,
Ulrich Huhs, Roger Huwyler
Željko Ivošević
Thomas Jehle, Dominik Joho, Otto Friedrich
Jungblut, Stefan Just
Dimitri Kaden, Tobias Kahl, Eva-Maria Kämpf,
Adrian Kast, Oliver Kaufmann, Fawad Kazi,
Claudia Keichel, Rea Keller, Sascha Kellermann,
Linda Kerschbaumer, Andrea Kieck, Maria Kinzel,
Mathias Klöpfel, Maria Klug, Lena Klusa,
Xaver Kollegger, Uta Könitzer, Aglaia Konrad,
Michael Konstanzer, Sabine Konstanzer,
Alexandra Kramer, Kathleen Krebs, Nicole Kreuzer,
Anne-Maria Kristokat, Julia Krug, Marcel Kubitz,
Wilfried Kühn, Alexander Kuhnert, Lars Kundert,
Thomas Künzle, Patrizia Kurda
Marie-Theresa Lampe, Barbara Lechner,
Jan-Ole Leistner, Kate Lemmen,
Magdalena Leutzendorff, Christian Lichtenwagner,
Hartmut Lissak, Regula Lüscher, Philipp Lutz
Robert Martinelli, Cornelia Mattich, Karoline Mayer,

Marcello Mazzei, Jürg Meier, Andreas Meili,
Jürg Meister, Franz Meisterhofer, Adam Melcher,
Julia von Mende, Margarita Mene Castineiras,
Sarah Miebach, Franz Moser, Adriana Müller,
Silke Multhaupt, Sebastian Murr
Werner Neuwirth, Valentin Niessen, Kaja Nowak
Susanne Ostertag
Luciano Parodi, Luca Pestalozzi, Thomas Peyer,
Karl Peyer-Heimstätt, Achim Pietzcker,
Manuel Plazuelo Caballero, Clemens Pöchacker,
Dana Pretzsch, Bente Prigge, Jan Proksa,
Gundula Proksch
Katharina Rabanser, Katharina Ráček, Florian Radner,
Jelena Radovi , Jana Raudnitzky, Annika Raugust,
Daniel Rebmann, Eric Red, Marcella Ressegatti,
Ole Ritzke, Henri Rochat, Adrian Roesli,
Claudia Rohrweck, Stefan Rudolf, Bahadur Rüegger
Nargjil Saipi, Lana Alex Sanders, Susanne Schaller,
Maike Schaper, Norbert Schingerlin, Gerhard Schlager,
Denise Schluderbacher, Dominic Schmid,
Tanja Schneider, Casten Scholz, Norman Schroeder,
Gunda Schulz, Fabian Schütz, Manuela Schwab,
Bela Schwier, Felix Siegrist, Harald Siemens,
Ines Sigrist, Sophie Stanek, Lorenzo Staude,
Katrin Steinbacher, Julia Steinert, Filip Steins,
Adolph Stiller, Mathias Stocker, Rainer Streule,
Anna Suter, Daniel Sutovsky, Michael Swazina,
Carola Tarmastin, Jay Thalmann, Volker Thurm,
Ulrike Tillmann, Karin Triendl, Wolfgang Tröger,
Niki Tselika, Gabriela Tucek
Vadim Unger
Valentina Valera
Markus Weck, Alexandra Weinhofer, Tobias Weske,
Anna Wickenhauser, Simone Wiestner, Ralf Wilkening,
Birgit Winkler, Andreas Wirz, Bernd Wölfel,
Wendy Wulff, Carmen Wurz
Rene Ziegler, Florian Zierer, Raphael Ziltener,
Katja Zimmermann, Markus Zimmermann,
Theo Zoller, Hannes Zweifel

Dank / Acknowledgments

Den folgenden Firmen, Institutionen und Personen sei für ihre hervorragende Unterstützung bei zahlreichen Planungs- und Bauprojekten gedankt: /
We are grateful to the following firms, institutions, and individuals for their outstanding support during numerous planning and building projects:

a.k.a. Ingenieure, Christoph Gengnagel; Adenbeck GmbH; Allreal Generalunternehmung AG, Bruno Bettoni; Alu-König Stahl, Andreas Pulides; architekturkanzlei langmayr - diessl, Pia Langmayr, Manfred Diessl; Atelier Auböck + Kárász, Maria Auböck, János Kárász; AXA Investment Managers Schweiz AG, Ernst Schaufelberger
b+p baurealisation ag; Ernst Basler+ Partner; BIG, Karl Dürhammer, Maximilian Pammer, Johann Kirschner; Nachhaltigkeit OeKB Eveline Balogh; Backhausen GmbH, Rainhard Backhausen; Baudirektion Kanton Zürich, Amt Für Raumentwicklung, Kantonale Denkmalpflege; Wolfgang Beer; Braun Lockenhaus GmbH, Jochen Joachims, Paul Lehner; Jos. Berchtold AG, François Schmid; Bundesdenkmalamt, Barbara Neubauer, Wolfgang Salcher; Friedrich Dahm; Burghauptmannschaft, Ursula Jörg, Roland Lehner
Caretta + Weidmann
DnD Landschaftsplanung ZT KG, Anna Detzlhofer; Österreichische Doka Schalungstechnik GmbH
EBG, Manfred Pagler; Eckelt Glas GmbH
Foamglas, Christine Sommer
gmeiner haferl zivilingeniere zt gmbh, Manfred Gmeiner, Martin Haferl und Team; Hans-Jörg Gress Heimatschutz Winterthur; Sven Hinrichs, Holzbau Kast GmbH, Florian Kast;
Jungbunzlauer Austria AG, Josef Gaß, Winfried Macho
Gabriele Kimla; klösch & richter gmbh, Josef Klösch, Gerhard Richter und Team
Laborplan; Lafarge Perlmoser; Gertrude Lazar, communication agency prihoda GmbH; Licht Kunst Licht; Willibald Longin Holzbau GmbH
Museum Rietberg, Katharina Epprecht, Albert Lutz
Büro Ing. Walter Naderer, Walter Naderer sen.; NÖ Landesregierung, Abteilung Kultur und Wissenschaft, Joachim Rössl; Novartis AG, Reto Naef
Franz Oberndorfer GmbH & Co; ÖSW, Michael Pech
Palmers AG, Gernot Essl
RMO-VIS, Rico Obermoser
Salfinger-Bauabwicklung; Schiedel GmbH; Robert Schmiedlehner; Schöberl & Pöll OEG, Helmut Schöberl; Schreiner, Kastler Büro für Kommunikation GmbH, Gerhard Kastler, Susanne Schreiner und

Team; SFL Technologies; Spiluttini Bau GmbH; Stadt Winterthur, Departement Bau und Amt für Städtebau; Friedrich Steinbacher & Sohn, Max Eisenberger; Synaxis AG Bauingenieure
TB Eipeldauer & Partner GmbH, Alfred Eipeldauer; Thermo Projekt, Erich Szczur; Tischlerei Karl Walter GmbH, Karl Walter sen.
UTA Telekom AG
Daniel Vasella; Villeroy & Boch Austria GmbH, Andrea Leifert
Wittmann Möbelwerkstätten, Heinz Hofer-Wittmann
ZFG-PROJEKT GMBH; Wolfdietrich Ziesel; Zimmerei Sieveke GmbH; Zumtobel Lightning GmbH; Zürcher Heimatschutz ZVH

Bildnachweis / Image Credits

Architekt Krischanitz ZT GmbH: S. / pp. 15, 42, 48/49, 55, 57, 60, 64, 66, 96/97, 104/105, 107, 110, 122/123, 141/142, 146, 150, 152, 156, 160/161, 200/201, 206, 216, 218, 227 sowie alle Perspektiven, Zeichnungen und Grafiken / as well as all perspectives, drawings, and graphics
Archiv Krischanitz / Kapfinger: S. / pp. 17/18, 20/21, 50–54, 56, 98, 100–103, 109, 144/145
katrin bernsteiner: S. / p. 119
BEV Bundesamt für Eich- und Vermessungswesen: S. / p. 147
Blom ASA: S. / pp. 56, 117
Braun Lockenhaus GmbH: S. / pp. 222/223, 225/226
Gilbert Bretterbauer, o.T. (Netz), 2006 © Gilbert Bretterbauer 2015: S. / pp. 82
Anna Detzlhofer: S. / p. 116
Gisela Erlacher: S. / p. 247
Marina Faust: S. / p. 244/245
Helmut Federle, Ohne Titel (für Johannes Itten und Andy Hug), 2006 © Bildrecht, Wien 2015: S. / pp. 62, 76
Roger Frei: S. / pp. 112, 130–133
Pez Hejduk: S. / pp. 80, 113, 134, 138/139, 210
Heinrich Helfenstein: S. / pp. 6, 60, 62, 68–72, 76
Candida Höfer © Bildrecht, Wien 2015: S. / p. 246
Roger Huwyler: S. / pp. 184/185
Gerhard Koller: S. / p. 32
Helmut Krischanitz: S. / pp. 113, 135
Allora & Calzadilla, Compass, Installationsansicht: Temporäre Kunsthalle Berlin 2009, Foto: Jens Ziehe, Berlin © Temporäre Kunsthalle Berlin / Allora & Calzadilla 2015: pp. 40/41
John Bock, FischGrätenMelkStand, Ausstellungsansicht: Temporäre Kunsthalle Berlin, 2010, Foto: Jan Windszus © Temporäre Kunsthalle Berlin, John Bock, Courtesy Klosterfelde, Berlin; Anton Kern, New York: S. 2015 / pp. 27, 36
Kunsthalle Wien / © museum in progress www.mip.at: S. / p. 33 (oben / top: Ed Ruscha, 17th Century – 20th Century, Kunsthalle Wien, 1993 © Ed Ruscha 2015; Mitte / middle: Gerhard Richter, River, Großbild, Kunsthalle Wien, 1995/96 © Gerhard Richter 2015; unten / bottom: Douglas Gordon, raise the dead, Großbild, Kunsthalle Wien, 1996 © Studio lost but found / Bildrecht, Wien 2015)
Luftaufnahmen Hausmann: S. / p. 120
Karoline Mayer: S. / pp. 118, 233
Johannes Michaelis: S. / pp. 114/115
Christian Pfaff: S. / p. 26
Pierrot Le Fou. Orphée © 1950 SNC (Groupe M6): S. / p. 58
Kurt Prinz: S. / pp. 194/195

Oskar Putz, Ohne Titel 09, 1979 © Oskar Putz 2015: S. / p. 107
rmo-vis: S. / p. 155
Gerwald Rockenschaub Fassade Temporäre Kunsthalle Berlin 2008 © Gerwald Rockenschaub 2015: S. / pp. 34/35
Paolo Rosselli: S. / p. 166
Dieter Roth, Grosse Tischruine (Large Table Ruin), Secession Wien, 1995 © Dieter Roth Estate Courtesy Hauser & Wirth 2015, Foto: Margherita Spiluttini: S. / p. 85
Lukas Roth: Umschlagabbildung, S. / pp. 34/35, 37–39, 83/84, 87, 111, 124–129, 136/137, 143, 148/149, 151, 153/154, 162–165, 167–180, 186–193, 196–199, 214/215, 219, 231/232, 234–244, 248/249
Stefan Schadenböck: S. / p. 121
Alfred Schmid: S. / pp. 22, 26, 106, 108, 217
Schreiner Kastler: S. / pp. 204/205, 224
Sol LeWitt, Wall Drawing #393, 1983 © Bildrecht, Wien 2015: S. / p. 167
Margherita Spiluttini: S. / pp. 19, 23–25, 26, 28–31, 33/34, 59, 63, 73–75, 77–79, 81/82, 85, 181–183, 203, 208/ 209, 211–213, 217, 221, 224, 228–230
Wolfgang Thaler: S. / pp. 65, 86, 250
Walter Vopava, ohne Titel, Jahr unbekannt / no date © Walter Vopava 2015: S. / p. 82
Wiesner Hager: S. / p. 220